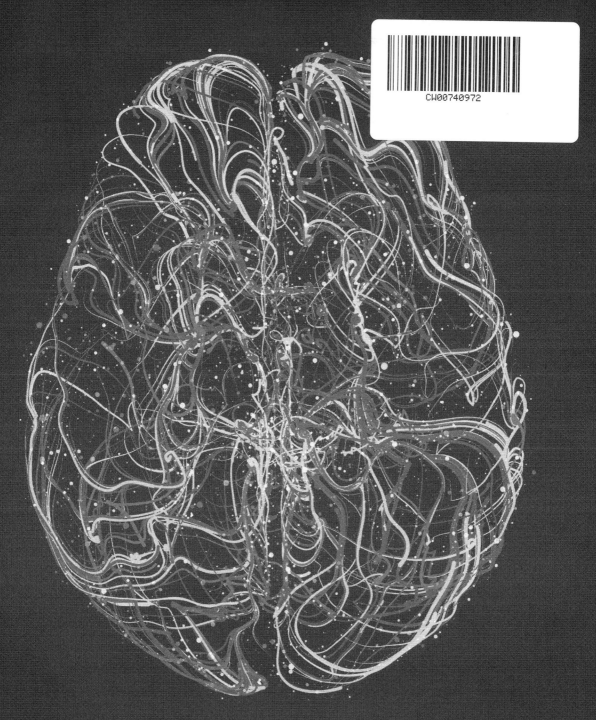

The Neurodiversity Reader

Exploring concepts, lived experience and implications for practice

Lead Editor: Dr. Damian Milton

Editors: Dr. Susy Ridout, Prof. Nicola Martin, Prof. Richard Mills and Dr. Dinah Murray

Pavilion

The Neurodiversity Reader

Exploring concepts, lived experience and implications for practice

Published by:
Pavilion Publishing and Media Ltd
Blue Sky Offices, 25 Cecil Pashley Way
Shoreham by Sea, West Sussex
BN43 5FF

Tel: 01273 434 943
Email: info@pavpub.com
Web: www.pavpub.com

Published 2020

ISBN: 978-1-912755-39-4

Pavilion Publishing and Media is a leading publisher of books, training materials and digital content in mental health, social care and allied fields. Pavilion and its imprints offer must-have knowledge and innovative learning solutions underpinned by sound research and professional values.

Editors: Dr. Damian Milton, Dr. Susy Ridout, Prof. Richard Mills, Prof. Nicola Martin and Dr. Dinah Murray
Production editor: Mike Benge, Pavilion Publishing and Media Ltd
Cover design: Phil Morash, Pavilion Publishing and Media Ltd
Page layout and typesetting: Emma Dawe, Pavilion Publishing and Media Ltd
Printing: CMP Digital Print Solutions

Contents

Biographies

Angie Balmer has worked in many different sectors. She is a Director and has recently launched her new training and consultancy business 4Neurodiversity, whilst simultaneously creating a supportive community group in Calderdale.

Zyggy Banks was a research partner on an autistic-led research project in which they investigated the strategies used by autistic people to overcome obstacles and empower themselves as well as the barriers that they faced both generally and specifically. He is also a specialist mentor for students with autism in the HE setting and a member of a service user advisory group.

Anna Barzotti studied creative arts at Manchester Metropolitan University, creative writing at Chichester University and screenwriting in New York. Anna has worked in health, education and arts settings in roles spanning theatre performer, arts and health coordinator, workshop facilitator, researcher and writer. She has worked as a specialist mentor for autistic students since 2017 and is currently writing a book about her experiences as a late diagnosed autistic adult.

Louis Bishopp-Ford was diagnosed Autistic with attention differences as an adult. He believes not knowing he was Autistic when he was younger meant that he could not ask for the support he needed to complete a university degree. Now that he knows about the support he needs, he is currently in his final year of an English and Creative Writing undergraduate degree, and hopes to write better fiction once he finishes!

Tania Browne was made redundant after 17 years in the hospitality industry in her early 40s, and subsequently returned to education where she completed a BSc (Hons) in Health Sciences with The Open University, and an MRes in Health Research at the University of Stirling. Her Master's dissertation focused on alcohol and substance use in autistic adults, and her chapter is a version of that work. Tania is currently a researcher working for The Salvation Army Centre for Addiction Services and Research at the University of Stirling. Her research interests include substance use, vulnerable populations, health inequalities, harm reduction and qualitative methodology. She is hoping to start a PhD in the field in the near future.

Carl Cameron is autistic and has been working with other autistic adults and children across the autism spectrum for the past 20 years both in residential and educational settings. Carl is a qualified teacher and taught health and social care for a few years. He has writing and delivering autism training sessions for the past 10 years and has worked with several organizations including the National Autistic Society, the NHS and CAMHS. Most of Carl's work these days is in pre and post-diagnostic support at Matthew's Hub, a unique autism charity in the city of Hull. Carl is the deputy chair of the Hull Autism Partnership Board.

Maura Campbell is Senior Editor and Features Writer for *Spectrum Women Magazine*, a free online magazine by and for women on the autism spectrum, and she served for two years on the board of directors of Specialisterne Northern Ireland. She was one of the contributors to *Spectrum Women – Walking to the Beat of Autism* (2018), an international collaboration by 15 autistic women, and she is one of the three co-authors of *Spectrum Women – Autism and Parenting*, published in August 2020. Maura has also written for a number of other autism and disability publications and for the BBC (*Tales of the Misunderstood*, filmed at the 2017 Edinburgh Fringe Festival, and BBC Radio 4's *Four Thought*). Maura is a civil servant and lives in Northern Ireland. She was professionally identified with Asperger Syndrome in 2011 when she was 44 years old.

Robert Chapman wrote his doctoral thesis on the ethics of autism at the University of Essex before coming to the University of Bristol, where he is currently a Vice Chancellor's Research Fellow working on the concept of neurodiversity. He is proudly neurodivergent and disabled.

David Cowan volunteers in the third sector and is a board member of Glasgow Access Panel where seeks to expand accessibility for the people with autism and other neurodiversity conditions.He is also the Secretary of Merchant City and Trongate Community Council which administrates on a wide range of issues from planning, government initiatives and social affairs. He is a live long student and attended a range of university courses, recently completing the first year module in Social Policy at Strathclyde University.

Lisa Cromar is a Person-Centred Counsellor who specialises in working with autistic clients, she runs autism training workshops, both face to face and online for counsellors. Lisa has also cofounded a lively and interactive Facebook forum called 'Counsellors Working with Neurodivergence.' She is currently studying towards a PhD at the University of Chester where she aims to advance research in the area of counselling for autistic people. Her mission is to increase awareness and acceptance of autism in the counselling field and to improve the counselling experience for autistic people. Whilst studying at the University of Derby, Lisa won multiple academic awards, including Professional Learner of the Year, a Deans Award and the prestigious Vice-Chancellor's Award. Lisa also has a personal interest in autism as she was diagnosed as autistic in her late thirties and has autistic children. To find out more, please visit www.lisacromar.com.

Paul Davies is 57 years old and is a BILD accredited trainer and instructor in Positive Support within a National charity organisation. He received his diagnosis late in life and has spent the last 20 years working within a range of equality projects, now focussing full time of autism and human rights. In 2019 he was commissioned, with his life partner Dr. Allison Moore from Edge Hill University, by Bild to co-create and co-present a contemporary approach to training about autism. Entitled, 'Valuing Autistic People – Valuing Difference' it advocates for a neurodiversity and Critical Autism Studies approach. The launch of this national training package has been impacted upon by COVID 19 but will call for a rights based, autism positive approach predicated on the 'controversial' notion that autistic people are actually human beings. He lives in the North West of England with 9 dogs and a friendly visiting Magpie.

Dr Sharon Elley has worked full-time in 12 workplace-settings, both professionally and non-professionally, including various Youth Services, and is currently a lecturer in Sociology and Social Policy at the University of Leeds, UK.

Dr Chloe Farahar is an Autistic academic whose research interests revolve around her Autistic specialisations (not 'special interests'). Chloe's specialisations include: reducing mental health stigma with a neurodiversity script *Stigmaphrenia*© (Farahar, 2012); supporting Autistic people with her co-founded *So, You're Autistic?* post-diagnostic support programme; reimagining the spectrum as a three dimension Autistic space; and educating both Autistic and non-autistic learners about Autistic experience in her training courses. Diagnosed at age 32 after a lifetime of being told she was 'weird', 'stand-offish', and 'unapproachable', Chloe struggled to make friends, and experienced bouts of depression and constant anxiety. It was only once she realised that she was Autistic that she found her 'group of weird' – the Autistic community, and her new friend Annette. Together, Annette and Chloe explored what being Autistic meant for them. Now they work on projects and research to help other Autistics learn to find their 'group of weird'.

Susan Harrington is currently a PhD researcher at the University of Strathclyde Business School in Glasgow, studying threshold concepts and transformational learning, with a focus on autistic people. Although not officially diagnosed autistic, for reasons many people seeking late diagnosis will be familiar with, she self-identifies as autistic, and is keen to make a difference for those who find themselves in a similar position. Aside from autism, Susan is interested in machine learning, and how people learn, and is hoping to combine these three areas of interest in her own research. Informal chats about any of these topics are always welcomed. In her personal life, Susan lives with her two sons in Central Scotland, and spends her free time reading, learning to code, and spending far too much time getting lost in rabbit-holes online.

Marion Hersh is a senior lecturer in biomedical engineerng at the University of Glasgow and autistic. Marion has a degree in mathematics, a PhD in engineering and finds their knowledge of foreign languages particularly useful in their international research. This has included the travel experiences and spatial perceptions of blind people in various countries, most recently Brazil, and a study of the employment, education and other experiences of autistic women in several European countries. They have organised a series of conferences on assistive technology for people with sensory impairments and a workshop in Brazil on accessible infrastructures for education and mobility of blind people. They have authored/edited two books on assistive technology, two on engineering ethics and one on mathematical modelling for sustainable development. They were a partner in the An Auternative research project on autistic people, strategies and barriers and have delivered several workshops in Poland with a blind friend on communication between autistic and neurodiverse people.

Donna-Lee Ida, School of Social Policy, Sociology and Social Research, University of Kent, has a background in many care roles, from residential and day care to holistic practices. She has worked at the University of Kent since 2011, initially as an educational support assistant and then as a specialist mentor with neurodivergent students from 2016. Currently she is in the process of a collaborative, emergent, relational research project about neurodivergent student wellbeing to complete an MA in Sociology. Her developing research interests centre around the paradigmatic framing of knowledge production and becoming, particularly with respect to the marginalisation of neurominorty groups. It is intended for her current MA research to inform a PhD further developing these interests.

Mike Lesser (d. 2015) was a mathematical philosopher and political activist. The youngest member of the anti-nuclear weapons, direct action, Committee of 100, he was sent, aged 16, to Wormwood Scrubs Prison along with most of the Committee. He served two spells as contributor to London's underground journal *International Times*. In 1992 he was the co-author of, *The Global Dynamics Of Cellular Automata*, an atlas of emergent forms evolving from the apparently chaotic product of a set of iterated logical operations. He worked with Professor, P. Allen, at the Institute for Ecotechnological Research at Cranfield University and co-authored several scientific papers on dynamical systems theory with him.[3] He worked on super computers at NASA's Goddard Jet Propulsion Lab, USA, and at Rutherford Appleton Laboratories, UK. With Dinah Murray, he published papers on Autism and a dynamic interest based model of mind, and ran not for profit Autism and computing.

Jessica Leza is a board certified music therapist originally from Houston, Texas, USA. She graduated with a Bachelor of Music in Music Composition from the University of North Texas and a Master of Arts in Music Therapy from Texas Woman's University. Jessica completed a music therapy internship at Banner Good Samaritan Medical Center in Phoenix, AZ and has received additional training in Neurological Music Therapy (NMT). Jessica provides music therapy for developmentally disabled students in north Texas public schools, addressing the skills described on their IEPs through singing, instrument playing, movement to music, and familiar songs played on guitar. In addition to her work in music therapy, Jessica enjoys canoeing, spending time with her spouse, and pursuing special interests such as ducks, permaculture, or the visual arts.

Prof. Nicola Martin is a neurodiverse academic who has worked with disabled pupils and students since 1982. She is Professor of Social Justice and Inclusive Education at LSBU. Nicola has a National Teaching Fellowship for her work on inclusion. Her research is underpinned by the principle 'nothing about us without us' and the idea of usefulness, collaboration and fairness. She has numerous publications focusing on inclusive education across the age range, many of which are co-authored by autistic colleagues. Alongside Damian Milton Nicola was instrumental in getting The Participatory Autism Research Collective (PARC) off the ground and continues to play a supporting role. She is editor of The Journal of Inclusive Practice in Further and Higher Education (JIPFHE) and a founder member of The National Association of Disability Practitioners (NADP). Both NADP and JIPFHE exist to promote inclusive adult education. Nicola is a member of The Westminster Autism Commission.

Michael McCreadie was a founding Director and Associate Consultant of AT-Autism London and practice lead on the Synergy programme. For many years Michael was a consultant health Psychologist for Studio 3, UK, working on programmes for understanding and responding to behaviours that of concern. He worked nationally and internationally for both organisations on their Synergy and ATLASS programmes. Previously, Michael had been the founding Depute Principal of Daldorch House School, Ayrshire, a residential school for autistic children, run by the National Autistic Society. Michael's long-term passion had been on the effects of stress on behaviour and he was instrumental in setting up the AT-Autism/ Laskaridis Foundation Synergy programme. Michael was also extensively involved with Scottish Autism as a consultant and member for the Centre for Practice Innovation. Michael died aged 52 years in the Summer of 2018.

Panda Mery is an almost too calm productive irritant, neurodivergent researcher, bricoleur and flâneur. He was a research partner on the autistic-led project 'An Auternative' investigating the strategies used by autistics to understand social situations and other people's reactions, and to empower themselves; and the barriers to participation in decision making, the economy and communities. Panda is an Independent Custody Visitor, making unannounced visits to police stations to check on the treatment and welfare of detainees; an advisor to Autism Injustice, a support and campaign group set up to hold the government and other public bodies accountable for injustices and abuses against autistics; a team member of AutAngel, an organisation run by and for autistic people to strengthen autistic community; a volunteer with the Restart Project, a social enterprise that aims to change our relationship with technology; and a human rights campaigner. His personal website is at https://gizmonaut.net

Prof. Richard Mills is Associate Consultant and Advisor to the board of AT-Autism London and practice lead on the Synergy and SPELL Programmes. He is also a Research Fellow in the Dept of Psychology at the University of Bath. He holds several overseas appointments; in Australia, Malta, Greece, Singapore, Jersey, and Japan, where is Professor of Applied Autism Research at Taisho University, Tokyo. For over twenty years Richard was with the National Autistic Society, first as Director of Services and later as Director of Research, jointly with Research Autism. He was a member of the NICE guideline development groups on autism in adulthood and behaviours that challenge. He is an editor of Autism, the International Journal of Research and Practice, and Advances in Autism and a member of Scottish Autism's Centre for Practice Innovation. His current research is in autism and justice and behaviours of concern. He is a trustee of the John and Lorna Wing Foundation, London.

Dr. Damian Milton works part-time for the Tizard Centre, University of Kent as a Lecturer in Intellectual and Developmental Disabilities. Damian also teaches on the MA Education (Autism) programme at London South Bank University and has been a consultant for the Transform Autism Education (TAE) project and a number of projects for the Autism Education Trust (AET). Damian's interest in autism began when his son was diagnosed in 2005 as autistic at the age of two. Damian was also diagnosed with Asperger's in 2009 at the age of thirty-six. Damian's primary focus is on increasing the meaningful participation of autistic people and people with learning disabilities in the research process and chairs the Participatory Autism Research Collective (PARC).

Linus Mueller is the founder of Autismus-Kultur, a German project that educates about autism and helps autistic people and their families to live their lives the autistic way in a mostly non-autistic world. Linus studied Gender Studies and African Studies at the Humboldt University Berlin. Upon discovering he was autistic, autism and neurodiversity became his main research interests. In his master's thesis he gained insight into the influence our ideas of nature, technology, and gender have on the concept of autism. Linus worked for several autism organizations in Germany until he founded Autismus-Kultur in 2007. He lives in Berlin with his partner and a fabulous kid.

Dr. Dinah Murray is an independent researcher with a PhD re Language and Interests (1986); a campaigner, and a former support worker for people with varied learning disabilities including autism. The PhD was the basis of an interest account of mind using ecological modelling of interest/ attention as a scarce resource. Based on her PhD, Dinah first published about autism with "Attention tunnels and Autism" in 1992, a conference paper, and most recently in Monotropism, an interest based account of autism in ed Volkmar, 2018, 2020. Dinah's autism-related research interests have included the nature of the human being, with a particular focus on the distinctive pattern of interests in autism. She has been assessed as autistic, and if growing up today would certainly have attracted an autism diagnosis. See also www.productiveirritant.org

Fergus Murray is an autistic science teacher, writer and co-founder of AMASE (Autistic Mutual Aid Society Edinburgh) who is involved in various autism-related projects at the University of Edinburgh, most recently Learning About Neurodiversity at School (LEANS), developing and piloting resources for primary-school pupils. Special interests include school inclusion, public education on autism and the role of cognitive theories, particularly Monotropism. When not wrapped up in autism things, Fergus takes a lot of photos, writes miscellaneous non-fiction, and occasionally makes tiny sculptures, giant puppets and web toys based on science and maths. Fergus has been published in The Psychologist, openDemocracy and Thinking Person's Guide to Autism.

Dr Susy Ridout's knowledge and expertise have been built in the UK and abroad (Spain and Cuba), and she currently works as an Associate Lecturer (Neurodiversity and Inclusion) in the School of Architecture, Oxford Brookes University exploring ways in which the [built] environment impacts on wellbeing. In addition, she holds a wider portfolio which embraces mentoring and also writing and research in neurodivergence and sexual violence. Susy has mentored for over a decade around the themes of autism, disability and wellbeing in a range of settings and advocate mentoring as an approach to examining barriers to learning, developing coping strategies and terminology used to voice these and challenging systemic injustices. She is a confident speaker, trainer and facilitator working across fields such as: autism, neurodivergence and disability, minority groups and intersectionality, and the Criminal Justice System and its impact on and interrelationship with victim-survivors. Her work ethic is resolution-based and taps into the skills, interests and abilities of people of all ages, abilities and backgrounds.

Akiva Secret (alias) is presently an Associate Professor in higher education and previously worked in secondary, further education and the media industry. Akiva wishes to remain anonymous.

Olatunde Spence is a mother, an art psychotherapist and a community activist. She worked for many years supporting the development of Black groups and networks to improve health, education and employment opportunities. She is a member of the International Hearing Voices Movement, a movement that challenges the very idea of human distress and or difference as pathology. Since her children were diagnosed with autism in 2017, Olatunde has struggled with the notion that they have a diagnosable psychiatric 'disorder'. This struggle continues. She currently works in private practice with children and adults whose lives have been impacted by PTSD and C-PTSD. In response to #Black Lives Matter protests taking place around the world, Olatunde is raising awareness of the issues affecting Black autistic young people in education. African Caribbean boys who are autistic are disproportionately facing permanent exclusion from education because of the systemic failures to identify and respond to their unmet needs.

Paul Wady was diagnosed autistic at the age of 41, in events detailed in the Guardian newspaper online. He tours the UK training professionals for the National Autistic Society and performs around the UK (and other parts of the planet) with his Guerilla Aspies audience autism mass conversion show. He also founded the Stealth Aspies 100% autistic theatre company. He wrote Guerilla Aspies – a neurotypical society infiltration manual book and produces advocacy badges and t shirts. His goal is to support other advocates and contribute towards the ongoing development of the Neurodiversity paradigm. He lives in London and is married to another autistic. www.paulwady.com. @paulwady @GuerillaAspies.

Callum Watson grew up in a household where the phrase "AS rules, OK" was frequently heard with no small amount of humour, which led to an early understanding of Autism and pointed him towards a degree in Psychology. He spent six years working with students with ASD and AD(H)D, over time he felt that the needs of his incoming students were becoming more complex and the system was missing or struggling to adapt to them. He decided to bite the bullet and try the clinical psychology route to see where he could bridge those gaps. This has led to a whirlwind tour as an AP working in neurorehabilitation services and now on to children's residential, alongside working with the Auternative Project through the University of Glasgow.

Gemma L Williams is an autistic, final year cognitive linguistics PhD Studentship awardee at the University of Brighton. Her research investigates the breakdowns in mutual understanding that can occur between autistic and non-autistic people from the perspective of relevance theory and the double empathy problem. Her doctoral research has also included a focus on loneliness in autism, and the use of both creative and participatory methodologies. Beyond her academic work, Gemma is a musician and a beekeeper. A piece of her autoethnographic fiction from her thesis, 'We're All Strangers Here', was awarded Honorable Mention in the *Society for Humanistic Anthropology 2019 Ethnographic Fiction and Creative Nonfiction Prize* and her short story 'm a r a c a' appeared in *Stim: An Autistic Anthology* (2020).

John Wilson is a former solicitor who set-up his own successful law company after realising that he needed to work according to his own management style, working patterns and organisational rules.

Dr Rebecca Wood is a former teacher and autism education practitioner who is a Senior Lecturer in Special Education at the University of East London. She completed her PhD at the University of Birmingham with the support of a full-time scholarship. Rebecca was also Project Manager of the Transform Autism Education project which was funded by the European Commission. This was followed by an ESRC postdoctoral Fellowship at the Social, Genetic and Developmental Psychiatry Centre of King's College London. Rebecca speaks at national and international conferences and has a number of publications in peer-reviewed journals. Her book 'Inclusive Education for Autistic Children' is published by Jessica Kingsley Publishers.

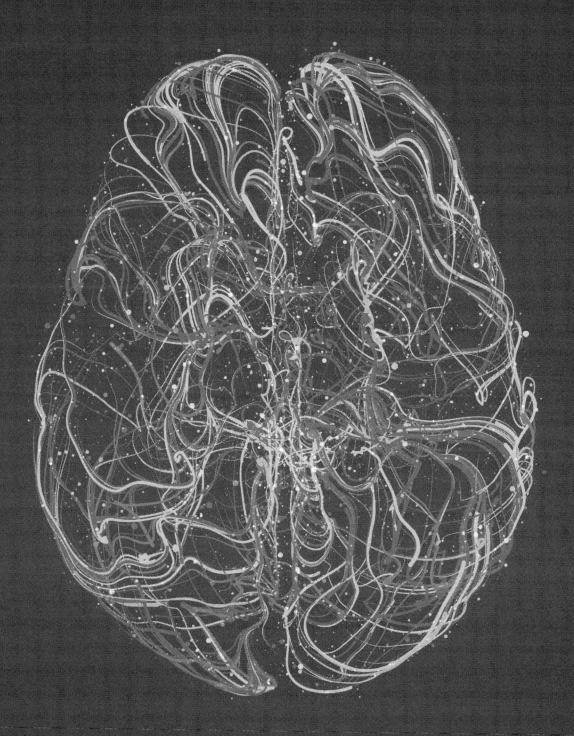

Section 1

Chapter 1: Neurodiversity past and present – an introduction to the neurodiversity reader

By Damian E M Milton

The term 'neurodiversity' originated initially in 1998 from the work of Australian sociologist Judy Singer, who proposed it as a new category for intersectional analysis, and to suggest it as a banner term for emerging social movements for civil rights for people with various devalued, medically labelled neurological conditions. She based it on the concept of Biodiversity, and its broad argument that the more diversity within an ecosystem, the more resilient and sustainable it would be. She did not define the term, thinking it self-evident, and moved onto the main body of her thesis, which included an evaluation of the social versus medical models of disability, and also explored the notion that perhaps an "ethnicity" or "minority" model was better suited to conditions like "Asperger Syndrome" and "ADHD". This idea was taken further by others, albeit often taking an approach more aligned with the social model of disability (or variations thereof – for example see Oliver, 2013).

Walker (2014) suggested using the terms 'neurodiversity', the 'neurodiversity movement' and the 'neurodiversity paradigm'. Here neurodiversity is stated as a 'brute fact' that all brains are to a degree unique, with the embodied development of people being differently disposed in their experiences and actions. In contrast to an individualised medical model of disability, which contrasts 'normal' development with that of 'abnormal', traditionally framed in terms of deficiency and dysfunction, such a view would not place value judgements of such diversity. The 'neurodiversity movement' as a term having been adopted by those arguing for the equal human rights of those deemed divergent from the idealisation of neuro-normativity. It is perhaps the concept of the 'neurodiversity paradigm' however that has created the most controversy (and misunderstanding) in this history, described by Walker as:

1. *Neurodiversity is a natural and valuable form of human diversity.*

2. *The idea that there is one 'normal' or 'healthy' type of brain or mind, or one 'right' style of neurocognitive functioning, is a culturally constructed fiction, no more valid (and no more conducive to a healthy society or to the overall well-being of humanity) than the idea that there is one 'normal' or 'right' ethnicity, gender, or culture.*

3. *The social dynamics that manifest in regard to neurodiversity are similar to the social dynamics that manifest in regard to other forms of human diversity (e.g., diversity of ethnicity, gender, or culture). These dynamics include the dynamics of social power inequalities, and also the dynamics by which diversity, when embraced, acts as a source of creative potential.'* (Walker, 2014).

The immediate antecedent to the development of the neurodiversity movement could be said, however, to have been the coming together of primarily autistic people who were challenging the dominant ways in which autism had been classified, often referred to as the autistic rights and/or self-advocacy movement. Through both online and in-person encounters, a small but highly influential community began to grow, such as through the online networks of ANI (Autism Network International) and InLv (Independent Living on the Autism Spectrum), and the setting up of the Autreat conference in the US (and later the Autscape conference in the UK). These networks included pioneers such as Jim Sinclair, Mel Baggs, Donna Williams, Martijn Dekker and Judy Singer (among others). A seminal essay in this development was 'Don't Mourn For Us', written by Sinclair (1992), in which concerns were directed to the parents of young autistic children.

'Grant me the dignity of meeting me on my own terms – recognise that we are equally alien to each other and that my ways of being are not merely damaged versions of yours.' (Jim Sinclair)

Such work was followed by the publication online of satirical guidance in the form of the Institute for the Study of the Neurologically Typical (Tisoncik, 2019), coining the term 'neurotypical' and framing such 'normalcy' in terms of medicalised symptomology. This was followed by campaigns critiquing the work of non-autistic-led major autism organisations and campaigns that framed autism as a tragedy and even epidemic.

This burgeoning of autistic culture and community has thus been central to the formation of the neurodiversity movement, which can be seen both historically and within this collection. Yet the concept of neurodiversity was never meant to apply to just autistic people, and in more recent years more and more disability advocates have found interest (and sometimes critique) in this movement and related concepts. Over 20 years since its inception, the neurodiversity movement could be said to be 'coming of age' with a wealth of books, blogs, films and events, and an ever-growing international reach. One can even see progression into what might be thought of the mainstream media, especially in the UK with pro-neurodiversity television series such as 'The Autistic Gardener' and the children's programme 'Pablo'.

Since its inception, the autistic community and neurodiversity movement has also provided a space for neurodivergent scholarship to emerge. Early examples of this can be seen in the work of Dinah Murray (see Murray *et al*, 2005) and Wenn Lawson (2010) regarding the topic of 'monotropism' or an 'interest model of mind' (captured in the next two chapters of this collection) and Scott Robertson (2010) regarding autism and quality of life. Other notable examples being the setting up of the *Autonomy Journal* (Arnold, 2012), the AASPIRE group (Raymaker *et al*, 2019), work relating to what has been called the 'double empathy problem' (Milton, 2012; Milton et al, 2018), influence through mainstream research conferences (Robison, 2019), general texts on autism theory (Chown, 2016), critical work on autism interventions (Milton, 2014; Kupferstein, 2018) and more recently regarding autism and culture (McGrath, 2017; Yergeau, 2018; Rodas, 2018). This can also be seen throughout this collection and particularly the first section of this book.

In recent times, neurodiversity and related concepts have come under criticism from various stakeholders. Whilst some criticism may be more well founded (e.g. Russell, 2019), much of this criticism has reduced these concepts to simplistic mischaracterisations (for a discussion of which, see Milton, 2019).

This collection involves three sections. First there are a set of articles that explore various conceptualisations of neurodiversity or aspects thereof. The second section concentrates more on the lived experience of being 'neurodivergent', whilst the third section reflects on the implications of neurodiversity and related concepts on practice. No collection such as this can be exhaustive of relevant topics, and it is suggested here that this volume be seen as complementary to other such collections, particularly that of the *Loud Hands* collection (Bascom, 2012), the two autism and intellectual disability annuals also published through Pavilion Publishing (Milton and Martin, 2016; 2017), and the superb recent collection edited by Steven Kapp (2019) reviewing the history of the autistic community and the neurodiversity movement (including articles from many of the pioneers of the neurodiversity movement). This book has thus attempted to collate work which seeks to explore key issues and yet also point to the future and where the neurodiversity movement may go from here, including chapters from a number of 'up-and-coming' voices.

References

Arnold L (2012) Autism, its relationship to science and to people with the condition. *Autonomy, the Critical Journal of Interdisciplinary Autism Studies* **1** (1).

Bascom J (Ed) (2012) *Loud Hands: Autistic people, speaking.* Autistic Self-Advocacy Network.

Chown N (2016) *Understanding and Evaluating Autism Theory.* Jessica Kingsley Publishers.

Kapp SK (Ed.) (2019) *Autistic Community and the Neurodiversity Movement: Stories from the frontline.* Springer Nature.

Kupferstein H (2018) Evidence of increased PTSD symptoms in autistics exposed to applied behaviour analysis. *Advances in Autism* **4** (1) 19–29.

Lawson W (2010) *The Passionate Mind: How people with autism learn.* Jessica Kingsley Publishers.

McGrath J (2017) *Naming Adult Autism: Culture, science, identity.* Rowman & Littlefield International.

Milton D (2012) On the ontological status of autism: the 'double empathy problem'. *Disability & Society* **27** (6) 883–887.

Milton D (2014) So what exactly are autism interventions intervening with? *Good Autism Practice (GAP)* **15** (2) 6–14.

Milton D (2019) Disagreeing over Neurodiversity. *Psychologist* **32** (8).

Milton D & Martin N (2016) *Autism and Intellectual Disability in Adults* (Vol. 1). Pavilion Publishing and Media.

Milton D & Martin N (2017) *Autism and Intellectual Disability in Adults* (Vol. 2). Pavilion Publishing and Media.

Milton D, Heasman B & Sheppard E (2018) Double empathy. *Encyclopedia of Autism Spectrum Disorders* 1-8.

Murray D, Lesser M & Lawson W (2005) Attention, monotropism and the diagnostic criteria for autism. *Autism* **9** (2) 139–156.

Oliver M (2013) The social model of disability: Thirty years on. *Disability & Society* **28** (7) 1024–1026.

Raymaker DM, Kapp SK, McDonald KE, Weiner M, Ashkenazy E & Nicolaidis C (2019) Development of the AASPIRE Web Accessibility Guidelines for Autistic Web Users. *Autism in Adulthood* **1** (2) 146–157.

Robertson SM (2010) Neurodiversity, quality of life, and autistic adults: Shifting research and professional focuses onto real-life challenges. *Disability Studies Quarterly* **30** (1).

Robison JE (2019) My Time with Autism Speaks. In *Autistic Community and the Neurodiversity Movement* (pp221-232). Palgrave Macmillan, Singapore.

Rodas JM (2018) *Autistic Disturbances: Theorizing Autism Poetics from the DSM to Robinson Crusoe.* University of Michigan Press.

Russell G (2019) Critiques of the Neurodiversity Movement. In *Autistic Community and the Neurodiversity Movement* (pp287–303). Palgrave Macmillan, Singapore.

Sinclair J (1992/2012) Don't Mourn for Us. *Autonomy, the Critical Journal of Interdisciplinary Autism Studies* **1** (1).

Tisoncik LA (2019) Autistics. Org and Finding Our Voices as an Activist Movement. In: *Autistic Community and the Neurodiversity Movement* (pp65-76). Palgrave Macmillan, Singapore.

Walker N (2014) *Neurodiversity: Some basic terms and definitions* [online]. Neurocosmopolitanism: Nick Walker's Notes on Neurodiversity, Autism, and Cognitive Liberty. Available at: https://neurocosmopolitanism.com/neurodiversity-some-basic-terms-definitions/.

Yergeau M (2018) *Authoring autism: On rhetoric and neurological queerness.* Duke University Press.

Chapter 2: Mind as a Dynamical System – Implications for autism

By Mike Lesser and Dinah Murray
Autism & Computing, London, UK

In the last 20 years there has been an intensive study of non-linear dynamical systems (Abrahams & Shaw, 1988; Allen, 1998; Eigen & Winkler, 1983; Thom, 1975; Prigogene & Stengers, 1987). The flow of fluids, the collapse of engineering structures, the development of the phenotype from the genotype and human imagination are examples. These systems, although subject to smoothly varying controlling parameters, exhibit sudden changes including the emergence of formerly non-existent features.

Such revelations of formerly invisible qualities of a system mark are the spontaneous appearance of new information. We should beware of thinking of information as a locally conserved quantity. There is no law about the conservation of information. We should expect to observe the spontaneous appearance and disappearance of information. Once there was no life on this planet. Once there was no planet. Now all this has emerged.

The interest system

We believe that mind models its environment, thus increasing the ability to predict. We assume that mind links sensation, both present and previous, with action. Our model provides a description of the underlying workings of Tolman's cognitive map (Tolman, 1948; Artigiani, 1993).

In our model, we describe the link between experience and activity by an algebraic equation derived from ecological studies carried out by Peter Allen and Mike Lesser (Allen & Lesser, 1991). In the ecological model, a fundamental and limited resource, solar radiation, is competed for by a spontaneously arising hierarchy of life forms. In our model, the fundamental and limited resource is mental attention. Mental

---

Note: the figures in this chapter are reproduced from originals which could not be enhanced in any way to provide clearer images for the reader.

events, which we describe as interests, using the word in its everyday sense, compete for and consume attention. Interests are emergent properties of the mental process.

Interests have the following properties:

- Interests may be more or less aroused.
  - The degree of arousal of an interest is a function of the magnitude of its emotional charge.
  - Interests are aroused in as many different ways as there are emotions, but to reduce the volume of computation, and simplify presentation, we only model attraction, a fundamental reduction of all other emotions.
- Interests compete for attention, which they consume.
- The arousal of interests is modified by sensation.
- Interests arouse each other.
- An individual's personality is determined as much by the pattern of the interests' inter-arousability as by the nature of the interests themselves.
- The arousal of interests is autocatalytic.
- Interests engender activity.
- Interests are consumed by the activity they engender.

A model of the interest system

The model is expressed as a pair of spatially discretised differential equations. Our mathematical model of the interest system is a densely interconnected and highly diffusive matrix. Nonetheless, the equations produce entities which are recognisably distinct both from one another and from their common background. That is to say, despite the equations' strong diffusion terms, the model generates a landscape of distinct features. We refer to these distinct features as interests. Interests are dynamical objects, patterns of briefly stable flow, produced by fields of positive and negative feedback and the accidents of history. They have no independent existence. The particular role each one plays is dependent on the state of the entire system.

Where: N = Attention, $x(ij)$ = Interest, $y(ij)$ = Activity, bx = the rate at which attention becomes interests = the rate at which interest becomes activity, mx = the rate at which interest arousal decays, my - the rate at which arousal decays, w = the rate of positive feedback, f = basal rate of associational excitation of interests, p = decay factor in resource overlap with distance, d = distance from $x^{\wedge}jj$ to $X(i'j^*)$-

$$\frac{dx_{i,j}}{dt} = \left(bf\left(x_{i,j} + wx_{i,j}^2\right) + b\frac{(1-f)}{4}\left(\left(x_{i-1,j} + wx_{i-1,j}^2\right) + \left(x_{i+1,j} + wx_{i+1,j}^2\right)\right.\right.$$

$$\left.\left. + \left(x_{i,j-1} + wx_{i,j-1}^2\right) + \left(x_{i,j+1} + wx_{i,j+1}^2\right)\right)\right)\left(1 - \frac{\sum_{i',j'} x_{i',j'}\,e^{-\rho d(i,j:i',j')}}{N\sum_{i',j'} e^{-\rho d(i,j:i',j')}}\right) - mx_{i,j}$$

$$\frac{dy_{i,j}}{dt} = \left(sf\left(x_{i,j}y_{i,j} + wy_{i,j}^2\right) + s\frac{(1-f)}{4}\left(\left(x_{i-1,j}y_{i-1,j} + wy_{i-1,j}^2\right) + \right.\right.$$

$$\left.\left. \left(x_{i+1,j}y_{i+1,j} + wy_{i+1,j}^2\right) + \left(x_{i,j-1}y_{i,j-1} + wy_{i,j-1}^2\right) + \left(x_{i,j+1}y_{i,j+1} + wy_{i,j+1}^2\right)\right)\right)$$

N= attention $\qquad$ $x_{i,j}$= interest $\qquad$ $y_{i,j}$= activity

b= the rate at which attention becomes interest

s= the rate at which interest becomes activity

m= the rate at which arousal decays

w= the rate of positive feedback

f= the basal rate of associational excitation of interests

ρ=the decay factor in resource overlap with distance

$d(i,j:i',j')$= the distance between $x_{i,j}$ and $x_{i',j'}$

Figure 2.1: Mind as Dynamical System

We model the environment of mind by a small perturbation in the value of each cell in the matrix at each time step. This is a strategy used in ecological mathematics to create a neutral environment. We use this strategy in the version of the model in the illustration in order to preserve its general features. In fact, we believe that the environment of mind is not neutral but information bearing. Information in the environment would be represented by a bias in the perturbation. Social transactions are modelled by using the output of one model to contribute to the bias of the input of another model with which it shares an environment.

The correspondence between model and mind

I said earlier that the value of a model relies on both its conformity to and its difference from its object. Our model of mind differs from mind itself primarily in that it is happening in culture space, and in the circuits of a computer, rather than as part of our ideas about the functioning of a living person. The value of this difference is that repeatable experiments can be performed with the model.

Clearly, however, what the model has to teach depends on the model's correspondence to its object. I will now survey some of the salient features of this model's conformity with the contemporary understanding of mind.

Mental development

We model the emergence of the landscape of everyday mind as a fiction of sensory input and the pertaining state of the system itself, which is effectively its past. We model three distinct learning processes. The result of each of these processes is that new interests become established in the system.

2.1.2

Interests occupy more than a single cell in the matrix. They are compound, various and multifaceted, rather than homogeneous or monolithic. They are gestalts rather than ideals. New interests enter the system as sub-components of existing interests, as differing aspects of the same thing.

2.1.3

Interests come into being in the model by a process of intermittent, rapid and crisp bifurcations. The creation of interests by bifurcation models the simple linear learning process that might be described as Pavlovian. Such interests are spatially associated within the model.

2.1.4

There is, in addition to simple association, another way in which new interests may come into existence within the system. The population of interests is occasionally augmented by the sudden emergence of clusters of new interests. Our growing ability to describe sudden emergence – that is, how new attractors suddenly appear in complex systems – is illuminating many formerly obscure aspects of the development of natural objects.

We are beginning to learn how complex systems undergo transformations of their fundamental identity. Furthermore, our ability to describe complex and sudden emergence provides us with tools to describe the mechanisms that underlie inspiration, insight and intuition, and to rebut the argument that mind is simple and linear. The equations develop smoothly but also generate discontinuities, modelling both systematic thought and spontaneous mental creativity.

2.2

The propensity of the system to harbour new interests, and the consequent density or quantity of interests present in the system at any one time, is a function of the strength of the system's inhibitory feedback fields. We believe that the density of interests sustained by the system is of fundamental significance in the understanding of the behaviours identified as, and associated with, autism. We will return to this point shortly.

2.3

Our model maximises its symmetry when it is unperturbed. That is to say, whilst the model is not being perturbed, it spontaneously seeks to minimise its informational content. It does not do this by the simple extinction of interests (forgetting), but by minimising internal differences present in the entire interest system. If global symmetry acquisition is the sort of thing that happens to our minds when we sleep, then dreaming may be a vestigial awareness of the process.

2.4

The one-dimensional Voltaera-Lotke equation comes to a cyclic attractor at equilibrium. Our (spatialised) version of the equation can exhibit both micro and macro cyclic behaviour. We speculate, therefore, that cyclic behaviours such as the sleep/waking cycle and the breathing cycle may be generated by similar mechanisms to rocking, flapping and tapping. Cyclic behaviours of this kind may also be linked to such psychological cycles as adventure/reassurance and transgression/forgiveness. We speculate that cyclic behaviour may be part of the stage rather than part of the play. In the very broadest of terms we might say that we feel there just is not enough room for all the stuff in our heads to go in straight lines. It seems easier to imagine that our minds go round and round. In more formal terms, we believe that the mental landscape is comprised of processes rather than states, and that these processes are bound by strange cyclic attractors rather than by point attractors.

2.5

At this stage in the development of our equations we have attempted to map only essential mechanisms. Language and self are two areas of the proposed system which, although not specifically modelled, require special mention. We believe that embedded within the general interest system, most people have an elaborate sub-system of interests which is what they know of language. The manipulation of interest systems is an important function of language and a direct consequence of language as an amplifier of the imagination. Embedded within the language system is an elaborate sub-system which is what we think we know of ourselves. Language brings greatly enhanced detail, durability and communicability to the system of self interests, but these interests are identical in structure to the rest of the interest system.

Ego, ourselves to ourselves, is not the prime mover in our model. We believe that it is the alchemy of language which generates the apparently independent agent, transforming activity into transitive behaviour. We think that the idea of the doing and the done to is one way, just one amongst many ways, in which the world can be imagined. In our model, ego is the spontaneous emergence of a system of images of the imaginer in the imagination. Ego is an emergent property of language, far from the central machinery of mind. In our model, social actions emerge from the play of our interests, including self-interests, from our images of other people, and from the situation in which we find ourselves (Murray, 1997; Stern, 1985).

2.6

Although this model owes little to Freud, we feel that a plausible model of mind should provide some account of the notion of the unconscious mind and the idea of psychological conflict. We do not explicitly model the unconscious mind. However, we propose that just as a minimum level of arousal of an interest is required to trigger an activity, there is a level of arousal so low that it fails to trigger awareness. We do not see this threshold as being sharp or sudden, but imagine that interests at a certain low level of arousal exist at the corner of our mind in the same way we may just see something from the corner of our eye.

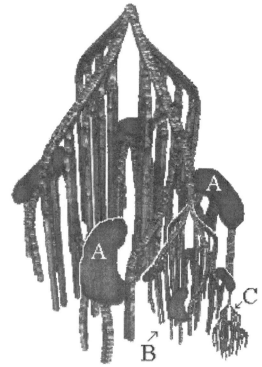

Figure 2.2: A computer graphic of development of interest system showing sudden events A. With added language system B and ego C.

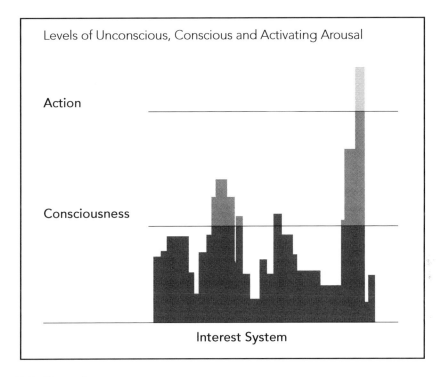

Figure 2.3: Consciousness

Interest system

Among sub-aroused interests are those at the vitally important interface with motor and other low level functions. This interlace requires interests at minimal emotional arousal, certainly below the threshold of consciousness. Indeed, its functioning is often impaired by continuous awareness, as the sportsman or the artist will attest. In our model, competition between interests is not a symptom of mental disease, but the fundamental condition of a functioning system. Behaviours are vectors whose components are conflicting interests. Psychological conflict does not arise unless attractive and aversive interests are simultaneously aroused.

2.7

The final area of correspondence that I will mention in this brief overview is biochemical. There is a parameter, N, in the model that controls the amount of attention available. Attention is the primary resource of the model. Increasing the value of this parameter N increases activity, without affecting the state of the model in any other way. This may be an idealised representation or an increase in the quantity of available excitatory neurotransmitters.

3. Born to Forage – a Model of Autism

I have outlined some of the areas in which our model resembles everyday mind to make it easier to understand what 1 mean by the model having an Autistic calibration. We believe that the attention tunnel or Monotropic Condition is a central feature of behaviours in the Autistic spectrum (Abrahams & Shaw, 1988; Williams I, 1994; Walker, 1997), In our model, the degree to which a mind exhibits the Monotropic Condition is controlled by a single parameter, Ro, which governs the strength of the feedback between interests. If the parameter Ro is set to a low value then many interests are aroused to a moderate degree. If Ro is set high then a few interests are very highly aroused. When many interests are aroused, multiple, complex, behaviours emerge. When few interests arr aroused then a few, intensely motivated, behaviours are engendered.
(Abrahams & Shaw, 1988)

Everyday Parameterisation

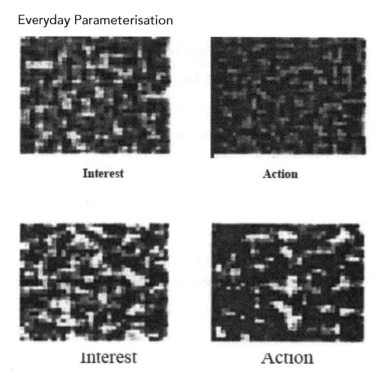

Interest　　　　Action

Interest　　　　Action

Figure 2.4: Broad arousal

Our understanding of the mechanisms which underlie the attention tunnel have informed our intervention in cases of diagnosed autism. Our work with the animator Ferenc Virag emerged from our attempts to, start where the child is, to enter his attention tunnel, to share with him a set of mutually aroused, common interests. Our choice of the personal computer as the environment in which to set up the attention tunnel also sprang from our understanding of these mechanisms (Lesser & Murray, 1997).

However, in addition to providing a theory which can be tested by experiments, certain general features of the situation have recently become apparent. We observe that, in the model, the Monotropic calibration is a particular region in a continuum of types of mind which includes everyday mind. We observe that the Monotropic Condition is merely a possible calibration of the model. It is not associated with the content, or arrangement of the contents of the model.

A theory of autism

It seems to us that the autistic spectrum of behaviours is evidence of one extreme of the normal distribution of types of mind that we would expect to find, given the environment in which the human race has evolved. It is a mind optimised for searching for sustenance in a dangerous environment in which resources are scarce. The attention tunnel which links the unarmed hunter to the prey must be optimised for the immediate high-gain, high-risk opportunity. It must have a propensity to accept what is seen, even when this contradicts what was formerly thought to be known.

It must be sensitive to immediate data rather than to pre-existent or received information, sensitive to clues to where future food resources might be concealed, rather than to knowledge of where food is presently known to be available. Such a mind must have a propensity for actual rather than literal information. It is a mind adapted for heterodoxy, rather than orthodoxy.

Such a mind seems to have the will to error, but is in fact the only sort of mind capable of discoveries that go beyond the known and transform situations (Allen & Lesser, 1991). Only error making leads to metamorphic discovery. In the light of this understanding, several paradoxes of the condition become less puzzling. The capacity for a high degree of sensory acuity is essential in the hunter. Spatial abilities are an obvious requirement. The ability to endure pain, to ignore the agony of the long-distance chase and to go without sleep have also emerged in the selection process.

The skills required in food foraging are similar to those required in war. The stories of Enkido, Achilles, CuChoran, Hercules, Perseval, boy Cornwall on the burning deck, and many other military heroes provide a lexicon of aspects of the syndrome. The stories of heroes also provide examples of exploitation of the weaknesses inherent in the condition. We believe that, where there is the capacity for extreme depth of arousal, there is often less capacity for breadth of arousal. The advantages of adaptation for depth, not breadth, of awareness are apparent in the field not in the camp, at the edge not in the centre, in crisis not in stability. People with the ability to concentrate very hard typically lack the capacity to sustain large numbers of simultaneously aroused interests.

People with the capacity for great depth of interest, adapted for pathfinding at the edge of the known, are poor at elaborate low risk/low gain social activity. This is because language and self are the most dense and complex areas of the interest system, requiring maximum breadth of modelling. We postulate that self and language tasks as they are habitually performed may require more breadth of arousal than is available in some interest systems. Many of the problems in relating to society experienced by people described as autistic are the result of different modalities of language use and of the modelling of the self, other and the words between.

The other extreme of this normal distribution of types of mind consists of people with very broad but not very deep minds. This category includes those most highly rewarded by society, chat show hosts and politicians. Such people do not possess outstanding specific talents, but have great ability to model other people, giving them power to manipulate social, rather than actual, situations.

We cannot think of autism as an illness for which a cure can be discovered (Jordan, 1998). We do however observe in people described as autistic a cast of mind that renders them unsuitable for conventional forms of employment. However, we see this economic frame of reference as holding the key to a happy outcome. In benign circumstances, people with the capacity for deep concentration have a great capacity to learn skills which are beyond the broad mind. Mass production culture may have deprived the deep minded of occasion to contribute to society as the pathfinders to physical resources, but it has opened a vast spectrum of new opportunities. It is the deep mind that has the capacity to read, understand and apply the technical manual, to enter into the intricate labyrinth of the logic of the integrated circuit and the computer program. It is the forager mind, insensitive to the way everybody knows things should be done, which creates the paradigm-transforming technologies.

Appropriate education would enable many ingenious and creative people who are now totally excluded from the mainstream of society to contribute to the economic and cultural life of the community. Education based on understanding could transform this apparent problem into an opportunity.

References

Abrahams RL & Shaw CD (1988) *The Visual Mathematics Library*. Santa Cruz, CA: Aerial Press.

Allen PA (1998) *Cities and Regions as Self-Organizing Systems*. Gordon and Breach.

Eigen ME & Winkler R (1983) *Laws of the Game*. London: Allen Lane.

Thom R (1975) *Structural Stability and Morohoeenisis*. Reading, Ma.: Benjamin Inc.

Prigogene l & Stangers I (1987) *Order Out of Chaos*. New York: Bantam Books.

Tolman EC (1948) Cognitive maps in men and rats. *The Psychological Review* **55** (4) 189-208.

Artigiani R (1993) *From Eoislomoloev to Cosmology: The evolution of cognitive maps*. Amsterdam: Gordon and Breach.

AlIen PA & Lesser M (1991) *Evolution: Traveling in an imaginary landscape parallelism, learning and evolution*. Berlin: Springer-Verlag.

Murray DKC (1997) *Normal and Otherwise Living and Learning with Autism*. Conference Proceedings, ARU Sunderland.

Stern DN (1985) *The Interpersonal World of the Infant*. New York: Basic Books.

Murray DKC (1992; 1993) Companion volumes to this one.

Williams I (1994) In the Real World. *Journal of the Association for Persons with Severe Handicaps* **19** (3).

Walker A (1997) Sep\rate Realities. In: Living and Learning with Autism. Conference proceedings. ARU Sunderland.

Blackburn J & Andrews DN (YEAR) in our poster presentation (this volume).

Lesser M & Murray IC (1997) '*/!utism and Computing*' Video Tape. London: Autism and Computing.

Allen PA & Lesser M (1991) *Evolutionary Human Systems: Evolutionary theories of economic and technological change*. Routledge.

Jordan R (1998) *Is Autism a Pathology?* this volume.

Chapter 3: Dimensions of difference

By Dinah Murray

This chapter is based on an ecological, embodied, enactive and exploratory account of minds. It offers an alternative to both medical and social models of disability, as it assumes that autistic differences have an embodied material basis that relates to resource allocation, and that those differences are not usually a medical matter. Like the social model, it sees the environment as often disabling. It locates both strengths and issues within an interest model of mind (and society) that amplifies the narrative about intense interests which threads through every set of diagnostic criteria that has ever been proposed. It proposes that flow, force, direction and distribution of energy are essential features, and that this directed force can be thought of as emotional (see Asma & Gabriel, 2019).

Outline of model

In both life and theory, information, attitudes and points of view are welded together in interests; interests are what change when new information arrives. There are material correlations of this; they change by ruling out possibilities and assuming a new form as a result. The process is more like digestion – sorting out the valuable from the waste – than the application of logic to propositions (see Asma & Gabriel, 2019)

All humans have only partly overlapping concerns and histories (Murray, 1986). The integrated account of minds as interest systems proposed here, argues that the varied nature of interests – in focus, in topic, in subjective including sensory experience, in intensity, in motility, in use of feedback loops, in longevity, in social acceptability, in capacity to tolerate inconsistency – can be seen to underpin the varied personalities and dispositions of all human beings.

Mainly, I use the word 'interest' in a way that fits with its very wide range of ordinary meanings, i.e. more as a natural than a scientific term – but this chapter is partly meant to show how thinking about it within a dynamic mathematical model can be illuminating. 'Interests' range from fleeting moments to lasting passions, from narrow fixations and self-seeking plots, to duties and universal concerns; and communities of interest can extend from family and friends, teams, gangs, brands and nations with long histories, to casual folk at bus stops; and from mutual aid to the self-seeking vested interests of corporations and their actors, and the bureaucratic interests of the state. Interests prepare us for action and for interaction. Though this is mainly about humans, all living things have survival interests and act to further them. Interests are where you direct your energy: energy is a scarce resource (Lesser & Murray, 1998, Goldknopf, 2013) which is constantly needed and must be distributed effectively and with minimum waste, both cognitively in the brain, and through processes of actual digestion.

Basic idea regarding autism as a human variant

This model depicts a system that is far from equilibrium, which in autism I suggest tends towards more extreme polarisation across whole systems, with steeper gradients that create strongly differentiated positions in contrast to areas with an absence of defining information. This hyper/hypo pattern seems to recur at many levels (Holiga *et al*, 2019; Cohut, 2018; Xu *et al*, 2018; and see a multitude of personal reports). It must, I think, have a deep physiological basis that is hinted at in the research of Pfaff and Barbas (2019), which suggests an 'imbalance in the fundamental dichotomy between behavioural approach and avoidance' may be crucial to understanding autism.

Distinctive intensity of interest has been in the diagnostic criteria for autism at every stage, yet has been little explored (see, though, Wood, 2019; Leatherland, 2018; Russell *et al*, 2019; Lawson, 2010; Murray, 1992; Murray *et al*, 2005; Goldfarb *et al*, 2019). We think self-generated activity in autism, including the activity of seeking (see Asma & Gabriel, 2019), has a mono thrust (Lesser & Murray, 1998; Murray, 2018): more processing resource goes to the focal interest with higher levels of subjective intensity and perhaps of objective local arousal, contrasting with areas lacking in structure and focus that have not yet been explored and hence not yet been sculpted by relevant experiences or transformed into 'priors' (i.e. prior beliefs) and competencies.

That sharp contrast is a key part of the overall picture which tends to be pervasively forgotten because of the negative shadow that pathology casts over interpretation. There is a wealth of anecdotal evidence about a phenomenon that implies the opposite of Pellicano and Burr's 'weak priors' (2012) – i.e. the extreme distress and emotional meltdown of many, especially younger, autistic people when confronted with unexpected change. In autism the contexts for interpretation, when they are active, may be atypically vivid rather than weak – in extreme contrast with areas in which 'priors' may be completely absent. I suggest that the less autistic a person is the more thinly spread and tenuously connected their 'priors' will be over all, versus being connected strongly or not at-all. The strength of those socially typical priors will tend to derive from their being widely shared, rather than from their inherent reliability, consistency or vividness. This is a way of interpreting the 'weak central coherence' idea that allows for inherent compensations (Chown, 2014; Leatherland, 2018).

Areas of lack tend to be the dominant focus in the autism industry. These are where the money goes, so the wider their mouths the more they can swallow. Caveat emptor! Let the buyer beware: the pressures to buy are huge, the ads seem authoritative and the criteria for atypicality are presented as pathological: all set to embrace more and more types of human as essentially ill just for being who they are. So those who care about these diseased people must be obliged to make them better if it's humanly possible (see Russel *et al*, 2019).

The intensity of interest that is seen as criterial to identifying autism in all Diagnostic and Statistical Manuals of Mental Disorders (DSMs 1-5) may enhance speed, accuracy, volume, duration, thoroughness, dedication, engagement and commitment. These are known features of autistic people who have been blessed with the chance to contribute those qualities to the human pot. If they are lucky enough to recognise and appreciate them in themselves – as I have always been – that can make the difference between chronic depression and the ability to act effectively in the world (Russell *et al*, 2019b; Shah, 2019).

The impact of this intensity on emotional state is likely to be either 'very X' or 'not X at all' (Pfaff & Barbas, 2019). This can be associated with catastrophic despair and a polarised desire for permanent avoidance. Or the opposite may occur, as super ecstatic joy thrills through the whole body and bursts out in excited expression, likely to be way beyond what anyone around is tuned to expect. From the outside, both these types of emotional expression are likely to be stigmatised as inappropriate and unwelcome; that means that the exchange of emotional support which is a feature of happy communication and mutual connection is much less likely to occur (Sasson *et al*, 2017; Milton, 2012; Bolis *et al*, 2017; Goffman, 1959, 1964; Stern, 1985; Jaswal & Akhtar, 2018).

Extreme polarisation may be the key to monotropic patterns of resource distribution in autism (Murray, 2019; Lesser & Murray, 1998 Goldknopf, 2013), creating areas of relative consistency and stability (i.e. 'priors') – enduring within a highly dynamic n-dimensional system, which alternate with unstructured and untuned areas or 'gaps'. These patterns guarantee extreme variation within and between individuals; accepting that is key to understanding where and how one can intervene when those idiosyncratic patterns are causing social disruption and attracting the concerned gaze of parents, teachers and clinicians. Because of problems with social embeddedness there is a strong tendency for other people's concerns to be magnified and elevated at the expense of the individuals' who are being worrying. Parents are there to know best and all children are on a learning curve that needs support. However lovingly these concerns are felt and expressed, they can impose negative expectations which become part of a person's identity, perhaps sometimes to the detriment of their lifelong well-being.

It follows from the extreme variety of autistic skills, preferences and dispositions I have been describing, that interpreting large scale results in autism research is a hazardous business in which much information can be too easily lost if the sensitivity to individual detail is not preserved. Being distinctive is what the diagnosis of autism itself requires, which strongly hints that understanding autism will be furthered by examining rather than discarding the qualities that make the distinction.

The small exploratory study by Høgsbro (2011) comparing ABA with other approaches in a Danish primary setting showed up how important it is to look at individuals whose distinctive profiles will be ironed out in a statistical analysis. It is clear that some children had experienced negative effects of intervention, in some cases to an extreme degree; some had also benefited. The much larger PACT study methodology (Green *et al*, 2010; Charman, 2018) has similarly allowed the researchers to go on fruitfully mining the data from varied angles – and revealing some extreme differences between individuals. There are often unexpected findings in research seeking to follow up on averaged results – autistic research subjects tend to fall into polarised categories of response, which is in line with the long-recognised, distinctively autistic and very 'spiky' skills – and preferences – profiles. We consider that this is the key to understanding and integrating other features of the highly varied autistic population.

One of the consequences of applying a dynamic interest-focused model of minds (and in fact of all living things) is that it has strong implications for improving practice. For example, it implies that new learning and new understanding, and the noticing and filling in of previously un-noticed gaps, may in principle happen *any* time. 'Development' is a lifelong process, not just a stage: learning more is a lifelong project. From personal reports, including my own, I know that even among the most obviously able young people, noticing such qualities as being gendered, or the fact that other bodies are being directed by other minds, or the fact that those other minds may have other thoughts, or that one can't directly feel other people's pains, can all be experienced as sudden discoveries after several years of being exposed to the evidence. People report that in retrospect it seems extraordinary to them that they missed out on these central facts for so long.

Capacity is highly fluctuating both in relation to inner states and environmental engagement: this is recognised in the UK's Mental Capacity Act and its guidelines, and is a frequently reported and commented on aspect of life for autistic people. It is also why 'spoon theory' – which has limited processing resources as its key theme (Miserandino, 2003; Memmott, 2018) – is so popular, i.e. because it provides a neat way of describing the phenomenology of autistic daily experience. I return in Points to Ponder at the end of this chapter (p31), to how seeing autism in the context of interests can affect practice for the better.

Unfortunately, the fundamental idea of monotropism has to some extent been misunderstood and misrepresented since we first published it (Murray, 1992; Lesser & Murray, 1998; Murray et al, 2005) because it has not been understood in the context of minds as interest systems. Positive hyperfocusing abilities – giving more to an individual's leading interests and less to others – can make for enhanced processing, not diminished, as portrayed in Tony Attwood's description (2007) of it being like 'looking down a rolled up piece of paper' and only seeing through that while not seeing the rest. This is partially true, but it leaves out the complementary positives, and is thus much closer to the weak central coherence hypothesis than to monotropism conceived within an interest model of mind.

The weak central coherence idea overlaps with a monotropism approach but pathologises some of the same phenomena while tending to ignore enhancements like those found by Mottron and colleagues (Mottron *et al*, 2006; Samson *et al*, 2012) or which were singled out by autistic participants in Russell *et al* (2019b), such as the ability to hyperfocus, and the disposition to accuracy. I would add to those a fierce desire to be right, which can be a productive goad in the right context. Seeing autistic nature fanatic Chris Packham getting answers wrong on the BBC's Curious Creatures TV quiz is a striking illustration of this, provoking much amusement in his colleagues. When one has both prioritised accuracy and done a lot of discovering and concluding things for oneself, there is more staked on being right, and commensurately greater distress at being wrong, than if one has merely borrowed one's certainties from others.

Psychiatrists Rutter and Pickles (2016) say, 'Howlin, Goode, Hutton, and Rutter (2009) showed that about a third of individuals with autism had exceptional cognitive or savant skills. *This was a much higher rate than had been previously considered. What we do not know is why these appear to be more frequent in individuals with autism* and what is the biological basis for the phenomenon' (emphasis added). We believe this shouldn't be a surprise, because the ability to have exceptionally focused attention involves being able to devote more processing resource at any given moment to whatever is of interest. In that light, the tendency to monotropic thinking is a transparent explanation for these exceptional abilities.

In a study led by Ginny Russell in Exeter (Russell *et al*, 2019b), autistic participants reported, regarding their own perceived traits:

'The ability to hyperfocus, attention to detail, good memory, and creativity were the most frequently described traits. Participants also described specific qualities relating to social interaction, such as honesty, loyalty, and empathy for animals or for other autistic people. In thematic analysis we found that traits associated with autism could be experienced either as advantageous or disadvantageous dependent on moderating influences.'

The enhanced processing by autistic people found by Mottron et al is also consonant with this model, though portrayals such as Attwood's (2007) would suggest the opposite. The monotropism idea has been attacked for implications it does not have because the working model within which it has been interpreted is poorly adapted to represent the role of interests, as the nature of interest and interests has been so little explored. For example, lots of research has revealed that switching attention is often but not always slower in autistic research subjects of various ages: 'In those with autism, brain connections remained synchronized for up 20 seconds, while they disappeared faster in individuals without this condition' (Cohut, 2018) Yet *within-task* switching may even be superfast and co-ordination no problem.

Michelle Dawson (2018) has tweeted that monotropism is contradicted by findings tested using some specific Ravens matrices, which show no problem for autistic participants in integrating and switching between different strands of information. When the task is clear, and completing it involves switching attention, then if task uptake has been achieved, an interest model would predict no problem because the switching is *within* interest not *between* interests. In fact, *so long as task uptake has occurred and been engaged with*, then – all other things being equal – the monotropism account of autism predicts likely superior performance.

Despite more than half a century of pathologised framing of autistic and other atypicalities, current world views tend to recognise that variety in every species benefits that species, and that 'error making' is in effect the same as exploration, be it at an individual or a reproductive species level (Allen & McGlade, 1987). From this perspective, predictability crucially frees up energy for exploratory behaviour towards the less predictable (Stern, 1985). Cutting out the unexpected and providing stability are sometimes put forward as the key ingredients for autistic contentment, education and provision. But that view (which can be seen as supported by predictive coding's emphasis on reducing energy expenditure and restoring homeostasis through predictability) needs balancing against the value of spending energy on purposes other than reassurance that things have not changed. An interest system is necessarily a value system as its job is to allocate attention and action potential *to what one cares about getting right*.

Unfortunately, care providers tend to use a need for predictability as an excuse to avoid adventure; anxiety about health and safety responsibilities also plays into this shutting down of experience (rather often along with personally dampening prescribed drugs, supposed to help control 'challenging behaviours'). Instead, emotional security should underpin adventure to the max.

Pathologising human traits – and trying to fix them

There is no fully functional rational type of being against which a pathologised autistic phenotype can be measured, and there has never been such a type. The search for 'normal' is a fundamental error in understanding diversity – an explanation for every specific sort of deviation seems called for. From that angle, the disability industrial complex, which has been massively boosted by the inclusion of every labelled vulnerability, spots fertile niches, and pathologies sprout ad lib. Any *similarities* that emerge between such varied people may be as much in need of explanation! That said, as I've been arguing, I do think there is a common thread that unites autistic dispositions and perspectives: namely a tendency to give more to one's current self-generated, authentic, interest – whatever that is – and commensurately less to all other processing needs. That creates a steep contrast between areas of excellence and areas of ignorance. That can have dramatic impact on a person's life course, both positive and negative. Chances to learn and explore should be ensured at every stage of life.

From this perspective, wide dynamic diversity is an inevitable feature both of the overall population of human thinkers and actors across time and space, and of individual thinkers and actors. Yet in relation to autism, if a difference is identified, it will be automatically classed as a defect (Gernsbacher, 2006[2]).

Interest is a quality that tends to elude measurement – except when it is deliberately (and perversely) reduced to 'behaviours'. The third diagnostic criterion has always been about interests; within ABA and its variants, that has been reframed as about behaviours. Behaviourism is a reduction of dimensions which creates an illusion of scientific worth by focusing only on what we can 'know for sure'. However, the effects of what we don't *exactly* know can be as ramified and real – and use up more real energy to integrate – while also sometimes being fun to pursue (Stern, 1985).

A main mistake of behaviourism is to deny value to what cannot at this point be measured. New ways of measuring newly defined events have always been

---

2   See also various tweets by Michelle Dawson – tweets such as this: https://twitter.com/autismcrisis/status/703582386102149120

technology dependent (Grant, 1986; McCluhan, 1964) and it looks likely that at least some of the behaviourist resistance to acknowledging the hidden life of minds must crumble as new light is constantly being shed on how much is happening in brains (if not on the meaning of those events), thanks to digitised opportunities. Instead of obstructing and diverting autistic flow states, those should be integrated into the life flows of all around them: that is what inclusion should be about, not about fitting in through loss of self.

Understanding the new findings that are constantly being published in a coherent manner is one of the great challenges of psychology – or should we just be calling it bioenergetics? I believe that the material basis for these systems is all about flow, force, direction and distribution of energy (Murray, 2018, revised 2019; McDonnell & Milton, 2014). Natural variation in those, as well as in the highly varied topics that interest different people, implies a radical rethink of how autism results are understood and reported and contextualised with other atypicalities.

Gernsbacher, a well-established US research psychologist, was one of the first to communicate directly and equitably with autistic adults such as Janet Norman-Bain, Michelle Dawson and Ralph Smith, and was one of the first to publish about the pathologising bias of research reports (Gernsbacher, 2006). She demonstrated that when identical features are found in the non-autistic subjects the polarities of supposed normality are reversed: *Oh dear! Autistic X has a thin brain lining; Oh good! typical Y has a thick brain lining. Oh dear! Autistic X has a thick brain lining; Oh good! typical Y has a thin brain lining…* is a light parody of this way of thinking.

Dawson herself has long noted that bias, and she regularly comments on positive research findings with a wry 'Interventions sure to follow'. Over and over again, observed differences are reported as defects when attributed to autistic people: but in our model, major differences can occur in many different ways and should be objectively noted, not assumed to be inherently functional or dysfunctional.

Recall that in the diagnostic criteria everything is a pathology, including strong and passionate interests. This casts a dark shadow over the concept of autism: not everything is a problem and seeing it that way is itself disadvantageous, even though there are some real extreme difficulties that must not be discounted. Even intense interests are frequently targeted in behavioural interventions despite the evident pleasure they bring.

One of the versions of social dysfunction autistic people are accused of is 'seeking attention'. That is wrong in more ways than one. Firstly, for some autistic people, perhaps especially women, being focus of attention is an acutely uncomfortable situation. I am such a person, and I can testify that when people assume my loss of emotional control is actually evidence of manipulative intent, the situation becomes instantly catastrophic. A combination of projected inauthentic 'mind reading' from others, and extreme autistic reactions of derailment or meltdown can cause profound and lasting distress to all concerned with cataclysmic effects on both individuals and relationships. As so often, we also find opposite patterns in autism, where the structured and predictable attention directed at performers on a stage can be handled by many autistic people with relative ease and pleasure.

Secondly, it is not rational to view attention seeking as a pathology in itself when typical people are constantly and skilfully extracting attention from others, presumably because they seek that attention. They do it with words and they do it with gestures: they do it competently because others respond warmly. On those daily life occasions when we may have to actively seek attention ourselves, we are typically seen as awkward and possibly hostile, or not noticed at-all. Then we are likely to be punished for succeeding if we eventually do get noticed. These blatantly inconsistent attitudes do not encourage trust and serve only to confirm prejudice and reinforce stigma.

Tending to behaviour that seeks to gain attention, to inauthenticity via 'masking', and to being 'unable to read minds' or 'mind blind', are routinely conceptualised as distinctively autistic trends. These accusations are often internalised and can lead to distressing states of mind, ruminations and even suicidal thoughts. It is no surprise that many autistic people see themselves as distinctively bad or worthless when this is the narrative they find themselves in. Yet each of those descriptions is just as true of people who are not autistic. As discussed above, communication routinely entails attention seeking; masking, too, is constantly deployed by most people most of the time. For an account of the complexities of presenting oneself in everyday life, Goffman's (1959) book on the theme from a sociological perspective remains unbeatable – Shakespeare on the theatrical nature of human performance is also a great source. What appears to be most distinctive about autistic masking is that we notice doing it, and we really don't like the sense of inauthenticity it gives us; also, we may hide by curtailing expression entirely rather than try to adjust our presentation subtly when we know we don't know how; or we may try to do the latter by mirroring. As I once wrote, 'I build myself a house of glass. You look, and thinking you see me, you see yourself...'

I suggest that the discomfort of inauthenticity is pervasively more disturbing and distressing for autistic people. It is bound up with why extrinsic rewards are likely to be less effective for autistic individuals than the intrinsic value of engagement: for example, 'On a prospective memory task, autistics perform as well as typical controls when asked to help others, but not when offered a reward... In contrast to our predictions' (Atagassena *et al*, 2019) – but not to the predictions implicit in the model of mind proposed in this chapter.

Sports psychology is one of the most successful areas of professional expertise – it has rather clearly visible results. Deci & Ryan (2000) holds that 'Intrinsic motivation represents the most self-determined or autonomous behaviour regulation by inherent interest, enjoyment and satisfaction.' It recognises that:

'There are three types of intrinsic motivation:
1. *Intrinsic motivation toward knowledge is observed if an activity is performed for the pleasure or satisfaction of learning or understanding something.*
2. *Intrinsic motivation toward accomplishment is defined as engaging in an activity for the pleasure of accomplishing or creating something.*
3. *Intrinsic motivation toward stimulation occurs when an activity is performed to obtain stimulating experiences.'*

In my experience, autistic people typically share all those intrinsic motivations. These are what we are most likely to do to enhance our flow states such as Csikszentmihályi (1990) and McDonnell and Milton (2014) describe. Among implications of that, it seems self-stimulation is just a special case of a universally valued feedback loop, and yet another case of inappropriately stigmatised and targeted behaviour, along with a futile struggle to block and frustrate it. We seek what we feel a need for – there is nothing unusual in that: our methods are atypical but our needs are human needs.

As Dutch researchers Späth *et al* (2019) put it, autistic people:
'*...usually do not deny their own needs, values and interests. This makes them less prone than non-autistic people to adapt their preferences to external influences, which might be seen as sticking to an authentic way of living.'*

They say we are 'independent in [our] own way by following [our] genuine interests'. To me these are central points to recognise if successful connections are to be made between autistic and non-autistic people.

Given the positioning of all people within external power structures, forced inauthenticity creates even greater vulnerability by damaging self-belief in one's own capacities. I suggest that it is both more disturbing for autistic people – as all felt disturbances will tend to be greater and all noticed contradictions more dramatic (see above and Murray, 2017) – and more likely that autistics will be subjected to it, given the pervasive hold of behaviourist thinking within the autism industrial complex and given the lowly positioning of those of all ages subjected to it.

The guidelines to the Care Quality Commission (CQC) advocate the nice sounding 'Positive Behaviour Support' (PBS) approach to the difficult ('challenging'!) cared for adults whose provision is monitored by them. This has meant that even the best care providers, who might once have questioned the compatibility of this behaviour-fixing approach with the official aspirations of person-centred attitudes and plans, have generally succumbed to the pressure to show they are using PBS, as the imprimatur of the CQC is essential for their survival. (Because it is vaguely defined, that may not always mean much regarding what providers actually do, but is vital 'window dressing' for monitoring purposes.)

Another frequent accusation is of 'mind blindness' – apparently a 'dysfunction' that is especially prominent in autistic pathology. This is fundamentally wrong from two very different angles. It is wrong because nobody can actually 'read' or 'see into' another person's mind. Tuning in to another's interests and substantially sharing prior assumptions can situate people in a comfortable dialogue in which good hunches happen about each other's hopes and fears. This is not much like reading, it is a lot more like dancing or sailing or improvising music together, and concerns reciprocal noticing, intuition, engagement and attunement (Stern, 1985; Bolis *et al*, 2017; Milton, 2012; Green, 2011; Constant *et al*, 2018).

This ability to tune into another's interests is intact for autistic people, *so long as the interests and background are authentically shared*. Indeed, many autistic people feel that when attunement is successful it can be truly excellent (it tends to involve acceptance and appreciation – see Hallett, 2019). For example, a significant number of people report that time at Autscape, the UK's autistic-led annual conference-cum-retreat, has a quality of mutual support and understanding that they rarely experience in other settings (www.autscape.org.uk). At Autscape, one is in the company of unpressurised other autistic people[3] in a pleasing setting with shared interests to the fore and the capacity to control interaction to an unusual degree, thanks to the interaction signal system of coloured cards that is in place. Like all social encounters anywhere, even at Autscape interactions can go horribly wrong. Yet most of the Autscapees have an experience of belonging and of generously supportive kindness for which they feel permanent nostalgia the rest of the year (personal communications, many, over many years).

Heasman *et al* (2019) demonstrates that this mutual empathy is observable in other settings and with less obviously able autistic people, as does my own friendship with non-speaking autistic artist Ferenc Virag. We shared many insights and pleasures through shared activities and viewpoints – and he identified me as autistically on his side of the normal/abnormal boundary before I had identified myself. We met at his autism specialist school when he was 13. I used to spend some time once a week in the classroom with him. After a few of these sessions, Ferenc was meant to be doing some writing before we explored other interests together,

---

3   That does not include the noble souls who are helping run the event.

and he pushed the pencil and paper towards me – very clearly inviting me to take over the task. I replied that, 'I think I might be in trouble myself if I did it for you,' and he responded immediately by taking them back.

That Milton's well known 'double empathy problem' (Milton, 2012) can reflect general differences between autistic/autistic and typical/autistic communications has been nicely demonstrated by Crompton and Fletcher Watson (2020). As well as being of similar 'neurotypes' helping effective communication, there is a pervasive need for shared interests at least partly shaped by common experience (contexts and 'priors'). Without that commonality, all minds are 'blind' to one another: it is not a reading of propositions but a sharing of interests and projects – and thus of attitudes and experience – that is missing. Understanding another person really is not much like having a theory.

Real problems

Part of relating honestly and authentically to autistic people is recognising the real difficulties and struggles we can encounter. Assuming that if we just 'tried harder' these could be overcome without social assistance is unfair for two reasons: because we are likely already trying as hard as we can; and because other people typically can easily access social assistance as they have been busily prioritising social relations since they were born.

The real problems include a greater likelihood of intensely felt experience, which must increase risk of acute pain and distress, and also of widespread numbness and confusion: these may have significant parallels with recognised trauma states. 'Having autism can sometimes mean enduring a litany of traumatic events, starting from a young age. And for many, those events may add up to severe and persistent post-traumatic stress disorder' (Gravitz, 2018). In a personal communication, Sonny Hallett wonders if autistic ways of thinking may 'make us more vulnerable to developing the signs of trauma?... Does the impact of trauma exaggerate what are understood as autistic traits?' My guess is that the increased risk of phenomenally intense negatives and positives I propose must boost the risk of trauma responses, and our poorly understood expressive behaviours' impact on others must increase the likelihood of negative feedback further entrenching a trauma response.

That numbness and confusion which entail lack of clear direction may also underpin problems of inertia that can escalate into full-blown life-threatening catatonia. Dr Amitta Shah's (2019) psycho-ecological approach to restoring function to people stuck in this negative state involves significant structuring of the environment to scaffold action. She has often found this to be an effective approach to what have been seen as medically intractable problems. A more intermittent but also inimical pattern to desirable action may be associated with events of high importance which can seem to form a resource drain around themselves.

As well as highlighting patchy individual excellence as a puzzle in regard to its relationship with autism, Rutter and Pickles (2016) also single out as a perplexing feature 'the frequency of temporary developmental regression involving language loss, which Pickles *et al* (2009) showed applied to over a quarter of individuals with autism'. Loss of language use tends to happen at one of two stages: during the initial baby to toddler process of acquisition; and in the teens when the will to emit speech sometimes seems to evaporate. Both of these phases are widely seen as mysterious, and – unlike most features of autism (Murray, 2019) – how they fit in with monotropism is no more obvious than how they fit with any other story about autism. However, if we consider that language is standardly used as a tool for manipulating interest systems (Mey, 1985; Murray, 1986) we may gain some insight into the problems with it at these different stages, which are likely related to the upsetting – discombobulating – nature of surprise.

Chomsky (1965) rightly made much of the infinite productivity of language systems: they are a wonder! But the downside is that, except in a number of ritualised or scripted contexts such as meeting and greeting, or chanting responses, outside those predictable moments speech unleashes high degrees of unpredictability into the world. When speech is lost in young children, perhaps that's sometimes a sign of being troubled by its unpredictability, and that may be especially troubling because it has the power to wrench one's attention any which way, obliging a sudden unexpected refocusing. Complementary features of the surprise potential of speech emerge later in life if the limits of a speaker's control over the impact of what they say become obvious to them or others. Speech is meant to be used to express one's own interests, yes, but also to manipulate other people's, not steamroll or shock them. Speaking 'without due care' can have a catastrophically unpredicted effect on hearers. When this enters a speaker's awareness they may well be drawn to avoid its associated risks as they have become convinced they cannot work out how to exercise 'due care'. So, one way or another, speech is a high-risk activity and that may provide an ecological explanation for its loss at these different stages.

Some wild speculation: a further real set of problems follow from seizure risk, which is elevated in autism – another autism puzzle mentioned by Rutter and Pickles (2016). Similarly puzzling is the correlation that also seems to obtain with Ehlers Danlos Syndrome, a problem that makes people stretchy and over flexible, and also often co-occurs with epilepsy. Although it seems far-fetched, could there be hints at parallels in both these undoubted pathologies, to alternating hyper and hypo activities seen in the monotropic pattern? And could that in turn be connected to some deep level extremes of neuronal polarisation such as those seen in attraction and aversion as reported by Pfaff and Barbas (2019)?

Points to ponder: how to fix your own behaviours

- Remember how different others are from you, within a shared humanity.
- Consider that everyone likes truth, enjoyable experiences and stimulation.
- Be frank, be clear and as honest as you can, including being open about uncertainties:
  - neither over-praise nor over-blame: doing either will undermine trust – be authentic yourself.
- Consider your relative powers.
- Consider how easily you can tap into social support systems compared to the other person.
- If a person can tell you how they feel and what they can cope with, then assume they know better than you about that, and about what they can manage:
  - please do your best to find those out by polite probing as required
  - be supportive, with humility.
- Try not to worry about the behaviours of others, either for themselves or for their impact on you: there's probably not much you can really do except patiently expect better when more has been understood.
- Do not rush, processing time and sometimes recovery time are often needed by all parties.
- Do not assume all behaviours are communicative or in some way directed at you:
  - Sometimes they are, sometimes they aren't: cultivate alertness to this.
- Try to notice it when you project your own interests and experiences into interpreting others' – this is harmful to your chances of making an authentic connection.
- Do not assume ill-will unless you have very strong evidence.
- Do not assume unsupported competence; do assume potential competence.
- Allow for lifelong learning.
- All people need to get others to align with their interests. This can easily not work however skilfully attempted, due to the essential unpredictability and incomplete knowableness of humans, and their potential resistance to being realigned.

- Comfort and discomfort are part of the highly varied overall picture which should be factored in to understanding:
  - Promoting comfort enhances confidence and exploration potential
  - Creatures thrive in a comfort + excitement dynamic
  - Opportunities to explore and learn need to be part of everyone's lives – Imagine how you would feel without them
- Remember, nobody's perfect and that includes you.

References

Allen PM & JM McGlade (1987) Evolutionary Drive: The effect of microscopic diversity, error making & noise. *Foundation of Physics* **17** (7): 723–728.

Atagassena M, Sheppard D & Hendriks M (2019) Do importance instructions improve time-based prospective remembering in autism spectrum conditions? *Research in Developmental Disabilities* **90** 1-13.

Asma ST & Gabriel R (2019) *The Emotional Mind: The Affective Roots of Culture and Cognition*. Harvard University Press.

Attwood T (2007) *The Complete Guide to Asperger Syndrome*. Jessica Kingsley Publishing.

Bolis D, Balsters J, Becchiod NC & Schilbacha L (2017) Beyond Autism: Introducing the Dialectical Misattunement Hypothesis and a Bayesian Account of Intersubjectivity. *Psychopathology* **50** 355–372

Charman T (2018) Address to the Autistica Discover Conference, London UK.

Chomsky N (1965) *Aspects of the Theory of Syntax*. MIT Press.

Chown N (2013) The mismeasure of Autism. Autonomy vol 1.2 http://www.larry-arnold.net/Autonomy/index.php/autonomy/article/view/AR5/html update?

Cohut M (2018) *What does autism look like in the brain?* https://www.medicalnewstoday.com/articles/323741

Constant A, Bervoets J, Hens K *et al*. (2018) Precise Worlds for Certain Minds: An Ecological Perspective on the Relational Self in Autism. *Topoi* **39**, 611–622

Crompton CJ & Fletcher-Watson S (2020) Autistic peer-to-peer information transfer is highly effective. *Autism: International Journal of Research and Practice* OnlineFirst https://doi.org/10.1177/1362361320919286

Csikszentmihályi M (1990) *Flow: The Psychology of Optimal Experience*. Harper & Row.

Deci EL & Ryan RM (2000) The 'what' and 'why' of goal pursuits: Human needs and the self-determination of behaviour. *Psychological Inquiry* **11** 227–268.

De Jaeger H (2013) Embodiment and sense-making in autism. *Front. Integr. Neurosci*. March. Available at: https://www.frontiersin.org/articles/10.3389/fnint.2013.00015/full

Gernsbacher MA (2006) How to Spot Bias in Research. Association for Psychological Science, Presidential address. Vol 19.

Gernsbacher MA & Pripas-Kapit S (2012) Who's missing the point? A commentary on claims that autistic persons have a specific deficit in figurative language comprehension. *Metaphor & Symbol*, **27**, 93–105.

Goffman E (1959) *Presentation of Self in Everyday Life*. Anchor Books.

Goffman E (1964) Stigma: Notes on the Management of Spoiled Identity Englewood Cliffs, NJ: Prentice-Hall.

Goldfarb Y, Gal E & Golan O (2019) A Conflict of Interests: A Motivational Perspective on Special Interests and Employment Success of Adults with ASD. *Journal of Autism and Developmental Disorders*.

Goldknopf (2013) Atypical resource allocation may contribute to many aspects of autism. *Front. Integr. Neurosci.* Available at: https://doi.org/10.3389/fnint.2013.00082

Grant GP (1986) *Technology and Justice.* Notre Dame: Canada.

Gravitz L (2018) *At the intersection of autism and trauma* [online]. Spectrum. Available at: https://www.spectrumnews.org/features/deep-dive/intersection-autism-trauma/ (accessed January 2020).

Green J et al (2010) Parent-mediated communication-focused treatment in children with autism (PACT): a randomised controlled trial. *Lancet* **375** (9732): 2152–2160.

Green J (2011) Art and Mental State: An interpersonal approach to painting. *Manchester Memoirs* Vol 148.

Hallett S (2019) Intense Connections. Autscape. https://link.medium.com/ywNqoJZLm7

Heasman B and Gillespie A (2019) Neurodivergent intersubjectivity: Distinctive features of how autistic people create shared understanding. *Autism* **23** (4) 910–921.

Hogsbro K (2011) *Ethical consideration following an evaluation of preschool programs for children with autism spectrum disorders* [Thesis]. Aalborg University.

Holiga et al (2019) Patients with autism spectrum disorders display reproducible functional connectivity alterations. *Science Translational Medicine.*

Jaswal VK and Akhtar N (2018) Being vs. Appearing Socially Uninterested: Challenging Assumptions about Social Motivation in Autism. *Behavioural and Brain Sciences* **42.**

Lawson W (2010) *The Passionate Mind: How People with Autism Learn.* Jessica Kinglsey Publishers.

Leatherland J (2018) *Understanding how autistic pupils experience secondary school: autism criteria, theory and FAMe™.* Doctoral thesis, Sheffield Hallam University.

Lesser M and Murray D (1998) Mind as a Dynamical System. In: Psychobiology of Autism: current research and practice. Durham University. Conference papers: obtainable from Autism Research Unit, School of Health Sciences, University of Sunderland, UK.

McDonnell A and Milton D (2014) *Going with the Flow: Reconsidering 'repetitive behaviour' through the concept of 'flow states'.* In: Jones, Glenys and Hurley, Elizabeth (Eds). Good Autism Practice: autism, happiness and wellbeing. BILD, Birmingham, UK, pp38–47.

McLuhan M (1964) *Understanding Media, the extensions of man.* Routledge, London.

Memmott A (2018) *Autism and Spoon Theory* [online]. Available at: http://annsautism.blogspot.co.uk/2018/02/autism-and-spoon-theory.html (accessed January 2020).

Merleau Ponty M (1945) Phenomenology of Perception, trans., Colin Smith, London and New York: Routledge.

Mey J (1985) Whose Language: A study in linguistic pragmatics. Benjamin's Paperbacks, Amsterdam/Philadelphia.

Miserandino C (2003) *The Spoon Theory.* https://butyoudontlooksick.com/articles/written-by-christine/the-spoon-theory/

Milton DEM (2012) On the ontological status of autism: the 'double empathy problem'. *Disability & Society* **27** (6). Pp 883–887.

Mottron L and Burack JA (2001) Enhanced perceptual functioning in the development of autism. In: (Eds.) Burack JA, Charman T, Yirmiya N & Zelazo P. *The Development of Autism: Perspectives from theory and research.* New Jersey: Lawrence Erlbaum Associates Publishers.

Mottron L, Dawson M, Soulières I, Hubert B and Burack J (2006) Enhanced perceptual functioning in autism: An update, and eight principles of autistic perception. *Journal of Autism and Developmental Disorders* **36** (1) 27–43.

Murray DKC (1986) *Language and Interests (unpublished thesis).* London: University of London.

Murray DKC (1992) 'Attention Tunnelling and Autism', in Living with Autism: The Individual, the Family, and the Professional. Durham Conference Proceedings, obtainable from Autism Research Unit, School of Health Sciences, University of Sunderland, UK.

Murray DK (2017) Liberating Potential – The Future I'd like to See [online]. National Autism Project. Available at: http://nationalautismproject.org.uk/liberating-potential (accessed January 2020).

Murray Dk (2018) Monotropism – an interest based account of autism. In F. Volkmar (Ed) *Encyclopedia of Autism Spectrum Disorders*. https://link.springer.com/referenceworkentry/10.1007/978-1-4614-6435-8_102269-1

Murray DK, Lesser M, Lawson W (2005) Attention, monotropism and the diagnostic criteria for autism. *Autism* **9** 139–56.

Murray FG (2019) Monotropism and me, a unified account of autism. *The Psychologist* **33** 44-49.

Pellicano E and Burr D (2012) When the world becomes 'too real': a Bayesian explanation of autistic perception. *Trends Cogn Sci* **16** (10) 504–10.

Pfaff D and Barbas H (2019) Mechanisms for the Approach/Avoidance Decision Applied to Autism. *Trends Neurosci* **42** (7) 448–457.

Russell G (Ed), Milton D, Bovell V, Timini S and Kapp S (2019) Deconstructing Diagnosis: four commentaries on a diagnostic tool to assess individuals for autism spectrum disorders. *Autonomy* **1** (6).

Russell G , Kapp SK, Elliott D, Elphick CM, Gwernan-Jones RC and Owens C (2019b). Mapping the autistic advantage from the accounts of adults diagnosed with autism: A qualitative study. *Autism in Adulthood.* **1**(2) 124-133.

Rutter M and Pickles A (2016) Annual Research Review: Threats to the validity of child psychiatry and psychology. *Journal Child Psychology and Psychiatry* **57** 398–416.

Samson F, Mottron L, Soulieres I and Zeffiro T (2012) Enhanced visual functioning in autism: An ALE meta-analysis. *Human Brain Mapping* **33** (7) 1553–1581.

Sasson NJ, Faso DJ, Nugent J, Lovell S, Kennedy DP and Grossman RB (2017) Neurotypical Peers are Less Willing to Interact with Those with Autism based on Thin Slice Judgments. *Scientific Reports* **7** 40700.

Schulz SE and Stevenson RA (2019) Differentiating between sensory sensitivity and sensory reactivity in relation to restricted interests and repetitive behaviours. *Autism*. Available at: https://journals.sagepub.com/doi/abs/10.1177/1362361319850402?journalCode=auta

Shah A (2019) *Catatonia, Shutdown and Breakdown in Autism.* Jessica Kingsley Publishers.

Späth E, Karin MA, Jongsma R (2019) Autism, autonomy, and authenticity. *Medicine, Health Care and Philosophy*. pp 1–8.

Stern D (1985) *The Interpersonal World of the Infant: A View from Psychoanalysis and Developmental Psychology*. Karnac Books.

Wood R (2019) Autism, intense interests and support in school: from wasted efforts to shared understandings. *Educational Review.*

Wood R (2019) *Inclusive Education for Autistic Children: Helping Children and Young People to Learn and Flourish in the Classroom*. Jessica Kingsley.

Xu et al (2018) Both Hypo-Connectivity and Hyper-Connectivity of the Insular Subregions Associated With Severity in Children With Autism Spectrum Disorders. *Frontiers in Neuroscience*. https://doi.org/10.3389/fnins.2018.00234

Yufik M and Friston K (2016) Life and Understanding: The Origins of 'Understanding' in Self-Organizing Nervous Systems. *Frontiers in Neuroscience.*

Chapter 4: Perceptual deviants: understanding autistic subjectivities in a (not so) predictable world

By Gemma L. Williams, University of Brighton

There is a woman I know who can hear a simple melody and promptly replicate it on any instrument. Languages come naturally to her; so naturally, in fact, that she became fluent in French overnight, over the course of a dream. She has friends and excels at most things she tries… at least for a time. She *hasn't* managed to hold on to any job for more than a couple of years, doesn't recognise faces out of context, is perpetually bruised on account of not being able to perceive depth, is bamboozled by facial expressions and becomes wildly disorientated by the clangour and chaos of public spaces. This woman is autistic. This woman also happens to be me.

Despite its increasing prevalence – the conservative estimate is that more than one in 100 people in the UK are known to be autistic – the medical, social and neuro-sciences have yet to agree on what autism actually is and what causes it. Is it a distinct 'thing' at all, or a collection of many things? Is it a disorder, a disability or simply one expression of human *neurodiversity*? One factor muddying the issue is its heterogeneity. The way autism manifests in one individual is often very different from the next, although modern diagnostic definitions all include reference to the famous triad of 'impairments': in communication, social interaction and social imagination. And yet while genes, failed theory-of-mind modules, different cognitive styles and structural brain abnormalities continue to battle it out in a bid to explain autism, 'autism' remains elusive.

We are still, too, trying to make sense of how we (humans) make sense of the world more generally. Predictive processing is a top-down model of cognition, its roots traceable back to 19th century German thinker Helmholtz, that has been gathering increasing traction. According to this model, the brain has developed a savvy mechanism to most efficiently manage the vast and constant stream of continuously updating information relating to its surrounds – either those of the body, via *interoception* and *proprioception*, or those of the external environment, via *exteroception* (sensory perception). Bottom-up theories of perception and cognition argue for raw sensory data as the starting point, laboriously integrated and analysed with progressive complexity from percept through to a series of conceptual wholes. Predictive processing flips this view, and in so doing provides an answer to the seeming intractability of information management in a highly complex world. The brain is instead seen as perpetually generating and updating informed predictions about its surrounding environment. Perception and cognition work as feedforward mechanisms, with only the data that serve as prediction errors feeding back up to tweak the signal.

For perception, at least, you don't need to look far for every-day examples of prediction errors in action. Think of sitting on a stationary train, watching the adjacent train pull away, and *feeling* that it is your train, instead, that is moving; the laundry-pile monster of your childhood looming at the end of your bed in the shadows; the McGurk effect, where visual information shapes and alters what you hear... The list goes on. Although predictive processing was first applied to the domain of (visual) perception, its scope has been broadened so that it now also offers a persuasive theory of higher-order cognitive functions. However, as an explanation it makes most sense when cognition is seen as *embodied* and *enacted*.

Modern conceptualisations of cognition have traditionally been heavily influenced by the kind of dualism made famous by René Descartes in the 17th century. Minds and their properties are made of a different stuff to that of the physical body and, as such, are distinct. Against this, theories of embodied cognition argue that mental processes cannot, in fact, be easily teased apart from the constraining influence of the body. An emphasis is placed on the online relationship between brain, nervous system and external environment, where the environment is understood to be, at least in part, enacted (created) by the intelligent inter-relation of sensorimotor faculties and whatever it is that is actually 'out there'. The world, *as experienced*, is carved up into meaningful chunks based on how a person (or organism) interacts with, and is attuned to, it. What is shared then, in both predictive processing and an embodied, enacted view of cognition is a phenomenological framing of an individual's external reality as inextricably linked to their experience of it, as filtered through their body.

Echoed within the above is the concept of 'umwelt'; a term coined by late 20th century German biologist Jacob von Uexküll, as a means of describing the environment as perceived by any living organism. Umwelten (the plural) are those distinct phenomenal worlds in which organisms are perceiving, acting subjects. Picture, if you can, the umwelt of the honeybee. Her position in space is determined by the relation between herself, the hive entrance and the position of the sun as it moves through the sky in a constantly recalibrating equation. Star and cross shapes leap out of the landscape while compact round shapes fade into the background, thus directing her flight across the meadow to opened flowers rather than to shut buds. Ultraviolet landing strip patterns on petals, invisible to humans, direct her to nectar-filled cups at the heart of the flower. Of many and varied phenomena in the natural world, it is only those that are biologically meaningful to an organism that will leap out and catch its attention: the world, is carved up into meaningful chunks based on how a person (or organism) interacts with it.

But how is this relevant to our understanding of autism? Well, for a start, one of the things we do know about autism is that it is usually characterised by perceptual and attentional differences that are present from (at least) birth. Autistic people tend to possess an idiosyncratic palate of sensory experience; presenting as variously hyper- or hypo-sensitive to external stimuli (sound, vision, smell, taste, touch, depth perception…) or internal ones (pressure, balance, temperature, thirst, hunger, emotion, pain, etc…). They inhabit umwelten that can set them significantly apart from their peers. Dr Temple Grandin, famous female autist and renowned animal scientist, opened the world's eyes to the possibility of thinking not in words but pictures. Naoki Higashida, a Japanese poet, author and essayist, surprised and deeply touched an international readership with his evocative account of an intensely and often excruciatingly vibrant inner life in his autistic memoir *The Reason I Jump*. At the time of writing Naoki was 13 years old, non-verbal, and had displayed behaviour all his life that, until he had discovered means of communicating via an alphabet grid, had been read by all as indicating a profound inability to connect with the outside world or others.

Recognising that autistic people perceive and process information – and therefore experience the world – differently, is crucial. However, doesn't everyone have their own unique experience and perspective? *Qualia*, the introspectively qualitative properties of experience, are largely seen as scaffolding and elaborating our *subjectivity*; what it is to be conscious of being a 'me'. Jill and Jane may gaze at the same sunset, and agree on the gloriousness of its peachy-red hues, but there is no way of knowing whether Jill's 'peachy-red' is the same Jane's, or if it is actually closer to Jane's 'pale pink', her 'orange', or even her 'electric blue'. The phenomenal character of experience is wholly subjective, although language allows us to yoke our subjective experience to a common coin sufficiently enough so as to forget this most of the time.

One major problem, then, thrown up by us each having our own subjective experience of the world, is that we cannot ever be *sure* that we know how or what another is thinking or feeling. Fortunately, humans are widely accepted as having 'theory of mind'; the capacity to recognise that others also have minds that differ from our own, and to attribute mental states to them. We can 'mind-read' (a skill considered unique to our species, give or take the handful of concessions cautiously afforded for potential, if reduced, theory of mind abilities in some other apes). Whilst 'theory of mind' has been readily absorbed into our accepted depiction of human minds, and is often described as the humanising feature of cognition on account of its assumed role in empathy, the clue is in the name: *theory* of mind. Jim's ability to understand and *feel* that Jack is sad, when Jack tells him, with a quiver in his voice and his eyes downcast, that his pet tarantula has died, really comes down to an act of inference. Jim may draw on his own experiences – perhaps from when his own pet canary died two years ago (a 'simulationist' account of theory of mind). Alternatively, he may draw on his world knowledge of how people typically seem to feel in such a situation, displaying such behaviour (a 'theory-theory' account). Either way, a *theory* – as opposed to a telepathic transmission – is produced that can be applied to the present moment in order to make sense of what is unfolding.

Despite this, when it comes to autism, the dominant narrative has been for a long time that autistic people lack theory of mind where non-autistic people do have it. Putting aside for now the damaging, dehumanising nature of this rhetoric, how could anyone, autistic or not, correctly infer the mental state of another, when there is a marked phenomenological gap between subjective experiences?

Something of this notion is reflected in British autistic scholar Damien Milton's 'double empathy problem'. Starting from the position that communication is a social phenomenon, and an inherently two-sided affair, Milton argues that the lack of understanding underpinning the communication breakdowns that often occur between autistic and non-autistic people run both ways. And research is beginning to back this up. A number of recent studies have begun to highlight the difficulties that non-autistic people have in understanding autistic people; including difficulty in inferring autistic affective and mental states (Brewer *et al.*, 2016; Edey *et al.*, 2016; Heasman and Gillespie, 2017; Hubbard *et al.*, 2017; Sheppard *et al.*, 2015) and a tendency towards negative thin slice judgements about autistic people (Morrison *et al.*, 2019a; Sasson *et al.*, 2017). Others have shown the ways in which autistic people can demonstrate highly successful and nuanced socio-communicative abilities when among others of a similar neurotype (Crompton, Fletcher-Watson and Ropar, 2019a, 2019b; Heasman and Gillespie, 2019; Morrison *et al.*, 2019b).

American philosopher Thomas Nagel grappled with a similar issue in his 1974 paper 'What is like to be a bat?'. His argument went as follows. Any conscious being must have some subjective sense of what it is like to be itself, and that is what we may say consciousness is. A bat uses sonar – a sense that humans do not (naturally) possess

– as its principal means of interpreting and navigating the world. If we were to try to imagine the subjective experience of a bat, we would only achieve a poor approximation as we are lacking in the necessary faculties to accurately represent a bat's way of being in the world. Imagination is anchored in experience and experience is hewn by the axe of the body. Autistic people clearly experience the world in ways that diverge beyond the central range agreed upon as the 'norm' within any given culture or society. In this way, we are perceptual deviants, the proverbial bats (in the belfry).

From the very start of life, sensory input data lattices and guides, up through multi-sensory processing to perceptual and 'higher order' cognitive processes, and establishes the bases of future predications of the world around us. Neuroconstructivism, an embodied-cognition-compatible alterative to the long-held nativist perspective on brains and minds, takes the view that genes, brain, cognition and environment all interact multi-directionally. Brain connectivity is shaped and changed across an individual's lifespan in response to the bodily and external environments and to life experiences. All of which, of course, are filtered through our means of experiencing them. Is it any wonder that the world, as *enacted* by an autistic individual, is characterised by divergent patterns of salience? Framed this way, could autism simply be the combined set of traits that develop and occur when an individual experiences reality in a particular way, and this particular way, in its atypicality, sets them outside of the reality shared by the majority of their peers? To live as a bat among birds, and in an aviary, would not be easy work.

At the heart of the autistic experience is the sense of being 'other', of being outside of being human. Autistic people in the UK report four times the amount of loneliness as the general population (NAS, 2018), and a large Swedish study found that death by suicide is ten times more likely among 'high-functioning' (sic) autistics than non-autistic people (Hirvikoski *et al*, 2016). For myself, at least, part of this throbbing disconnect from the world of people and things comes from the inability to be seen and understood on our own terms, as people, as individuals, as relatable humans. The difficulty is that we don't just see the world differently; our worlds are different, and different from each other's. Untranslatability between realities can make it feel as though we are each a lonely species of one, gazing across at our close cousins around the fire, all able to share in some common humanhood inaccessible to us and the other, equally unreachable, outliers. And yet a fear of isolation and aloneness is perhaps one of the most unifying human experiences there is and what drives people to contrive group identities in the first place, to forge a sense of belonging. To a greater or lesser extent, we are each alone, autistic or not, in our uniquely detailed umwelten, with our uniquely woven personal histories. It is, counter-intuitively, the loosening of our grip on those identities, the dropping of assumptions, that allows us to feel into the spaces between people, between species, even. It is in this neither-neither space that we can see other beings for what they are; other, but relatable. It is here we can experience true theory of mind.

References

Brewer R, Biotti F, Catmur C, Press C, Happé F, Cook R & Bird G (2016) Can neurotypical individuals read autistic facial expressions? Atypical production of emotional facial expressions in autism spectrum disorders. *Autism Research* 9 (2) 262–271.

Crompton CJ, Fletcher-Watson S & Ropar D (2019a) "I never realised everybody felt as happy as I do when I am around autistic people": a thematic analysis of autistic adults' relationships with autistic and neurotypical friends and family. *OSF Preprints*, 24 September. Available at: https://doi.org/10.31219/osf.io/46b87.

Crompton CJ, Fletcher-Watson S & Ropar D (2019b) Autistic peer to peer information transfer is highly effective. *OSF Preprints*, 24 September. Available at: https://doi.org/10.31219/osf.io/j4knx.

Descartes R (1998) *Meditations and Other Metaphysical Writings* (Clarke, D. trans.) London: Penguin.

Edey R, Cook J, Brewer R, Johnson MH, Bird G & Press C (2016) Interaction takes two: Typical adults exhibit mind-blindness towards those with autism spectrum disorder. *Journal of Abnormal Psychology* **125** (7) 879.

Grandin T (1995) *Thinking in Pictures: And Other Reports from My Life with Autism.* New York: Doubleday.

Heasman B & Gillespie A (2017) Perspective-taking is two-sided: Misunderstandings between people with Asperger's syndrome and their family members. *Autism* p.1362361317708287.

Heasman B & Gillespie A (2019) Neurodivergent intersubjectivity: Distinctive features of how autistic people create shared understanding. *Autism* p.1362361318785172.

Helmholtz HV (1860) *Treatise on Physiological Optics.* New York: Dover.

Higashida N (2013) *The Reason I Jump.* (Yoshida, K. and Mitchell, D. trans.). London: Sceptre.

Hirvikoski T, Mittendorfer-Rutz E, Boman M, Larsson H, Lichtenstein P & Bölte S (2016) Premature mortality in autism spectrum disorder. *The British Journal of Psychiatry* **208** (3) 232–23.

Hubbard DJ, Faso DJ, Assmann PF & Sasson NJ (2017) Production and perception of emotional prosody by adults with autism spectrum disorder. *Autism Research* **10** (12) 1991–2001.

Morrison KE, DeBrabander KM, Faso DJ & Sasson NJ (2019a) Variability in first impressions of autistic adults made by neurotypical raters is driven more by characteristics of the rater than by characteristics of autistic adults. *Autism*, DOI:10.1177/1362361318824104

Morrison KE, DeBrabander KM, Jones DR, Faso DJ, Ackerman RA & Sasson NJ (2019b) Outcomes of real-world social interaction for autistic adults paired with autistic compared to typically developing partners. *Autism*: 1362361319892701.

Nagel T (1974) What is it like to be a bat? *The Philosophical Review* **83** (4) 435–450.

National Autistic Society (2018) *Hidden Crisis: Autistic people four times more likely to be lonely than general public* [online]. Available at: www.autism.org.uk/get-involved/media-centre/news/2018-04-25-hidden-crisis-autism-and-loneliness.aspx (accessed January 2020).

Sasson NJ, Faso DJ, Nugent J, Lovell S, Kennedy DP & Grossman RB (2017) Neurotypical peers are less willing to interact with those with autism based on thin slice judgments. *Scientific Reports* **7** 40700.

Sheppard E, Pillai D, Wong GTL, Ropar D & Mitchell P (2016) How easy is it to read the minds of people with autism spectrum disorder? *Journal of Autism and Developmental Disorders* **46** (4) 1247–1254.

Von Uexküll J (1992) A stroll through the worlds of animals and men: A picture book of invisible worlds. *Semiotica*, **89** (4) 319- 391

Chapter 5: What kind of thing is autism?

By Robert Chapman, Department of Philosophy, University of Bristol

Introduction

I often hear other neurodiversity advocates refer to autism as a different 'brain wiring'. This is a rather unclear term, and I am not fully sure where it originally came from. But I take it the point is that we have something different about our neurology that makes us autistic – some kind of essential difference that provides the basis of and legitimisation for our shared autistic identity. In turn, this claim is often accompanied by the further notion that 'autism is genetic', a claim which is often justified with a link to some newspaper article or another that reports how yet another a new study has 'shown' or 'found' that autism really is genetic after all.

There is something obviously right in these claims. Studies do, after all, indicate that there is a strong genetic basis for autistic traits. And it is of course true that autistic minds stem in significant part from autistic brains in some sense. Beyond this, it is easy to understand why people feel the need continually to emphasise the naturalness of autism in the face of false and harmful claims that autism is a product of, say, so-called 'refrigerator mothers' or vaccinations. When compared to those alternatives, reducing autism to genes and neurology is preferable.

Still, these claims can also be highly misleading, especially when taken together. For they often give the impression that autism is some kind of biological thing, a copy of which is inside all autistic people. Moreover, the impression is often given that this is what grounds our shared autistic identity and voice. If we understand the claim to be that all autistic people share, and are grouped by, a genetically-based neurological essence, this framing encounters two highly significant sets of issues.

Here I first want to highlight these issues, and then to argue that it is important for the neurodiversity movement to work towards adopting a constructivist perspective, both of autism, but also of neurominorities more generally. When I say constructivist, I do not mean that autism is not real, but rather than it is the kind of thing whose reality is constituted by how we construct the human world, rather than it simply being a product of nature. My own suggestion will be that autism is constituted by the external world as much as internal traits, in such a way where it is both a construct and objective part of the world.

Is autism a scientifically valid concept?

The first set of problems regard the validity of the concept of autism. In short, although one would not think this from reading news articles about autism, there is no known biological basis that is clearly definitive of autism at all, and neither does it have much use as a disorder classification from a medical perspective.

First, consider the notion of the autistic brain. True, some studies have indicated certain tendencies in neurological functioning or structure (Brambilla *et al*, 2003). But these findings are typically either based on very small samples that are not reproduced; or they only show very general tendencies across extremely large samples that don't tell us much about autistics as individuals (Timimi & McCabe, 2016 Waterhouse, 2013). Moreover, what has been found is that each autistic brain is unique, rather than being the same as other autistic brains (Coleman, 2005, p30). In line with this, the same is true at the psychological level. Although there are a rough cluster of traits vaguely associated with each of the (many) various autism classifications (both historical and contemporary), there is no single cognitive trait that is exhibited by all autistic people (Happé *et al*, 2006; Cushing, 2013). Even traits that are highly prevalent in the autistic population (e.g. sensory sensitives) are somewhat different in each case.

These problems re-emerge with the genetic and hereditary evidence for autism too. Up to 1,000 genes have been identified as increasing the likelihood of autism (Ramaswami & Geschwind, 2018), and they rarely, if ever, come in the same combinations or through the same epigenetic processes (Coleman & Betancur, 2005, p15). This makes it very hard to claim that there is anything like a shared genetic basis for autism, or at least any more so than there is for, say, being vegetarian, or supporting a certain sports team. Moreover, while it is true that autism has high heritability, as indicated in many twin studies, this does not provide any support for the notion that autism itself is a scientifically valid construct. By analogy, it is well known that our racial classifications have no scientific validity, but it is still the case that any set of twins will presumably be the same race as each other. Likewise, as Keller and Miller (2006) have noted:

'*...finding positive heritability for a mental disorder does not vindicate the mental disorder as a diagnostic category. To a first approximation, every reliably measured behavioural trait shows positive heritability – even constructs such as television viewing and political attitudes. Any arbitrary 'disorder' composed of unrelated but heritable symptoms will show credible heritability.*'

Putting aside the pathologising vocabulary, the point here is that pretty much *any* arbitrary grouping of traits can be similarly mapped. Hence, such findings do not vindicate our actual grouping together of any given vague cluster of traits as a kind. We could have grouped together different traits at random and still found similar results.

To be clear, the issue is not about whether the traits are real or not (clearly, they are real), or whether they are biologically-based (clearly this is often a significant factor). Rather, it is about how we decide to construct various clusters of traits into different classifications, and in turn to claim that these classifications themselves are naturally grounded rather than being human constructs. The upshot: although there are very general *population* tendencies when it comes to autism, and although these do reflect underlying, to some extent naturally occurring traits, there is nothing like an essential, defining neurological or genetic marker shared by all autistic people as *individuals*, which thereby separates them from non-autistic individuals. Given this, as well as other factors I discuss in more detail elsewhere (Chapman, forthcoming), it is far from clear that the concept has scientific validity. And the claim that any two autistic people share the same 'wiring' as each other, unless they have literally gone to a lab and been tested to verify this, is largely unsupported by the scientific research. Equally unsupported, then, is the (often implicit) notion that shared wiring is what grounds our shared identity or political voice (I'll return to this below).

Is a naturalist framing of autism politically useful?

The second set of problems are more social, political and ethical. On the one hand, it seems important to admit that biologised framings of autism have sometimes been politically helpful for neurodiversity proponents. In short, because terms like 'neurotype' *sound* clinical and scientifically legitimised, this sometimes makes people take those who use them more seriously. Because of this, such terms have also been helpful for us to develop solidarity and to organise resistance to the pathologisation of autism. Nonetheless, there is also a number of ways in which biologising and essentialising classifications such as 'autism' often tends to reinforce social processes that are at odds with the emancipatory aims of the neurodiversity movement. I will just note two here.

First, consider the findings of a 2011 review article on the geneticisation of human kinds and the socio-political effects of this. As the authors (Dar-Nimrod & Heine, 2011) summarise, evidence consistently shows that:

'People's understanding of genetics with relation to life outcomes is shaped by their psychological essentialist biases – a process termed genetic essentialism – and this leads to particular consequences when people consider the relations between genes and human outcomes ... genetic essentialist biases have played in eugenic ideologies and policies, and ... these biases shape and are in turn shaped by contemporary discussions of genetic research.'

In other words, what they found was that the practice of geneticising socially constructed human kinds (whether regarding race, gender or disability) in popular discourse ultimately functions both to support a thing like eugenics, and to increase stigma. For this often helps what are socially-caused issues to seem like they are simply natural. Although only a partial analogy, consider how women have often been excluded from education based on the false notion that women are naturally irrational, and have then in turn been framed as naturally irrational in light of not exhibiting the benefits of education. While it is clear to most people now that that this reasoning is viciously circular, to many people it has seemed to simply be a natural fact that women were naturally irrational. So too do we run a similar risk with naturalising autism: doing so can tend to make the limitations autistic people often exhibit that are a product of social exclusion (e.g. from education, work, etc.) seem like they are naturally grounded internally, in autism itself. But this kind of undue, harmful pathologisation is, of course, precisely the kind of thing that the neurodiversity movement has emerged to resist.

Second, any single attempt to reduce autism to any specific genetic, neurological, or psychological traits, if it were widely accepted, would thereby exclude some autistic people. This is perhaps especially important when it comes to psychological theories of autism that attempt to explain autism in light of one key trait. For instance, if we define autism in the light of specific sensory processing differences, this definition will exclude those who don't have those specific traits. Or if we define it in light of, say, hyper-systemising, or monotropism, or weak central coherence, our definition will exclude those who do process information in these ways. In turn, even if we adopt a laxer naturalist definition of autism, this would exclude others still. Although it is clear that the traits associated with autism are largely genetic, there are a small number of people with what researchers refer to as 'quasi-autism' (Rutter *et al*, 2007) who have developed autistically due to abuse and neglect[4]. But why should we count this as mere 'quasi' autism just because of its different genesis? What if some of those given this label wanted to be included in the autistic community? If they are functionally and experientially autistic, then would it not be better to develop a definition of autism that didn't automatically exclude them? Of

---

4   This is not the same as Bettleheim's incorrect theory that autism itself is caused by abuse and neglect, it is just that researchers have identified a small number of people for whom this seems to be the case.

course, this is somewhat hypothetical, but my point is that any attempt to reduce such a heterogeneous group to internal essential traits will automatically exclude some or other of the group's members. In short, while I do not think autism is *merely* a matter of identification, the issue here is somewhat akin to how biological-reductionist accounts of gender exclude trans people. Overall, then, there are good political reasons to move away from essentialist reductionism.

Towards a constructivist perspective

I just criticised the tendency to essentialise and biologise autism. To be absolutely clear: I certainly do *not* conclude from this that autism is not real, or that the term is not meaningful. But I do believe that certain proponents need to be more careful about the biological reductionism and essentialism that they have too often uncritically adopted from biological psychiatry. Here, we need to follow those such as autistic sociologist Damian Milton, who has long resisted such temptations. For Milton (2016), the notion that autism is 'scientifically valid as a natural kind' is untenable, and we are 'unlikely ever to find … a simplistic explanation of what autism 'is' at a biological level'.

The alternative view holds the classification of autism as a human construct that emerged within certain power dynamics and a specific social and historical context, rather than being a natural grouping that we simply discovered (Hacking, 1999; 2007). What this means is that the way we have classified these traits, and how such classifications continually change, is more closely a product of power-dynamics, ideology and social norms, than simply being a matter of picking out a pre-existing natural classification (Chapman, forthcoming). This framing does then still have room for associating autism with a rough cluster of psychological traits (although no singularly essential ones), and admits that these each of these likely has a significant biological underpinning (Chapman, 2019a; forthcoming). It just also acknowledges that the way we group and frame these is more related to social processes than simply being a matter of trying to understand nature.

Of course, just as there are different conceptions of the nature of autism from a naturalist perspective, so too are there different constructivist perspectives. In one view, autism as a classification is mainly constructed by human agreement, much in the way that coins only have specific values because humans agree what those values should be. According to anthropologist Ben Belek (2019), for instance, who is autistic or who is not is constituted by an 'authoritative other' (p238), typically a medical professional. But this is not my view. I have argued in detail elsewhere (Chapman, forthcoming) that autism reflects a material social reality rather than being a product of the human mind or medical expertise. In particular, what binds autistic people together is our shared relationship to external factors, for instance, disabling sensory barriers, the structure of working and learning environments, and so forth (Chapman, forthcoming). This would make autism what feminist philosopher Iris Marion-young (1994) refers to as a 'serial collective', a term which indicates collectives who are bound together though sharing is a specific relationship to external factors, as much as shared internal traits. Autistic people, then, are bound together most primarily though being disabled in ways which combine us, given the way our societies are organised. Who falls within this will be determined in part by objective internal factors (e.g. cognitive traits) but also by the objective external factors (e.g. human-made sensory environments) that disable us. This combination, I believe, is what our shared voice, our culture, and our emerging autistic vocabularies and form of life is most fundamentally based on.

What are the benefits of this view? I would suggest at least three, primarily for autism but also, perhaps, for many other neurominorities. First, this view fits better with the evidence presented above. For the serial collective understanding of autism would predict that there would be no essential internal autistic trait, while simultaneously predicting that there would likely be rough clusters of traits for most members of the collective at any given time. Second, in avoiding essentialism we also avoid the problems associated above in terms of excluding certain autistic people, dividing our community, and inadvertently contributing to stigma. Third, by conceptualising autism in a way that draws attention to the external as well as the internal, this helps us understand autistic disablement as an external societal issue rather than an internal medical one (also see Chapman, 2019b). On this view, then, autistic people can have a shared voice, and shared interests, and have the basis for a say in how autism is represented. However, this is not based on some elusive shared biological essence or 'wiring'. Rather, it is based on our similar social positioning, our shared history, our emerging culture, and our irreducibly complex manifold of psychosocial similarities, in what we might call our shared autistic form of life. So this perspective is both superior from a scientific perspective and is likely to be more practical from an advocacy perspective.

In the long run, I have no doubt that eventually it will become standard for neurodiversity proponents to admit that autism and other 'neurominorities' are social constructs, rather than natural kinds (except perhaps one or two, for instance, Down syndrome, which do seem to be natural kinds). This will be just as all the earlier civil rights movements regarding other kinds of minorities similarly deconstructed the purportedly natural classifications they were based on, whether regarding gender, race or sexuality. The question is more when this happens. For me: the sooner the better. For I believe that a widespread acknowledgement and exploration of the constructed nature of autism and other neurominorities will be necessary for the emancipatory aims of neurodiversity proponents to become fully realised.

References

Belek B (2019) An Anthropological Perspective on Autism. *Philosophy, Psychiatry, and Psychology* **26** (3) 231–241.

Brambilla P, Hardan A, di Nemi SU, Perez J, Soares JC, Barale F. Brain anatomy and development in autism: review of structural MRI studies. *Brain Res Bull.* 2003;61(6):557-569. doi:10.1016/j.brainresbull.2003.06.001

Chapman R (2019a) Autism as a Form of Life: Wittgenstein and the Psychological Coherence of Autism. *Metaphilosophy* **50** (4).

Chapman R (2019b) 'Neurodiversity Theory and its Discontents: Autism, Schizophrenia, and the Social Model'. In: S Tekin & R Bluhm (Eds.) *The Bloomsbury Companion to the Philosophy of Psychiatry* (371–389). London: Bloomsbury.

Chapman R (forthcoming) 'The Reality of Autism: From Disorder to Diversity'. *Philosophical Psychology.*

Coleman M (2005) *The Neurology of Autism.* Oxford: Oxford University Press.

Coleman M and Betancur C (2005) Introduction in M. Coleman (Ed.) *The Neurology of Autism* (pp3–39). Oxford: Oxford University Press.

Cushing S (2013) Autism: The Very Idea. In JL Anderson & Simon Cushing (Eds.) *The Philosophy of Autism* (pp17–45). Rowman & Littlefield.

Dar-Nimrod I & Heine SJ (2011) Genetic essentialism: on the deceptive determinism of DNA. *Psychological bulletin* **137** (5) 800–818. doi:10.1037/a0021860

Hacking I (1999) *The Social Construction of What?* Cambridge, MA: Harvard University Press.

Hacking I (2007) Kinds of People: Moving Targets. *Proceedings of the British Academy* **151** 2006 Lectures. pp285–318.

Happé F, Ronald A & Plomin R (2006) Time to Give Up on a Unified Theory of Autism. *Nature Neuroscience* **9** (10) 1218–20.

Keller M & Miller G (2006) Resolving the paradox of common, harmful, heritable mental disorders: Which evolutionary genetic models work best? *Behavioural and Brain Sciences* **29** (4) 385–404.

Milton D (2016) Re-thinking autism: diagnosis, identity and equality. *Disability & Society* 31:10, 1413-1415.

Ramaswami G and Geschwind DH (2018) Genetics of autism spectrum disorder. *Handbook of Clinical Neurology* **147** 321–329.

Rutter M, Kreppner J, Croft C, Murin M, Colvert E, Beckett C, Castle J and Sonuga-Barke EJS (2007) Early adolescent outcomes of institutionally deprived and non-deprived adoptees. III. quasi-autism. *Journal of Child Psychology & Psychiatry* **48** (12) 1200–1207.

Timimi S & McCabe B (2016) What Have We Learned From the Science of Autism? In: K Runswick-Cole, R Mallett & S Timimi (Eda.) *Re-thinking Autism: Diagnosis, identity and equality* (pp30-48), London, Jessica Kingsley Publishers.

Waterhouse L (2013) *Re-thinking Autism: Variation and Complexity.* New York: Elsevier.

Young, Iris Marion (1994) Gender as seriality: thinking about women as a social collective. *Signs: Journal of Women in Culture and Society* **19** (3) 713–738.

Chapter 6: Stigmaphrenia©: Reducing mental health stigma with a script about neurodiversity

By Chloe Farahar | SoYoureAutistic.com | SoYoureAutistic@outlook.com |University of Kent

Louis Bishopp-Ford

'Neurodiversity may be every bit as crucial for the human race as biodiversity is for life in general. Who can say what forms of life can prove best at any given moment?' (Blume, 1998; Farahar, 2012, p11)

Following background and overview, this chapter is structured thusly:

4. A problem in society: the stigmatisation of psychologically-divergent ways of managing distress (commonly referred to as 'mental illness').

5. Neurodiversity: not just about autism. How neurodiversity applies to psychologically divergent, reasonable responses to a disordered society.

6. Neurodiversity: for psychological-diversity in practice. How a play reframing 'mental illness' as neurodivergent responses can reduce public stigma and, importantly, self-stigma. Here I will introduce the play Stigmaphrenia© as a means of Experiential (experiencing) Intergroup Contact with the 'mentally ill' outgroup. More simply put: how roleplaying the mentally ill outgroup in a play reframing these experiences as neurodivergences under the neurodiversity of humanity reduces mental health stigma.

Background and overview

I am one of a growing number of late-diagnosed autistics, discovering my autistic identity in 2015 and diagnosed a year later aged 32. Before discovering my autistic identity, I had entered higher education as a mature psychology student (at age 26 years) to learn *why* my mum was 'bipolar' (although I now believe she is autistic with voice hearing and delusional beliefs), and *why* my dad was 'schizophrenic' (more accurately and respectfully, a voice-hearer). A further reason for wanting to study psychology was a desire to learn *how* I might be able to affect these disorders – to cure my parents and others like them. I quickly became disillusioned with, and disabused of, the pervasive narrative of mental illness I had been fed since growing up in care. Quite simply, the evidence I was learning via my psychology degree did not substantiate claims that those of the population who experience psychological and emotional distress were ill. This was cemented by my 'Abnormal Psychology' lecturer (formerly a clinical psychologist), who provided fantastic critical reading lists that included *Anatomy of an Epidemic*, by journalist Robert Whitaker (2010)[5].

At this point I hit an impasse: my parents and people like them were recipients of stigma based on the narrative that they were mentally ill, and yet the evidence suggested they were not ill. How could I hope to improve the attitudes, feelings and behaviour toward them if the dominant narrative was one of inherent disorder?

The problem: the stigmatisation of 'mental illness'

Building on the Greek and biblical origins of the term 'stigma', sociologist Erving Goffman (1963; 1991) defined mental illness stigma as a severe social disapproval of personal characteristics or beliefs that go against cultural norms and expectations. As such, society stigmatises people who are considered 'mentally ill' due to the belief that they have personal traits which deviate from the 'norm', and this diverse group is considered 'among the most deeply discredited of all stigmatised conditions' (Stuart, 2012, p455; Goffman, 1963)[6]. Social psychologists expanded on this initial definition of stigma, identifying the cognitive and behavioural processes of public and self-stigma (e.g. Corrigan & Shapiro, 2010; Link & Phelan, 2001) (see Table 1). These processes include cognitive stereotyping; prejudicial attitudes and emotional responses arising from learnt beliefs; and discriminatory behavioural consequences of being labelled 'other'.

---

5   In a nutshell, Whitaker critically discusses the creation of chronic mental health issues due to psychiatric drugs that create chemical imbalances, not reduce them – a startling and disturbing finding corroborated by further reading in journal articles during my undergraduate degree.

6   Also see Bos *et al*, 2009; Corrigan, 2005; Heflinger & Hinshaw, 2010; Johnstone, 2001.

Table 1: Recreation of Corrigan & Shapiro's (2010) processes of mental illness stigma			
Construct	Definition	Public stigma	Self-stigma
Stereotypes (cognitive)	Learnt beliefs	■ E.g. dangerous; ■ responsible; ■ incompetent	■ E.g. I am dangerous; ■ I am to blame; ■ I am incompetent
Prejudice (cognitive)	Attitudes & emotional responses	■ E.g. benevolence; ■ anxiety; ■ Fear	■ E.g. I am childlike; ■ low self-esteem (not worthy); ■ low self-efficacy (not able to achieve)
Discrimination (behavioural)	Behavioural consequences of prejudice	■ E.g. loss of opportunity; ■ failure to support; ■ remove empowerment; ■ segregation	■ E.g. 'why try' effect; ■ why try to get a job – not worthy

Critically, the language used to identify and label the mentally ill as deviant (e.g. diagnostic labels, and the very term 'mentally ill' itself) creates the categorical 'them' and 'us' distinction – not some objective, physical mark. While not all labels are inherently negative (e.g. we have many important social identities, e.g. mother; employee; student), being labelled with a disorder and being considered mentally ill carries certain connotations of dangerousness, weakness and unpredictability (Corrigan & Shapiro, 2010; Henderson, 2017). This labelling brings with it status loss and discrimination.

Problematically, given how there are no physical marks of being 'mentally ill', and the reliance on labelling to be 'othered', it is entirely possible for individuals to conceal their given identity as mentally ill – to mask their difficulties (Chaudoir & Fisher, 2010; Quinn & Chaudoir, 2009; Quinn, 2017) – as a means to avoid stigma. This masking is known to reduce or limit disclosure of one's struggles, which can impact individuals in some cases more than their mental health experience itself (Corrigan & Wassel, 2008). This demonstrates both structural and psycho-emotional disablism. The former is social oppression which can exclude the labelled from employment, housing and appropriate healthcare. The latter 'restricts who people can be' (Reeve, 2015), due to stigma stereotyping, prejudice and discrimination by others. This causes people to feel they cannot express how they experience the world, which can be turned in on the self as self-stigma.

One argument for the endurance of mental illness stigma is the recent tendency for stigma-reduction strategies to compare mental illnesses to physical illnesses. It has been found that insisting that 'mental illness is an illness like any other' (Longdon & Read, 2017; Read *et al*, 2006) paradoxically reduces public perceptions of blame yet increases a need for distance from those labelled mentally ill (Corrigan, 2016; Haslam & Kvaale, 2015; Schomerus & Angermeyer, 2017). This neurobiological 'othering' has arguably proliferated the stability of, and increase in, stigma (Schomerus & Angermeyer, 2017). So, what does this pathologisation do?

Within the dominant pathology paradigm, psychological and emotional distress equates to illness. This pathologisation assumes that there is one right, normal, and healthy brain, and any variations from such are necessarily deemed abnormal and unhealthy. This assumes that people – their brains – are disordered, and so the person is the thing to be treated, changed, altered. Ultimately, this boils down to the controlling of behaviours – and thus people – that society feels do not adhere to an ideological standard of normality (e.g. in interactions; relationships; work):

'When we function in ways that go against the norm and wants of society [e.g. we cannot contribute to working life and relate to others, we are]… called ill due to functioning in ways that [violate] the social contract.' (Kelmenson, 2018)

The dominant pathology paradigm (that psychological and emotional distress is the result of biological illness – the 'biogenetic' explanation) does not, then, reduce stigmatising attitudes and behaviour, but increases them (Haslam & Kvaale, 2015; Kvaale *et al*, 2013). And the medical language, this pathology paradigm, shapes attitudes and behaviour (walker, 2013). While many outside of psychiatry (i.e. the public) believe diagnostic labels placed on individuals represent real biogenetic differences between healthy and unhealthy brains, and so the labels and the paradigm should be seen as useful tools, this pathology narrative does not stand up to scrutiny. Definitive biogenetic causes of mental illnesses are simply not found, for *any* mental illness (Kelmenson, 2018; also see Moncrieff, 2009). And if this finding is difficult to grasp, perhaps knowing that Dr Kupfer, the Chair of the committee for the DSM V (a clinician's tool for diagnosing), admitted that:

'In the future, we hope to be able to identify disorders using biological and genetic markers that provide precise diagnoses that can be delivered with complete reliability and validity. Yet this promise, which we have anticipated since the 1970s, remains disappointingly distant…We've been telling patients for several decades that we are waiting for biomarkers. We're still waiting.' (Kupfer, 2013)

And the previous DSM IV task force wrote in their introductory chapter how what are called mental disorders are fuzzy, descriptive constructs, not diseases with clear boundaries or causes.

'In DSM-IV, there is no assumption that each category of mental disorder is a completely discrete entity with absolute boundaries dividing it from other mental disorders or from no mental disorder. There is also no assumption that all individuals described as having the same mental disorder are alike in all important ways.' (American Psychiatric Association, 1994)

So, if mental illnesses are not illnesses at all, where does that leave us when people experience very real psychological distress?

Neurodiversity: not just about autism

I thus came to the neurodiversity paradigm disillusioned by the pathology paradigm of 'mental illness', and first read about neurodiversity in regard to people I now refer to as psychologically-divergent[7] in Susanne Antonetta's 2007 book *A Mind Apart: Travels in a neurodiverse world*. Antonetta solidified the critical thoughts I had about the pathology paradigm, riding on the back of my enamoured feelings toward Dave Horrobin's *The madness of Adam and Eve: How schizophrenia shaped humanity* (2002)[8] (the latter picked up in a public library as the only thing they carried on the subject of schizophrenia when I was 17 and eager to learn). These two influential books helped me articulate and expand my critique of the pathologising of understandable human responses to trauma. I had come to a psychology degree ready to learn about *why* 'mental illness' existed and what could be done to combat these 'illnesses', but found that the more I scrutinised the evidence for the pathology paradigm, and the pathologisation of, for example, 'schizophrenia' (more accurately and respectfully 'voice-hearing') and depression, the more shaky the ground of the paradigm became. On a more personal note about this disillusionment, I had only ever witnessed a decline in my parents' capabilities as a result of (among other things) their chronic anti-psychotic treatment and general pathologisation – there had to be a better, more humane way of approaching them and their struggles[9]. So,

---

7 Latterly, I have come to distinguish between neuro-divergences (e.g. developmental differences such as autism; ADHD; dyslexia) and psychological-divergences (e.g. voice-hearing; anxiety; depression), in relation to neuro- and psychological-typicality.

8 Horrobin details an evolutionary adaptive take on psychosis, in opposition to the pathology narrative. As a 17-year-old trying to understand my parents it was revolutionary to consider the possible adaptiveness of what I had been led to believe was an inherently maladaptive human condition.

9 And actually, the World Health Organisation found that developed countries with technologies (i.e. medications) to address mental illness fare worse on long-term schizophrenia outcomes and have higher mortality rates in comparison to developing countries where these technologies are not readily available or used; Jablensky & Sartorius, 2008; Whitaker, 2010.

how can the neurodiversity paradigm approach what are currently considered mental illnesses or disorders?

I shall not go into great detail about the neurodiversity paradigm (not to be confused with the neurodiversity civil rights movement) as there are some very well written descriptions on the subject (Graby, 2015; McWade *et al*, 2015; Walker, 2014), but for those who may be new to it, or perhaps not sure what the paradigm is precisely (something that I come across regularly is people's misunderstanding of the paradigm), next is a brief breakdown.

The first thing to state emphatically is that while the word *neurodiversity* implies neurological, neurobiological, *physicality*, the paradigm is a social model. Discussions and polite (and some not-so-polite) disagreements I have had with people over the paradigm typically stem from the misunderstanding that the paradigm is based on physical science or neurobiology. It is not. In a nutshell, the neurodiversity paradigm states that all human brains are different from one another, and this is biological fact in the same way that biodiversity is fact. And so, as a species we are neurologically diverse[10], and there is no such thing as a normal brain[11] (if we all had the same brain, we would not make it far, evolutionarily speaking). As a social model, the paradigm discusses how people whose behaviours, ways of being in and interacting with the world that society *currently* deems acceptable, as the social 'norm/s', can be considered *today's* neurotypical. Conversely, people whose behaviours and interactions with the world that are *currently* deemed unacceptable are *today's* neurodivergent. What I believe confuses people with the paradigm is the word neuro, referring to neurology. What the paradigm means when it calls behaviours and ways of interacting with the world neurodivergent from neurotypical is not in relation to observable brain differences, but in relation to those in society whose behaviours and ways of interacting are not considered acceptable, and so those individuals – their behaviour and interactions – diverge from the 'norm', and, ipso facto, so too must their brain[12].

Importantly, due to the neurodiversity of all humanity, and the fact that there is no such thing as a 'normal brain', there is no negative judgement or connotation placed

---

10 To be clear, *only* a group (i.e. two or more people) can be neurodiverse. We cannot talk about individuals being neurodiverse as we only have one brain each! This is a battle of semantics, grammar and definition that many neurodiversity advocates are constantly embroiled in. As a community we do like to be precise!

11 Yale scientists Holmes and Patrick (2018) '[use] evolution to show that uniformity in our brains is totally abnormal. The point [they] argue is that there is no universal, unconditionally optimal pattern of brain structure or function... any given behavioural, psychological, or neurobiological trait is typically neither good nor bad... rather, the context a person is in, their age, social network, and environment, can have a huge influence on the costs and benefits of particular traits'; Livni, 2018.

12 Although at present there is no evidence to suggest consistent brain differences shared between members of any given neurominority; Kelmenson, 2018; Moncrieff, 2009; Pua, Bowden, & Seal, 2017

on being divergent (excluding those brains that experience, for example, physical trauma), and today's neurodivergent is tomorrow's neurotypical, as dependent on the whim of society and what is deemed the 'norm'. Some lament that this still maintains a 'them' versus 'us' narrative, but I argue that divergence does not equate to 'bad', because different means *different*, not less, while also acknowledging the inequality that the divergent experience in a society that currently does view and treat, for example, autistics, as 'other' and less than. If society were to get to a point where all ways of experiencing and interacting with the world were treated equitably, then simply all would be typical *or* divergent under the umbrella of human neurodiversity – dependent on if you are a 'glass half full' or 'glass half empty' kind of philosopher. But that is all about autism, attention differences, dyslexia. What has that got to do with mental illnesses?

What cemented my understanding that people respond to life in neurologically – or, more accurately, psychologically diverging and thus divergent ways – was work identifying that the variables correlating (e.g. factors linked) strongly with what have been referred to as mental illnesses are not in fact genetic or biological factors[13], but traumatic experiences (Johnstone & Boyle, 2018; Johnstone, 2014; Kinderman, 2014; Moncrieff, 2009; Read *et al*, 2009). When it comes to trauma, our brains are capable of responding in any given number of reasonable ways – we cannot pick which psychological response we have to trauma, and nobody gets to determine what constitutes a traumatic experience. One individual experiencing poverty, racism, assault, neglect and so on, may respond in an entirely different way to another experiencing a similar trauma. As a species we have a number of psychological responses in our arsenal, some more distressing than others, and these responses include voice-hearing, post-traumatic stress responses, anxiety, depression and so on. These psychological mechanisms arising from trauma are psychologically-divergent ways of responding to a disordered society, and in and of themselves are not disabling. A trauma response such as voice-hearing or extreme low mood are not disabling until experienced in relation to social contracts: interpersonal relationships, employer-employee relationships, community relationships, independent self-care etc. Attempting to understand these responses in relation to unknown biogenetic causes removes the responsibility from the traumatising society and places it on the individual. The hunt for possible (if improbable) biogenetic reasons why person X responds to trauma with voice-hearing and person Y does not, is quite frankly not an interesting or important question when the trauma response is caused by a disordered society[14].

---

13   Phenomena can be statistically identified as having a genetic component without actually knowing what exactly is inherited – something that confuses many when they are told that something is genetic/inherited, but not what is inherited.

14   For me, this was a key point raised by Professor Peter Kinderman at a talk of his I attended during my PhD, and one I hope I have not misrepresented here, Peter.

'But schizophrenia isn't normal or a reasonable response', I hear some bemoan. Consider the following analogy I use to explain this point when I deliver training about mental illness, stigma, neurodiversity and trauma. Take a room of 10, 20, 80, 500 – any number – of people, and pose the question: 'If I were to go around and punch you all in the face, how would you respond?'. You will receive any number of responses, and in the six-plus years I have delivered this training I have received them all, from being shocked and stunned, to punching back (and some more violent suggestions!). Then I ask, 'and which of those responses was unreasonable?'. The answer is always that none were unreasonable responses to being punched in the face. Quite simply, there are few unreasonable responses – unreasonable for the traumatised anyway: my being assaulted back is not necessarily reasonable to some, but we are not talking about legal responses, but adaptive, personally reasonable responses. Any of these responses are determined by a number of factors: past experience, general personal and individual differences in character, individual cognition and so on. Importantly, regardless of *why* an individual responds the way they do, no response is unreasonable – and often they are unconscious and automatic.

The same can be said about responses to trauma such as voice-hearing, depression, anxiety, post-traumatic responding and so on. One individual's psychology may respond to perceived threat with unconscious, involuntary voice-hearing, while another experiencing a similar perceived threat responds with unconscious, involuntary anxiety. Again, reiterating my previous point: it is unhelpful, and arguably scientifically so, to ask *why* we respond in certain psychological ways that society deems abnormal. The fact is if we address the cause of distressing yet reasonable psychological responses such as poverty, racism, neglect (and all other indicators of a disordered society), we may be more likely to reduce the number of people experiencing reasonable trauma responses.

The pathology paradigm framing trauma responses to a disordered society as 'illnesses' is only one narrative to explain psychologically-divergent experience, neurodiversity is another. The former has dehumanised, and physically and chemically incarcerated those with different neurologies, different responses to trauma. The latter, if given the chance, can free the same people, yet still offer real, *human* support to those whose psychologies have tried to protect them in ways that society struggles to understand or accept. But how to use the neurodiversity narrative? How can we create empathy toward those with psychologically-divergent experiences where the pathology paradigm has failed?

Neurodiversity: for psychological-diversity in practice

In 2012 the charitable organisation Time to Change called for university students to tackle mental health stigma on campuses, a subject dear to my psychology undergraduate heart. I thought hard about things I could do on my campus. After considering possible methods to get across an anti-stigma message, I decided to be creative and tell the alternative and still very real story about the experiences of those with mental health conditions, one that is not often told on television or in the media. In the summer of my first undergraduate year I took the neurodiversity narrative and cognitively scripted and imagined the scenarios, dialogue, and staging for my neurodiversity play, coming up with the play Stigmaphrenia© (Farahar, 2012).

The Stigmaphrenia© script narrative follows 9-year-old Max and his mother, Alice, as she attempts to break down the mental health stigma with which her son is preoccupied. Max accompanies his mother to a waxwork android display where he is introduced to the curator of the 'Exhibition of Neuro-Divergence'. Here, Max discovers his mother's diagnosis of bipolar, and learns to embrace neurodiversity and neurodivergent experiences as a non-pathologising perspective of mental illness (see Appendix on page 65). With script in hand, over the course of the summer of 2012, I solicited the expertise of a retired drama teacher for some constructive criticism on the dialogue, formatting of the script, and eventual direction of the actors taking on the roles. Toward the end of the summer I advertised online and within the university for actors who could rehearse and perform the script as a play in the early part of 2013. I advertised the project on Time to Change via a blog[15], drumming up enough interest locally and nationally that the play was very successfully attended over the two performances in February. It was my hope that the play would affect some sort of change in the audiences who attended, but something far more interesting and important happened.

When I began Stigmaphrenia© I intended to affect the attitudes and emotions of the audience. What I consequently found, however, was very real changes in the attitudes and language of those who took on the roles – the actors themselves. My actors, it seemed, had empathised, and took on the perspective of the neurodivergent roles they embodied[16]. My introducing the neurodiversity paradigm to 'am-dram' actors led to significant changes in attitudes, emotions, and behaviour toward others erroneously labelled 'mentally ill', but more importantly, toward the actor's selves (self-stigma reduction). It seemed that my extrapolation of the neurodiversity narrative from

---

15 For a blog hosted by Time to Change, see https://www.time-to-change.org.uk/blog/stigmaphrenia-play-mental-health-stigma

16 The original script only used the terms neurodiverse and neurodiversity. The expansion in neurodiversity language now includes terms such as neurodivergent and neurotypical. This is reflected in the latest Stigmaphrenia© script, updated in 2018 to incorporate the evolution of the neurodiversity paradigm and consequently the expansion of the language that accompanies it.

autistic experience, where the paradigm was born, to the area of 'mental illness'[17] shifted the narrative from one of biological disorder to one of reasonable responses to unreasonable life situations, helping in practice to reduce public- and self-stigma. This finding led to theorising about a new form of positive, simulated contact where those considered mentally well role-play the 'mentally ill' outgroup with my Stigmaphrenia© script as a means of stigma reduction. I was fortunate that the Economic and Social Research Council saw the possible impact my theory and practical stigma-reduction method could have and funded my PhD research to investigate Stigmaphrenia© as a novel form of *Experiential Intergroup Contact*.

So, what is Experiential Intergroup Contact and how does it work?

Simply put, Experiential Intergroup Contact is a simulated, role-playing form of positive contact between two groups, one present as actors, the other absent. The actors are typically those *without* personal experience of a mental health diagnosis and they role-play the 'mentally ill' outgroup as a means of developing empathy and perspective taking. This is all accomplished with my Stigmaphrenia© script. The underpinning theory of Stigmaphrenia© as a form of intergroup contact between neurotypical and neurodivergent groups (those with and those without 'mental illness') is based on the processes of *experientially roleplaying* the outgroup, and *re-categorising* the mentally-ill as part of shared neurodiversity. But why is re-categorising the mentally ill as neurodivergent important?

Research shows that when we consider our own, personally important ingroup/s and an outgroup (e.g. the mentally ill) to belong to a shared, overarching common ingroup (e.g. neurodiversity: humanity), we are far more likely to develop positive attitudes, emotions and behaviours toward that outgroup (Gaertner *et al*, 1989; Gaertner & Dovidio, 2000). This is because we understand that we are connected, and in effect this shared common ingroup makes us stop seeing others as an outgroup altogether: they become cognitively closer to us. This is still the case if the subgroups (e.g. mentally well and mentally ill) are maintained, but with the understanding that both groups belong to the shared, common ingroup (which is called a dual identity (Gaertner & Dovidio, 2000; González & Brown, 2003)).

Stigmaphrenia© manages to bring the ingroup and outgroup cognitively close to one another by depicting those with mental health problems as part of the superordinate category neurodiversity. This particular category is a rare form of social identity as it is 'optimally distinct': neurodiversity provides a shared common ingroup, which by its very nature simultaneously affords individual divergence and variation (Brewer, 1991; Gaertner & Dovidio, 2000) (the need for both uniqueness and belonging is a paradoxical need in Western societies). However, it is not enough

---

17 Walker also discusses this in *Neurocosmopolitanism*; Walker, 2016

to present the idea of re-categorisation; we need stronger, experiential methods if we want to make real change and have it stick.

When I developed my Experiential Intergroup Contact with Stigmaphrenia©, I looked at the praxis of theatre for change, which followed in the wake of Boal's Theatre of the Oppressed (circa 1979) (Boal, 2000). Theatre for change considers it important to be an actor involved in the process of rehearsal, as opposed to being an audience member viewing the product of performance. This is an important actor-process versus audience-product distinction. Roleplaying with the Stigmaphrenia© script allows neurotypical actors the opportunity to learn and embody the neurodiversity narrative as a means of reducing stigma. This actor-process method is known to elicit affective empathy and cognitive perspective-taking, and I argue this is because roleplaying outgroup members solicits the same sensory cues that embody intergroup interactions – you can *see*, *smell*, *touch*, and *hear* other actors. More simply, actors get experience both *with* and of *being* the 'outgroup', which helps them to no longer perceive those with mental illness labels as an outgroup. And this method not only works for ingroups without mental health diagnoses, but also improves the self-perceptions of those with diagnoses, and these effects *last*.

In 2018, as part of my PhD, I interviewed four of my original actors from 2013 and one later actor who took part in a filmed version of my script in 2015. Given the neurodiversity narrative embedded in the Stigmaphrenia© script, I wanted to see how the interviewees – the past actors – constructed their realities before and after involvement with the script. What I found was how experiential, embodied involvement with Stigmaphrenia© and its neurodiversity narrative was a main factor contributing to interviewee mental health awareness; positive mental health attitudes, language, and behaviour; and the pre-emption or reduction of personal self-stigma, leading interviewees to disclose to friends and family. And these effects were found some three-to-five years following their involvement with the script. Importantly, those past actors with their own mental health problems, either at the time or developed later, found their involvement beneficial in terms of understanding their mental health in relation to neurodiversity; an increased inclination to disclose their experiences; a change in attitude and behaviour toward others they encounter who are neurodivergent; and an improvement in personal self-esteem. Interviewed actors cited the neurodiversity narrative as a reason for and means of approaching stigmatisers in their workplaces, and one actor only disclosed their own psychological experiences to those who had seen the play or understood neurodiversity, wanting to avoid the stigma he knew existed from the pathology narrative:

'*I only disclose it to the people I'd also talked about the play with them, about. So the people I told were my parents, my best friend. And my partner, and all of them had been, had seen the play. I kind of felt that they were the right kind of people to also tell.'* (Russ[18])

What I was seeing was past actors managing a potentially discreditable and discredited identity by adopting the neurodiversity narrative and neurodivergent identity. Two of my original actors, Cassandra and George[19], talked about their experiences of anxiety and depression, experienced both at the time of their involvement with Stigmaphrenia© and at the time of interview. However, they embedded these experiences in two different narratives – *before* and *after* Stigmaphrenia©. Both actors talked about how *before* Stigmaphrenia© they considered their mental health as pathology, and experienced self-stigma:

'Yeah, it was too easy to be just explained away. Like, just like, oh, you just have mental, you know, I didn't really. I didn't really believe in it.' (Cassandra)

'[B]efore I did the play, erm, I knew that I definitely had what I perceived as mental health issues, mental health problems. Erm, but because I also sort of misunderstood mental health and what it meant I would keep very quiet about it.' (George)

These same actors described how after Stigmaphrenia© they reframed their experiences within the neurodiversity narrative – a narrative that empowered them to disclose and actively combat public stigma:

'[R]ather than mental health being almost like a dirty word, it is now just something that is, you know, it's a simple to me something I check, I check on, like the weather… And it's carried on, you know, here we are, six years later, five years, and it is it is something that I actively encourage people to talk about, because it only helps to talk about it.' (George)

'So yeah, I think I think the whole experience, to be honest, has been what it's been rewarding for me, because I feel I can handle it better now. And I'm fine with talking aloud about it. And it's just, it's just how it is really.' (Cassandra)

The future for my method of Experiential Intergroup Contact to reduce stigma with Stigmaphrenia© looks bright. Following its investigation during my PhD, and Stigmaphrenia's© effectiveness in education settings in the UK[20] and the USA[21],

---

18 Russ is a pseudonym.

19 Cassandra and George are both pseudonyms.

20 In 2013, at Canterbury Christ Church University; Neupauer, 2012

21 In 2013, at Parkland High School, Winston-Salem, North Carolina; The Paisley IB Magnet School, 2013; and in 2014 at the University Theatre at UW-Sheboygan, University of Wisconsin, Sheboygan; University Theatre at UW-GB, Sheboygan, 2015

I plan to co-create scripts for further marginalised groups, to continue to tackle self-stigma with the neurodiversity narrative, and take my methods into highly stigmatising contexts such as clinical settings with professionals.

This snapshot of one of my PhD studies demonstrates how the experiential role-playing element of my Experiential Intergroup Contact strengthens a neurodiversity cognitive narrative, providing a new representation about those with mental health problems. Through a process of re-categorisation, actors come to view themselves as neurodivergent in an overarching human neurodiversity, and this improves their sense of self and well-being. My Experiential Intergroup Contact method thus demonstrates the practical application potential of neurodiversity.

Summary

Having initially discussed a problem in society – the stigmatisation of psychologically divergent ways of managing distress (commonly referred to as 'mental illness') – I have hopefully demonstrated how neurodiversity is not just about autism, or even neurodevelopmental conditions. Neurodiversity as a paradigmatic narrative also applies to those with psychologically divergent, reasonable responses to a disordered society, because all psychological responses are reasonable, which shows the variable and diverse ways in which humanity has evolved to deal with unreason. As a means of tackling the stigma that surrounds those with psychological-divergences, I have outlined a method in which the neurodiversity narrative can elicit empathy and perspective-taking for those who take part in the process of script rehearsals with my play Stigmaphrenia©. This method demonstrates how neurodiversity holds implications for practice, both as an experiential form of intergroup contact between psychologically typical and psychologically divergent groups, and hopefully as a narrative we can more broadly embrace in our everyday lives and interactions.

On the 20th anniversary since neurodiversity was coined (Singer, 2017), its influence on theory and practice is tangible. Neurodiversity and neurodivergence have played, and continue to play, a fundamental part in our evolution as a species, and closer to home in our present society. As a paradigm, ultimately, neurodiversity *allows for* and *accepts* difference, it encourages the *support* of difference, and importantly it *humanises* difference. The neurodiversity paradigm is not a movement in and of itself (Walker, 2014), and people will interpret it as they see fit, as driven by personal values (normality vs difference and uniqueness), assumptions (normal brains and pathology vs diversity), and practices (change the person vs change the environment) (Prilleltensky, 1997). For those who value the pathologising of human experience – human experience in all its guises – there will be personal assumptions and practices that follow suit. The neurodiversity of humanity is an irrefutable fact (Livni, 2018; Holmes & Patrick, 2018), the paradigm, like the pathology paradigm, however, is one narrative among several that can be adopted for those who have lost faith and been harmed by the pathologisation of human emotional and psychological suffering.

I have given talks, trainings and workshops, all based on the psychological-diversity of human experience. Those who attend are seeking something to explain and voice their disillusionment with the pathologisation of their, or their loved ones', experiences. The neurodiversity paradigm offers an alternative narrative for those who seek it, for those harmed by the mainstream, dominant medicalisation of human experience[22]. Attendees of my training have wept with validation that they are not ill, disordered or broken. They may be disabled by our society following their (involuntary) psychological responses to trauma, and neurodiversity does not alter this fact. What it gives them is hope, and an understanding of the impacts of trauma that they have felt and experienced, but which the dominant narrative of pathology did not allow for or voice, simply stating that they had a 'chemical imbalance' and a 'mental disorder'. For those who fear the neurodiversity paradigm, fear that it will ignore or silence the most disabled in our society, I hope that someday you will see that this is not built into the paradigm, that the paradigm comes in peace and with good intention to improve the lives of those most vulnerable in our communities. It comes to humanise the lives of those whom the pathology paradigm makes less than. Our very interaction with a world we cannot control will always mean that there are those of us still disabled. The neurodiversity paradigm seeks only to lessen suffering at the hands of pathologisation, and this is something we can readily embrace.

Acknowledgements

The research presented in this chapter was conducted while Chloe Farahar was a full-time postgraduate student in the School of Psychology, University of Kent (September 2015 – September 2019), on an Economic and Social Research Council awarded scholarship from the South East Doctoral Training Centre (now the South East Network for Social Sciences Doctoral Training Partnership).

Bibliography

American Psychiatric Association (1994) *Diagnostic and statistical manual of mental disorders (DSM IV)* (4th ed.). Washington, DC, USA: American Psychiatric Association.

Blume H (1998) *Neurodiversity: On the neurological underpinnings of geekdom*. Retrieved September 2015, from The Atlantic : www.theatlantic.com/magazine/archive/1998/09/neurodiversity/305909/ (accessed January 2020).

---

22 Of which there are unfortunately many – see the psychiatric survivor's movement, for example; World Network of Users and Survivors of Psychiatry, n.d.

Boal, A. (2000). *Theater of the Oppressed* (2nd ed.). (C. A. McBride, M. L. McBride, & E. Fryer, Trans.) London, UK: Pluto Press.

Bos, A. R., Kanner, D., Muris, P., Janssen, B., & Mayer, B. (2009). Mental illness stigma and disclosure: Consequences of coming out of the closet. *Issues In Mental Health Nursing, 30*(8), 509-513. doi:10.1080/01612840802601382

Brewer, M. B. (1991). The social self: On being the same and different at the same time. *Personality and Social Psychology Bulletin, 17*(5), 475-482. doi:10.1177/0146167291175001

Chaudoir, S. R., & Fisher, J. D. (2010). The disclosure processes model: Understanding disclosure decision making and postdisclosure outcomes among people living with a concealable stigmatized identity. *Psychological Bulletin, 136*(2), 236-256. doi:10.1037/a0018193

Corrigan, P. W. (Ed.). (2005). *On the stigma of mental illness: Practical strategies for research and social change.* Washington, USA: American Psychological Association.

Corrigan, P. W. (2016). Lessons learned from unintended consequences about erasing the stigma of mental illness. *World Psychiatry, 15*(1), 67-73. doi:10.1002/wps.20295

Corrigan, P. W., & Shapiro, J. R. (2010). Measuring the impact of programs that challenge the public stigma of mental illness. *Clinical Psychology Review, 30*(8), 907-922. doi:10.1016/j.cpr.2010.06.004

Corrigan, P. W., & Wassel, A. (2008). Understanding and influencing the stigma of mental illness. *Journal of Psychosocial Nursing and Mental Health Services, 46*(1), 42-48. doi:10.3928/02793695-20080101-04

Crisp, R. (2015). *The social brain: How diversity made the modern mind.* London, UK: Robinson.

Farahar, C. T. (2012). Stigmaphrenia©. 1, 1-22. Canterbury, UK.

Gaertner, S. L., Mann, J., Murrell, A., & Dovidio, J. F. (1989). Reducing intergroup bias: The benefits of recategorization. *Journal of Personality and Social Psychology, 57*(2), 239-249. doi:10.1037/0022-3514.57.2.239

Gaertner, S., & Dovidio, J. (2000). *Reducing intergroup bias: The Common Ingroup Identity Model.* East Sussex: Psychology Press.

Goffman, E. (1963). *Stigma: Notes on the management of spoiled identity.* New York, USA: Simon & Schuster, Inc.

Goffman, E. (1991). *Asylums: Essays on the social situation of mental patients and other inmates.* Harmondsworth, UK: Penguin.

González, R., & Brown, R. (2003). Generalization of positive attitude as a function of subgroup and superordinate group identifications in intergroup contact. *European Journal of Social Psychology, 33*(2), 195-214. doi:10.1002/ejsp.140

Graby, S. (2015). Neurodiversity: Bridging the gap between the disabled people's movement and the mental health system survivors' movement? In H. Spandler, & J. Anderson (Eds.), *Madness, distress and the politics of disablement* (pp. 231-244). Bristol, UK: Policy Press.

Haslam, N., & Kvaale, E. P. (2015). Biogenetic explanations of mental disorder: The mixed-blessings model. *Current Directions in Psychological Science, 24*(5), 399-404. doi:10.1177/0963721415588082

Heflinger, C. A., & Hinshaw, S. P. (2010). Stigma in child and adolescent mental health services research: Understanding professional and institutional stigmatization of youth with mental health problems and their families. *Administration and Policy in Mental Health and Mental Health Services Research, 37*(1-2), 61-70. doi:10.1007/s10488-010-0294-z

Henderson, C. (2017). Disorder-specific differences. In W. Gaebel, W. Rössler, & N. Sartorius (Eds.), *The stigma of mental illness - End of the story?* (pp. 83-109). London, UK: Springer.

Holmes, A. J., & Patrick, L. M. (2018). The myth of optimality in clinical neuroscience. *Trends in Cognitive Sciences, 22*(3), 241-257. doi:10.1016/j.tics.2017.12.006

Horrobin, D. (2002). *The madness of Adam and Eve: How schizophrenia shaped humanity.* London, UK: Transworld Publishers.

Jablensky, A., & Sartorius, N. (2008). What did the WHO studies really find? *Schizophrenia Bulletin*, **34**(2), 253-255. doi:10.1093/schbul/sbm151

Johnstone, L. (2014). *A straight talking introduction to psychiatric diagnosis.* (R. Bentall, & P. Sanders, Eds.) Monmouth, UK: PCCS Books Ltd.

Johnstone, L., & Boyle, M. (2018). *The Power Threat Meaning Framework: Overview.* Leicester: British Psychological Society.

Johnstone, M. J. (2001). Stigma, social justice and the rights of the mentally ill: Challenging the status quo. *Australian and New Zealand Journal of Mental Health Nursing*, **10**, 200–209. doi:10.1046/j.1440-0979.2001.00212.x

Kelmenson, L. (2018, January 22). *If 'Mental Illnesses' aren't real illnesses, what are they?* Retrieved February 26, 2018, from Mad in America: Science, psychiatry and social justice: https://www.madinamerica.com/2018/01/mental-illnesses-arent-real-illnesses/

Kinderman, P. (2014). *A prescription for psychiatry: Why we need a whole new aporach to mental health and wellbeing.* Basingstoke, UK: Palgrave Macmillan.

Kupfer, D. (2013). *Chair of DSM-5 task force discusses future of mental health research. Public statement, released May, 3* . Arlington, USA: American Psychiatric Association.

Kvaale, E. P., Gottdiener, W. H., & Haslam, N. (2013). Biogenetic explanations and stigma: A meta-analytic review of associations among laypeople. *Social Science & Medicine*, **96**, 95-103. doi:10.1016/j.socscimed.2013.07.017

Link, B. G., & Phelan, J. C. (2001). Conceptualizing stigma. *Annual Review of Sociology*, **27**(1), 363-385. doi:10.1146/annurev.soc.27.1.363

Livni, E. (2018, March 15). *Yale neuroscientists debunked the idea that anyone is 'normal'.* Retrieved from Quartz: https://qz.com/1229137/yale-neuroscientists-debunk-the-myth-of-normalcy-in-life-and-psychiatry/

Longdon, E., & Read, J. (2017). 'People with problems, not patients with illnesses': Using psychosocial frameworks to reduce the stigma of psychosis. *The Israel Journal of Psychiatry and Related Sciences*, **54**(1), 24-28.

McWade, B., Milton, D., & Beresford, P. (2015). Mad studies and neurodiversity: A dialogue. *Disability & Society*, **30**(2), 305-309. doi:10.1080/09687599.2014.1000512

Moncrieff, J. (2009). *A straight talking introduction to psychiatric drugs.* Monmouth, Wales, UK: PCCS Books.

Neupauer, V. (2012, September 17). Time to Change: CCCU PsySoc is supporting Mental Health Day by putting on a play. *UNIfied*, pp. 23-23. Retrieved from Issuu: https://issuu.com/ccsu/docs/unifiedseptember2012

Prilleltensky, I. (1997). Values, assumptions, and practices: Assessing the moral implications of psychological discourse and action. *American Psychologist*, 52(5), 517-535. doi:10.1037/0003-066X.52.5.517

Pua, E. P., Bowden, S. C., & Seal, M. L. (2017). Autism spectrum disorders: Neuroimaging findings from systematic reviews. *Research in Autism Spectrum Disorders*, **34**, 28-33. doi:10.1016/j.rasd.2016.11.005

Quinn, D. M. (2017). Identity concealment: Multilevel predictors, moderators, and consequences. *Journal of Social Issues*, **73**(2), 230–239. doi:10.1111/josi.12213

Quinn, D. M., & Chaudoir, S. R. (2009). Living with a concealable stigmatized identity: The impact of anticipated stigma, centrality, salience, and cultural stigma on psychological distress and health. *Journal of Personality and Social Psychology*, **97**(4), 634-651. doi:10.1037/a0015815

Read, J., Bentall, R. P., & Fosse, R. (2009). Time to abandon the bio-bio-bio model of psychosis: Exploring the epigenetic and psychological mechanisms by which adverse life events lead to psychotic symptoms. *Epidemiologia e Psichiatria Sociale*, **18**(4), 299-310.

Read, J., Haslam, N., Sayce, L., & Davies, E. (2006). Prejudice and schizophrenia: A review of the 'mental illness is an illness like any other' approach. *Acta Psychiatrica Scandinavica*, **114**(5), 303-318. doi:10.1111/j.1600-0447.2006.00824.x

Reeve, D. (2015). Psycho-emotional disablism in the lives of people experiencing mental distress . In H. Spandler, J. Anderson, & B. Sapey (Eds.), *Madness, distress and the politics of disablement* (pp. 99-112). Bristol, UK: Policy Press.

Schomerus, G., & Angermeyer, M. C. (2017). Changes of stigma over time. In W. Gaebel, W. Rössler, & N. Sartorius (Eds.), *The stigma of mental illness - End of the story?* (pp. 157-172). London, UK: Springer.

Singer, J. (2017). *NeuroDiversity: The birth of an idea*. New South Wales, Australia: Judy Singer.

Spandler, H., & Anderson, J. (Eds.). (2015). *Madness, distress and the politics of disablement*. Bristol, UK: Policy Press.

Stuart, H. (2012). The stigmatization of mental illnesses. *The Canadian Journal of Psychiatry*, **57**(8), 455-456. doi:10.1177/070674371205700801

The Paisley IB Magnet School. (2013, October 27). *The Paisley Pipeline. Retrieved from The Paisley* Pipeline: https://www.mynewsletterbuilder.com/email/newsletter/1411889741

University Theatre at UW-GB, Sheboygan. (2015, February 24). *'Stigmaphrenia' by Chloe Tyler - a staged reading by University Theatre at UW-Sheboygan*. Retrieved from YouTube: https://www.youtube.com/watch?v=axGrvw5zf58

Walker, N. (2013, August 16). *Throw away the master's tools: Liberating ourselves from the pathology paradigm*. Retrieved February 26, 2018, from Neurocosmopolitanism: Nick walker's notes on neurodiversity, autism, and cognitive liberty: http://neurocosmopolitanism.com/throw-away-the-masters-tools-liberating-ourselves-from-the-pathology-paradigm/

Walker, N. (2014, September 27). *Neurodiversity: Some Basic Terms & Definitions*. Retrieved October 9, 2016, from Nick Walker's Notes on Neurodiversity, Autism, and Cognitive Liberty: http://neurocosmopolitanism.com/neurodiversity-some-basic-terms-definitions/

Walker, N. (2016, June 23). *Autism and the pathology paradigm*. Retrieved February 26, 2018, from Neurocosmopolitanism: Nick Walker's notes on neurodiversity, autism, and cognitive liberty: http://neurocosmopolitanism.com/autism-and-the-pathology-paradigm/

Whitaker, R. (2010). *Anatomy of an epidemic: Magic bullets, psychiatric drugs, and the astonishing rise of mental illness in America*. New York, USA: Crown Publishing.

World Network of Users and Survivors of Psychiatry. (n.d.). *Welcome to the website of WNUSP*. Retrieved July 2019, from World Network of Users and Survivors of Psychiatry: http://www.wnusp.net/

Appendix

Stigmaphrenia© synopsis and scenes

Scene 1. Opening scene, a poem adapted from Robert Burton's Anatomy of Melancholy (1651). The poem depicts a 'madman', but also implies there is no difference between the 'mad' and the 'sane'.

Scene 2. We are introduced to nine-year-old Max and his mum, Alice. Max is dejected and in a funny mood. He explains he is upset and confused. He is being bullied at school for wearing a bear onesie, with his peers calling him 'Mad Max', and is confused by the portrayals of madness everywhere – in books and on television. Alice tries to explain it is not madness, but neuro-divergence.

Scene 3. Max goes to bed, and Alice tells him The Wise King/The Madman Parable by Kahlil Gibran (1883–1931; depicted in the play as shadow puppetry). The moral of the story is that we are only mad if a group of people tells us that we are. Alice convinces Max to come to her place of work, the museum, that weekend.

Scene 4. Max meets Alice's co-worker and curator of the museum, George. George shows Max around the 'Exhibition of Neuro-Divergence' (END) – the END Stigma waxwork android display. At the exhibition Max hears from waxwork 'droids who depict famous persons who are neuro-divergent, such as Adam Levine, lead singer of Maroon Five, who has attention differences ('Attention Deficit Hyperactivity Disorder').

Scene 5. Having fun, Max wonders off and finds a closed exhibit depicting a 'droid scene about the evolutionary importance of neuro-divergent experiences, such as 'schizophrenia'. The exhibit depicts how '[n]euro-diversity may be every bit as crucial for the human race as bio-diversity is for life in general. Who can say what forms of life can prove best at any given moment?' (Actor; quoted from Blume, 1998; Farahar, 2012, p11).

Alice and George catch up with Max and explain the 'Evolution and Neuro-diversity' room is closed at present because '[s]ome of the Museum Board think it's too controversial to be seen' (George; Farahar, 2012, p14), indicating those who may disagree with a non-pathologising theory of mental health.

Scene 6. Max, Alice and George head into a work-in-progress room where there is a family of 'droids. The family of 'droids introduce themselves as a mother, father and son, each with their own neuro-divergent experience. As well as descriptions of themselves similar in tone to the famous 'droids exhibit, the 'droid family also depict the distress that these experiences can cause.

Scene 7. Max, Alice and George head to a local pub to meet Max's dad, John. Here the adults explain to Max, in simple terms, what bipolar, schizophrenia and autism are, and also why they may exist in the first place. It is here that Alice discloses to Max that she has a diagnosis of bipolar. Max reaffirms his love for his mother, and how he thinks of her as 'normal'. Alice and John explain that when she gets low or has a 'manic' episode she seeks support.

Scene 8. Back in school Monday, Max confronts his classmates during his turn to 'show and tell' what he did that weekend. He describes himself in a similar way that the 'droids did in the exhibition, ending by saying 'I like being me' (Max; Farahar, 2012, p20). The opening poem is reiterated, but with contemporary language.

Epilogue. The cast speak to the audience:

'GROUP 1	Like anything, there are good and bad points to the neuro-diversity of the whole human race.
GROUP 2	Those who are considered mentally ill are actually a part of the diversity of human minds.
GROUP 3	So let's stop calling them illnesses and think of them as divergent experiences…
GROUP 4	…A part of the person, both a significant and insignificant part.
MAX	While not all neuro-divergent experiences are positive or easy to live with …
ALICE	… neuro-diversity across all of humanity can create art, solve maths problems, or write beautiful poetry and music.
GROUP 5	Our abilities are only limited by our creative imaginations.
MAX	So let's not limit it with labels, let's just be.' (Farahar, 2012, p21).

Chapter 7: Neurodiversity: not just about autism!

'What more can the neurodivergent community do to support those with learning disabilities?'

By Maura Campbell

Introduction

The neurodiversity paradigm embraces all kinds of minds, and people with learning disabilities[23] are as much a part of the neurodivergent family as any of us. And, like any of us, each person with a learning disability is a unique individual with their own interests, talents and challenges. Each has intrinsic value as a human being and deserves to be treated with as much dignity and respect as anyone else. There are an estimated 1.4 million people with learning disabilities living in the UK.

However, this part of our community tends to be significantly underrepresented within advocacy and activism, particularly on social media. This draws criticism from our opponents, who claim it as evidence that proponents of neurodiversity are only interested in so-called 'high-functioning' individuals who see neurological difference solely as a 'gift' – an incorrect but persistent assumption about our core values.

So, what should we do? I believe we can, collectively, do more to highlight and address the particular challenges and systemic barriers people with higher support needs face – not just as a defence against our critics, but because it is the right thing to do.

---

23 I am using 'person-first' terminology throughout this article since those I consulted said they prefer this to 'identity-first' language, and I wish to respect their right to choose how they should self-identify.

Why does this matter?

My son just had his 12th birthday. He is a happy, healthy, wonderful boy who has brought more joy to my life than I could ever have imagined. In just two years, we will formally start the process of preparing for his transition from special school into adult services.

And I am terrified.

The ground-breaking *NeuroTribes* (Allen & Unwin, 2015) exposed the dark history of disability and the eugenics movement, recounting heart-breaking stories that chilled me to the bone. It graphically illustrated how people with disabilities are generally used as the 'canary in the mine' for those intent on pursuing an agenda to usurp the basic human rights of marginalised groups of people.

Unfortunately, the mistreatment and neglect of people with learning disabilities is not a thing of the past. In the UK alone, there has been a litany of disturbing accounts of abuse in institutional settings in recent years. In 2011, six care workers at the Winterbourne View care home in South Gloucestershire were given prison terms for the 'cruel, callous and degrading' abuse of disabled patients and a further five staff members received suspended sentences. The abuse came to light after being secretly recorded by a reporter for the BBC's Panorama programme in response to a whistleblowing allegation.

On 4 July 2013, 18-year-old Connor Sparrowhawk was found unconscious in the bath in Slade House, an NHS assessment and treatment unit in Oxfordshire. He had diagnoses of autism, learning disability and epilepsy. An independent investigation demanded by Connor's family concluded his death could have been prevented (Death of 18-year-old Connor Sparrowhawk was preventable, 2014).

Mendip House in Somerset, the first specialised care facility for autistic adults in the UK, was closed in 2016 after an anonymous tip-off triggered an investigation which uncovered a culture of 'laddish' and neglectful behaviour on the part of care staff.

In June 2017, 13 care workers were convicted in court after an inquiry into organised and systemic abuse, including false imprisonment, at two care homes for adults in learning disabilities in Devon.

In December 2018, a leaked report obtained by the BBC revealed shocking levels of abuse inflicted on patients with severe learning disabilities in Muckamore Abbey Hospital in Northern Ireland, some of which had been captured on CCTV.

In May 2019, the Panorama programme went undercover again, this time in Whorlton Hall hospital in County Durham. Ten staff were subsequently arrested on a range of charges relating to the neglect and abuse of patients.

This torrent of abuse shows no sign of abating. Cases like these are regularly reported around the world, and may only be the tip of the iceberg, and highly vulnerable people continue to be warehoused in settings that are meant to be places of safety but have been shown time and again to be unsafe.

There are, of course, many risks within community settings as well. According to Victim Support UK (Rossetti *et al*, 2016), people with 'limiting disabilities' are almost three and half times more likely to suffer serious violence (violence with injury), twice as likely to suffer violence without injury, 1.6 times more likely be a victim of personal theft, and 1.4 times more likely to be a victim of household theft than adults without a 'limiting disability'.

While people with a learning disability are believed to be more likely to experience hate crime, they are less likely to report it, for a number of reasons. They may not recognise they are being abused, for instance, since this is a group which is particularly susceptible to 'mate crime'. They may have experienced abuse so often in their lifetime that it's become normalised. They may fear not being believed, they may not have the language to express the harm that's occurred, or they may have been conditioned to feel that their opinions don't matter.

Hate speak may be directed towards either individuals or whole groups of people and can be dressed up as something else; with the advent of austerity, for example, disability has increasingly been represented as an economic burden on the rest of society.

I am focusing here primarily on the abuse experienced by people with a learning disability but there are, of course, other inequalities that impact more acutely on this group of people. These include lack of access to education, housing, employment and healthcare. On average, the life expectancy of women with a learning disability is 18 years shorter than for women in the general population and the life expectancy of men with a learning disability is 14 years shorter than for men in the general population (NHS Digital, 2017). These inequalities between those with or without learning disabilities are simply not acceptable in a modern society.

So why are people with learning disabilities so much more likely to suffer abuse or neglect, or to be denied proper access to services? It's tempting to blame it all on a group of evil people or government agencies. The latter must shoulder at least some of the blame if systemic problems are identified or regulatory regimes are shown to be ineffective, but it is a much wider problem than that.

The real question is, I think, what creates the conditions in which this type of abuse can take place? What makes it seemingly okay to demean people with learning disabilities?

What we really need to do is consider what part is played by societal attitudes to this type of difference. It is not that long ago that it was standard practice to take people with learning disabilities away from their families and lock them up, out of sight and out of mind. Now that they are more often part of the community, society is still coming to terms with how to react to this group of people. That partly explains (though hardly excuses) why a significant minority of people will admit they are uncomfortable with the idea of sharing a restaurant, office, pub or public transport with someone with a learning disability or autism (Londoners least comfortable when sharing spaces with people who have learning disabilities or autism, new survey finds, 2019).

What is ableism?

Ableism is the term used for discrimination or prejudice against people with, or perceived to have, physical, mental or developmental disabilities, and it is grounded in the idea that disability makes a person inferior. Or, as Julie Zeilinger, puts it: 'This interpretation of difference as defect is the true root of ableist acts that cause far too many to feel marginalized, discriminated against and ultimately devalued in this society.' (Zeilinger, 2015). Making the level of intelligence or neurological conformity the measure of someone's worth as a human being is a slippery slope, not to mention the foundation of the eugenics movement.

Ableism may be conscious or unconscious, deliberate or unintentional. It can take many forms, some of which are more obvious (failure to provide a wheelchair ramp or propelling a blind person across the road without asking whether they even wanted your help, for instance) and others that are much subtler – like seeing the achievement of a common task by a person with a disability as 'inspirational' or thinking that it's okay to ask extremely personal questions. We get a lot of intrusive questions from complete strangers when we're out with our son, especially whenever he's attached to his assistance dog. Most people are simply curious, but some are downright rude – like the man who stared at my son and demanded to know, 'What's wrong with him?'. Having a visible disability can sometimes make people see you as public property and expect you to explain yourself.

We all like to think of ourselves as good people, especially those of us who are active in the world of autism or disability advocacy. We call out institutional abuse whenever it's uncovered or condemn violent attacks in the community, and we demand that action is taken. But is that enough? Can you swear that you have never, ever, said or done anything, even unintentionally, that could be construed as being disrespectful towards people with higher support needs, or failed to challenge someone else who did? Ever?

I know I have. Being disabled yourself doesn't inoculate you against ableism. One phenomenon I've observed, for example, is autistic or physically disabled people being very quick to point out that they are, in fact, highly intelligent. Often this is, legitimately enough, in an effort to debunk the myth that all autistics have intellectual disabilities. But, if we are too quick to disassociate from this part of our community, the risk is that we inadvertently reinforce the stigma against them.

What's in a name?

Perhaps one of the most common (and subtlest) forms of ableism is ableist language. Our attitudes to intellectual disability are reflected in the language we use, but because of the extent to which ableist language has been normalised it can be extremely difficult to tackle.

I thought of myself as a perfectly nice person until the day I stumbled upon an article on ableist language that stopped me in my tracks (Brown, 2012). I started to search out other articles on ableism. There weren't that many, and most were concerned with physical disability. Then I found one particular article containing an infographic which illustrated how terms that I had been using in my everyday speech for years – 'idiot', 'imbecile' and 'moron' – were actually cruel slurs with their origins in the clinical terms for intellectual disability (Gold, 2020). These terms were replaced with levels of 'mental retardation', which means that they have exactly the same meaning as 'r*tard' (which many people now accept is problematic terminology). Mental retardation was subsequently replaced by 'mental handicap', with its connotations of begging 'cap in hand' for charity. This constant updating of terms as they inevitably become corrupted for what is now known in the UK as learning disability, and in the US as intellectual disability, is sometimes referred to as the 'euphemism treadmill' (Pinker, 2003).

In the UK, the word 'idiot' is especially popular. People tell me it's 'not meant like that anymore' or that it's just an archaic meaning of the word and language changes. Yes, that is true, though the following legal definition was only repealed in the Republic of Ireland (an hour's drive from where I live) in December 2015:

'And the word 'lunatic' shall be construed to mean any person found by inquisition idiot, lunatic, or of unsound mind, and incapable of managing himself or his affairs.'

That feels pretty recent to me.

The reality is that it is not just about particular words. It is, fundamentally, about the idea that people with a learning disability are inferior, intrinsically flawed and consequently not worthy of respect. The question to ask is not so much 'is this word offensive?' as 'is saying this disrespectful towards people with learning disabilities?'.

What role does unconscious bias play?

People tend to be extremely resistant to the idea that the language they commonly use is disrespectful. If your core belief is that you are a good person, anything that might challenge that self-perception can create real cognitive dissonance. We rarely pause to consider the role that unconscious bias plays in our attitudes.

All of us experience unconscious bias on a daily basis. It is hard-wired into the human brain as part of our survival mechanism and causes us to prefer people who are like us, since they make us feel safer. It is part of the reason why encountering someone who is very different from us can provoke irrational fear or discomfort.

One form of unconscious bias is the herd effect, or 'group think' – if a critical mass of people believes a thing to be socially acceptable, including friends and family, it effectively makes it so.

Ableism is insidious and pernicious. It is so commonplace that it is difficult to get people even to acknowledge its existence. If challenged on the language they use, people may cite freedom of speech, which is commonly misunderstood as the right to say whatever the hell you like. Freedom of expression is, actually, about the right to express an *opinion* without interference by the *state*. It is also a qualified right, which means that it needs to be balanced against other fundamental human rights, such as the right not to be discriminated against on grounds of disability as enshrined in the United Nations Convention on the Rights of People with Disabilities. All rights carry responsibilities, and freedom of expression does not justify the ill-treatment of others, either directly or indirectly.

Another common defence is that querying the use of ableist sentiments is 'political correctness' (usually said with an eyeroll) or 'tone policing'. If that is the case, is condemning misogynistic, racist or homophobic language also just 'political correctness'?

We have a long way to go to tackle ableist attitudes to intellectual disability, or even to get people to the point where they realise these exist. It is only relatively recently that disability has started to reframe itself as a civil rights movement and it is earlier in its journey than other minority causes. Added to that, within the disability movement, learning disability is lagging behind other forms of disability. That brings me back to my son. Right now, he is in an environment in which he is safe, well-supported and valued. He's happy there. The staff have genuine affection for him and work hard to help him reach his full potential, while remembering to have fun as well. He'll be devastated when the time comes for him to have to leave the school he loves. And so will I. How can I, his mother, prepare him for the challenges of navigating a confusing and hostile world as an autistic adult with a learning disability? And how can I prepare the rest of the world for him? One thing is for certain – I can't do it alone.

Hopefully, I won't have to.

What is already happening?

There are, I am glad to say, some great examples already of neurodivergent leaders taking the initiative in this area.

The National Autistic Taskforce, led by Dr Damian Milton, was launched at the farewell event of the National Autism Project (NAP) in December 2017. The NAP, generously supported by the Shirley Foundation, was established 'to provide authoritative recommendations on autism research and practice which have demonstrable effectiveness in benefitting autistic people and their communities'. The Taskforce, which is autistic-led, aims as its primary focus 'to help empower autistic adults, including those with less autonomy and higher support needs, to have a stronger voice in the decisions and direction of their own lives'.

In pursuance of this important goal, the Taskforce has produced a new guidance document setting out the key elements of quality care, with a strong emphasis on promoting autonomy, fighting stigma and discrimination, and accepting difference. One of the themes in the guidance that particularly appeals to me as a parent is the reframing of what are usually referred to as 'challenging behaviours', as distress and an indication of unmet needs.

Dr Milton has claimed ownership of the description of him and his colleague Dr Dinah Murray as 'positive irritants' on the NAP with pride, as well he should. As badges of honour go, it's a good one. Both are on the of the National Autistic Taskforce Strategy Board, alongside Dr Yo Dunn, who delivered a comprehensive and thought-provoking presentation at Autscape 2017 entitled 'The Other Half', on the legal framework and policies which apply to autistics, and which impact most acutely those with co-occurring learning disabilities (Dunne, 2017). Dr Dunn used the presentation as an opportunity to call on autistic adults to help those with no family, friends or caregivers, or whose caregivers are no longer able to look after them – the issue which keeps most parents like me awake at night – by lobbying for the development of community services, new legislation and positive reform.

Autistic UK, which is the largest autistic-led national organisation in the UK, has been campaigning for autistic rights, including those of autistics with learning disabilities, since 2009. While most of their previous work has been behind the scenes with local and national governments, the NHS, Equality and Human Rights Commission and other organisations, during their recent organisational change to become a Community Interest Company, they have now shifted much of their focus to reach out to the autistic community through campaign initiatives to give their members a chance to be directly involved in making lasting positive changes with these and other institutions and to provide a platform for those groups who often go unheard. With the coming formation of working groups, forums and workshop events for learning disabilities and other marginalised groups, A-UK hopes to attract volunteers to run and participate in these groups who have lived experience. As one of Autistic UK's former directors, Kat Humble, has said: "The best people to ask what needs to change are the people directly affected by the outcomes. A-UK is a firm believer in intersectionality, so it's not enough to actively seek autistic rights generally, as each intersection has different experiences, barriers and support requirements. We must never forget that every autistic person is an individual."

What more can we do?

Building on this positive work, there are practical actions all of us can take. We can:

7. *Allow people with learning disabilities to take the lead*

   This is a group of people who tend to be spoken for, talked over and infantilised.

   We should directly support the efforts of intellectually disabled advocates. They exist, and when given a platform their message is all the more powerful by virtue of being based on lived experience.

   We should amplify their voices, include them in group discussions and involve them in setting the agenda for neurodiversity activism. Their views should have primacy on matters that directly impact on or are important to them. These *may* include education, employment, social inclusion or self-determination (getting to decide for yourself what to have for dinner, for instance), but will of course vary across groups of people or individuals.

8. *Be a good ally*

   We are all fellow travellers, seeking to debunk the idea that 'different' means 'defective'.

We should defend the human rights and civil liberties of people with learning disabilities, as enshrined in the United Nations Convention on the Rights of People with Disabilities.

We should lobby for better provision for those wishing to remain in the community and for additional safeguards for those who do require institutional care.

We should lobby policy-makers and service providers to take proper account of the needs of people with intellectual disabilities.

9. *Realise that if neurodiversity doesn't challenge you, you're not doing it right*

    Consider your own attitudes first and foremost, before you challenge the views of others. I say this because I've had to do it. I hadn't a clue how ableist some of my former attitudes were before I knew better. I had to learn from great disability activists and advocates like Autistic Hoya and my fellow *Spectrum Women* sister, Jen Elcheson.

    We should open our minds to the idea that we might not be quite as 'woke' as we like to think we are.

    We should learn more about how to recognise and avoid ableism.

10. *Mind your language!*

    Language directly impacts how people are treated. Whether we think certain words are ableist or not, if people with learning disabilities believe they are, we should avoid them.

    We should always endeavour to be respectful in how we speak about intellectual disability.

    We should set the bar high for ourselves when it comes to our choice of language.

    We should educate others.

11. *Make sure that it's 'Access all areas'*

    The principle of 'nothing about us without us' should apply to all parts of our family. Research has shown that contact between people with and without a learning disability is the best way to increase positive attitudes (Scior & Werner, 2015).

    We should make information accessible. There is so much excellent material out there now on neurodiversity but it's rare to see Easy Read versions. I understand it can be hard to distil a lengthy, tightly argued piece into a short, simplified version, but it's also a good test of whether the piece was actually saying anything of real consequence. Albert Einstein is credited with saying: 'If you can't explain it simply, you don't understand it well enough'.

We should make events and online discussions accessible. We should be mindful of the need for practical accommodations, such as accessible parking.

We should allow people to give their views without fear of being mocked or corrected if they are finding it difficult to express themselves properly. If we are unsure whether someone may have an intellectual disability, we should give them the benefit of the doubt.

We should give people the time they need to respond.

12. *Ask, don't assume*

Even the most committed ally can fall into the trap of assuming they know what people with higher support needs think, want or need. However well-intentioned, we must avoid such paternalistic behaviour.

An Easy Read version of this article has been produced by Positive Futures[24], a fantastic all-Ireland based charity which supports people with a learning disability, those with acquired brain injury and people on the autistic spectrum, by transforming their lives and moving issues important to them further up society's agenda. Their Advisory Board, comprising individuals with lived experience of learning disability, kindly reviewed the Easy Read version and one member made the point that she likes to be independent, like many others, and felt she doesn't need others to stand up for her. The Board recommended, therefore, that allies should stand up for them only if they ask for our help.

Another member of the Advisory Board said: 'Our voice is powerful and we should be listened to'. I agree. We should take the time to listen: we might learn a lot.

---

24 https://www.positive-futures.net/

Conclusion

Becoming the parent of a child with high support needs has been a humbling experience. My son might be the one with the learning disability, but I am the one who's had the most to learn.

What I have offered here is a personal perspective. Whether you have been on a similar journey to mine or not, I invite you to consider this a call to action, or at the very least the opportunity to continue an important conversation.

My goal is to harness the energy, capability and dedication of our big, noisy, occasionally dysfunctional neurodivergent family in order to support the good work that is already underway. Let's all be 'positive irritants'.

When there is unity in our community on an issue, together we really can make a difference.

References

Bindmans LLP (2014) *Death Of 18-Year Old Connor Sparrowhawk Was Preventable* [online] Available at: www.bindmans.com/news/death-of-18-year-old-connor-sparrowhawk-was-preventable (accessed July 2020).

Brown LXZ (2012) *Ableism / Language* [online] Autistichoya.com. Available at: www.autistichoya.com/p/ableist-words-and-terms-to-avoid.html (accessed July 2020).

Dunne Y (2017) *Autscape: 2017 Presentations* [online] Autscape.org. Available at: www.autscape.org/2017/programme/presentations (accessed July 2020).

Gold CM (2011) *Morons, Imbeciles and Idiots* [online] Campbellmgold.com. Available at: www.campbellmgold.com/archive_esoteric/morons_imbeciles_idiots.pdf (accessed July 2020).

National Autistic Taskforce (2019) *'An Independent Guide To Quality Care For Autistic People'* [online]. Available at: https://nationalautistictaskforce.org.uk/ (accessed July 2020).

NHS Digital (2017) *Health and Care of People with Learning Disabilities: Experimental Statistics: 2016 to 2017* [online] Available at: https://digital.nhs.uk/data-and-information/publications/statistical/health-and-care-of-people-with-learning-disabilities/health-and-care-of-people-with-learning-disabilities-experimental-statistics-2016-to-2017 (accessed July 2020).

Pinker S (2003) *The Blank Slate.* East Rutherford: Penguin Publishing Group.

Rosetti P, Dinisman T & Moroz A (2016) *VS Insight Report – An easy target.* Victim Support UK.

Scior K & Werner S (2015) *Changing Attitudes to Learning Disability: A review of the evidence.* Mencap and University College London.

Silberman S (2015) *Neurotribes: The legacy of autism and how to think smarter about people who think differently.* Allen & Unwin.

United Response (2019) *Londoners Least Comfortable When Sharing Spaces With People Who Have Learning Disabilities Or Autism, New Survey Finds* [online]. Available at: www.unitedresponse.org.uk/news/public-attitudes-survey-learning-disabilities-autism-londoners?utm_campaign=socialsignin&utm_medium=social&utm_source=twitter&fbclid=IwAR0ztEf9l-kL8kz8eCvxfBy7WM1Fn2QPagI6EcJmyS_NoWjNclScUYEy9Hc (accessed July 2020).

Zeilinger J (2015) 6 Common Forms of Ableism We Need to Retire Immediately. *Mic.* [online] Available at: www.mic.com/articles/121653/6-forms-of-ableism-we-need-to-retire-immediately (accessed July 2020).

Chapter 8: Multiplicity and neurodiversity – exploring potential in Deleuzoguattarian social theory for furthering a paradigm shift

By Donna-Lee Ida, BSc. (Hons), UMHAN

This is a work in progress, the explorations of a Sociology MA student, an idealist and enthusiast of the neurodiversity paradigm. My life's work has centred around well-being, from a holistic perspective, always seeking to lift the whole person up from a medicalised backdrop. I am passionate about neurodiversity and have treasured working alongside neurodivergent individuals in many roles. My academic journey now is full of hope for solidarity and greater freedom in our attitudes to difference. I hope my efforts here are at least interesting, and ideally poignant, for current developments.

I'll start by declaring that it is my nature to try and bring a lot together into one project. I am attracted to sociological and philosophical thinking for this reason, for its expansiveness and multidisciplinary nature. I recognise my limits as a postgraduate student but endeavour for my attempts at bringing a lot together to be accessible and follow clear threads of both inspiration and pragmatism. I hope the reader will find this to be so.

Introduction

My intention here is to bring together a range of philosophical ideals with my experience of working with neurominority groups[25] in the hope of developing a pragmatic approach for applying theory to practice. I attempt this firstly by viewing the neurodiversity paradigm through lenses of social theory and considering mechanisms involved in one paradigm transforming into another. Attention is given to the neurodiversity movement being akin to other civil rights and equality movements because, as Singer (2017) states on the front cover of *Neurodiversity*, we are concerned here with 'the last great liberation movement to emerge from the 20th century'. Foucauldian influences found in the social model of disability, and the development of a neurodiversity perspective from that discourse are outlined, leading into an exploratory presentation of emerging social theory that promotes a greater openness towards encountering difference. An openness that is both complementary to the neurodiversity paradigm and can build upon it. Conclusions are drawn from how paradigmatic shifts in thought and our resulting attitudes might be harnessed for best practice by means of a Deleuzoguattarian theory of multiplicity. Examples are discussed from current accessibility and ethnography approaches that inform my work in progress, particularly as I look towards developing valid new research.

The neurodiversity paradigm is underway, casting off the shackles of an overly simplified, stigmatising and disempowering pathology paradigm (Walker, 2012). Yet there is consistently a theme witnessed when working with neurodivergent individuals of a kind of battle with the ethereal, with unconscious attitudes that hem them in by maintaining a sense of feeling 'there is something wrong with me', maddeningly amidst a public narrative of equality, diversity and inclusivity. A tension is felt between services 'providing support' – a premise that in itself maintains a top down approach, and individuals' needs being met. In service provisions we talk about collaborative, empowering, user-led services and then, often unconsciously, we talk about 'disorders' ,'recovery' and 'support' and limit the scope of services due to procedural and market driven bureaucracies rather than recognising and appreciating differences as a part of the individual, and of the whole that makes up our human diversity. The resulting muddle of this scenario is services often being experienced as 'inaccessible, limited and fragmented' (Kaufman *et al*, 2019, p422). I advocate a commitment to carving out new pathways for adjusting procedure and practice accordingly.

---

25 Defined as groups of neurodivergent people sharing a form of neurodivergence that is 'largely innate and … inseparable from who they are, constituting an intrinsic and pervasive factor in their psyches, personalities, and fundamental ways of relating to the world', and tends to involve experiences of discrimination associated with a stigma-inducing pathology paradigm classification (Walker, 2014). People experiencing mental health difficulties, specific learning difficulties and autistic people are examples of neurominority groups.

The main point here is about attitudes towards neurodiversity remaining stifled by unwittingly, or otherwise reinforcing negatives. Instead, I wonder if we could bring together aspects of former, current and emerging paradigms to be multiplicitous in our attitudes around service provision. A nurturing of appropriate attitudes intended consciously for bringing together the abundance of neurodiverse human potential could equate to more co-ordinated networks of services, or to quote Jane Addams[26] (1910, p98), to 'democracy in social terms'.

A challenge is put forward here to examine lingering presupposed norms of an old paradigm and make way for a more ethically oriented approach to emerge from promotion of a greater reflexivity and responsibility-of-self. The notion here of a responsibility-of-self is not the kind that makes the marginalised take responsibility for societies' disabling infrastructures, but instead encourages everyone to consider what they bring to any encounter with difference. In line with Addam's emphasis on the importance of shared experience and responsibility in the development of ethical and radical democratic processes, I consider what thoughts and attitudes we are held by that reduce our capacity for openness. Or, how our expectations of what is fair and possible are shaped (Bruce, 2017; Ahmed, 2012). The hope is for differences like neurodivergence to become further accepted and appreciated in an atmosphere that nurtures multiple possibilities.

The neurodiversity paradigm has begun to open us up to the multiplicity of human potential. To think in terms of neurodiversity, rather than in crude binaries of being normal or not, is already leaps and bounds forward from a history of medicalising and demonising. I ask, can we make use of emerging social theory (namely of Deleuzoguattarian, feminist, and new-materialism lines) to further the transition from binary, hierarchical thinking into more open attitudes that allow for solidarity with all our experiences of human neurodiversity. To quote Jane Addams (1922, p85) once more:

*'What after all has maintained the human race on this old globe despite
all the calamities of nature and all the tragic failings of mankind,
if not faith in new possibilities and the courage to advocate them.'*

In order to consider how to advocate for new possibilities, let us start by looking at the nature of social movements and their relationship to the paradigm they are set within.

---

26 A particularly inspiring feminist sociologist who pioneered social reform during the late 19th and early 20th centuries by establishing settlement housing as a refuge for the poor that emphasised solidarity and community action (Addams, 1910). She advocated for social justice and created unprecedented, radical social services.

Social movements and paradigms

Social movements develop as a means of rectifying social inequalities and struggles amongst marginalised groups of society. Where solidarity is not readily experienced a striving to emancipate struggles into a sense of 'civic solidarity' occurs (Alexander, 2017, pp325-326). A variety of individuals will make up the membership of social movements, who may be invested in the cause for a variety of reasons, but underlying principles hold this heterogeneity together into a unified movement (Peters *et al*, 2009). In the case of neurodiversity, the unifying principle has centred around how civil rights, equality, social inclusion, respect and experiences of citizenship might result in solidarity with all neurominorities (Walker, 2014). The paradigm within which a movement originates is pivotal and more so here as we are concerned with a movement that provokes a depth of engagement with a new paradigm. The way that we think about our reality, or what we consider as normative, is shaped by the paradigm we are functioning within (Walker, 2012).

The social model of disability and the neurodiversity movement are enmeshed within normative modes of thought and knowledge production that affect our attitudes and approaches to diversity. Modes of thought currently reflecting how we understand neurodiversity and the formation of its social movement have shifted from discourse initially intended to move away from medicalised paradigms and towards more social contexts of resistance and diversity. From a Foucauldian perspective, it is perceived that a balance exists between institutional and cultural mechanisms that maintain inequalities, at the same time as potential existing within those mechanisms for enabling a more inclusive social experience (Peters *et al*, 2009). In the social model of disability this centres upon how society constructs disablement, but in the case of neurodiversity- whilst entirely related to social constructionism in respect to normative measures, the paradigmatic element is also about moving beyond binaries of abled and disabled, or normal and not normal, by drawing from a range of medical, social and political parameters, and most importantly by encompassing everyone, because we are all diverse, neurodiverse, racially diverse, culturally diverse and so on (Walker, 2014; Booth, 2019; Singer, 2017).

When Judy Singer coined the term neurodiversity in 1999 with respect to autism spectrum conditions and associated experiences of not being considered 'normal', she was following on from a social model of disability by emphasising the role of institutionalised discrimination in creating practical obstacles to participating in society (Singer, 2017). By outlining constructions of normalcy from the implementation of statistics 'as a tool of governance' and drawing from theories of disability as ethnicity, because disability is about a political minority rather than a medical category, she defined the 'neurologically different as representing a new

addition to the familiar political categories of class/gender/race' (Singer, 2017, p9 &
pp35-37). The resulting development of a neurodiversity movement as inclusive of
all neurominorities recognises the Foucauldian premise of inequalities maintained
by social dynamics of power alongside a latent potential for embracing difference
(Walker, 2014; Booth, 2019).

Various intersectionalities can be called upon to demonstrate the implications of
assumptions like normative measures of ablemindedness and how these modes of
categorisation separate out difference from 'normal', rather than difference being a
part of 'normal'. For instance, Swain and Cameron (1999, p68) compare normative
modes of declaring categorisations of disability to heteronormative parameters of
'coming out'; as having to reveal oneself as differing from 'normal'. Another example
is found in issues of gender subordination resulting from 'unmarked categories',
the unmarked category being the normative one, with which males are typically
more likely to identify with, and females are historically more likely to feel Other to
(Schauwer *et al*, 2018, p608). This is echoed by Walker's (2012, p232) discussion of
'the most insidious sort of social inequality' stemming from a 'normal' group having
no label, which unashamedly highlights the imbalance of power implied inherently
in not even needing a label. Intersectionalities like these outline the ways in which
discourse is embodied throughout the nuances of everyday life and why our choice
of words and use of appropriate language are so important.

The importance of words

Foucault's (1979) theory of governmentality, through which we can view experiences
of difference as resulting from power structures within society, is demonstrated
by the relationship Singer (2017) identifies between statistical approaches to
governmentality and the construction of normalcy. The bureaucratic administration
of populations according to moral averages and normative measures become a tool
of governance distinguishing us into categories of what it means to be 'an average
man' (Singer, 2017, p37). The perfect instrument for finding Others where there is a
below or above average status identified. This in turn informs the language we use
to think about and discuss our experiences of being 'normal' or 'different'. Particular
attention is drawn to the misuse of neurodiversity terms by Walker (2014)[27] in
respect to an increased risk of Othering when neurodiversity is mistakenly used to
imply separation from a privileged (neurotypical) group.

Continued use of medical language and administration within services founded
on social models of disability serve as a further example. In my current role as
a specialist mentor for autistic university students or students experiencing

---

27 I strongly urge anyone working with issues of neurodiversity to read and re-read this blog entry until
    the fundamentals of accurate language are fully grasped. Even then, it cannot be read too many times.

mental health difficulties, notably a service categorised administratively as being
'non-medical help', each student must nonetheless provide medical evidence of a
disability.[28] In my experience this forms part of the backdrop for neurodivergent
individuals describing themselves as 'not being well' or having an 'inability'
to be 'normal'. This often results in feelings of guilt or embarrassment, which
Foucault (1967) points to as informing discourse around the binaries of reason
and madness. Guilt results from feeling judged, from a sense of wrong-doing
inherent in being Other, or non-normative. An ideological exclusion from integral
infrastructures of society (education, employment, etc) is maintained in this way
(Oliver & Barnes, 2012).

Service provisions for neurodivergent individuals need to go beyond the shackles of
overly simplified and stigma-inducing medical categorisations for the ways in which
we think about and engage with neurodivergence to better fit proposed inclusivity
and equality intentions. An individual labelled with a disability[29] category of
neurodiversity is likely to describe themselves in the same medicalised language
that 'disqualifies them' (Foucault, 1978, p101) however, doing so might also generate
awareness in neurotypical people of the marginalised experience of neurodivergent
people and therefore be a means of hope for greater solidarity.

We can think in terms of needing to 'imagine disability[30] differently' (Fritsch, 2015)
whereby heeding a call from Karen Barad (cited in Schauwer *et al*, 2018) to consider
'what is being made to matter' when we encounter difference presents a hope for
stepping outside of a governmentality imposed by assigned categories. Ableism
incorporates a predetermined neoliberal concept of what constitutes 'a life worth
living', which amounts to disability being considered as undesirable. If parameters of
diversity exist within narratives of inclusion and equality, and are therefore worthy
forms of living, it doesn't make sense for it to be nonetheless undesirable (Fritsch,
2015). It follows that alleviating experiences of negativity and inequality require a
shift in perspective around what is deemed desirable and worthy. Otherwise we are
at risk of diversity narratives being essentially empty promises, or as Sara Ahmed
(2012, p110) says, 'equality can participate in concealing inequalities'.

With this in mind, it is worth considering what Walker (2012, p228–235) refers to as
throwing away the 'masters tools'[31] – the tools in this case are made up of language

---

28 To be clear, I do not personally equate neurodivergence with disability, I am highlighting the confusing
and often negative impact of neurodiversity and disability being used as interchangeable terms.

29 See footnote 3

30 I refer again to footnote 3, and highlight that excellent studies exist that are relevant for discussing
neurodiversity but use disability terms owing to the crossover of medical and neurodiversity paradigms.

31 This is actually a reference to the feminist poet Audre Lorde's speech, 'The Master's Tools Will Never
Dismantle the Master's House', at an international feminist conference in 1979.

originating from a pathology paradigm. Later, in 2014, Walker's definitions
of neurodiversity appear more multiplicitous by acknowledging pathology as
relevant, when it is appropriate and consensual, by acknowledging whilst there
is no 'normal' within the multiple presentations of neurodiversity, pathology
language is appropriate in some cases of neurodivergence. Booth (2019) echoes
this by encouraging us not to 'throw out the impairment baby with the medical
model bathwater', otherwise we risk alienating groups for which a pathological
language applies. This emphasises that pathology is not conducive to defining what
is normal but in some cases pathology and impairment exists within experiences of
neurodiversity.

However, Ahmed (2000) identifies a tendency in our encounters with difference
that equate to a kind of 'fetishism' for forming illusions of proximity or distance
that equate to Othering. Moreover, this tendency is likely to be at work even when
we utilise 'new tools' -we might still be steered into maintaining 'the master's
house' (Walker, 2012). From this, and the afore mentioned tensions within service
provisions for neurodivergent individuals, we notice a performativity around
diversity that is implicit particularly within market driven institutions, such as in
higher education. If performativity is still possible, even with new terms, we need
to take heed of Ahmed's concerns all the more. This is exactly why the philosophy of
Deleuze and Guattari becomes relevant in a call for revolution, or paradigm shift,
because 'social relations of the capitalist order [have] repressed and limited the
multiplicity and potential of the world' (Ryder, 2018).

Deleuze and Guattari seek to determine a new praxis of thought production
that appreciates a kind of creative multiplicity within and around how people
and society are experienced. Examples of this are found in their work with
international social movements, such as the French gay liberation movement
and The Workers Party movement of Brazil, both of which sought liberation from
modes of representational thinking that maintained division, or identity politics,
where there could instead be a civic solidarity through multiplicity (Ryder, 2018).
To balance out social equality movements resulting in an identity politics that can
perpetuate a 'them and us' rhetoric, we need to establish how resistance can go
beyond highlighting difficulty and towards overcoming it (Runswick-Cole, 2014). It
is my opinion that the neurodiversity movement inherently reaches beyond binary
traps of identity politics because it is about recognising a diversity inclusive of all
humans. However, the overall point remains that our approach needs to go beyond
highlighting difficulty and towards integrating the currently non-normative into a
new normative narrative.

Multiplicity has a greater capacity over intersectionalities, and associated identity
politics, to reduce representational thought from contributing to difference being

perceived as separate to 'normal', or to what is included within concepts of diversity. Again, let us not lose the usefulness of outlining intersections in the first place, by not 'throwing out the baby with the bath water' but at the same time let's recognise the positive implications for developing emergent thinking as well. In his essay on the *The Function of Autonomy*, Ryder (2018) elucidates why Deleuzoguattarian theory:

*'... can help us think of struggles around anti-racism and gender
expression not as battles for representation or inclusion, but the
reshaping of desire toward practical solidarity and creative activity.'*

If this is the same as we hope for with the neurodiversity movement, we can find solidarity by being wholly conscious of how discourse permeates our knowledge production and therefore our social movements. The premise of 'nothing for us without us' for instance is vulnerable in a performative sense when the emphasis of representation is on numbers rather than skills; when a diversity quota becomes tokenistic in the governance of organisations (Fittler, 2015). Co-ordinated networks of care designed to be a response to the voices of neurodivergent 'consumers' are found to be more provider-led than consumer-led (Kaufman *et al*, 2019) and marginalised groups are expected to attain conscientisation[32] (Cuddeback-Gedeon, 2018). How do we join up the fractured aspects of these problems? How do we become more ethically accountable in our bureaucratic settings? Perhaps a reflexive and pragmatic approach that brings together ethics, market forces, medical models, social models, and neurodiversity requires a further paradigmatic element – a paradigm of multiplicity?

Multiplicity: some new terms

As with all paradigms, a new lens of thought production requires some new terms, which I hope to make accessible here (Walker, 2012; 2014). I'll begin with a familiar term, openness, which is not specific to a concept of multiplicity, but bear with me as the terms become more Deleuzoguattarian, especially as they have a reputation for being difficult to grasp, but everything new can be difficult to grasp at first.

In texts grappling with how normative attitudes might develop ethically, openness is a key theme (Ahmed, 2012; Schauwer *et al*, 2018; Fritsch, 2015). As a philosophical concept, openness is found prominently within the work of Deleuze and Guattari (1987) for developing a way of thinking about multiplicities instead of divisive categories. We will find a need for openness in Ahmed's (2000) ideal of ethical encounters, and as mentioned already, Barad's vision of appreciating

---

32 A concept coined by Brazilian anthropologist Paulo Freire acknowledging that people enduring
oppression are required to have a certain level of reflexivity, enabling them to recognise structural
oppression and desire social justice and transformation.

difference equally depends upon openness, because difference cannot be properly understood, or encountered, when it is trapped within a discourse of normative representational thought (Fritsch, 2015; Schauwer *et al*, 2018; Ryder, 2018). We lose potential for stepping beyond norms that confine our thinking about difference when we rely on confirmatory modes of discourse. Instead, an appreciation for a creative, open and ethical multiplicity within and around how people and society are experienced is called for.

From what I have outlined so far it is apparent that Ahmed (2000), Fritsch (2015), and Schauwer *et al* (2018) would all ask us to consider what is already present in our experiences to constitute a sense of difference in the first place? An intrinsic facet of openness can be found in the kind of responsibility-of-self introduced at the outset of this essay as attainable through developing reflexivity around our unconscious assumptions. In this light, an aim of facilitating real engagement is determined, a means of truly listening to Others, from a non-normative position, as much as possible. A position from which we can't even assume our ears will hear what is spoken to us, because:

'*...such encounters always conceal as much as they reveal, they involve traumas, scars, wounds and tears that are impossible to beget (they effect how we arrive or face each other...) ... In my notion of ethical encounters, hearing does not take place in my ear or in your yours but in between our mouths and our ears, in the very proximity and multiplicity of this encounter.*' (Ahmed, 2000)

An intriguing notion in line with listening 'between our mouths and ears' comes from Schauwer *et al* (2018, p611) in the form of 'emergent listening'. A listening that transcends 'moralistic judgements that trap us inside endless repetitions, and towards an ethical recognition of the other and affective openness to emergent entangled differences' (Schauwer *et al*, 2018, p611). In this sense we move away from categories of difference and instead into tracking how difference is constituted. Shining a light on the collective experience amounting to multiplicity, rather than separate identities trapped in any pre-supposed norms. This kind of emergent listening intends to be open to the experience of others without having any precognition of what should or could be (Shauwer *et al*, 2018). We could say that the essence of a multiplicity paradigm would be to achieve an openness about our perceptions of difference and our resulting attitudes, instilling a more communal way of thinking[33] honouring Addams' pioneering emphasis on the importance of shared experience and responsibility (Bruce, 2017).

---

33 Deleuze and Guattari believed they 'had rediscovered a more communal way of thinking that preceded the subordination of thought to capital accumulation' (Ryder, 2018).

To engage further with the essence of shared experience, responsibility and multiplicity that occurs in any encounter with difference we need to acknowledge that long established normative measures will have a way of re-asserting themselves, even within work aiming to deconstruct it. We can understand this by drawing on Deleuzoguattarian concepts of de- and re-territorialisation as modes of repetition by which we organise ourselves socially. This would encompass the tensions highlighted above in my own experience of current service provisions as both oppressive in nature whilst also embracing how comfort is generated in a chaotic existence. A full awareness of limits existing concomitantly within (typically ableist) comfort zones brings our focus more onto emergent states of experience and possibility, rather than any distinct expectations (Shauwer *et al*, 2018).

How we currently imagine neurodiversity or difference are part of what Deleuze and Guattari would define as machinic assemblages[34] that are constrained by normative repetitions in our day-to-day experience (Clough, 2007). The kind that de- and re-territorialisation stem from. These would affect what Ahmed refers to as 'how we arrive or face each other' and how 'the encounter itself involves a form of remembering' (Ahmed, 2000, p158). A 'violence of assimilation' is how Ahmed (2000, p. 156) terms oppressive modes exerted within language intended to empower but tending instead to fall into performative traps. But, whilst we can be conscious of oppression happening in processes of assimilation that dilute the essence of embracing diversity, we can also appreciate it happens in order to incorporate a sense of order into what we can achieve and expect. Therefore, we can make use of feeling limitations by acknowledging them as part of our experience, and then additionally, purposefully incorporating that feeling into a light beckoning us forward, bridging the gaps between what is currently considered feasible and what potential exists beyond these experiences. Promoting reflexivity around the limits of machinic assemblages enables us to embrace them as a comforting means of homeostasis, in order to navigate better the multiplicity of a rhizomatic[35] type of assemblage – a more fluid and chaotic thought production, which certainly exists but we tend to avoid because it's difficult to rationalise and pin it down (Clough, 2007). 'Multiplicities are rhizomatic' (Deleuze & Guattari, 1987, p7) in the sense that we can explore connections between relational networks of thought that are at the same time not set in stone in their relationship to one another (Colman, 2010).

A rhizomatic theory of neurodiversity would enable an inherently non-assumptive openness to all manner of possibilities, or multiplicities through a commitment to

---

34 Assemblages (of machinic or rhizomatic nature) are a territory of circumstances and lines of thought (Deleuze & Guattari, 1987, p584). More about this can be understood from Marcus & Saka, 2006.

35 A kind of analogy is understood here with the biological term of rhizome referring to a type of plant that extends itself underground, in a seemingly chaotic fashion to develop new plants, seemingly sporadically, on the surface (Colman, 2010)

reflexive responsibility-of-self that recognises each self within the neurodiversity
of human existence. A depth of engagement with thought production through and
between all the proposed aspects within neurodiverse perspectives (medical, social,
reflexive, ethical, emergent…) would better recognise the (often ableist) discomfort
present in currently normative attempts to comfort ourselves with machinic
assemblages. Ahmed (2012) suggests that where we come up against 'holding
patterns', especially within institutional organisations, we need to nurture a different
perspective of what is flowing, rather than simply going with the flow, or resisting
it. In this sense a metaphorical bridge might emerge as a new vantage point for
the paradigm shift we are seeking and promote a rhizomatic-type of thinking as
conducive to shifting our perspectives. By respecting our interconnectedness, we
can find new territories to explore together, in solidarity, which may at times be
uncomfortable, but everything new can be uncomfortable at first.

Having now outlined a few brief, hopefully manageable terms, without losing the
depth and expansiveness of these philosophical ideals I come now to how we might
begin grounding such ideals into practice. Some existing examples of multiplicity in
action will be presented alongside a call for imagining how this might grow.

Praxis: ethnography, accessibility and inclusivity issues

Applying theory to the everyday to establish a 're-engagement with the real' is
required because 'survival depends upon the production of useful knowledge in the
real world' (Oliver & Barnes, 2012, p30). We can all benefit from a reflexive, ethical
perspective around what is normative, why it is normative and how we might
further shift our normative narratives.

Rumblings of pragmatic multiplicity can be found in current developments within
university accessibility policy. For instance, a range of assistive technology initiatives
at the University of Kent under the umbrella project of OPERA (Opportunity,
Productivity, Engagement, Reducing Barriers, Achievement) demonstrate how:

'…*mainstreaming accessibility by catalysing a shift in culture from
individual adjustments via Inclusive Learning Plans (ILP) towards anticipatory
reasonable adjustments and inclusive practice by design [is] the preferred
means to tackle accessibility barriers at source.*' (University of Kent, 2019)

Implementing digital tools that encourage student resources to be more diversely
accessible are ways that OPERA seeks to undo normative repetitions within existing
administrative practices for teaching. A UCAS roundtable recently established a need

for updating applications processes specifically with respect to how mental health difficulties are categorised, implying it is increasingly apparent that neurodiversity doesn't necessarily mean identifying as disabled (UMHAN, 2019).

We are also stepping towards the reflexivity and responsibility-of-self required for multiplicity in Equality, Diversity and Inclusivity (EDI) training that increasingly highlights issues of unconscious bias. Even so, in the same way that the social model of disability was incorporated extensively into 'newly emerging disability equality training' (Oliver, 2013, p1024) in the 1980s, it would be ideal if greater emphasis on notions of multiplicity, openness and responsibility-of-self, particularly regarding neurodiversity could be further incorporated into current EDI training.

A call from Kleinman (1998) for an ethnographic[36] way of thinking and engaging with morality strikes me as a mode of encountering difference in keeping with a multiplicity movement. Indeed, Deleuze and Guattari's work has had crossovers with ethnography by being integrated into research and political movements with indigenous communities[37] (see Ryder, 2018). Ethnography, as a form of participatory research and action, is conducive to the shared experience and radical responsibility that Addams (1910, p98) calls upon for creating 'democracy in social terms', and in keeping with Schauwer et al's (2018) concepts of emergent listening. Kleinman's (1998, p415) description of the ethnographer as 'attentive to the new and unexpected possibilities that can (and so often do in real life) emerge' is in line with the emphasis put forward here on reflexivity around what is emergent in our attitudes.

What Kleinman (1998, p418) particularly suggests is that the ethnographic approach 'be developed more generally as a means of teaching about moral processes and examining their practical implications'. I wonder about systems of decision making that involve a 'walk a mile in their shoes' kind of strategy but whilst I am aware of an increased emphasis on participatory research and action within policy developments, I understand that the application of such work in practice is contentious. For instance, endeavours springing up from the 'nothing for us without us' campaign demonstrate strategies that are more inclusive and hold great possibilities for solidarity and accountability, but an atmosphere persists of difficulties with implementing participatory methods and yielding sufficient outcomes (Fittler, 2015; Kaufman et al, 2019; Cuddeback-Gedeon, 2018; McIntyre et al, 2019; Knight, 2015). Insightfully, in reference to ethnographic work in the field of intellectual and developmental disabilities Cuddeback-Gedeon (2018, p83) warns us that we 'must be aware of the places where the theories underpinning our praxis might continue to exclude', and generic problems of pre-specific outcomes leading to

---

36 A method of research whereby the researcher immerses themselves in a social setting (Bryman, 2016).

37 Examples of this are found particularly in the radical politics, clinical psychology and anthropology of Brazil (Ryder, 2018).

tokenism are highlighted by Allen *et al* (2018), and Fittler's (2015) concerns around numbers outweighing skills, as discussed already.

Of course, the reality of participatory work is going to appear messy at times, messy in the sense that multiplicity is not a linear, easy to track approach. Knight (2015, p103) draws our attention to Nancy Fraser's refusal to pin down 'what counts as a legitimate mode of participation' because participation will take multiple forms. I advocate it is important to distinguish between the difficulties that arise due to market forces however, and those that are to be embraced as a part of the multiplicity present in our lives. To return to Ahmed's (2000) issues of assimilation and performativity it is imperative for efforts towards inclusivity to separate out and then utilise the strands of bureaucratised market forces and the multiplicity of reality in a rhizomatic application for neurodiversity advances. I hope to explore in my imminent postgraduate research how we might apply rhizomatic thought to honouring the multiplicity of existing and emerging modes of inclusivity that incorporate real-life dimensions of bureaucracy and diversity in practice.

Conclusions

I have attempted to make accessible a theory of multiplicity, because all humans are diverse, and because an attitude that celebrates difference and generates a shift in attitudes, from assumed outcomes to an openness beyond assumptions, paves the way for greater wellbeing for all. I hope the potential for multiplicity theory to complement and build upon the ground gained already by emancipatory pioneers (Addams, Oliver and Singer in particular) and specifically by the neurodiversity movement can be clearly perceived from what I have introduced.

The relevance of multiplicity theory is initially sparked by its background in paradigm shifting mechanisms associated with other civil rights movements. To demonstrate how multiplicity might be found relevant in practice for neurodiversity issues we have considered examples of how real voices are increasingly considered in the development of effective networks of services (Kaufman *et al*, 2019; University of Kent, 2019; UMHAN, 2019) and how ethnography, or participation, can be utilised as a means of greater shared experience (Kleinman, 1998; Cuddeback-Gedeon, 2018; Allen *et al*, 2019). The incomplete nature of what exists already is acknowledged nonetheless whilst celebrating steps in the right directions. I go on to stress the importance of bridging gaps between market forces that permeate our service facilitation and the reality of multiplicity in meeting the needs of neurominorities and how rhizomatic thinking might be a means worth incorporating for this end.

Where we have been prone to intersectional politics expounding a rhetoric of emancipation by inclusion and diversity, in justified condemnation of exclusion and homogeneity, we can begin to look further beyond ideas of them and us. Putting down the simplicity of binaries in terms of pathologizing versus social constructs requires us to embrace dualistic notions, as organising principles, of a bureaucracy-friendly, machinic mode of thought. At the same time, extending into multiple potentialities of difference that are not categorised against normative assumptions and therefore are not limited to old, fragmented, ableist outcomes. It needn't be one or the other. Rhizomatic thought is a possible way forward.

Established assumptions stemming from normative measures need not facilitate our approach to neurodiversity, and our shifting narratives around what is normative need not be in simple resistance to existing parameters for service provision. The key is in generating a creative, bridging multiplicity approach by rhizomatically thinking about what is possible and emerging. Taking a conscious stance to share responsibility for where we find ourselves in normative terms, and to nurture full recognition of 'how we arrive and face each other' (Ahmed, 2012, p158) shifts our focus from what is considered different or divergent to what constitutes our perceptions of difference and divergence and how we can broaden our thinking to increase experiences of solidarity, equality and inclusivity for neurominority groups.

This is merely an opening up of what is conceivable. I recognise there are limitations in the scope of theory and practice considered here, leaning more towards the higher education sector of wellbeing I currently work in. I acknowledge the overlap between my choice to apply specific Delezoguattarian terms and existing efforts in research and practice for similar notions framed as reimagining, emergent listening, ethical encounters and incorporating participatory research and action (Fritsch, 2015; Ahmed, 2000; Schauwer *et al*, 2018; Kleinman, 1998; Knight, 2015). Writing this has been a steppingstone for me to carve out further research plans, by tracking what is already in motion and what might emerge from where we find ourselves.

Ultimately, I am exploring how we ground idealisms for embracing multiplicity, as a complementary concept for neurodiversity. My suggestion is that we need to start with our attitudes, as territories to be explored with as much openness and reflexive responsibility-of-self as we can. Admitting when we find ourselves in unknown territory is encouraged because it is here that we can find solidarity, by working together to map out new pathways.

So much more could be discussed around how our attitudes towards difference are formed and I would have like to give more emphasis to a progression of philosophy that can be traced through Foucauldian to Deleuzian theory, but what is most

important here is how we look ahead and grow, possibly rhizomatically in our
thinking. Foucault (cited in Marks, 1998, p122) says:

*'What is philosophy today…if it is not the critical work that thought
brings to bear upon itself? In what does it consist, if not the
endeavour to know how and to what extent it might be possible
to think differently, instead of legitimating what is already known.'*

In our current political climate, where even conservative notions of democracy can
be in question, we need more than ever to consider how thinking differently might
bring about a neurodiverse solidarity to ensure experiences of radical 'democracy in
social terms' (Addams, 1910, p98) for all of us.

References

Addams J (1910 [1960]) *Twenty Years at Hull House.* New York: The New American Library, Inc.

Addams J (1922 [2002]) *Peace and Bread in the Time of War.* Chicago: University of Illinois Press.

Ahmed S (2000) *Strange Encounters: Embodied others in post-coloniality.* Routledge, London, UK.

Ahmed S (2012) *On Being Included: Racism and diversity in institutional life.* Dukes University Press,
Durham, UK.

Alexander J (2017) 'Reconstructing Democratic Theory in an Age of Disillusionment'. In: *Contested
Knowledge; Social Theory Today.* Seidman S (Ed) John Wiley & Sons Limited, Chichester, UK.

Allen K, Needham C, Hall K & Tanner D (2018) Participatory research meets validated outcome
measures: Tensions in the co-production of social care evaluation. *Social Policy and Administration,* **53**
(2) 311–325.

Booth J (2019) *Two-and-a-half Cheers for Neurodiversity* [online]. Available at: https://www.janinebooth.
com

Bruce BC (2017) How Jane Addams Expands Our View Of Education As An Ethical Enterprise.
Educational Theory **67** (6) p677–692.

Bryman A (2016) *Social Research Methods.* Oxford University Press, Oxford.

Colman F (2010) 'Rhizome'. In: Parr, A. (ed) *The Deleuze Dictionary.* Edinburgh University Press.

Clough PT (2007) *The Affective Turn: Theorising the social.* Duke University Press, Durham, UK.

Cuddeback-Gedeon L (2018) 'Nothing About Us Without Us:' Ethnography, Conscientization, and the
Epistemic Challenges of Intellectual Disability. *Practical Matter Journal* **11** 70–87.

Deleuze G & Guattari F (1987) *A Thousand Plateaus: Capitalism and Schizophrenia.* Bloomsbury,
London, UK.

Fittler D (2015) Nothing About Us Without Us Is a Great Battle Cry but Good Governance Must Go
Beyond Inclusion. *Human Rights Defender* **21** (1) 22–27.

Foucault M (1967) *Madness and Civilization: A history of insanity in the age of reason.* Tavistock
Publications Limited, London, UK.

Foucault M (1978) *The History of Sexuality.* Billing & Sons, Guilford, UK.

Foucault M (1979) *Discipline and Punish: The birth of the prison.* Penguin, London, UK.

Kleinman A (1998) Experience and Its Moral Modes: Culture, Human Conditions, and Disorder. In: *The
Tanner Lectures Series On Human Values,* Stanford University.

Fritsch K (2015) 'Desiring Disability Differently: Neoliberalism, Heterotopic Imagination and Intracorporeal Reconfigurations', *Foucault Studies*, No. 19, p43–66, York University, UK.

Kaufman JS, Schreier A, Graham S, Marshall T & Bracey J (2019) Nothing About Us Without Us: Authentic participation of service recipients in system development. *Children and Youth Services Review* **100** 422–427.

Knight A (2015) Democratizing Disability: Achieving Inclusion (without Assimilation) through 'Participatory Parity". *Hypatia* **30** (1) 97–114.

Marcus GE & Saka E (2006) Assemblage. *Theory, Culture and Society* **23** 101–106.

Marks J (1998) *Giles Deleuze: Vitalism and multiplicity*. Pluto Press, London.

McIntyre G, Cogan N, Stewart A, Quinn N, Rowe M, O'Connel M, Easton D, Hamill L, Johnston G, McFadden A & Robinson J (2019) *Understanding Citizenship Within a Health and Social Care Context in Scotland Using Community-Based Participatory Research Methods*. Sage Publications Ltd.

Oliver M & Barnes C (2012) *The New Politics of Disablement*. Palgrave Macmillan, New York, USA.

Oliver M (2013) The Social Model of Disability: 30 years on. *Disability & Society* **28** (7) 1024–1026.

Peters S, Gabel S & Symeonidou S (2009) Resistance, transformation and the politics of hope: imagining a way forward for the disabled people's movement. *Disability & Society* **24** (5) 543–556.

Runswick-Cole K (2014) 'Us' and 'them': the limits and possibilities of a 'politics of neurodiversity' in neoliberal times. *Disability & Society* **29** (7) 1117–1129.

Ryder A (2018) *'The Function of Autonomy': Felix Guattari and New Revolutionary Prospects*. Accessed online at http://salvage.zone/online-exclusive.

Schauwer E De, Van de Putte I, Blockmans IGE & Davies B (2018) The intra-active production of normativity and difference. *Gender and Education* **30** (5) 607–622.

Singer J (1999) 'Why can't you be normal for once in your life?' in *Disability Discourse*. Open University Press, UK.

Singer J (2017) *Neurodiversity: The birth of an idea*. Amazon Fulfilment, Poland.

Swain J & Cameron C (1999) Unless otherwise stated: discourses of labelling and identity in coming out. In: Corker, M. & French, S. (eds) *Disability Discourse*. Open University Press, Buckingham, UK.

UMHAN (2019) UMHAN summary of discussion at recent roundtable, *UMHAN Newsletter*, received by email on 31/07/19.

University of Kent (2019) OPERA (Opportunity, Productivity, Engagement, Reducing barriers, Achievement) [online]. Available at: https://www.kent.ac.uk/studentsupport/accessibility/opera.html (accessed January 2020).

Walker N (2012) Throw Away the Master's Tools: Liberating Ourselves from the Pathology Paradigm. In: *Loud Hands: Autistic people, speaking*. The Autistic Press, Washington, DC.

Walker N (2014) *Neurodiversity: Some basic terms & definitions*. Neurocosmopolitanism (http://neurocosmopolitanism.com).

Chapter 9: From neuronormativity to neurodiversity: changing perspectives on autism

By Linus Mueller

Neuronormativity

When we look at what is considered today to be normal or abnormal, healthy or diseased, we tend to assume that it has always been this way. Actually, these norms, and the concept of norm itself, only date back a few hundred years. Clinical medical discourse, psychiatry and contemporary concepts of disability are all rooted in the Age of Enlightenment.

Eighteenth century science was intent on measuring, classifying and categorizing – think about Linnaeus' biological taxonomy. During that time, the concept of a 'norm' was developed – and it wasn't merely descriptive. A telling example is the Belgian statistician, mathematician, sociologist and astronomer Adolphe Quetelet's idea of *l'homme moyen* – the average man. He measured the physical features of Scottish Highland regiment soldiers and recognised that they followed a bell-shaped curve, the so-called norm distribution. From there, he moved on to try to measure moral and intellectual, psychological and behavioural features including madness, suicide, crime and even poetic ability. Quetelet's *homme moyen* was an average of all human attributes in a given country, both physically and mentally.

Quetelet considered the abstraction of the average man as 'the model of beauty and goodness', while 'everything that instead of resembling his proportions or his way of being departed from them, would constitute deformities or diseases' (Quetelet, 1835).

Are Quetelet's ideas still relevant today? Well, we encounter one of his inventions and its normative impact on a regular basis: the BMI. In accordance with his idealisation of the norm, Quetelet didn't label the peak of the bell curve as merely average, he labeled it 'ideal', and the deviations 'overweight' and 'underweight', instead of merely heavier or lighter than average. His ideas probably influence us more than we are aware.

The concept of norms was appealing to medicine, a discipline focused on separating health from disease. In medicine, norms don't simply describe an average. They describe a desirable condition. If you have appendicitis you do not want to be 'appendix-diverse', you want to get treatment. Medical norms thus distinguish between health and disease, between those who are in need of treatment and those who are not. And while medicine speaks of the *discovery* of a condition, the discipline *creates* these conditions, thus establishes norms, and defines who is in need of treatment and who is not.

Not by chance psychiatry emerged as a new field during the Age of Enlightenment, or the Age of Reason: Michel Foucault calls the language of psychiatry 'a monologue by reason about madness' that could only emerge 'because modern man no longer communicates with the madman' (Foucault, 2013; 1961). Psychiatry was construed as a medical discipline and it adopted the medical concept of norms.

It was psychiatry that claimed authority over neurodivergent conditions, and it did not do so in a vacuum. The concept of neuronormativity (the paradigm that a particular mode of cognition and perception is superior to others) was a necessary precursor to the description of the neurological differences we know today, and it shaped the way they were (mis)understood. When we talk about the discovery of autism, we imply that autism has always been there, just waiting to be discovered. Yet, while people like those we call autistic today have probably been around since the beginnings of humankind, autism is a cultural construct.

Donna Haraway regards facts as 'types of stories, of testimony to experience', and notes that 'the provocation of experience requires an elaborate technology – including physical tools, an accessible tradition of interpretation and specific social relations. Not just anything can emerge as a fact; not just anything can be seen or done, and so told. Scientific practice may be considered a kind of story-telling practice – a rule-governed, constrained, historically changing craft of narrating the history of nature. Scientific practice and scientific theories produce and are embedded in particular kinds of stories' (Haraway, 1989).

Autism research claims to be rooted in science, merely to discover what is there. Yet autism is also a historical, and therefore narrative, field. When autism emerged as a scientific entity, it was shaped (and limited) by the traditions of the discipline. A specific (normative) way of looking at people, a specific (neurotypical) way of interpreting their behaviour gathers some aspects of a possible story, and misses or ignores others.

Under the normative paradigm, neurological differences could hardly be described as other than pathological deviations from the norm.

The DSM 5 criteria for autism spectrum 'disorder' list deficits (in social-emotional reciprocity, in non-verbal communicative behaviours, and in developing, maintaining and understanding relationships) that are rooted in the autistic person, without taking into account that reciprocity, communication and relationships need (at least) two people. The neurotypical side of the equation is overlooked: a lot of autistic people note that they have far fewer problems interacting with other autistic people, and neurotypical people clearly have a lot of difficulties interacting with autistic people. There is a good deal of literature to help neurotypical people understand autistic people – and these difficulties understanding are construed as the autistic person's deficits.

A non-neuronormative description might point out different styles of social communication and social interaction.

The neuronormative paradigm is explicit when the manual states, 'highly restricted, fixated interests that are abnormal in intensity or focus' (who defines what is (ab) normal and why would it even matter?). It is more implicit in 'restricted, repetitive patterns of behaviour, interests, or activities' and 'insistence on sameness, inflexible adherence to routines, or ritualised patterns of verbal or non-verbal behaviour' – but both are only noteworthy in terms of their deviation from the norm.

Another item in the DSM criteria is 'hyper- or hypo-reactivity to sensory input or unusual interest in sensory aspects of the environment'. This construes (and simplifies) autistic people's sensory sensitivity as being either above or below an idealised (and unnamed) norm. Just like the terms 'overweight' and 'underweight', they are not merely descriptive.

Neuronormative statements implicitly or explicitly express that it is better to be neurotypical than to be neurodivergent; and for neurodivergent people, inherently better to be closer to the norm, i.e. better to be 'high-functioning' than 'low-functioning'. There is no objective reason for this assumption. I am not aware of a study looking into the quality of life of autistic people and concluding that the level of support they need determines their well-being (while excluding the effects of a neuronormative society as a factor).

How does a discourse mold a subject? Foucault notes that a discourse has underlying rules of what can be said and thought, and what cannot, a 'separation, not of the true from the false, but of what may from what may not be characterized as scientific' (Foucault, 1980).

One thing that *can* be said within the neuronormative discourse is that autistic people have strengths and positive characteristics as well, and that these are directly related to the person being autistic – one early example of this is Hans Asperger who states: '... the basic fault sheds a characteristic light on all expressions of the personality, explains the difficulties, the failure, as well as the special accomplishments', and, 'The special accomplishments and the special difficulties of these people are founded in this – like for every man his merits and flaws belong inextricably together' (Asperger, 1944).

Stating that a disorder comes with talents does not challenge the normative paradigm – actually, there are many articles linking schizophrenia with creativity[38], or stating that Williams syndrome involves strengths in language and communication, empathy and socialisation skills (Mervis & Klein-Tasman, 2000).

Yet to say that autism is not a disorder is considered advocacy, not a valid statement in a scientific discourse. (It's not a question of being off-topic: they do consider it a valid scientific statement to say that autism *is* a disorder.)

Also, while the norm is idealised, it usually is unmarked and unnamed, only defined and created by its deviations. The deviations are under scrutiny, yet we cannot talk about the invisible norm, and thus cannot challenge it. (How many research papers have been published about neurotypicalism? Would such a paper be considered scientific within the medical discourse?)

We need to rethink autism from a non-medical perspective, and the paradigm of neurodiversity provides a framework to do so. The neurodiversity paradigm asserts that neurodiversity is a valuable form of human diversity; exposes neuronormativity as a cultural construct; and analyses neurological differences in terms of social dynamics (Walker, 2014). Thus, the concept of neurodiversity is an attack on neuronormativity.

To change a discourse

James MacGrath, autistic author of *Naming Adult Autism: Culture, science, identity*, notes that:

---

38 To give just a few examples: Karlsson J, 1970; Power *et al*, 2015; Keefe & Magaro, 1980; Sass, 2001; Hartmann *et al*, 1981; Hasenfus & Magaro, 1976; Richards, 2001; Andreasen, 1997.

*'[a]cross psychiatry, society and culture, autistic people have had their
critical perspectives and even just their voices ignored for way too long.
Even now, although progress is visible, it's still mostly neurotypicals
(or allistics) who exercise almost all the power over whether, when
and where autistic people are given a public voice.'* (Sara, 2018)

To paraphrase Foucault, the mainstream discourse on autism is a monologue by
neurotypicalism on autism that can only exist because the researchers don't talk
with autistic people. Too many of them study us as they study mice, not as equal
communication partners – and frequently, they actually study mice to learn about us.

I said earlier that some things can be said in a discourse, and others cannot. Of course,
this is not set in stone. The rules of a discourse can be challenged and changed.

For Donna Haraway, science is 'a contestable text and a power field' (Haraway,
1988). She argues that '... redistributing the narrative field by telling another
version of a crucial myth is a major process in crafting new meanings. One version
never replaces another, but the whole field is rearranged in interrelation among all
versions in tension with each other' (Haraway, 1984).

To change the autism discourse, we need to make autistic people heard, to expose
and label the norm and neuronormativity as culturally constructed, and analyse
autism in the context of social dynamics. There are many autistic researchers who
are already doing this.

Does autism look different from an autistic perspective? Let's have a look at some
research works by autistic people or teams including both autistic and non-autistic
people. (These examples are somewhat arbitrary and definitely incomplete, but they
give a good idea.)

Autistic research on autism is deeply rooted in lived autistic experiences. Looking
at Jim Sinclair's 'Being Autistic Together' (Sinclair, 2010) shows how much this
autistic view can change the story of autistic social interaction.

Sinclair points out that, while autistic people 'are generally seen as lacking
in ability to share common interests with others, disconnected from social
participation and fellowship, and inaccessible to social transmission of behaviours
and attitudes', this looks different from an autistic perspective: while '[s]ome of us,
at some times in our lives (generally early childhood), really aren't aware of other
people or their activities or their attempts to connect with us', most autistic people
have various other reasons for avoiding interaction. Sinclair notes difficulties
understanding others or interacting with others, different sensory experiences,

different fields of interest, as well as 'a lifetime of difficulties and disappointments with interpersonal connections'.

Sinclair notices that many autistic people do want social interaction in spite of these barriers:

'After a lifetime of such distressing and discouraging experiences, it would be little wonder if autistic people did choose to withdraw from human contact. Yet during the past 20 years, facilitated in large part by the availability of the Internet, more and more autistic people have been reaching out and forming connections, creating community, and discovering our own styles of autistic togetherness.' (Sinclair, 2010)

Sinclair then explores the different experiences of being autistic in a neurotypical space, in one's own space, in shared autistic space, in virtual or physical space. This view on autistic social interaction, which takes into account autistic people's experiences in a world structured by neurotypicals, has been virtually missing in decades of neurotypical research on autism.

Not being understood is an experience that most, if not all, autistic people share. Yet mainstream autism research does not address this, other than viewing autistic people being a puzzle to be solved. While neurotypical researchers were quick to attribute a lack of Theory of Mind or empathy to autistic people, it didn't occur to them question their own Theory of Mind when they couldn't understand autistic people. It was autistic Damian Milton who formulated the 'double empathy problem':

'A disjuncture in reciprocity between two differently disposed social actors which becomes more marked the wider the disjuncture in dispositional perceptions of the lifeworld – perceived as a breach in the 'natural attitude' of what constitutes 'social reality' for 'neuro-typical' people and yet an everyday and often traumatic experience for 'autistic people' (Milton, 2012).

Michelle Dawson *et al* (2007) discovered that a standard intelligence test systematically underestimates autistic intelligence. Since access to education for autistic students is often based on (perceived) IQ, the usage of that test is likely to deny autistic people chances in life.

Dinah Murray, Wenn Lawson, and Mike Lesser (2005) developed the monotropism theory, a non-pathologising theory that accounts for most or even all autism characteristics.

In *Naming Adult Autism: Culture, science, identity*, James McGrath (2017) interrogates autism clichés in literature, cinema and television, and points out that not all autistic people are gifted at maths and indifferent to fiction.

In *Embodied Semiosis: Autistic 'Stimming' as Sensory Praxis*, Jason Nolan and Melanie McBride (2015) explore the discursive construction of autism as a disease rather than a difference, and how within this paradigm, autistic sensory experience is construed as a sensory integration 'disorder' that produces a normative sensory ideal.

In *Authoring Autism*, Melanie Yergeau (2018) uses a queer theory framework to look at neurodivergence as an identity – neuroqueerness – rather than an impairment.

Instead of asking how to make autistics more normal, autistic people's research interests tend to involve various aspects related to autistic quality of life. Dora Raymaker researches about health care (in)accessibility for autistic people. Jac Den Houting explores anxiety in autistic children. Chloe Farahar investigates innovative ways to reduce neurodivergence stigma[39].

What do autistic research works on autism have in common? For one thing, they tend to take a neurodiversity perspective by challenging the norm. For another thing, they tend to take a contextual view on autism.

Mainstream autism discourse has a blind spot, and it's neurotypicals. Autism would not exist if there was no neurotypicalism, or no neurological norm. Social interaction, understanding, and communication with autistic people usually involve non-autistic people as well, and the interpretation of any kind of behaviour is generally shaped by neuronormative ideas of human behaviour. Thus, autism cannot be studied without taking into account neurotypical people and a world structured by a neuronormative paradigm. Neurotypical researchers mostly ignore this part of the equation – the neurological norm stays invisible.

By presenting a contextual perspective on autism, autistic researchers add what Donna Haraway calls 'situated knowledges' to the autism discourse. Like all perspectives, these are partial, but they are contextual, and including them to the autism discourse will provide a more objective view:

'So, not so perversely, objectivity turns out to be about particular and specific embodiment and definitely not about the false vision promising transcendence of all limits and responsibility. The moral is simple: only partial perspective promises objective vision' (Haraway 1988).

---

39 https://soyoureautistic.com/chloe-farahar/ and https://www.researchgate.net/profile/Chloe_Farahar

Only seeing the different perspective in autistic research makes us aware of what has been missing so far. To talk about autism, we need to talk about neurotypicalism.

Why it matters

As Haraway puts it, 'one story is not as good as another' (Haraway, 1989). The neuronormative approach also shapes autism research: what is the focus? Which questions do we ask? What approaches do we develop and how do we measure outcomes?

For example, the main reason why autism research focuses on children is not that adults don't need support; it is the idea that children have more potential for normalisation, especially young children (thus the wave of early intervention approaches).

Looking at the 'interventions' themselves, sometimes the normative concept is explicit – for example, Lovaas proclaimed that ABA would make autistic children 'indistinguishable from their peers' (Lovaas, 1987). Outside the neuronormative model, it would be absurd to consider this a success. Actually, ABA is a prime example for a neuronormative approach.

I was recently researching the effectiveness of various autism 'interventions' for an article. Unfortunately, many studies do not measure whether the method studied actually helps autistic children. Instead, they measure whether the children's autistic characteristics become less, using scales like the Autism Behaviour Checklist, ADI-R, ADOS, Childhood Autism Rating Scale, or the Gilliam Autism Rating Scale before and after the 'intervention'. If the latter makes toward the norm, the researchers count it as a success.

Clearly, normalisation was the goal of these studies.

I wasn't interested in whether the children stimmed less after the researchers intervened in their lives, whether they learned to keep their reactions to unpleasant stimuli to themselves, or whether they started to engage in pretend play instead of solving jigsaw puzzles. I would have liked to know whether the methods and approaches studies made these kids' lives better.

Reading these texts as an autistic person, I have to conclude that the researchers prioritise conformity to our well-being. Thus we need to evaluate outcome measurement scales from a neurodiversity perspective and find new ways to measure the effects of the approaches and methods used on autistic people.

Communication, for example, is vital. If an approach helps autistic people to communicate their needs that is wonderful – no matter whether they talk, or sign, or use picture cards.

Stimming, on the other hand, is not a useful indicator. There are many reasons why people stim. One person might mostly stim when they're stressed, so for them an approach that leads to less stimming might mean that they are less stressed. Yet it might also mean that they stopped using stimming as a means to cope with stress, and might actually be more stressed as a result. For another person, stimming might be a source of joy. For them, less stimming would obviously not be a desirable result.

So, the neurodiversity paradigm does not mean leaving autistic people without support. But the aims are different, yes.

Furthermore, what does it do to autistic people to identify with a neuronormative concept of autism, versus one within the neurodiversity paradigm? Research in this area is limited, but a study by Edward Griffin and David Pollak (2009) divided 27 neurodivergent students in higher education into two groups based on their views on themselves: one group with a 'difference' view – they saw neurodiversity as a difference incorporating a set of strengths and weaknesses, and another group with a 'medical/deficit' view – they considered neurodiversity to be a disadvantageous medical condition. Griffin and Pollack found that, while both groups shared equally difficult experiences in their school careers (due to exclusion, abuse and bullying), those students who saw themselves from a difference perspective expressed greater career ambition and academic self-esteem.

One could also conclude that the pathologising view actively harms neurodiverse students.

What is more, the neuronormative paradigm is limiting regarding the understanding of autism. Describing stimming and echolalia as 'abnormal behaviour' doesn't tell us much about autistic people, apart from the fact that they are considered to be outside the norm. Yet, if we look at these behaviours from a functional perspective ('what purpose does that behaviour serve?'), a whole new multi-faceted world opens up. An example for this is Prizant and Duchan's work on the functions of echolalia (1981).

In essence, taking a neurodiversity perspective on autism as the potential to change the way neurotypical people treat autistic kids (and adults as well), it can change the way neurodiverse students see themselves and their abilities, and it can help us understand autism and autistic people better.

As Haraway writes:

'We exist in a sea of powerful stories: They are the condition of finite rationality and personal and collective life histories. There is no way out of stories; but [...] there are many possible structures, not to mention contents, of narration. Changing the stories, in both material and semiotic senses, is a modest intervention worth making.' (Haraway, 2004)

I am convinced that we can change the stories we tell about autism and autistic people.

We are already doing it.

References

Andreasen NC (1997) Creativity and mental illness: Prevalence rates in writers and their first-degree relatives. *Eminent creativity, everyday creativity, and health* 7-18.

Asperger H (1944) Die „Autistischen Psychopathen' im Kindesalter ['Autistic psychopathy' in childhood]. *European Archives of Psychiatry and Clinical Neuroscience* **117** (1) 76–136.

Dawson M, Soulières I, Ann Gernsbacher M & Mottron L (2007) The level and nature of autistic intelligence. *Psychological science* **18** (8) 657–662.

Foucault M (1980) *Power/knowledge: Selected interviews and other writings*, 1972-1977. Vintage, p197.

Foucault M (2013, 1961) *History of madness.* Routledge.

Griffin E & Pollak D (2009) Student experiences of neurodiversity in higher education: Insights from the BRAINHE project. *Dyslexia* **15** (1) 23–41.

Haraway D (1984) Primatology is politics by other means. In: PSA: Proceedings of the biennial meeting of the philosophy of science association (Vol. 1984, No. 2, pp. 489-524). Philosophy of Science Association.

Haraway D (1988) *Situated knowledges: The science question in feminism and the privilege of partial perspective. Feminist Studies* **14** (3) p577.

Haraway D (1989) *Primate Visions: Gender, race, and nature in the world of modern science.* Routledge.

Haraway D (2004) Modest_Witness@Second_Millenium. Haraway, D. The Haraway Reader. Routledge.

Hartmann E, Russ D, Van der Kolk B, Falke R & Oldfield M (1981) A preliminary study of the personality of the nightmare sufferer: relationship to schizophrenia and creativity? *The American Journal of Psychiatry.*

Hasenfus N & Magaro P (1976) Creativity and schizophrenia: an equality of empirical constructs. *The British Journal of Psychiatry* **129** (4) 346–349.

Karlsson J (1970) Genetic association of giftedness and creativity with schizophrenia. *Hereditas* **66** (2) 177–181.

Keefe J & Magaro P (1980) Creativity and schizophrenia: an equivalence of cognitive processing. *Journal of Abnormal Psychology* **89** (3) 390.

Lovaas, OI (1987) Behavioural treatment and normal educational and intellectual functioning in young autistic children. *Journal of Consulting and Clinical Psychology* 55, 3–9.

McGrath J (2017) *Naming Adult Autism: Culture, science, identity.* Rowman & Littlefield International.

Mervis CB & Klein-Tasman BP (2000) Williams syndrome: cognition, personality, and adaptive behaviour. *Mental retardation and developmental disabilities research reviews* **6** (2) 148–158.

Milton DE (2012) On the ontological status of autism: the 'double empathy problem'. *Disability & Society* **27** (6) 883–887.

Murray D, Lesser M & Lawson W (2005) Attention, monotropism and the diagnostic criteria for autism. *Autism* **9** (2) 139–156.

Nolan J & McBride M (2015) Embodied semiosis: Autistic 'stimming' as sensory praxis. In: *International Handbook of Semiotics* (p1069). Springer, Dordrecht.

Power R, Steinberg S, Bjornsdottir G, Rietveld C, Abdellaoui A, Nivard M & Cesarini D (2015) Polygenic risk scores for schizophrenia and bipolar disorder predict creativity. *Nature neuroscience* **18** (7) 953.

Prizant B & Duchan J (1981) The functions of immediate echolalia in autistic children. *Journal of Speech and Hearing Disorders* **46** (3) 241–249.

Quetelet A (1835) Sur l'homme et le développement de ses facultés. Paris: Fayard. Vol.2, p266.

Richards R (2001) Creativity and the schizophrenia spectrum: More and more interesting. *Creativity Research Journal* **13** (1) 111–132.

Sara (2018) Exclusive interview: Dr. James McGrath, autistic author. Seeking Sara [online]. Available at: https://seekingsara174.com/2018/08/19/639/ (accessed January 2020).

Sass L (2001) Schizophrenia, modernism, and the' creative imagination': On creativity and psychopathology. *Creativity research journal* **13** (1) 55–74.

Sinclair J (2010) Being autistic together. *Disability Studies Quarterly* **30** (1).

Walker N (2014) Neurodiversity: Some Basic Terms & Definitions [online]. Neurocosmopolitan. Available at: http://neurocosmopolitanism.com/neurodiversity-some-basic-terms-definitions/ (accessed January 2020).

Yergeau M (2018) *Authoring Autism: On rhetoric and neurological queerness*. Duke University Press.

Chapter 10: Neurodiversity is for everyone

By Fergus Murray

Ecosystems are richer when they are diverse: biodiversity makes for a more resilient system, better able to deal with shocks and to fill niches. Diversity is good for groups of humans, too, from the level of committees up to societies. It helps us make better decisions. We thrive on cross-pollination, learning from people with different perspectives who bring new ways of doing things and thinking about problems. Diversity is also just an unavoidable feature of human societies, which we need to deal with whether we like it or not. People have very different experiences of the world, and unless we listen to them when they tell us what makes their lives difficult and what helps, we often make things worse.

Acting as if everybody conforms to some idea of the 'default human' fails most people. Not that many of us are white, male, well-off, cis, straight, abled *and* neurotypical, but those who are can rest assured that everyone from outside those boxes has at least some idea what it's like to be them. This is why we need to talk about privilege: some people's viewpoints are privileged over others, so we all hear about their challenges and triumphs, while the disadvantages of less privileged groups are largely hidden. If you've never experienced being an American white man, a million books, films and TV shows are jostling to tell you all about what it's like.

One aspect of human diversity is the variety of processing styles we have: what we call neurodiversity. Like other kinds of diversity, it is probably a net positive, but it comes with serious challenges for those who are seen as divergent. In many ways, society is built as if everyone's brain works in much the same way. If you stop to think about it, it should be pretty obvious that there is no one 'normal' way of thinking, but most people never give it much thought. We tend vaguely to assume that other people have similar sensory processing abilities, ways of imagining and executive functions. In fact, all of these things vary profoundly–try asking your friends about their internal monologues and visual imaginations if you want to get a sense of this, or about their experiences of noisy environments. There are few, if any, totally neurotypical people; but some are certainly more neurotypical than others. They think more like the average person, or, at least, like the type of person society treats as the default, and their lives tend to be easier as a result.

Figure 10.1: A bell curve

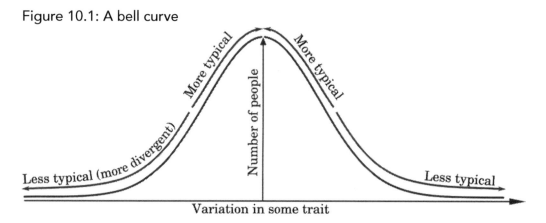

Given almost any trait, a minority of the population will diverge strongly from the average. There are many ways to diverge, so most people are atypical in some ways.

Atypical thinking is in fact highly valued in many contexts, because most kinds of neurodivergence bring strengths as well as weaknesses, and all bring unusual perspectives. It is generally understood that scientists and artists of all sorts are likely to be quite odd, for example, and their focus and unusual takes are often seen as a worthwhile trade-off for some non-conformity. If they are lucky, they may find that the advantages of their divergent thinking outweigh the disadvantages.

Still, on the whole, the more typical someone's thinking style is, the more they'll find the world set up to accommodate them. Those whose brains work strikingly differently from the norm – neurodivergent people, including autistics, dyslexics, ADHDers and so on – run into all sorts of invisible barriers, from inaccessible sensory environments to assumptions of incompetence to social exclusion. We regularly run up against people's expectations about how easy or how difficult things 'should' be. Either way can make our lives much harder.

Everyone has experienced being misjudged or misunderstood at some point in their lives. This is horrible for the person being misjudged, and bad for everyone else because it means that their strengths are being wasted. Schools and workplaces can be awful places for people who think and experience the world differently from their peers, where such misunderstandings are all too common, and human potential is recklessly squandered. This happens all the time, even to relatively neurotypical people, because most of the population has so little understanding of how differently other people think.

Disability, roughly speaking, is the inability to do things that people are normally expected to be able to do. That makes it a mismatch between a person and their physical and social environment–including other people's expectations. People don't usually think of themselves as disabled unless they are prevented from doing things *they* want or need to do. It is misleading to suggest that all disability is caused by other people's attitudes and the barriers put in disabled people's way, but it is true that disability can never be disentangled from its social context. In Britain in 2019, for example, most autistic people are disabled[40]. For the most part, people are only labelled as neurodivergent if they are seen as disabled, although they may not think of themselves that way.

Perhaps some autistic people would be disabled in almost any context, but it's hard to be sure: social expectations have been very different in different times and places, and sometimes changing someone's environment can make an amazing amount of difference to their ability to function. Either way, the existence of very disabled people is compatible with the idea that neurodiversity is not a bad thing. We can say that we don't want a 'cure' for the processing style that makes us who we are, without saying there is nothing we want to change about ourselves. Everyone has things about them that they'd like to fix or improve, unless they're convinced they're already perfect – in which case I guarantee there are still things that *other people* would like to fix about them. If someone wants to change something about themselves, and they have a chance to, that is usually okay, even though all change comes at a cost.

It is possible to accept wholeheartedly someone for who they are, while offering them the help and support they need to thrive in life. It is not possible to accept someone fully if you have a problem with who they are at a fundamental level, and that includes any neurodivergence they might be born with. You can help a child to grow and learn, but know that there are things you will never change about them, and appreciate what makes them unique.

Self-acceptance can be hard to come by, especially if we don't feel accepted by others. Without it, self-improvement is infinitely harder. It is by understanding our challenges and strengths that we learn how to live with them.

Further reading on the meaning of neurodiversity

What Neurodiversity Isn't (by me): https://medium.com/@Oolong/what-neurodiversity-isnt-591b1bd18ae0

---

40 See https://medium.com/@Oolong/autism-as-a-disability-14790520ef81 (accessed January 2020).

Neurodiversity: Some Basic Terms & Definitions (by Nick Walker): https://neurocosmopolitanism.com/neurodiversity-some-basic-terms-definitions/

Neurodiversity FAQ (by Thinking Person's Guide to Autism): http://www.thinkingautismguide.com/p/so-youre-doing-story-about.html

What the Neurodiversity Movement Does – And Doesn't – Offer (by Emily Paige Ballou): http://www.thinkingautismguide.com/2018/02/what-neurodiversity-movement-doesand.html

Disagreeing over Neurodiversity (by Damian Milton): https://thepsychologist.bps.org.uk/volume-32/november-2019/disagreeing-over-neurodiversity

Here's What Neurodiversity Is – And What It Means For Feminism (by Cara Liebowitz): https://everydayfeminism.com/2016/03/neurodiversity-101/

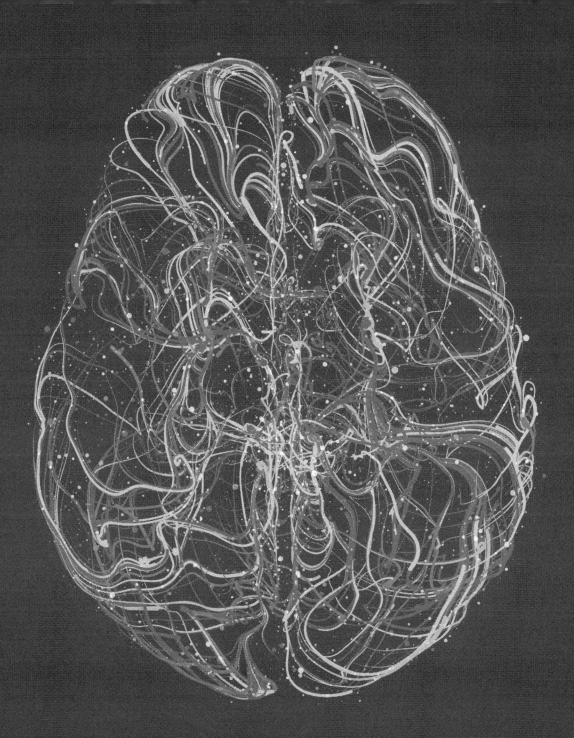

Section 2

Chapter 11: An act of resistance

By Carl Cameron

To disclose one's autism is a deeply personal and complex decision to make, and once revealed it's impossible to take back. To mask or not to mask, that is the question; but make no mistake, whether you decide to disclose or mask, there is a risk attached. Revealing you are autistic may change others' perceptions of you, particularly professionally, and it may leave you vulnerable to manipulation and perhaps open to exploitation. Non-disclosure leads to a life of stealth, pretence, exhaustion and a life in which no adjustment is made, where no one has any idea you are struggling. Before the reader reads on, and since we are here at the beginning and we're talking about disclosure, I suppose I should do the decent thing and disclose first.

I am a privileged person, just so you know. I shouldn't be, but I am. I am an openly autistic person (and with a diagnosis) who has worked for a number of autism charities over the past 20 years, including the National Autistic Society. Currently, I work as a specialist mentor at Matthew's Hub, an autism charity in Hull in the East Riding of Yorkshire. The bulk of the work I do is mentoring autistic people who are awaiting a diagnosis and those who have recently been diagnosed, but I also support autistic people into work. I have my own office and have complete control of my environment. I write my own diary, have a fair amount of autonomy, and as a result I have never been as happy at work as I am today. I am an openly autistic person who works for an autism charity, so when I run into difficulties (and I still do) they understand and support me. I am a privileged person and I can measure that privilege by the occasions when I overloaded, had no support and could not go on. I lost two jobs right at the end of probationary periods – and importantly, on both occasions shortly after disclosing (you've got a bit of autism yourself haven't you?) and where no problem had been flagged before (Carl, we've had complaints). I was emotionally challenged by these events; I was a mess.

I have been described as professionally autistic. I spend most of my working life in the company of other autistic people; I listen to them. I totally get how hard it is for others and the reasons why people don't feel comfortable that others know they're autistic. It's anyone's guess, of course, how comfortable I would feel disclosing if I didn't work in the sector, but since I am an open book it's hard to see how I wouldn't tell. What I would say with a degree of certainty, is that every time an autistic person discloses and is open about their diagnosis it makes it just that bit easier for the next person who decides they have had enough and does the same, but it takes courage and comes with risk. I want everyone to know, especially young autistic people, that being autistic, like the colour of your skin, is nothing to be ashamed of.

Now I have just shared with you a little of the car crash that my career (and by extension my life) went through a few years back, and you may also have gleaned that I have never quite recovered, because as I have already said, I am an open book. I am far from alone in this. As a people, as the distinct cultural group (for that is what I believe we are) we do have a tendency to over-share, I think we can all agree on that. We are a trusting bunch and tend to take people at face value. It's because of this, and because body language can be so tricky that we sometimes don't see the harm when it is staring us in the face. Information we share can be of value to those with a deficit of scruples, and not always when delivered to strangers either. The truth is we find people confusing enough as it is, without trying to predict how they might react to the news their work colleague has an interesting neurological condition. Instinctively, I believe, autistic people want to be open, we want to 'tell', and sometimes because we need help; sometimes we are not OK.

Several years ago, and for reasons which escape me, I disclosed badly to a couple who my wife had a family connection with. They got talking about work and told me they thought someone in the office was 'definitely on the spectrum'. I had been meaning to tell them for ages I am autistic, especially as our paths were about to cross professionally. I had expected that I would just casually drop the 'A' word and me into the conversation and now seemed the perfect moment to do it. Instead, I decided to blurt out, 'Did you know I am autistic? I am just telling you because I am on the autism partnership board and you are going to see my name at some point, we never need to mention it again!'

Why did I do that? I have spoken about autism for over a decade, delivered training to 100s of people, spoken on the radio – it's a documented fact I am autistic. I think it's often to do with perceptions of the competence of autistic people; some people look at you funny after disclosure. I have been talked to as if I was five years old, talked down to at meetings and gatherings connected to autism, not taken seriously. It's only in the past few years that autistic people have been paid to speak at conferences; we didn't have a value before that. Until you can prove differently, all kinds of assumptions will be made about you, even by people who are supposed to know better. One minute you are a colleague, the next a subject of interest, and it's hard sometimes not to feel you are being watched, studied. There has to come a time when to be autistic is a celebration of difference, there has to be a culture that goes beyond the lip service paid to such things at conferences.

I have been writing and delivering autism training for years. It's fun to do and I get to tell it like it is. Earlier this year I was asked, with a colleague, to deliver some autism training across the other side of the city. The session was to a medium-sized group of around 60 delegates for an NHS well-being thingy with various stakeholders and third sector organisations. My colleague (and boss), Gill Emerson, is a well-known personality in nursing and health board circles, so it was no surprise to hear her introduced first as we approached the stage. What was a surprise was when the facilitator asked, 'Is this one of your patients, Gill?'. It took me a moment... Wow, is she talking about me? Somewhat pricked by this statement, I muttered something about being neither a patient nor a service user before introducing myself. I told them that I am employed as a specialist mentor and deputy chair of the Hull Autism Partnership Board with 20 years' experience working with autistic people across the spectrum... oh, and I'm about to complete a Masters degree, an MA Autism.

She judged me! She called me a patient! She automatically medicalised me, and from that positionality made a whole set of assumptions about who she thought I was and what my capabilities were, and she made them instinctively, too. I know several professional people in the field of autism who won't disclose for fear of what might come next, that they would be treated differently.

It's not surprising we mask, we learned early, too, didn't we? We were not like the other kids and they knew it, and kids don't like kids who are different. I think it was Uta Frith who said that bullying among autistic children was so common as to be almost diagnostic. Much of my working life is spent working with autistic people who are awaiting an autism diagnosis, people who believe they may be autistic, often walking in straight off the street to ask questions, and sometimes to begin a new journey through life. It's a privilege to contribute to the referral process and follow their diagnostic journey through to assessment, diagnosis and beyond. One of the first questions I always ask of someone who believes they are autistic is, 'Were you bullied at school?' Most of us were, you see. I recently asked the 'Dungeons & Dragons' group at Matthew's Hub in Hull the same question. Out of a group of eight young autistic men, every person, including myself (number nine) had been bullied at school. Now, I am not saying that every autistic person has been bullied – of course not – but it feels rare and always comes as a shock when someone says they were not. I recently ran an autistic over 40s group with a dozen or so members of the Hub; all had been bullied at school and later went on to be bullied in the workplace. It seems adults don't like adults who are different either.

We mask for safety, despite the damage it causes. No, it doesn't make sense, but we do it all the same. Hiding/masking one's autism is about as helpful as a gay person staying in the closet – he/she are not less gay, just more miserable. If the reader might allow me to make the same analogy, the same is true of autistic people, yet most of us continue to mask on some level. To mask one's autism does not make you less autistic, it just means that you are covering up well and on the road to a mental health crisis: masking comes at a price. As famously adept at masking as women and girls on the autism spectrum are, masking is not the preserve autistic females alone: boys and men do it, too. We must, we don't have much choice if we want to survive in the schoolyard or the workplace. The harder we try to fit in, the better we are deemed to be coping and even less adjustment is made and the more we struggle. Autistic people are great people watchers, we watch and copy, it's how we build our masks and hide, it's how we get by. Masking is essentially camouflage, it's a well-practised survival technique that comes with an inner dialogue, an ear worm that says, 'I mustn't let 'em find out I'm a weirdo'; a soundtrack to accompany an environment which appears to be poorly organised chaos, the workplace.

As you may remember previously, mentoring autistic people into employment is an important part of my role. Recently, I supported a young autistic woman, newly graduated, and who had just been bullied out of her job from a well-known art space. Soon after commencing employment she disclosed she was autistic. Shortly thereafter, and I do mean shortly, questions began to be raised about her ability and suitability to perform certain tasks, to attend conferences and meetings. In time, her position became untenable and she could no longer work there. Sometime later she was able to secure a similar position at another gallery elsewhere, a city some 70 miles away. However, while she was comfortable disclosing that she suffers from anxiety, her sexuality, gender and other aspects of her neurodiverse life, she won't tell them she is autistic – once bitten, twice shy. This talented young woman continues to mask and tells me she struggles because no adjustment have been made.

When someone tries to converse with me, someone I don't know I may make little or no effort to engage. If I attempt to mirror them in conversation, they will view this as encouragement, and they end up wanting to talk even more. I struggle to maintain these interactions; I just can't keep the conversations going. I usually let my wife do the talking if we are out and about or on holiday and just chip in the minimum in an attempt to be polite. I find maintaining a conversation to be a poor use of resources. I have rarely found 'small talk' to be beneficial, only exhausting. When I am obliged to engage socially, the anxiety levels begin to rise days or weeks in advance. I find it almost impossible for the date or time of these proposed interactions to stick in my mind. It is almost as if my brain rejects them, and I am good with dates. I start the scripting process in the hours leading up to the event. It's such a confusing dilemma this socialising business, just how much information do I disclose about me? Do people want to hear? How much do I disclose? What's appropriate? How much detail do they want to hear? When is a good time to shut the hell up? If I don't find a way into a conversation quickly and find my place, I won't find my way in at all and may not say a word.

When I was young and someone asked me how I was when I met them, I told them, and in some detail, too. Now I have gotten a little older and I know now that they don't really want to know how I am, it's just a greeting like saying hello. Nothing has changed for me however: today when someone asks how I am, I am still bursting to tell them and find it difficult not to, but I know that it's not the 'done thing' and they don't really want to hear. Despite my age and all the societal practice, I still need to coach and script my way through social events, even family occasions. I still attempt to turn the conversation around to something I know about – either that or I might not talk at all. I still find social situations uncomfortable or unpleasant no matter how I try to cover up that fact. Tolerating social occasions does not make me less autistic. Unless I am on safe ground, and that tends to be autism talk, my global stability begins to shift, which in turn triggers my adrenaline and anxiety levels, and then there is the internal debrief from the interaction you never wanted to have in the first place. All of this processing is exhausting.

When forced to visit or be 'visited' by other people, I used to constantly be told, 'Just be yourself' or, 'You don't need to tell everyone exactly what you think all the time'. And, somewhat less charitably, 'You don't have to be a weirdo'. Really? Just relax and be myself? Do they really mean that? If I was to be myself, I wouldn't visit or interact with anyone outside the workplace or family in the first place; I just wouldn't go out. I don't enjoy social occasions in rooms full of neurotypical people and I do not believe it is wrong to seek solitude. It doesn't make me a bad person because I prefer to be on my own, it doesn't make me less because I don't need all that social stuff to make me a happy person. What my solitude does is give me lots of autonomy, which is anxiety free, safe and protected. I manage my own global stability; I maintain my spoon count (my units of energy and reliance), my well-being, and I take autonomous action for myself and the choices about my well-being about my life.

Just relax and be myself… Do they really mean that?

They really want me to talk at my natural volume and talk about topics and things which interest me? Are they sure they are comfortable with me doing that? People have been telling me my entire life to stop shouting (I have no volume control and hate the volume I naturally speak at) or to stop banging on and on about some interesting fact I have told them before. And are they *really* happy for me to say exactly what I think about whatever it is I feel strongly about?

What is so wrong about telling it like it is and being clear? Neurotypical parents tell their children not to lie, but they don't want them to tell the truth, either; to give an honest reply to a question they have been directly asked. (This is where things start to get confusing.) No, what they really want is an adjustment to the truth, just a tiny little lie, a lie which may or may not be made, dependant on the context of environments which are fluid and not ours. Why would anyone ask a question that they don't want to know the answer to? I sometimes think we don't stand a chance. When I am the only autistic person in the room I am an actor playing games I hardly know the rules to.

Just relax and be myself? They don't mean it. They don't want me to be myself. What they mean is, 'We want you to pretend to be someone else; we don't like you the way you really are'. Society does not want autistic people to be autistic. Society wants autistic people to appear 'normal' regardless of the damage it causes. Applied Behavioural Analysis, so beloved among professionals (sic) in the United States, brutally demonstrates the lengths to which society will go in order to obliterate autistic traits in what appears to be an obsessive drive for social conformity. To be autistic is to challenge neurotypical norms, our directness, focus, interests and honesty they find alarming.

I seldom leave the house unless I am going to work, and it is because of my work that, other than speaking to my lovely and rather patient wife, I rarely talk to anyone who is not either autistic or a genuine ally. I've worked with other autistic people across the spectrum for the past 20 years, mentoring autistic undergraduate students and autistic people into employment. Despite the belief that autism is something white boys 'have', I have worked with autistic people from many different cultures, genders, races and social classes. Why is it that the single most important detail in these interactions is that we belong to the same neurotype? Why is that intersection so important? Why are relationships between autistic people built quicker and more successfully than those with members of the predominant neurotype?

I have worked with people who had never spoken to another autistic person before and who expressed their relief at being able to talk to another autistic person for the first time, not having to explain and be understood. In the years before my own diagnosis I often said that I preferred being with autistic children and adults to socialising with the staff. Staff asked me how I built relationships and achieved the outcomes I did with autistic children who were considered 'complex' or 'hard to reach' when no one else could? I didn't understand why I succeeded when others failed. After all, I didn't seem to do anything. Now of course I have come to realise it was because I did nothing, didn't back kids into a corner with needless communication and interaction. I watched and worked with them when they were ready, I engaged by sharing interest and built bridges with them. Spoken language is overrated – you can do without it and still find mutual understanding. I later came to realise that I was the same as those children and that we were members of the same tribe.

Damien Milton talks about the 'Double Empathy Problem'. That autistic people have some difficulty understanding, interpreting and using reciprocal social communication as well as problems reading social cues used so instinctively by neurotypical people. Neurotypical people have similar difficulty understanding and interpreting autistic communication, culture and the reasons why somethings are so important to us. Milton argues that neurotypical people understand each other better than they understand autistic people and that autistic people understand each other better than we understand neurotypical people; that there is better empathy between us than between mixed groups.

Recent research by Crompton and Fletcher-Watson (2019) appears to confirm Milton's 'problem'. The study examined the transfer of information between neurotypes. Information or skills were passed through 'chaining' – exercises where information was passed between members of a group. The study found where the transmitted information was between autistic people, or non-autistic people, there was little 'noise' and the information was transferred successfully. When the communication transfer was between a mixed group of participants (Au – NT – Au – NT – Au – NT etc) the flow becomes corrupted and begins to fall into a state of decay. The autistic participants of the study also reported higher levels of relaxation and empathy when they socialised or worked together than when they were with neurotypical people. Autistic people have no need to mask in each other's presence; we are culturally the same. To be with other autistic people, on the whole (we can fight and fall out like everybody else), is to be free, free to be who we are without judgement or explanation. Watch what happens when groups of autistic people meet, like at autistic-led conferences, retreats, meetings, pride picnics and social occasions. We take off our masks and we throw them away, we have no need for them. Eye contact appears to be easier and stimming becomes the norm, it's an important part of our culture, heritage and well-being.

Autism is my life, my passion, interest and profession, but I do have other interests. I speak a little Swedish and have something of an interest in that post-punk band gem The Fall. I like The Fall; I have seen them dozens of times live since 1979. I own over 150 vinyl records and a hoard of over 300 live recordings. I like The Fall, and surprise, surprise, I know a little about them (try me out!). Of course, not every autistic person has the same passions and interests that I do. I might not have a thing for electricity pylons, a deep understanding of the Spanish Civil War or have a detailed knowledge of Norwegian Railways, but what I can do, what we as autistic people can do, is to understand and respect how important to us those interests are to us, why talking about them is important, why the drive to pursue them is so strong. To deny them or seek to restrict access to a special interest or item is a cruel thing to do. My wife understands I have to utter every part of my information distribution, including any preamble, back story or what-have-you, or I am unable to move on, or at least have great difficulty in doing so.

Now I need to say this and I need to say it loud (like I usually do) and clear: if we need a 'data dump', we need a data dump and that is all there is to it. If there is something we need to talk about then we need to talk about it, and it seems only fair that given that autistic people are exposed daily to the mindless banality of small talk, something which is painful for many of us and an inefficient use of spoons (our units of energy). It's a verbal avalanche of neurotypical flotsam and jetsam which we can do without but which we try to accommodate. If that accommodation was reciprocal I am sure the majority of the autistic community would be eternally grateful.

Autism is exhausting, but hardly anyone outside of the autistic community talks about it. Why is that? Organisation and planning is difficult for autistic people for many reasons, including anxiety – it's an anxiety provoking business. As autistic people we sometimes become so interested, so focused on a task or a subject that the rest of the world appears to disappear, and stuff we need to get done, doesn't. I believe autistic people are monotropic people. Monotropism, as described by Murray, Lesser and Lawson (2005), suggests that we have limited channels of attention that are available to us and these channels are used far more intensely than neurotypical people classically do, the polytrops of this world. Monotropism helps explain so many aspects of autistic life, such as our intense focus and interests and the flow states and attention tunnels we form as we pursue them. We are the Marmite people: either we are completely into something, or completely uninterested. Monotropism explains our black-and-white thinking styles and our polarisation in the way we process the environment, our hyper and hypo sensitivities to sensory stimuli. When we have a reaction to the environment, we usually feel it strongly.

Now if you want to make Carl sick, make Carl work in an open-plan office; the results are spectacular and quick. The hell hole which is your average open plan office serves no purpose except to save ground space, they do not improve efficacy. What they do is make life a living nightmare for autistic people and exclude them from the workplace. When I first went to work at Matthew's Hub, I didn't have a home, my own space, just a Chromebook which I wandered the building with. When the main office was rearranged and I was asked to take a desk at one end of the room – after all I was 'one of the team' – I knew it was going to end badly, but they were lovely people who for all the right reasons wanted me to feel like one of them. But of course I am not, I am not one of them at all. I was so completely overloaded by the end of the day, even with ear defenders, that I went straight to bed when I got home and stayed there. I woke in the morning wondering how in the name of God I had allowed this to happen, again. This was far from the first time I had overloaded like this; it's happened before, it always happens. For my lovely neurotypical colleagues the very thought that they might be on their own all day with no one to talk to fills them with dread, but I am not the same as them, I just don't need that level of interaction to function; I need control of my environment.

Before I went to work at the hub I worked in an open-plan office delivering health and social care qualifications remotely, a job I had done for years previous at the college in Lincoln. Despite having the light turned down over my desk, it was still too bright, the radio is turned on the moment anyone arrives and stays on all day. By five past eight the small talk has been turned up to full volume, some nonsense about TV. The heating has just been turned up full and has been on all night, again. The phone starts to ring and the volume of the office has begun to rise, the sharp 'ting' of text messages, emails, WhatsApp and eBay messages fill the air. I struggle to stay focused, to create my bubble, but I am disturbed again and again (would you like another coffee?). It feels like my head is fit to burst and all I want to do is focus and work. I was so overwhelmed and overloaded by the end of each day that I would retch hard from the effort of holding in my discomfort the moment I got to my car (cars are mobile safe spaces). I was exhausted – my work days spent in purgatory, my evenings trying to 'reset'… after all, tomorrow is another day.

If you are forced to work or learn in an environment which hums and bristles with sound, people endlessly talking about nothing in particular until the chatter becomes inaudible, your world is full of unpredictable events and you only have so many channels open to process them with, then eventually you (as an autistic person) are going to overload, meltdown or worse.

Autism + Environment = Outcome (Breadon, 2017)

Breadon argues that an autistic person thrives or fails depending on the environment they find themselves in, and that also includes the people who inhabit that environment. Masking sensory processing difficulties is like trying to mask a broken leg or a heart condition – not terribly useful and just perhaps a little dangerous. Inevitably, and out of fear, many autistic people will attempt to 'tough it out', at least in the short term, and I do mean short.

Masking is a one-sided activity. It's all about us making unreasonable adjustments for others, and it's hard work. Masking is exhausting. Autistic people are expected to engage in all aspects of neurotypical culture intuitively with little if any effort being made to understand ours. No one sees the damage we do to ourselves, twisting ourselves out of shape for the benefit of others. When we mask we become the allies of a culture which discriminates and which is neurologically imperialist.

We permit expectations of 'norm' and support our own discrimination. By 'being autistic', by taking off our masks and being true to ourselves, we are not only taking back control of our lives and celebrating our culture, we are also making a political statement. It's an act of resistance.

References

Beardon, L. (2017). *Autism and Aspergers Syndrome in Adults.* London : Sheldon Press

Crompton, C, J and Fletcher-Watson, S (2019a). *Efficiency and Interaction during Information Transfer between Autistic and Neurotypical People* [poster presentation] Retrieved from: https://insar.confex.com/insar/2019/webprogram/Paper30110.html

Milton, D. (2012) "On the ontological status of autism: The double empathy problem'," *Disability & Society*, **27**(6): 883–887. doi: 10.1080/09687599.2012.710008.

Murray, D, Lesser, M and Lawson (2005). Attention, monotropism and the diagnostic criteria for autism. Autism: *the international journal of research and practice.* **9**. 139-56. 10.1177/1362361305051398.

Chapter 12: New light through old windows

By Paul Davies

I'm autistic. I have a diagnosis of Asperger's syndrome. I'm neurodivergent. This isn't a 'poor me' article, nor is it an attempt to inspire. Inspiration porn does nothing for me. It is simply a description of experiences and an explanation of why, in my humble opinion, the neurodiversity movement is the only true hope for so many people. There are wiser people than I who can speak to the details, so I haven't tried to do this. Instead, I would suggest that it is almost inevitable if you are neurodivergent, or a true ally, that the movement is the best option for progress.

The term 'neurodiversity' and the neurodiversity movement have become synonymous with the Autism Rights Movement, but it is primarily a focus on neural and cognitive difference. As opposed to being an exclusively autism-focused approach championed by the Autism Rights Movement, it also includes people with diagnoses such as ADHD, dyslexia and bipolar disorder. The central theme is that, rather than being a disorder, these 'ways of being' are simply a natural part of human diversity. This does not deny the struggle that many people face, it never has, although it has been misconstrued or misunderstood that this is the case. It is an inclusive and liberating agenda that seeks to benefit everybody. The continued prominence of arguments and theories that view autistic cognitive processes as disordered or a biogenetic puzzle only serve to further alienate, disenfranchise and marginalise us.

As an inner-city child in the 1960s, I once asked a teacher why the other children seemed to understand the classroom social 'rules' and I didn't. She brought me a book on social etiquette to help me. Being eight years of age and knowing that the port decanter should only be passed from left hand to left hand and not touch the table saved me from many social faux pas. That said, I was never invited to any parties anyway. Never included.

For so long I searched for my place in the world. Alone. I fought my way through school, relationships and numerous jobs, and ultimately the mental health service meat grinder. I was told that it was positive to find out what was wrong with me. The reason I couldn't be like the normal people I was surrounded by. Once I was manic depressive, then I wasn't and I was suddenly bipolar. Then I wasn't again and I was Borderline Personality Disorder (BPD). When I challenged this particular diagnosis, I was told that by the very fact that I challenged the authority of the clinical psychologist I had simply proven my status as BPD. Then I was confused and angry, but I learned the importance of not challenging the experts and taking my medication to pacify me. In their eyes I was troubled, damaged and challenging. I was not viewed as a human being, though. Indeed, the older I get, the less human I appear to become in this society.

It's always been like this. Always. For as long as I can remember, and I'm 57 now with an amazing memory. All those decades of exclusion and pathologising my differences; so very long. This has always distressed me. I was lucky though. So many neurodivergent people throughout the last few centuries have been removed from the gaze of wider society. Medicated, institutionalised and habituated. Difference has always been demonised and therefore feared, intimidating or reviled. It still permeates our attitudes and treatment of disabled or different people today.

I try to be human; I really do. I have a job, I have a long-term relationship, I drive a car, own the right phone: all the vital qualities required to be considered human. But then comes the kicker; I'm autistic. I can only do those things because I have a well-crafted mask to hide my true self. A mask that declares 'I don't care!' caringly, as I care and feel deeply about everything. Overwhelmed by empathy and emotions in this intense world. Most people don't notice, I work very hard at that. It's exhausting. Some do; some see the differences and the judgement begins. Very few see the difference then accept and embrace them. Many claim to but they don't, and perpetuate the infantilisation of autistic adults. Those who do are special. Very special.

By a complete stroke of luck, or fate, 20 years ago I met somebody who didn't ask me to act. She accepted me and my strange friendship. That was totally bamboozling I can tell you. It isn't supposed to be like this. But she was, and still is, my best friend. As time and circumstances passed and changed, she also became the single great love of my life. She listened and included me in her life. In so doing, she saved my life. It is a debt I feel unable to even imagine how I can ever pay back, but I try every day. She saw beyond labels, the pathologised behaviour, and told me to simply be myself.

That was the by far the single biggest challenge I have ever faced.

I had to start at the very beginning and read everything I could about mentally ill people. It was educating, but ultimately frustrating, as I clearly wasn't very good at being mentally ill either. I had the depression and the anxiety. I could tick those boxes, but there was so much missing that couldn't explain why I did the stupid things I did, or was so angry and defensive all the time. It didn't explain why the world was always so loud, so bright, so smelly, and so full of people. So alienating. I kept reading.

When I realised I was autistic it was a revelation. It was as if the label was written for me. Just me. It went to the very core of who I was and why I was the person I was. Finally here was redemption, all the answers I had searched for. I finally knew which flag I was marching behind and that made so much sense for me. I didn't have a diagnosis yet, but I believed this was the start of a new chapter. In many ways it was, in others it was plus ça change…

'I have Asperger's syndrome!' I told myself. I 'had' it. But I didn't feel as liberated as I had initially hoped. I 'had' a disorder, which thereby, by logical extension, made me disordered. It made me less than the rest. I couldn't make friends, but clearly that was my fault for having Asperger's syndrome and that being a deficit in me. Clearly it wasn't other people's fault; the other people who spoke and thought differently to me just understood things that eluded me. No, it was all my fault.

'Having' Asperger's was clearly the problem for all the failed communications I had over the years. I was obviously too stupid to understand what people meant when they said one thing but they actually meant the opposite. I was baffled why people would say we Aspies lacked empathy, as that was the opposite of what I experienced. So maybe I wasn't autistic after all? Maybe I was rubbish at having Asperger's syndrome, too? It was probably for the best that I was mainly excluded and isolated by my peer group or work colleagues. All the broken relationships were clearly my fault; well, I had been told as much often enough over the years. It must have been true. Except, I was never actually 'me' during these times, I was what I thought the other person wanted. Masks and acts designed to make me less disordered or damaged and therefore less damaging. Propped up by continual medication, it never worked long-term; too hard to keep going. Another failure on my shoulders. 'Mea Culpa'. I got that tattooed on my leg.

In reality I was no longer 'disordered' or 'defective', I was actually just different. My brain was wired differently to other people. Tired old clichés about human machines or opposing computer operating systems aside, I knew this was the truth and pointed to the answer I had always been looking for. My true identity.

To achieve this I knew that I had to look for a definitive label, and that label was autism. Not ideal, given what I had read, but true. The NHS proved ineffective as all funding was going to children, and how can anybody begrudge that? I did. My shame deepened because of thinking, 'But what about me?' The decision to seek a private diagnosis was exacerbated by a workplace situation which was deteriorating and I was, once again, being cast as the agitator, the trouble maker, the disordered employee who was always asking for changes to be made. Changes that cost money. This was clearly unacceptable. I had to choose to declare myself disabled officially as this was the only legal route open to me to acquire the changes I needed. I felt stupid and worthless for asking for reasonable adjustments, but I did anyway. I was made redundant. They said it was unconnected and just economics. Another lesson learned. Don't be honest in the workplace – it will cost your livelihood.

My private studies continued while I watched the society I inhabit change and become more radical and extreme. I was born in a city that embraces socialism as a way of life and 'walks its talk' in this regard. It has always been part of my nature to challenge unfairness and look to the collective for strength. Why would my autism change this? It didn't and it hasn't. While politics has lurched to the right under Conservative and Neo-liberal governments, the status of all disabled people has diminished considerably. Given we have been the victims of eugenics throughout history, this was a low bar to begin with.

We have been demonised and targeted as benefit fraudsters and a drain on the 'good working people'. Clearly not having a job makes you bad. I have always held down a job, so clearly simply being disabled was presumably enough in my case to be deemed 'bad' and a 'life unworthy of life'. No longer a human being in the eyes of millions. The deaths of hundreds of thousands of vulnerable people due to austerity over the last decade raises little more than a shrug of the shoulders in many circles. So what? They couldn't work anyway. Why should we carry them? Why should my taxes support them? You have to have a job and 'work will set you free'. We all know this.

With the lurch to the Right and a market economy driven society, coupled with the growth of 'social media', individualism has become the norm. This politic of self-centredness will always be hostile to whatever isn't the accepted 'normal', where 'normal' equates to more of us than you. It is true that in actuality, very few people fit this and most of us are found on the intersections which act as barriers to participation or acceptance into society. A permanent liminal state. I have a diagnosis of Asperger's syndrome, and as such this renders me not autistic enough for some but not normal enough for others. This is often by neurotypical people who assert that their parental status subsumes my lived experiences, or that I don't fit a stereotype as I look 'normal' or can talk. The isolation of disabled people is key to our lack or influence. Divide and conquer; hardly a new tactic. It is our difference that is exploited.

The true hope for all disabled people is through collectivism and acceptance of the unique individual experiences we all have being merely a part of a spectrum. Factional thinking, however alluring, 'Yes it's OK for you… but you don't have to…' and a focus on individual struggle does nothing to further any of our causes. I once sat in a disability 'community' meeting and I heard a wheelchair user say about a profoundly deaf man, 'What's he complaining about hearing loops, at least he can use his legs!' Some people appear to value their 'disability' as it offers an excuse to live a limited life. Not everybody, but some. Of course, that said, the only way we can access support is to focus on our impairments and emphasise our helplessness: 'Prove you deserve our money'. This affects us all, irrespective of our differences. Factionalism dilutes the arguments and simply perpetuates the medical and deficit based system.

Neurodiversity is natural. It is the very basis of life itself. We are all different and this is universally accepted. Why then should a political movement based on this precept be challenged or dismissed as it is? I have always believed in science and have accepted that theories change or are dismissed when evidence is presented to the contrary. The earth isn't flat in the same way that vaccines don't cause autism. The science is there for all to see, but it is not accepted by some. The neurodiversity movement offers the only route towards understanding and acceptance and the potential to be viewed as human beings. Collectively. The view that we are all simply different shouldn't be controversial, and yet is. It absolutely is.

The social model of disability was a welcome addition to the debate as I grew up and it served to offer an alternative that brought with it a sense of redemption. It wasn't our fault. It was society that was hostile and thoughtless; it caused our problems. That was liberating, but in so many ways it isn't. My hyper-sensitivities are my own and society can do little to mitigate or ameliorate some of them. Admittedly, it would be nice if it tried, but there will always be some differences or challenges for me. I thought, 'If only there was a school of thought that said that so many of us weren't actually worthless lives and an economic drain on the good normal people'. This is what the Neurodiversity Movement addresses. I went from *having* to *being*.

The clarion call of the Neurodiversity Movement is 'Nothing about us without us!' That, again, shouldn't be controversial, but it is. The vast majority of research doesn't include the *actual* autistic voice at all, and even when we are research subjects. Our words are then viewed via a Neurotypical lens and with Neurotypical interpretations imposed upon them. The Health and Wellbeing Sector has now reached the point where the 'customer' is actually the funding body rather than the person receiving the service or support. The person supported rarely has a say in the most basic elements of their life. Autism Spectrum Conditions are individual and the unplanned consequences of planned actions of 'person-centred' approaches often actually serve to exacerbate our isolation. 'Well they are all different so you can't make overarching statements!' Focus on the individual, whilst welcome, reduces the collective bargaining power of the many. The weight of Neurotypical 'expertise' is stacked against us. All of us who are different.

The fact that the neurodiversity movement challenges medical supremacy and the lucrative autism industry is key to change. It is also a massive hurdle. Billions of pounds and dollars profit are 'earned' on the back of the differences found within the autism spectrum and wider neurodivergence. Ironically it is our neurology that sets many of us apart as disordered, yet, at the same time, our type of original, innovative and unconventional thinking is often highly prized within businesses and drives innovation and change. Yet only small numbers of disabled people hold down full time employment. Even when we do, we are faced with a neurotypical workplace. I've never known an autism-friendly workplace, ever. I am fortunate to work within a team that does work to support me but the wider organisation is still deeply neurotypical.

These days autism is very fashionable, it's everywhere. However, as representations on TV grow, we autists are either IT savants or super detectives or, more likely, just 'undateable'. Forever the quirky outsider. But we are educating people about autism so it's not exploitative, and if *they* can get a date then there is nothing stopping you, is there!? If not this, then on the news as the victims of yet another abuse scandal. There have been numerous policies and legislation introduced since Winterbourne View, but how much has changed? Well, Whorlton Hall, The Dene, Crawford's Walk, Mendip House... (I could continue) appear to demonstrate that little improvement has been forthcoming. If disabled people were to be considered human beings, and not just a 'person with autism', then at least this would be a start.

Countless medics, scientists, academics, pharmaceuticals, therapists, trainers, charities and governmental organisations take advantage of the stereotypes attached to autism to soak up huge amounts of grant money or family savings just to make us less autistic. We are subjected to therapies that cause PTSD symptoms in many of the recipients. We are given enemas of industrial strength bleach. We are given anti-psychotic medication instead of changing the environment we live in. We are sources of revenue. We are lab rats to find the cause of what we are. Neurodivergent. Professionals focus on person-first language despite insistent and constant calls from autistic people and their rights organisations to respect our chosen identity and to stop conflating autism with negativity. The initial call to 'see the person first' may have had some merit in the 1970s, but the continued use of this language merely serves to underpin the idea that you can only be a person if the autism, and its manifestations, is literally or metaphorically removed as being something negative or unwanted. The goal is to remove all traces of our difference as it is better for us not to have to live the lives we live. They state, and some believe, that are doing us a favour by eliminating our disordered ways. Eliminating us.

Education is distilled down to 'Bewareness Training'. Watch out because they aren't like other children and display 'challenging behaviour'. Challenging to who?

Sometimes this can simply be saying 'no!' to the adult, thereby gaining an extra label of PDA. Voices from within various disabled groupings assume the mantle of 'voice of…' or 'autism advocate', who promote finding a 'cure' for what they perceive as devastating disorder that not only affects their child but also negatively impacts upon them (as a neurotypical) and their family, and further factionalise our worlds with personal opinion. People fighting for the right to impose their credo or pseudoscientific theories on us. What is gained by labelling and marginalising a person and refusing to see another way? What is achieved by refusing to accept that neurodivergence is difference and not disability? They cannot, or will not, perceive that there could be any cause for pride within our life or way of being.

My purpose in writing this is to use a life lived through changing times to offer observations gained from hard-earned experience. I don't claim to speak for everybody, but I lived through the horrors of Britain in the 1980s and the 90s. I experienced the deliberate disenfranchisement of entire regions and groups of people by central government and political dogma. I have seen the 'group' lose its importance and been replaced with the individual and the 'greed is good' mentality. The cost of that change to the most vulnerable of us has been huge, and hugely damaging for the main. My life moved from mentally ill outsider and freak through to a person with Asperger's syndrome and finally an acceptance of self as autistic and just different. I believe there are points to be drawn from my experience.

Most people caught in an intersectional existence, be it gender, race, sexuality or any other, hope to be the last of their kind. The last generation to be caught in oppressive, regressive thinking and restrictive practice. I am no different. I want to see neurodivergent children treated as human beings and not just damaged or disordered human 'becomings' who will never achieve their true potential due to ignorance. The Neurodiversity Movement is the key to this evolution. Read about it. Please.

We need to put aside the minutiae of our differences and focus on our commonalities. As the late Jo Cox said, 'We are far more united and have far more in common than that which divides us'. Our neurodivergence unites us and we must be proud of our difference.

Chapter 13: Female neurodiversity and the emotional leeching boyfriend

By Anon

I was on Facebook the other day when a friend posted an article about the way in which men depend entirely on women for emotional intimacy while women, in contrast, are able to create emotional support networks and are able to delegate their needs between multiple people, avoiding putting all of the burden on one person. It struck me as a little callous, but I had a hard time putting my finger on what exactly bothered me about the article itself. For the most part, it spoke about the unspoken truth of contemporary heterosexual relationships in today's society. But something felt off, and I couldn't explain why until I revisited the concept of male-female socialisation. The article itself framed the issue as almost biologically or societally inevitable, with men as poor victims of not being the 'finer sex' and women as trained social mavens, all perfectly skilled at intuiting their own social circles. Nothing actually challenged how we frame socialising around gender in an article entirely about the intersection of social needs and gender.

The concept of the 'male' vs 'female' brain, whether to justify sexism ('men have bigger, more competent brains'), scratch a niche curiosity itch, or to actually try to improve health, has been an area of scientific interest since the 19th century (Hofman & Swaah, 1991). Simon Baren-Cohen was the first to bring this rationale into the lens of Autism Spectrum Disorders, a group of neuro-developmental disorders that affects the way an individual socialises and communicates with others (especially with same-aged peers).

During the 1990s, Baren-Cohen used the concept of almost entirely dimorphic gendered brains to explain both the way that autistic people process information, and the gender disparity in autism diagnoses (4:1 male:female when I was diagnosed in 1994) (Baron-Cohen, 1999). According to this theory, human brains fall on a spectrum of being stronger in 'empathising' or 'systemising', with stronger 'empathising' being connected more to women, and stronger 'systemising' being connected to men. Autistic people, in this theory, are so strong at systemising and so underdeveloped in empathy that the qualities of a 'typical' male brain are amplified, thus making it an 'extreme' male brain. Cohen's previous theory on 'mind-blindness' specifically studied autistic people's inability to conceptualise the thoughts and feelings of others from their own perspective (Baron-Cohen, 1995), but wasn't able connect this lack of skill to autistic people's 'shallow but specific' hyperfocused interests, repetitive behaviours and aversion to change (according to Baron-Cohen's previous research). Maybe this is why the entire system feels incredibly artificially stitched together. Having empathy and organising things neatly aren't opposites of each other. To say that they are makes as much sense as saying being tall and being thin are opposites, and that the only middle ground is being of average height and weight. This of course also implies that people who are short and fat or tall and lean do not exist at all.

Regardless of this, the Extreme Male Brain theory is thrown into piles of his other poorly-done research: e.g. his 1985 article speculating whether or not autistic children have the capacity to understand 'theory of mind', his work on the 2001 "Autism Spectrum Quotent"- a diagnostic tool working off stereotypes more than symptoms, or his 2005 book theorizing that autism could be caused or related to prenatal testosterone. However, out of all of Baron-Cohen's work, the "Extreme Male Brain" feeds into the idea that the major differences in the social skills between men and women are biologically wired and not socially learned or reinforced. Social skills have 'skill' in the name; a skill is something that can be taught. If this were not the case, then any kind of autistic based 'intervention' or therapy would essentially be useless snake oil (many of them are, anyway). It would make cases of feral children like 'Genie' (1970s) nonsensical, because isn't socialising something 'hardwired' and not taught or reinforced? We treat socialising like an SD card slot that one lacks or has, and not like an entire coding language itself (how is body language not language?).

In the case of autism, socialising would be a second language to us that we had to learn differently than 'native speakers'. Our fluency and ability to translate into this second language of socialising is incredibly varied because we all sit on a spectrum and have different needs and abilities. Maybe autistic women and girls are pushed harder to learn the second language, so not as many people notice that it's not our first. Obviously, the girls that are caught in the spectrum diagnostically speaking have to be 'worse' at this language for people to hear the difficulties, as research points to early diagnosed girls of the spectrum showing more 'severe' symptoms as well (Evans *et al*, 2018).

I emphasise that social skills can be taught, because there is a huge difference in having a 'learning disorder' when it comes to social skills, and simply not practicing them at all. Many neurotypicals conflate the two, and the brunt of this mix-up falls on autistic people.

Men have the capacity to be socially charismatic, suave and cunning if they need to be. Male-dominated positions such as lawyers, politicians and businessmen all need to learn how to get what they want while balancing delicate social rules and norms. They need to be aggressive without strong-arming people into taking positions. They need to make clients believe that their ideas were actually the client's idea all along. If men were as socially clumsy as they say they are, they could never dream of taking these positions. Even positions traditionally associated with women, because of our 'empathy', such as teaching, nursing and therapy, were originally dominated by men.

Men are socially clumsy in a calculated, specific way dictated by the needs of a capitalist society, and capitalism itself created a shift from dependence on one's community to a dependence on a small nuclear family. Men from middle class families, who could afford to have their wife not work, were expected to throw all of their energy, time and motivation into the nine-to-five, 40+ hour work week grind. Women, regardless of their actual vocation or lack thereof, were expected to then pick up the slack – cooking, cleaning and raising the children. In this pile of 'women only' responsibilities was the responsibility of maintaining the family's social circles and social affairs. It was the women who set up play dates for their children and scheduled dinners out with other couples. The specific social skills allocated to women dealt with creating emotional support networks, socialising with peers in a non-professional environment, and conflict resolution in domestic situations.

In 2019, the norms around women in the white and blue collar workplaces has shifted dramatically, and the way that we talk about social justice issues and the wave of feminism that we're on is drastically different. However, even with this change, there is still an old hang-up among heterosexual couples that the the woman is responsible for managing friendship groups and maintaining social ties, and everyone acts like this is a biological inevitability that came out of nowhere. Furthermore, the social skills required in and out of the office are regarded differently based on the gender associated with using them. The charisma/social ladder climbing required to manoeuvre major careers are considered to be viable skills that you invest in and develop over time. The social skills needed to cope with emotions in a healthy way or form healthy, intimate platonic bonds with peers are considered up to chance and something that women automatically have without having to put any work into.

Being autistic is constantly being aware that socialising is work, something that is easily missed by neurotypicals. Neurotypicals are assumed, as women are assumed, to have no problems picking up body language, reading between the lines of what someone is saying, and communicating their needs and desires clearly, without issue. And most of the time, this is fairly correct. These 'baby men without social skills' can still pick up dates and significant others, still find (albeit emotionally stunted) friendship groups at young ages, collaborate efficiently in school projects and wing job interviews. Unlike with autistic people, socialising is almost a game to them, a skillset they turn on and off when it suits them best. If I cannot find a romantic partner as an autistic person, I can't socialise well in other spheres either. I will not improvise on a job interview well, or socialise with my co-workers well; I will not do well in school projects or find lots of friends among my school-aged peer group. If I fail, I fail across the board.

This isn't to say that neurotypicals all have stellar social skills. A lot of them socialise at an 8th grade reading level. The issue comes when people associate this with actual autism. A lot of neurotypicals socialise poorly because they refuse to put in the work to get to understand other people better, or to stop behaviours that hurt friends and create toxic relationships (romantic or otherwise). Egotism and self-obsession aren't the exclusive domain of people on the spectrum, they are character flaws that neurotypicals and autistic people alike fall prey to. A lot of ways people fail at socialising are poor character traits the person has failed to develop or confront, and because people want to give unlikable people the 'benefit of the doubt', these traits become pathologised as 'autistic behaviours' and get thrown in with 'can't pick up body language' or 'doesn't make enough eye contact' (more of a western cultural issue).

The benefit of the doubt plays more into the favour of autistic men, however. The autism diagnosis exists in the public eye as a 'white male only' disorder, so as 'official' wearers of the diagnosis they garner the most sympathy. In an effort to be 'friendly towards disability' and accommodating, well-meaning disability advocates make excuses for asshole behaviour that autistic men exhibit because they make it a part of their diagnosis instead of seeing it as part of their personality or how they actively choose to treat people (sometimes with the autistic man exploiting the reputation of the neurotype to do so).

Autistic women have no such luxuries. If we are not as obviously on the spectrum as Temple Grandin, we're not pegged as having the disorder at all. Instead, opposite to our opposite-gender peers, our autistic diagnosis becomes a personality flaw that we're responsible for. Any understanding of sarcasm, nuance or humour in general becomes evidence that we're 'faking' our disorders because we're not the poster boy for 'Autism Speaks'. As an autistic woman, I have a constant nagging fear of being the 'emotional man' in all of my relationships. I lack in social skills because of the autism and yet have this intense pressure to socialise correctly anyway because that is just what women do. It has resulted in me learning every social skills workshop, workbook and cheat sheet ten times over. I could recite the skills of 'active listening' in my sleep. It has also caused me to constantly play back every interaction I have with people in my mind, similar to how Applied Behaviour Analysis (ABA) enforces playing back recordings of a child acting wrong in order to correct it. Every little conversation gets analysed, and I never think my reactions and responses are correct unless I have someone else confirm it, and it slowly poisons the friendships that I have. ABA constantly plasters the message that you have to change everything about the way you interact with the world in order to reach the ultimate goal of 'seeming normal', and only if you seem 'normal' or 'invisible' can you get to the auxiliary goals of having friends, a significant other, or the other trappings of the suburbanite white picket fence dream.

Half of my deepest terrors lie in seeing myself reflected back behind the lens of a camera and 'looking autistic'. On the other hand, because women are expected to be incredibly socially competent, enough to put up with men with the emotional maturity of a toddler throwing a tantrum, when relationships go wrong, it's always assumed its because the woman is 'defective' in some way. She's a 'crazy ex girlfriend', the man 'dodged a bullet'. Men cannot be socially wrong enough to warrant blame for their part in a two-person romance, no matter how much they do wrong. Between these two philosophies, comes the lesson that if something goes wrong socially with other people, I am always the culprit and I am always the responsible party. This comes at a weight unique to autistic women, who are hit on two fronts, of having to be responsible for both their own actions and reactions, and the actions of other people. It is a severity that is foreign to neurotypcial women, who can always counter claims of a mental disorder with the (diagnosable) fact that they don't have one.

When neurotypical women discuss autism, they gender it as this: a predatory autistic man tormenting an innocent, neurotypical woman doing nothing wrong. First of all, it doesn't make sense to portray autistic men as extremely predatory in the face of socially competent men. While autistic men are still men, and still fall prey to the traps of toxic masculinity, they also still have autism colouring their actions. Autism almost has its own 'disability accent' that neurotypcials can pick up through socialising with us, or even an autistic person's voice having a flat affect with very little change in tone. Some of us can hide it, some of us are not so lucky. With this accent, with an autistic man spouting Mens Right Activist (MRA) ideas with no filter, with sexism so cartoony and outlandishly out there, it can be very blatantly obvious whether an autistic man is predatory or not. Autistic predatory men are easy to avoid because they're easier to spot. Like a poisonous frog, his colours are bright and right in your eyes. A predatory neurotypical man wears camouflage without changing how poisonous he is when ingested. A neurotypical man would know better than to state sexism outright, he would know what liberal feminist hot takes and talking points he should pepper his speech with to sound 'woke' and 'progressive'. He is better suited to being sexist because he's more aware of what he thinks women think sexism is. That will always make neurotypical men 100% more dangerous to women of any neurotype, and women without the social skills themselves to counter this can count themselves as sitting ducks. Neurotypical men will always be more dangerous to neurotypical Women than autistic men, and they are also 100% less fun to ridicule or lampoon.

When these non-autistic women previously made fun of 'sexism', they made fun of things associated with autistic nerds because they're low hanging fruit (mostly around personal hygiene and fashion choices). Things like 'Dorito fingers', 'neck beards', and fedoras were popular targets. Even autistic info-dumping became conflated with 'man-splaining'; which is an ironic misstep, given that it's autistic people who have their own neurotype and life experiences explained back to them by non-professionals (especially, 'I have an autistic son/cousin/sibling/niece's cousin's dog's babysitter's librarian'). This is in the exact same manner and condescending tone that men mansplain topics back to women who are actually experts in their given field. The treatment of autistic men as the sole proprietors of sexism tells me alone that neurotypical women don't count us in their definition of woman or feminism. We are the unfortunate neuters of the blue puzzle piece, boy-only disorder.

Making fun of autistic people is the exact same thing as making fun of the entire male gender to them. Autistic women are never given lip space in talks about the expectations of socialising put on different genders (when we have socialising hurdles), the performative aspects of femininity in regards to self-grooming practices (with the issues of hygiene, fine motor skills regarding makeup, and even sensory issues regarding clothing, skin lotion and hair styling), not even in the hurdles of women in STEM spaces (which, given how stereotypical it is for autistic people to be good at math or science, is a little surprising). We only seem to be remembered by a Sir Simon Baren-Cohen when he goes to explain women, men, autistic women with a 'male brain' and autistic men with an 'EXTREME male brain'. Outside of Baren-Cohen, we live in the periphery of social justice spaces. Even in the real world, our disorders don't exist simultaneously because we don't act 'autistic enough' and because no one wants to admit that they're still picking on an autistic girl for explicitly acting autistic.

References

Baron-Cohen S (1995) *Mindblindness: An essay on autism and theory of mind*. Cambridge: MIT Press.

Baron-Cohen S (1999) The extreme-male-brain theory of autism. In: HTager-Flusberg (Ed.), *Neurodevelopmental Disorders*. Cambridge, MA: The MIT Press.

Evans SC, Boan AD, Bradley C, Carpenter LA. Sex/Gender Differences in Screening for Autism Spectrum Disorder: Implications for Evidence-Based Assessment. *J Clin Child Adolesc Psychol*. 2019;48(6):840-854. doi:10.1080/15374416.2018.1437734

Hofman MA & Swaah DF (1991) Sexual dimorphism of the human brain: myth and reality. *Experimental and Clinical Endocrinology* **98** (5) 161–170. DOI: 10.1055/s-0029-1211113. PMID 1778230.

Chapter 14: The perpetual bookworm – avid reading and the moment the penny dropped

By Susan Harrington

When I submitted a PhD proposal relating to autism, knowledge and transformational learning in early 2018, the intention was always to conduct the research based on lived experience. My (now) 15-year-old son is autistic, and when I approached my supervisor with an entirely unrelated topic, he pointed out the value that this lived experience could add to autism research. It is safe to say, however, that neither of us had any idea just how much lived experience I had to offer…

When research uncovers more than expected

Although I started researching from the point of view of an autism parent, being an unapologetic bookworm and devourer of information meant it didn't take long before I started reading about autistic women and girls, and the sheer number of undiagnosed autistic women. And then the penny began to drop. I had started mentioning my research to various people, leading a friend to open up to me about having recently been diagnosed in her early 40s, and I was curious. As mother to an autistic son, I had heard plenty of light-hearted (albeit, actually quite offensive) comments about him having inherited it from me, but never paid too much attention until this point. In fact, if I wasn't researching autism, I probably still wouldn't have paid much attention. I've always felt I was a bit of an outsider, that person who's not quite in a group but also not quite not in it, but that was just me. Even reading everything I could find about autistic women and girls wasn't out of the ordinary, as far as I was concerned.

I love reading. I will read anything, and once I start I cannot stop until I'm done. Ok, so my research wasn't specifically related to women and girls, but you know, I am a woman, and I have the seemingly inevitable middle-aged woman rage about being disadvantaged because of my sex, so off on a reading spree I went. I'm what you might call a completer-finisher. I get a bee in my bonnet and I'm not happy until I've sorted it. If you can see where this is going, you are already well ahead of where I was at the time. Anything I could get my hands on, I read it. Blogs, books, academic papers, none of it was safe from me and my curiosity. And eventually (because I may be reasonably intelligent and an avid reader, but I'm not always the quickest at realising what's going on beyond what is explicitly spelled out) it hit me. These people were writing about me.

I had essentially become thoroughly engrossed in reading checklist after checklist of how my own life had played out so far. Not only was I researching an as autism parent, with the hope of contributing to making the world a bit better for my son, I was researching as an autistic woman, based on over three decades of first-hand lived experience. I might not have known it, but perhaps that's even better. Maybe there's some added value in not knowing that there was a reason why I behaved (or didn't behave) in a certain way. From a research perspective, it feels purer that I am looking back on my history which was entirely unaffected by any accommodation or adjustment for my autistic traits. That means that, when I look at how this transformational learning occurs in autistic people, I'm looking at how it occurred in me while I was being treated as neurotypical. Would knowing I was autistic have made a difference to how I lived my life, and how my parents approached certain situations? Probably, just as I would treat my son differently if I did not know he was autistic. The world is full of should and should nots, all of which have been designed to accommodate NTs and, growing up as an NT, this is what I was expected to adhere to. From a personal point of view, and a mental health point of view, there have definitely been negatives to that, but, with my researcher hat on, I feel there is value to it.

Maybe that's something that I'm trying to convince myself is true as a kind of antidote to the feeling of not fitting in, being a bit weird, not always being quite sure why things I said were so funny… To be bluntly honest, trying to convince myself that the years of anxiety, depression, frustration and despair were worth it. I'm not for a moment claiming that my life has been miserable, of course, but there have perhaps been more troughs than peaks. Anyone who is neurodivergent – a term which spans much more than just autism – can more than likely relate to the feeling of 'why on earth can I not just do what everyone else seems to find so easy?'

This is not intended to be full of self-pity, so I'm not going to dwell on the feelings that being neurodivergent has either directly or indirectly contributed to throughout my life, but rather on how I can now use those feelings, emotions, and experiences to help ensure that it's better for those who come after me. If that's not motivation to put my all into this research, what is?

The dawning of my realisation

Going back to reading about undiagnosed autistic women, and what I now refer to (even if just in my own head) as the checklist of my life, here's some of what pushed me towards finding an online AQ test and getting some kind of confirmation of what I now strongly suspected. I am, of course, aware of the issues with the AQ test, and don't agree with the various empathising/systemising, mindblindness, and extreme male brain theories that are behind it (Baron-Cohen, 1995; 2001; 2002; 2009), but it's what I had to work with, so I used it. There is a definite need for better autism diagnostic tools, or perhaps a need to do away with the notion that autism is something that needs to be diagnosed, and not just a 'normal' variation of the human mind (after all, what is normal anyway?), but that's a discussion for another day. And one which I am more than happy to bore anyone to death with – open invitation to anyone who wants it. That's before I get started on the difficulty in having a GP take me seriously ('You're 36, what difference will a diagnosis make now?') and the incredibly long waiting list, which I am still occupying a space on. While I've been writing this, I've had a letter confirming that I am on the waiting list, and a questionnaire for my parents to fill in, so fingers crossed it won't be too much longer (although, that leads to the spiral of 'what if I don't get a diagnosis?).

If you're reading this and wondering what, exactly, it was that led me to this rather important moment of self-understanding, perhaps because you're having a similar experience yourself, here's my basic list. Much of it is random things I remember reading *somewhere* and identified with when I first began exploring the possibility of being autistic myself and, to be very clear, I am not attempting to generalise at all, merely to outline and explain what stood out to me, but here it is:

Married young, got divorced.

Diagnosed with anxiety and depression for pretty much my entire adult life (and, with hindsight, it was always there).

Difficulty maintaining friendships.

Terrible at exams, no matter how well I know the material (I also don't do well with being asked direct questions).

Sensory problems with food textures and certain sounds.

There are quite a few but they're not what's important about me. Neither are your own, or anyone else's, perceived deficits what defines you. In the interests of discussion, I will say some more about how and why I identified with these particular traits.

- **Being an avid reader.** Much as the stereotypical male autistic child lines up cars, or memorises facts about dinosaurs, I read absolutely everything. I learned how to read at a very early age (around three) and from that day onwards, I read. Everything. Cereal boxes, the small prints on ads, every book I could get my hands on… I read them all. One of my favourites was encyclopaedias, and my family still talk about how, aged around seven, I told my teacher that she was wrong, there is an animal whose name starts with Q, and it is called a quagga. To the teacher's credit, she believed me, wrote it on the board, and went home to find out if I did indeed have some very specialist knowledge. I did.

- **Being terrible at exams.** This is very much a divisive one, as a look at a recent thread on my Twitter account will show (@susanisainmdom), but one thing that struck a chord when I read it in Laura James' *Odd Girl Out* (James, 2017) and elsewhere, was my inability to perform well at exams. I never did badly as such, but I could never quite achieve what I was capable of. Hence starting university at 31, when my youngest child went to school and I could get in through an access course rather than relying on my Leaving Certificate results (360 points, for Irish people who know what that means and just how, well, mediocre, it is). On a similar vein, if you ask me a question, I'll stare at you blankly for a few seconds, even if I know the answer. This doesn't mean that I don't know, or that I can't remember, I just cannot retrieve what I know on demand. It took me four attempts (at the age of 34) to pass my driving test, because I cannot bear being watched or tested.

- **Being over sensitive.** This is another thing that was said about me a lot when I was younger. If you confront me, I will cry. If I am angry, I will cry. Basically, I cry. I cannot process emotion until I have cried and gotten past that initial feeling of 'OHMYGODMASSIVEEMOTIONANDTOOMANYFEELINGS' and been able to work out what I'm really feeling. This may be 10 minutes later, it may be a week later. Whenever it occurs, I'll want to talk to you about what I really meant when I said something that wasn't actually what I wanted to say. Chances are, you'll have forgotten by then, but I'll need to get it out of my system anyway. I also take on other people's emotion a lot. I over-empathise to the point where I am drained and exhausted. In fact, there are times when I would welcome some degree of not being able to empathise, but I can categorically state that is not a universal autistic trait.

There are also plenty of perhaps more stereotypical traits that I can now relate to. I've always been a picky eater because I cannot tolerate certain textures. When my sons were babies, the sound of them crying physically hurt me, to the point where I would dread them waking up. If plans get changed, I get a little panicky. I *definitely* have special interests. Much of what is said about autistic girls and their special interests being people rather than things seemed to describe me to a tee. I hate mess, but struggle to get the motivation to clean the house. I'm either unstoppable or unstartable, and can identify strongly with pretty much everything I've read about monotropism (Murray *et al*, 2005), in particular with the link between monotropism and flow made at a talk by Damien Milton I attended at PARC's 2018 conference in Glasgow. I've been diagnosed with, and medicated for, anxiety since I was about 19. I had PND after both births. I've always felt like I don't fit in, like I'm somehow different, and I'm always, *always* tired. This world is not made for me, or people like me, and it is exhausting. But this is all ok now, because I know why it happens, and I can make sense of it.

How my own autism helps shape my research

My PhD topic relates to threshold concepts (Meyer & Land, 2003) and transformational learning, and how these present in autistic people. Briefly, a threshold concept is an element of learning which transforms the learner. It's not just learning some new information, or acquiring new knowledge, it involves a significant personal change which is very difficult, if not impossible, to undo or unlearn. The 'downside' of this transformation is that the learner must go through a difficult process to get there. Just as a child becomes an adult only through navigating puberty (which can be a troublesome time for those around the young person in question, never mind the young person themselves!), and a caterpillar becomes a butterfly in the cocoon, I have been through a troublesome, transformative, and irreversible experience which has undoubtedly changed my sense of self, and how I appear to others.

When I first became interested in threshold concepts, I was under the impression that I was neurotypical and, as such, was experiencing life and its various challenges much as everyone else could be expected to. So, although my research topic has remained the same, my perspective on it was virtually turned on its head just a short time into the project. The thing that may seem surprising to anyone who has not had such a realisation about themselves is that this was an entirely positive experience. The preceding 36 years, however, could most definitely be described as troublesome and difficult to navigate…

Admittedly, I do have some minor concerns about being accepted for who I am, and some internal debates around just how open I should be about being an (for now, self-diagnosed) autistic woman. Although, in fact, realising that I am autistic myself has been infinitely less challenging than awaiting diagnosis for my son. After almost eight years of very little sleep, severely delayed speech, various other missed 'milestones', and a constant, overwhelming feeling of 'why on earth can I not just do what everyone else seems to find so easy?', his actual diagnosis was very much welcomed. I felt no shame in having an autistic son, but what I did feel was worried.

Worried about his future and how his life would turn out. Worried about how people would perceive him and treat him. Worried about how he would cope when I wasn't around anymore to help. Worried about how I could make sure that he, for want of a better phrase, lived his best life.

Although autism research was not my initial choice (ironically, I felt like I was living in an autism bubble and should do something different), I very quickly realised that I could make this experience count. As the psychiatrist who diagnosed Jack said, he wasn't doing (or not doing) specific things to be difficult, he was having a difficult time. Why would any parent not want to take the opportunity to make even the tiniest difference to that, not only for Jack, but for all the other autistic children and adults who are going to need to navigate this world at some point?

Who knew I was one of those autistic people? If reactions are to be believed, around half of my friends for a start. Especially the one who tried so hard not to head-tilt and say, 'Well, duh', that it was incredibly obvious that's what she was doing. That's still one of my favourite moments; it was hilarious. What I can say? Even just a few months on from the realisation that I am neurodivergent, accepting myself for who I am has been life-changing. I'm more comfortable in myself, I don't try to be what I 'should' be (most of the time, I'm still working on this), and I've now got a fantastic partner who accepts and loves me for who I am, and shares my disdain for the word 'should'.

Autism, in itself, is not necessarily a problem. There may be other co-occurring disabilities and health problems making the lives of autistic people difficult, but autism is, generally, a disability in a social sense, rather than a medical one (Woods, 2017). Autism is not something to be cured, or eradicated, or prevented, or whatever else the numerous proponents of devastatingly dangerous 'treatments' would like us to believe. The problem is the world we live in, where each of us is expected to conform to a sense of normal that doesn't really exist. We're supposed to act in a certain way, like certain things, enjoy being gregarious, extroverted, multi-talented, well, robots, who all come from the same mould. That isn't reality. What is real is that humans are individuals, and each and every one of us should be celebrated.

The importance of making a difference

It did not take long, once I became aware of autism, to also become all too aware of just how much misinformation there is about it. I was probably guilty of believing some of it myself, before I was to all intents and purposes forced to pay more attention to autism, what it actually is, and what it is not. I'm deliberately not going into detail about my son's autism, because that is his story to tell, if and when he decides he wants to.

I can't change the world. I can't single-handedly remove the prejudices, stereotypes and negativities about anything that is deemed to be 'other', whether that is autism, gender, religion, race… the list is endless because, when normal doesn't exist, the truth is that we are all 'other'.

I am enough. Both of my sons are enough. We are all enough.

That is why learning from lived experience is incredibly important, and that is why I, and numerous other researchers (not to put words in their mouths), are working to be heard. To have the value of all neurodivergent people recognised, acknowledged and actively embraced. Yes, we are different. Yes, some of us can be disarmingly blunt, or stim in a way that makes other feel uncomfortable, or have any number of annoying habits. But so can neurotypical people. Because diversity of any kind should be celebrated, and that is exactly what I intend to do. I have already learnt a massive amount from my own experience, and it's only been around a year since I realised that was, in fact, my personal experience of being autistic. Jack has taught me an incredible amount over the past 14 years too, not least of which is that autistic people can be just as caring, funny, bright and downright stubborn and annoying as their neurotypical counterparts. Much of my experience of parenting Jack is exasperating beyond words, but there is a lot of pride involved in knowing that I have created this person who has enough conviction in his beliefs to hand his mother his beloved Xbox and say, 'I'm not going to school'. As an aside, parenting his NT brother is also exasperating beyond words at times. I suspect it's the responsibility of raising decent human beings that is a problem, not their individual neurotypes.

So, how does this all fit in with my research, in terms of learning from my lived experience? Quite simply, although my research topic has not changed, the perspective from which I am approaching it has, vastly. The realisation that, despite thinking that I was NT for 36 years, I am actually one of the autistic people I was seeking to help. I'm deliberately not going into huge amounts of detail about my research, as I want this to focus on lived experience. For now. Through that experience, I have become both researcher and research participant, alongside mother of a potential research participant. I have an insight I did not know I had, and I continue to learn from that every day. Perhaps most importantly, I'm learning that my own experience is not the same as anyone else's and, although I can do my utmost to help as many members of the autistic community as possible with whatever my research output turns out to be, it won't apply to everyone. Just as the past and current theories of autism do not apply to everyone. At present, I do not believe that there is a single definition of autism, nor any one theory or model which can be applied appropriately and helpfully across the board. In fact, I'm not sure I believe there should be any single autism model or theory, nor that autism is anything which requires a theory.

I'm also left-handed and, while that would have been treated as 'wrong' in the not-so-distant past (Flatt, 2008), it's now just an accepted deviation from the 'norm' of being right-handed, although the world is still predominantly aimed at right-handed people (scissors and tin-openers, I'm looking at you). Left-handed tools and versions of everyday products have been made available, and nobody judges you as 'other' for being left-handed. Maybe this is the ideal for autistic people. Having said that, I reserve the right to change my mind on this, just as I've changed my mind on so many other things over the past year of research, and 14 years of parenting.

Recognising differences, learning from new knowledge and experiences, and being open-minded to the realisation that you've been wrong, and willing to put that right, are what I think are important about conducting research based on lived experience. And that research is essential. As Donna Williams put it, '...*Right from the start, from the time someone came up with the word 'autism' [it] has been judged from the outside by its appearances, and not from the inside according to how it is experienced*' (Williams, 1996, p14). It's time to start focusing on what it is, from the inside, according to those who really know. This is what my experience has taught me.

Finally, I would like to be clear that I am not at all stating that all autism research has been wrong. There's been a lot of excellent, relevant, truly helpful research done, particularly in recent years. I would perhaps even argue that many of those early researchers who got it wrong, did their best based on the knowledge and information which was available to them at the time. ABA I will never defend or excuse, but plenty of the now-outdated research probably came from good intentions. When we refine and rewrite the literature relating to autism, we do that due to learning from lived experience. Autistic researchers, and those NT researchers who truly involve and listen to autistic participants, are doing exactly that, and the importance of it cannot be stressed enough.

The special interests/hyperfocus/monotropism thing, though? That's true (in my experience). Take it from someone who's currently learning Arabic for no real reason, and has realised it's suddenly 3am more than once recently, following a totally oblivious few hours of 'just one more Duolingo lesson'...

References

Baron-Cohen S (1995) *Mindblindness: An Essay on Autism and Theory of Mind*. Cambridge, Mass: The MIT Press.

Baron-Cohen S (2002) The extreme male brain theory of autism. *Trends in Cognitive Sciences* **6** 248–254.

Baron-Cohen S (2009) Autism: The Empathizing–Systemizing (E-S) Theory. Annals of the New York *Academy of Sciences* **1156** 68–80.

Baron-Cohen S, Wheelwright S, Skinner R, Martin J & Clubley E (2001) The Autism-Spectrum Quotient (AQ): Evidence from Asperger syndrome/high-functioning autism, males and females, scientists and mathematicians. *Journal of Autism and Developmental Disorders* **31** 5–17.

Flatt AE (2008) Is being left-handed a handicap? The short and useless answer is 'yes and no.' *Proceedings* (Baylor University. Medical Center) **21** 304–307.

James L (2017) *Odd Girl Out*. London: Bluebird.

Meyer J & Land R (2003) Threshold Concepts and Troublesome Knowledge: Linkages to ways of thinking and practising within the disciplines.

Murray D, Lesser M & Lawson W (2005) Attention, monotropism and the diagnostic criteria for autism. *Autism* **9** 139–156.

Williams D (1996) *Autism: An Inside-Out Approach: An innovative look at the 'mechanics' of 'autism' and its developmental 'cousins'*. London: Jessica Kingsley Publishers.

Woods R (2017) Exploring how the social model of disability can be re-invigorated for autism: in response to Jonathan Levitt. *Disability & Society* **32** 1090–1095.

Chapter 15: A few words on a lot of living

By Paul Wady
September 2019

My name is Paul Wady. I had no idea I was autistic until I was diagnosed in May 2004. I was given the label of 'autistic'. Not even high functioning. Just autism. I remain feeling very happy about that. You can read about how this happened in my interview in *The Guardian* Weekend Magazine, October 2005.

By 2006 I was working for the much-loved National Autistic Society. I have been there ever since. I have held numerous roles such as teaching meditation to autistic people in one of their adult services. I have also worked in their head office. I've held a few part time roles there, set up and ran the Ladbroke Grove Autism centre social group, and ended up in training. I now tour the UK telling people what it is like to be me, with a presentation entitled 'Being Me'. I also talk about stress, anxiety and being autistic.

I deliver these talks to teachers, social workers, all manner of council employees, you name them. I once 'did' a rather rich company outside of London who were working on pharmaceuticals for autism, whatever that means. I did try and warn them it was all placebos and a waste of time. They took it quite well, I think. I will be covering curing later on.

During my talks I add anything I feel like at the time. So all the current thinking from online, and thus all of what everyone online and autistic tend to say, gets given to such people. I did a room full of psychiatrists in Leatherhead three years ago. I'd crack a joke and they would all go...HMMMMMMM very intensely. I thought, they are not going to let me go home.

I joined a group of autistic people, interchanging over the years, who have been trying to influence the NAS internally since they joined it. I made and narrated the *Ask Autism* training module films for them, together with Dr Dinah Murray, and voiced over the NAS's *Do you know what Autism is?* film. I've co-conducted countless job interviews as the 'autistic person on the panel' and been in more autistic colleague and feedback meetings than I can count. I've advised and spoken to staff, and, as I explained earlier, I set up and ran the Ladbroke Grove autism centre social group before going over to training.

Working part time meant I could put time and energy into other things. Back in 2007 there was an attempt at an autistic political self-advocacy initiative called the Politics of Autism group. This led to the London Autistic Rights Movement, which imploded five years later in 2012. It ended its days a small gang of dictators who did not need to listen to others. I wonder why? (Yes, that is sarcasm).

There was clearly a need for a self-advocacy movement to address governments and the National Health Service, that was 100% autistic led and represented. I have always tried to facilitate such initiatives rather than lead them.

So to these ends I have only tried to do two things: to make sense of everything, and to facilitate others. I have always tried to adhere to this mission statement, and as an attempted Buddhist, it has served me well. I try to be a conduit for others whom I consider to be more effective and positive, autistic self-advocates. I spend my life looking for better ideas than my own. Trying to zero in or focus on the best vision of being positive and healthy as an autistic person. Then going in that direction with my work.

In 2015 I published a book called *Guerilla Aspies – a neurotypical society infiltration manual*. The format was the best I could come up with to say everything I wanted to at the same time. It's been successful and I am now in my third round of self-publishing. That year I also started performing a show on the Edinburgh Festival Fringe, and around the country, which converted audiences to being autistic. It too is called 'Guerilla Aspies', and often has publicity taglines such as *BECOME AUTISTIC WITH PAUL WADY* or *THE WORLD'S LONGEST RUNNING NEURODIVERSIFICATIONAL SHOW*. Which so far it is.

In 2017 I started the Stealth Aspies theatre company with some autistic friends, and three (performing) and two (calendar) years on we have just finished a small tour funded by the Arts Council of Great Britain. (Well I just *had* to write that, didn't I, darlings…) Yes, everyone in the decision-making process and performances was autistic. We only used survey response material from other autistics, finding ourselves on stage through the words of other people we had usually never met before. Or using our own writing and poems.

We hope to continue indefinitely. I personally have become a yearly fixture on the Brighton and Edinburgh festivals, walking around day and night in my message t shirts. I wear these non-stop I get to the cities, and until I leave on the trains home.

I also produce and sell badges and even fridge magnets. I spend my life trying to think of any other things I could possibly produce…

The reason for all of this is that none of it existed before. So I created it all in order that it be part of history. That somewhere there was the presence of these messages, and that people of all neurotypes could at least be aware that such perspectives were being expressed in this way. The rise of the global internet has really facilitated and justified all of this.

I have performed my solo shows all over the country as well as in Dublin and New York City. The book has travelled far and wide, too. Apparently, in last year's Autscape, many people were walking around wearing my badges. Very touching. I have met so very many autistic people now. I swear that if you all go find a gathering of six ordinary people anywhere in this country, at least one will have a connection with someone autistic. Let alone be on the spectrum. A friend who runs a mentoring and supporting organisation was surprised at this figure. He had already decided it was more like a group of eight people. Minimum.

So, the point I wanted to make was that my advocacy has not taken the traditional role of academia or rote instruction of the properties of being on the spectrum. I have tried to invent and spread a conceptual advocacy. A creative and performance art one, in which the world can learn about us outside of the text – book and the lecture. The staid traditional formats of knowledge access.

2019 has been an eventful year for me. I organised the protest at the Southwark Playhouse and have spent a lot of time developing perspectives on Twitter. I found myself debating with what appears to be an organised cult of very depressed, mainly autistic people who do not like being autistic. They don't want anyone else to, either. There seems to be an attempt amongst them to make anyone out who tries to be positive about their autistic natures, as holding the rigid ideas of a cult which they named 'The Neurodiversity Movement'.

I hold such people to possess all the properties of a Neurodiversity Movement themselves. Publically identifying as autistic. Coming together as a group on the basis of that identity. Holding views and ideas in common and being bonded by such. Reacting and agitating towards others together in organised actions. Debating issues around the term autism and being autistic almost daily. Why that is funny – sounds like they are a schism of the very thing they reject?

They have done well for small numbers, and have recruited many unhappy parents and over intellectualising autistic people – usually single – into their group.

Together with the ABA, general therapy and treating autism etc. crowd. Oh, and rumour has it that Autism Speaks tends to pass on their Tweets?

All I see in the so-called ND Mob which I find myself a member of, is just a collection of individuals who hold some ideas in common. I am not aware of a rigid party line. Maybe no one will tell me about it? ☹ Autistics are the most self-defining and non-group member people you could meet, so I've no idea how you go around projecting the opposite onto us. If you believe in cures as many of the miserable group do, then off you go – get cured. Go on, try it! What's a little trauma, brain damage or death?

Personally I don't think the frame of reference of curing is real. I think it is a fantasy that has yet to be debunked. I think we are all made the way we are and aside from mental health issues which you can address, treat and actually cure, we are all hereditary neuroatypicals. That's all. So we have to make the best of it in life while we can.

So for me, 2019 was definitely the year when self-advocacy really came into play. When a social scene became apparent and many people figured upon it. All self-identifying as standing up for being autistic in a positive way. One reason was that we had a negative to contrast our positive. We saw the visible forming of a schism or reactionary opposite group which held that the only real autism was when you are severely disabled and qualify for a diagnosis. The publication of Jonathan Mitchell's ragingly paranoid Spectator article in January, announced the presence of this. (One thing I have to note is the strange, utterly polarised nature of this social group. Many people involved of course did not take the whole thing that seriously, but an element remain utterly devoted to a negative vision of neurodiversity that seems to define them as people. They do not realise that you can hold several opposing views about yourself at once).

Now, at this point I would like to ask you to do something. We all hear about treatments, interventions, cures, and just plain 'helping you with your autism' things. Okay, so can you go away and prove that all these things or however you may categorise them, do more than just these two points:

ONE – Alleviate anxiety and tension, then enable you to learn social skills, cope better with the world and mask really well.

OR

TWO – Are just smokescreens that look like they change you. When really you are just one more late developer like the rest of us who then catches up and develops social skills, and gets on top of the elements of your autistic nature that limit and disable you.

You see, I am convinced that these two explanations are all that ever goes on in the world of curing. That's it. Please prove me wrong?

This year I have had people make out I have a bad attitude towards people with mental health issues. Well, if I could get over my own constant anxiety and forget about my suicidal depression phase in the early 80s, then maybe I could manage one. But The Doctor, yes that doctor, always treated everyone he met the same way. So I have never seen any need to behave any other way.

I have always supported others and loved the most vulnerable, because I knew that was who and what I was. I know what it's like when you cannot stand up to others. When people don't relate to you and get nasty about it. I was also brought up to think that kindness was always the right thing. I know what it is like when you want to be different, but you cannot change. When everyone around you calls you names and ignores you.

To an extent I will always be like a small child. I know that. This is part of my autistic nature. I will always be vulnerable in ways I spend every day both hiding and denying to myself and others. Let alone working around.

Paradoxically, my internalised Ableism is an attitudinal mechanism that enables me to relate to certain kinds of hard core neurotypicals. To have the identity that I often use around people. A bad attitude to dysfunctionality and a claim to competency, ability and not being disabled. I do not know if I will ever recover from this. I am working on it, but I have to admit I think that it's always been a viable and irreplaceable protocol with which to go through the world. A means of being taken seriously and 'talking the talk' that Neurotypicals can relate to in that special way of communicating we as a kind can never quite get.

Paradoxically, I have always been anti ableist, and supported and loved everyone I met who was more vulnerable than me if I could. But the fact is that in order to function and relate, I have the capacity to aggressively reject the mistakes and lack of abilities of others. This paradox haunts me to this day.

So I admit I can be the bad guy. But I know that, and I only use this side of me to survive and get through. I am sorry if you were expecting me to make out I am a wonderful human being. This is what it did to me, not knowing I was autistic until I was 41. You end up a sordid thing in some respects.

I have met a huge number of autistic people of all ages. Children, teenagers and adults. The one thing they had in common was not just being autistic. It was also their trying daily to pretend they were not autistic.

There does not seem to be any research into masking as a way of life; as an inescapable effect that you embrace when you are born. Everyone does it. It takes the form of ordinary social skills. Relating to your community. Being British. Being from the South. Being from Eastbourne. We all try to be polite. We try to talk in a way that others can understand. Masking. Social skills. Survival. Being human.

An autism diagnosis, comments on specific clichés of being autistic such as personality traits, behaviours and responses. But they will all be mitigated by masking and social skills. So I think what we see as being on the spectrum is really this hybrid interpretation of our natures and our acts.

People whose autistic natures are on top of them and are dominated by them show us the truth about ourselves. People like myself, who are relatively skilled at neurotypical behaviours and relating, and don't have that many visible sensory issues, are socially acceptable liars: actors. (Well yes, I must be, because I just got an Equity card this year, Darling.)

The more you are on top of your autistic nature, the more you can do the ableist attitude and the more society will accept you. This is wrong. You know, before I knew I was autistic I used to talk about the 'tyranny of competence' in our society. About how people defined their identities just by what they could get right. This effect alone surely causes so many of us pain. Every day trying to do things socially that are not natural to us. Walking down streets, interacting with people, using public transport. All that. The things that the everyday folks take for granted. They expect us to, too. But we cannot. But we must. But we cannot. But we must. Round and round it goes in our lives, the eternal antagony of living in a neurotypical society.

If you want to know where autism really comes from, look for family members who are very good at not looking autistic. People who can relate really well to others and to their work. They may be using a skill rather than being naturally empathetic with others. Because behaving in a Neurotypical manner is a skill you can perfect. It's an art. That is how I think stuff like ABA works.

My point is that between ourselves we can de-programme from these maskings we practice. The maskings many of us hold as our identities and self-respect, and even abilities with which to survive and achieve. We can find our true natures in each other. Having spent a huge fraction of my life in a Buddhist movement, I am convinced this will do nothing but benefit our mental health. It is the disparity that causes problems; when you go against your true nature. I think that, in order to be well and healthy, we must make peace with our autistic natures; at least find a compromise.

Stim secretly. Be quietly obsessive. Allow our energies to run around in a socially acceptable way. Take into account your sensory issues and work around them and even appease them whilst integrating into the ordinary world. But do not deny and hate them. Find a way to embrace them positively.

Some of you may say that's impossible. But that, I think, is the challenge of being born autistic. The rest is a brave quest and personal effort.

Well done to everyone for being here in this book and for yourself for reading it this far. In solidarity as autistic people. Not as people 'with' being autistic. I am male, not a person with being a bloke. It's a defining part of my overall identity. To say we are people with our autistic natures has always for me been an attempt to estrange ourselves from what we are and how we were made in the first place. It's alienating you from you.

I see this as a state of being in denial, because you have an idea of how things should be, and you are not able to be entirely or partially like that. Everyone human can get that. It's called being unsatisfactory and not content with yourself. It is making a statement to yourself, that your autistic nature does not define you as a person. Some of us, of course, hate being autistic. We have a strong need to estrange ourselves from our autistic natures. So please beware of doing that to yourself. I think it will only cause you abstract pain. For me that is not a real thing.

By the end of the century all our frames of reference may be redundant. Humanity will be seen as a neurodivergent race of beings. Normal and abnormal, as I grew up understanding the terms in the 1960s and 1970s, will be gone. The idea that all people can be understood by having different hereditary brain types will, I believe, be the prevalent way of seeing humans. Simple as that.

This is because we've all grown up accepting frames of reference that we contributors, here, are now part of changing or denying. This is a radical gathering of authors. Writing history. It could be said, I think, that NeuroAtypical stereotypes of being, and the tyranny of competence and ability to do things and relate to others in certain ways, is being unmasked as the group fraud it is; that it is being challenged and changed by such books as this.

We all face mental health issues. All human's do. We must believe that we all have the potential to survive and be happy, to progress in our minds and become positive. As a Buddhist, I cannot emphasise enough how important that is. Anxiety seems to be a normal part of all our lives. It's one more enemy we face every day. We must be strong and find self-love. Do not give into depression and pain. Nor fall into addiction and take our frustrations out on others. Be brave and form friendships with other autistics. We relate to each other as we do ourselves. We can survive. Don't end up ruled by pain. Speaking of which…

Is there anyone on social media who does not find examples of others being lied about on there? Or at least others or themselves being misrepresented. My point is that some of the attempts to do this show the same recurring style.

1. People seem to relate to you, but really they are either relating to themselves or to a group of like-minded people.

2. You get ignored when you relate to them, and they just go around in their own circles. They state things without any regard to you.

3. There is this staged narrative going on. They think anyone reading what they write just sees things the way they want them to be seen. Without any of their tricks showing.

Actually they just cannot conceive of anyone smarter and more aware than they are and how they would read what they write. So do not worry if you get this.

I recommend that, if you get anything like this on social media, you just disengage and ignore it. None of it is real. It's not part of the real world at all. Just silly. But as autistic people we are prone to obsessing. So we must remember that. We must be able to stop ourselves and say no to drowning in online dialogues that are neurotic and basically abusive or, and possibly at the same time, which are ultimately self-destructive.

By now an entire culture of personality types has emerged that represent various clichés of being autistic people. I once drew up a series of tables for the National Autistic Society caricaturing such people. The young and hyper-active, the self-centred and without social skills. The mature and undiagnosed long-term 'in the closet' type. Perhaps they have survived inside themselves by being good at things that pay, or that rewarded them with contentment. Or both. Bookish, formal and rather parsimonious about getting facts right. Able to justify their ritualistic and rigid behaviours and hide them in plain sight.

Then there are those more determined by mental health issues, which ride their natures and express themselves through pain, a self-centred and negative interpretation of everyone and everything and, of course, have had a terrible time in life. Leaving them rather cruel and nasty, and some without conscience.

Previously we had no frame of reference to grow up with in terms of the personality types of our own kind. 'Rain Man' is not that impressive for your self-respect in our society. But I always found Faraday, Pasteur and Newton would have looked good on me. So what is autistic? Cool? Sheldon Cooper? Saga Noren, the brazenly autistic woman in the lead of the television series 'The Bridge'? The autistic Power Ranger in the most recent film, or Spock, the half human hero of the Star Trek franchise?

This is a major issue, dwelling as I do in my work with sub cultural images. Over the different years of my solo Guerilla Aspies show, I have given the world numerous tropes of myself on posters. One as a Che Guevara figure. Another as a Superman, with ASPIE on my chest instead of a Kryptonian logo. Then in 2018 I used an image that had me covering my face with the original Guerilla Aspies book. This year, 2019, it was a version of me as a puppet hero – Captain Scarlett. Drawn for me by the autistic artist Ash Lloydon. A comment on the All in a Row play protest I organised at the very start of this year.

I think that to survive and progress we must remain strong in the face of our own natures. We must remember that we can have better lives if we stay positive. Otherwise we self-destruct.

Crucified on the wheels of our OCD. Ground down with the energy of our ADHD. Destroyed by our sensitivity issues. So we must be positive about our lives, each other and our autistic natures. Find new ways to face each day. Forgive other people when they upset us, and find people to be with who do not. Consider how we hurt ourselves by being so self-focused and pedantic, obsessive and relentless in our feelings and energy.

Good luck and thank you.

Paul Wady, September, 2019.

Chapter 16: Communicating away the barriers

by Anna Barzotti

'Without deviation from the norm, progress is not possible.' – Frank Zappa

In my youth I struggled with communication. I was very shy and found speaking fluidly quite difficult. After leaving school, my subconscious mission was to learn about people. In my own quiet way, I set out to meet as many different people as possible so I could get a broad understanding of how humans communicate together and what makes someone an 'acceptable' member of a social group. By 'different' I mean people who I didn't go to school with, that didn't live in the same town as me and whose backgrounds I did not find familiar. I wanted to learn how to be like those people that seemed to be able to be their natural selves in any situation. I wanted to know how to live life fully and learn how to 'play the game' that everyone mentioned but never actually explained. I could not fathom it and was often told I came across as too quiet or too sullen or too moody or, from the age of 17, too aggressive.

In most situations I found myself on the periphery. I was there but not fully there. I was too timid or confused to immerse myself entirely. Occasionally I met people who I felt comfortable with but most of the time I was slightly on edge and always relieved to get back to a place where I could be on my own and escape into books or TV or whatever obsession was currently on my mind.

I realised that I needed to think about what to do with my life and I based that on what I felt needed fixing in me. After a series of misadventures in my early 20s, I decided that being an actress would help me to be more confident around people. I joined an amateur theatre group and went to acting classes. I applied for a place on a degree that I thought was acting but turned out to be creative arts, which was actually a much better fit for me. I made friends that seemed to like me even with all my foibles. I discovered that I was able to find my voice when deeply immersed in creating something and this was exciting. After that, I worked in theatre for a few years but this eventually lost it's appeal as I became frustrated that the words and actions I performed held no true meaning or clue to my own identity. I moved to a different city to find out what I could do on my own. I began writing my own material in the form of performance poetry, short stories, theatre and screenplays. I did an MA in creative writing. I facilitated many writing workshops but seemed to stumble when it came to making something of my own creative projects. Much of what I have written so far has gone no further than the page, but nevertheless it's my stuff, which I wrote.

I did not realise that the challenges I was and still do experience in this context, in addition to generally feeling like I was 'not quite right' and also 'not very good at life', were and are all part of having Asperger's Syndrome, or ASD (Autism Spectrum Disorder) as it is now often referred to. I found out about Asperger's Syndrome two years ago when I was reading a great deal about autism and working with students on the autism spectrum as I had begun a job as a mentor in this field. At the time it was a huge relief to have this knowledge. Many of the challenges I was reading about or that the students were telling me about correlated with my own experiences. It felt like I had finally been equipped with the correct brain manual. I could make sense of my life up to this point. I was elated and thought that I would be able to be much more productive now that I knew what works well and less well with the type of brain that I have. I am hopeful that this is what I will feel eventually, but in the meantime things feel a tad confusing as I am integrating this new knowledge into my persona, which means taking everything apart and rebuilding it from a stronger foundation.

Despite how disassembled I feel in this process, as I am not entirely rebuilt yet, I am glad that this has led me to discover neurodiversity. I had not heard of this concept until I began reading about autism, and it has now become one of my new obsessions. I think that neurodiversity has the potential to prompt us to re-evaluate everything that we know about humans, particularly our attitudes towards different ways of perceiving the world, being in the world and communicating with other human beings.

My understanding is that a neurodivergent person may be someone on the autism spectrum, someone with ADHD or Tourette's syndrome, they may have dyslexia or dyspraxia and they may have been labelled as someone with 'learning disabilities'. It is likely that a neurodivergent person may have had, or continues to have, a range of mental health issues or were previously misdiagnosed as having a mental health illness. The mental health issues are likely to have been influenced by the ongoing challenges of attempting to adapt to social constructs created by and for neurotypical people. Neurodivergent people have brains that fall outside of the perceived 'norm' despite the fact that society is made up of individuals who are neurologically diverse.

The rise in awareness of neurodiversity, and indeed the notable rise in people being diagnosed with a range of neurodiverse conditions, is bringing to light the rigidity of current social constructs, constructs that influence every public amenity that exists i.e travel and shopping, plus education, health and community settings. I believe that it is this rigidity that has led to a society that has become incompetent at communication.

Despite the increased technical possibilities for communicating, when it comes to connecting with humans that are in some way differently abled or neurodivergent, people are generally ill-equipped to navigate a successful interaction. A common example is someone assuming that a person in a wheelchair or a non-verbal person will naturally be of lower intelligence and treat them accordingly. On an almost daily basis new buzzwords or politically correct ways of referring to someone 'other' are added to the already huge vocabulary, so we stumble and stutter awkwardly. It is as though the neurotypical and/or the 'non-disabled' person are themselves becoming disabled in the context of communication.

However, as the social constructs described above become less effective with the ever-changing landscape of abilities/disabilities and neurodiversity, it is clear that there is no simple way of adapting existing systems but rather those systems in many cases, particularly education, need to be pulled down altogether and re-built entirely. Because if you keep putting new sticky tape over old sticky tape, it won't be long before your construction starts to wobble again.

As previously mentioned, I work as a mentor for students on the autism spectrum. Many of them also have related conditions such as those mentioned above. I have noticed that one of the challenges that seems to be a common denominator of many of these students is that of 'fitting in'.

There is a need to constantly question and vet how students present themselves or behave in a social situation. This applies to group work assignments, shared living arrangements, attending lectures/seminars, as well as actually going somewhere and socialising. It is yet another layer of challenge to what a neurodivergent person needs to deal with on a daily basis, in addition to the extra brain power needed to process sensory information and stay calm and focused until they can return to a less taxing space. These neurodivergent students are constantly being expected to learn the 'game' rules and play them well. But perhaps at this point it might be more useful to remove the game entirely and instead try to figure out how to become more flexible in how we communicate with each other, whether neurotypical or neurodivergent. In the neurotypical world a person can be judged harshly for things like not smiling; raising their voice slightly; giving too little or too much eye contact; being too direct; being too slow at answering questions, and so on. For a neurodivergent person a simple social outing can turn out to be as intense and nerve-wracking as going to a job interview. The so-called fun social event becomes debilitating and not fun at all.

Having spent much of my life prior to knowing what my brain type was attempting to 'fit in' somewhere, I now know better than to use camouflage i.e. play the neurotypical game, to conceal who I really am, as that leads to regular exhaustion, breakdowns and mental health issues. So rather than give students tips on how to communicate in a neurotypical way, I try to work with them on self-awareness and acceptance of who they are so that they can grow the confidence to apply that authentic self in every situation. In this way they will save themselves years of confusion, at least when it comes to knowing themselves, their needs and how to communicate these to other people. If neurodivergent people could be allowed to do this, neurotypical people would also become more flexible communicators. Indeed, in my opinion it is very odd that from the moment children start to learn they are not taught things like sign language and Makaton, which surely should be as common as learning French or Spanish or whatever the current popular language might be.

This would also make us understand more about how non-verbal people (whether on the spectrum or not) are not 'less intelligent' but simply use a different method to express themselves. Perhaps we could start thinking about creating non-verbal versions of every language on the planet and then make this an obligatory part of everybody's learning requirements!

Let's go even further. Imagine, if you will, your first experience of socialisation. Perhaps it was nursery school. You are about four years old and you are taken to this place that is new to you. You understand that you will stay here for a few hours without anyone familiar to look after you. Inside the space there are lots of things to do and there are lots of children doing them. Some of the children run, some of them use a wheelchair to move around, others are communicating with each other using different hand gestures. There is somebody who wears dark glasses and sits with a book in front of them feeling the pages. Another child is intent on lining up all the toys from one of the boxes in order of height and colour tone. A kind adult takes you by the hand and asks you what you feel like doing. You look around a bit and think that the Wendy house in the corner of the space, where another child is playing, looks most appealing. So the kind adult takes you over there, introduces you to the other child who looks at you briefly, hands you a teddy bear and says it is called Pom Pom and it is a magic bear.

You are glad about this and carry Pom Pom with you for the whole day. During your time at nursery school you learn about playing and using your imagination. You learn that Plasticine feels nice but you really don't like Lego bricks. You learn that some children cannot see with their eyes like you can, but they can use their fingers to read and can move around the space as fast as anyone else. You learn that some children use a few words, some use none at all, but somehow everybody manages to get their point across. The adults are always patient and seem to know the best way to get a child interested or ready to go home when it is time to. Your young brain absorbs all of this like a little sponge and it never occurs to you that this is actually a wholly imagined scenario that is far removed from our current reality.

From an early age, people are categorised into boxes. New boxes are created every day, it seems, with different labels on. And these boxes will keep on increasing as we find out more about neurodivergent brains and what they can do. Unfortunately, up to this point the boxes and the labels have done little that is positive for those who do not fit the neurotypical or 'able-bodied' criteria and therefore are deemed as someone with 'special needs', as one example, which will put them at a disadvantageous point from the outset. This categorising of people has created a society rife with inequality and confusion. It is time to rethink pretty much everything about society, and a good starting point would be education. What is it really that we should be teaching to children and young people? What values do we want to uphold? If we want to positively evolve as a human race i.e. a race where everyone is treated humanely; where capitalism is not the master of opportunity; where we can stop destroying the planet; and where inequality is the outdated relic it ought to be, then at the very least we have to be better communicators. We have to stop judging or holding back people who are 'different', and attempt to listen and learn from them rather than try to change them to fit outdated constructs or, if they fail, exclude them completely. I think the only way to prompt the metaphorical meteor to come and destroy the dinosaurs is to stop creating boxes and labels in order to fit a social construct that is no longer fit for purpose.

There are some schools of thought that believe neurodiversity is a stage in evolution. If this is true then I think that there is hope for positive change as, if neurodivergent people become the majority, how will it be possible for our social constructs to remain as they are?

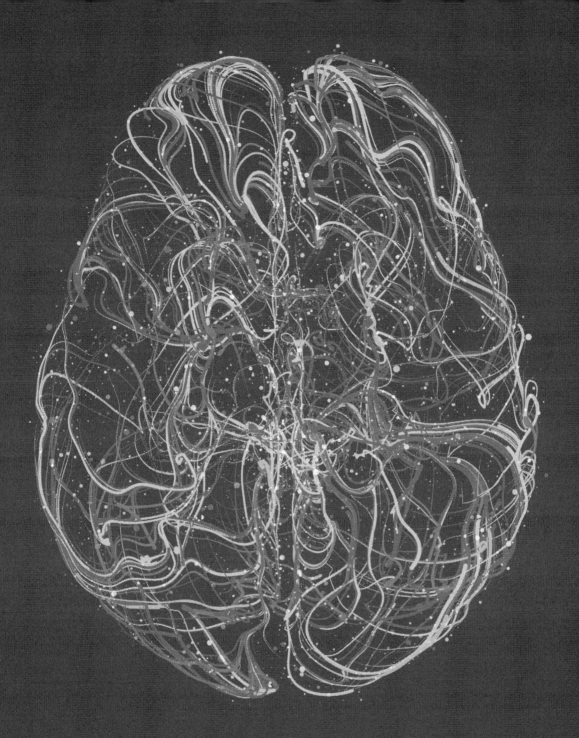

Section 3

Chapter 17: Autism: understanding behaviour

By Dr Michael McCreadie and Dr Damian Milton

Introduction

Being a parent is a demanding role. It places demands on our tolerance, our time, our energy levels, our coping skills and our physical stamina. But in the end the large majority of us consider that the attachments we form with our children, the pleasure they give us, the opportunities to contribute to their lives and the affection we receive back is all worth it. From the moment of our child's birth we attune to their movement and vocalisation, and in the dance of interaction we hope they attune to us.

As our daughters and sons develop, we observe changes in the nature of our interactions. Development necessitates changes in bodies and minds, and so we adapt our own expectations and anticipation of our child's behaviour to retain synchronicity and share common experience. The changes in our engagements reflect the development in reaching common milestones in the nature of parent-child interaction, primarily initiated by the anticipated development of the child.

Ultimately, we expect that our children will become adults and each family may have a set of expectations that may or may not be reached. For a range of cultural, ethical and legal reasons, our children generally become adults in their own right at the age of 16, but it should be remembered that they never stop being our sons and daughters, and the bonds developed in childhood are equally as strong when our children become adults.

Most of us cope well with the demands our children make of us, although we can feel an overwhelming sensation of frustration from time to time. However, some of us find it difficult to cope at times. Irrespective of disability, some parents are just more able to cope than others, and from time to time all of us need help, whether it be from family members, friends or outside agencies.

Parents of autistic children are no different in their coping resources than any other parent, but they can be faced by a range of what they may see as confusing behaviour from their child that can alter how they engage. For some families this can place unanticipated demands, create challenging situations and stress within parent-child interactions, particularly when in public settings where the stakes are high and social cost significant.

This chapter discusses the demands placed on parent-child interactions. It aims to provide some guidance as to how to derive meaning through interaction and offer some tips and strategies that will facilitate engagement.

While this chapter is primarily aimed at parents and carers of autistic children as well as practitioners working with autistic children, not all of the information or strategies will be relevant or appropriate for a particular child. Each person and situation is unique, so it's important to think about how the issues discussed here relate to your own context.

Finding meaning in behaviour

Human behaviour is complex, can serve many purposes and often has multiple causes. Fundamentally, it is an expression of our own experience of our internal world. Historically, some have described behaviour as a means by which we communicate. But this is not the full picture and does not explain behaviour related to illness which may be beyond our conscious control. Rather, behaviour is an outward expression of what we experience. However there remains a problem: while we express our own experience, it is others that are required to interpret that experience and to derive meaning from it in order to respond in the most efficient and appropriate way. It can be like breaking a code so that your child and you can share experiences.

For human beings to engage with one another we must move in synchrony, pausing at appropriate times, observing, listening, not judging or jumping to conclusions, but paying close attention to the other's expression. All of this allows us to respond appropriately and share meaning.

Let us for a moment consider how we may care for an elderly relative that we know is unwell. We adjust our verbal communication, demanding little of them but listening intently. Perhaps we may even pay close attention to how they are breathing looking out for any changes showing them compassion.
In this way we approach the child, pausing, observing, listening and responding to them when they are able to listen rather than interjecting, giving direction or instructing, which can be difficult for a child to process, particularly when they are in a high state of distress.

Challenged by behaviour?

We often hear the term 'challenging behaviour' applied to a whole range of behaviours that are described in terms of how the behaviour makes us feel or its impact upon our health and well-being. Moreover, many parents of children with autism report that they are continually exposed to stressful events involving their child that have elements of both low and high perceived controllability.

What does this mean?

Perceived controllability means how much control we **feel** we have over a situation. It does not necessarily mean that we are correct in our estimation. This is important, as the strategies we use will be influenced by how much we perceive we have control over the situation.

Let us for a minute consider the following scenario involving Child A who self-injures:

We know that her self-injury (which involves slapping her face) is more likely in the presence of unfamiliar people. As such we take steps to avoid areas where there are unfamiliar people. This is called *problem-focused* coping. Here we perceive that in preventing self-injury we have a high degree of control and use coping strategies in which we try to control exposure to certain environments where unfamiliar people may be present. We are viewing the situation as a problem that we can influence. This seems a fairly reasonable strategy and we observe that, in general, it seems to work.

However, there are times when things may happen that we have no control over. On one occasion the doorbell rings and we open it to find that someone campaigning on behalf of a political party is standing there and they launch into a speech regarding a current local issue. By coincidence, Child A is standing in the hallway and observes this. In response she lets out a scream and runs through the house shouting 'stranger danger' and slapping herself hard on her left cheek. In this situation we realise there is very little we can do (low control) and so we switch to an *emotion focused coping strategy*. Such a strategy requires us to read the emotional distress of the other and ensure that we remain focused on keeping our own emotions in check. By correctly assessing that there is little control over the situation we keep our voice low, use minimal language, ensure that we provide Child A with space and minimise any feelings they have of being under threat. This may be achieved by offering gentle re-assurance until Child A is calm. Here it has been necessary that we keep calm and are aware of how we present in the situation. To do otherwise may have maintained the distress felt by Child A or have made it worse. Knowing when to switch between the two coping styles and being able to do this across situations is called *adaptive coping*.

In considering the situation above, we can see that, had we been unable to identify the change in controllability when Child A became distressed, we would have maintained a *problem-focused* coping style. In so doing we may have attempted to provide instruction to Child A by telling them to calm down or stay calm, have followed them closely through the house and tried to prevent them from hitting themselves, or offered them objects or food as a means of distraction. As we engage in desperately seeking out solutions to fix the problem, we may notice that our own distress increases and that we become more psychologically and physically aroused. This increase in our own arousal can result in us speaking faster, being less clear in our communication and choosing options that are less helpful to the situation. As such we become out of synch with the child.

We have now learned that, perhaps rather than using terms such as 'challenging behaviour', it is really the notion of *threat* that is more important here. In the situation above, Child A feels under threat by the unfamiliar person and we, as the adult, feel under threat by the child's response. The result being that we can both become highly stressed.

We have now learned that in starting to address the issue of behaviour that challenges us we must first examine how we have traditionally responded to those times we have felt stressed by the child's behaviour. It is important then to ask ourselves the following questions:

How good am I at correctly identifying the amount of control I have in a situation?

How good am I at switching between problem and emotion focused coping as the situation changes?

How much time do I spend discussing with my own support network how I respond to stressful encounters?

How do I bring myself back on-line when I feel under threat?

Are there strategies that work across all situations?

The scenario of Child A may be familiar to you, or you may say, 'Well, that's not how my child behaves'. This raises the question, are there any strategies that work with everyone in every situation? The answer is, of course, no. Human behaviour in general is complex and is not the result of any single factor. Our behaviour is caught up in our thinking and emotion and how we feel about ourselves in our own bodies. It is far more productive to learn about our own reactions in situations that threaten us so that we can adapt as situations arise.

That is not to say that we cannot have some general sense of how our reactions also depend on how we are feeling at the time: if we are under a lot of pressure we are likely to become annoyed more quickly than we would if we were relaxed.

Common assumptions

Culture plays a significant role in our interpretation of others' behaviour, the intentions we ascribe to their behaviour and, ultimately, our responses. In UK culture we observe a number of common beliefs surrounding behaviour, which often places the problem within the child rather than seeing behaviour as a result of the interaction between the child and their environment. These include:

- 'He's just doing it to get attention.'
- 'She should have known better.'
- 'He knows exactly what he's doing.'
- 'If I let him get away with it this time he'll think it's OK to behave like that all the time.'
- 'I shouldn't let him win.'
- 'If I give her what she wants then that just rewards the behaviour.'

It can be easy to find yourself locked into a battle of wills, to think that someone is behaving that way deliberately, or that you must 'win'. This is especially true if you are feeling anxious, tired, scared or frustrated.

It is important that we question our beliefs, especially in a challenging situation when our emotions are running high. If you can, it is more helpful to focus on helping a child to cope with a situation or to regain control. It is also helpful to remember that autism is a different pattern of development, no worse or better than typical development, but this may mean that your child has problems understanding the consequences of their own or others' actions. Equally, a parent may have difficulties understanding the consequences of their own actions on their autistic child.

Common underlying causes of distress

For some autistic people, distress is often brought on by stress, anxiety, sensory differences, or difficulties with communication, all of which can create difficulties in interaction and mutual understanding.

Stress and anxiety

'I get anxious and I'll stop eating and I'll be sick every day. Anxiety attacks, they're called. So I make myself not worry about anything.' (Ian)

Earlier we discussed the concept of threat and how this can result in a stress response that affects the quality of interactions. The behavioural scenario of Child A illustrates that the stress experienced by Child A in response to a perceived threat has an impact on the stress experienced by her parents.

Stress occurs when we feel under threat and while stress and anxiety are not characteristic of autism itself, many autistic people experience unprecedented levels of stress as a response to a situation they find threatening. While there may be some common threats for autistic people, the important thing is to identify situations where the child in your care feels under threat.

In contrast to stress which occurs as a response to threat, anxiety is more closely aligned with worry. When an individual is worried, they tend to spend a lot of time thinking about a potential threatening situation. Here, it is the act of engaging with thoughts of threat and the experience of them going around in our mind (rumination) that causes distress. This can be more harmful to our physical and psychological well-being as we cannot run away from our thoughts. As such we experience more distress over time and this can lead to mental and physical illness.

By viewing a child's behaviour as a means of coping with threat. It becomes more obvious to us that their behaviour that we find challenging is generally a means of coping with that threat. For example, let us consider ritualistic behaviours. This may involve repetitive movements such as rocking, flapping or spinning. We may have a desire to prevent our child from engaging in this as we perceive it to be socially undesirable, but in fact this may be a coping mechanism to manage stress (McDonnell & Milton, in Jones & Hurley, 2014). In fact, there is a growing body of evidence that suggests preventing a child from engaging in these behaviours increases the release of damaging stress hormones (Hirstein *et al*, 2001).

Change

Many autistic children find change difficult. Sometimes changes that seem apparently small and insignificant, such as changing clothes for a PE lesson at school, may cause more difficulties than a significant change, such as moving house.

Change can lead to an increase in stress and this can quickly become overwhelming for a child.

Escape or avoidance

A child's behaviour may be an indication that they want to escape or avoid a situation. This may be due to being overwhelmed by sensory information, which can be threatening and can prevent them forming a coherent picture of the world. In some children this can trigger a dramatic stress response, and so running away from or avoiding the situation may be the only means the child has of coping with it.

Transition

People in general can find unstructured time particularly stressful. For autistic people, who may have difficulty predicting activities, transition times, where they are moving between activities and places, perhaps seeing different people, can be especially stressful. Some examples of transition times include break times or moving between lessons at school, waiting for an activity to start, leaving work or school and going home. There is an element of uncertainty at these times and a child may not be sure what they should do; this is likely to cause anxiety. Sometimes the anxiety can become so overwhelming that it results in distressed behaviour.

Mood or physical state

Our mood affects our level of tolerance for others and our ability to relate to ordinary day-to-day situations. If a child is tired, hungry, stressed or ill, they may become more agitated or frustrated than usual, or more sensitive to sensory stimuli. Just like you, their tolerance may be less at such times and we should consider how we relate to them, perhaps placing less demand at that time, or providing them with more space and time to engage in preferred activity.

Sensory differences

Many autistic people experience sensory processing difficulties. In some environments, certain sensory stimuli such as noise, smells, tastes and colours can be overwhelming.

If a child is sensitive to noise in some environments, they may cover their ears to block it out or become very distressed. They may even experience physical pain. On the other hand, if a child does not receive enough auditory sensory feedback in certain environments, they might seek out loud noises, or make a lot of noise in order to reach some kind of sensory equilibrium.

As autistic children can have a different pattern of development, it may be that their perception of sensory experience is organised and perceived in different ways. This means that the way that a child responds (their behaviour) may not always be the same across each situation and so it is worth observing your child's response to sensory stimuli across many environments.

Communication difficulties

Some autistic people have a degree of difficulty with communication. Some people are non-verbal or have limited expressive vocabulary; others are highly articulate but may still have difficulty understanding what other people mean at times, as well as understanding the common etiquette associated with social situations.

Your child may be unable to communicate their feelings and needs effectively through conventional means for their age, and may lack speech and gesture. For example, they may lead someone to a door to indicate that they want to go out of the door and across the hall to use the toilet, a means of communicating common in very young children. Here it can be beneficial to create a rich communicative environment where speech, gesture and visual supports are all available to the child to help them express their needs. We must be patient with the child as they may be frustrated by their difficulties in expression that may cause an increase in feeling stressed.

Losing control

Losing control is scary, challenging and upsetting for anyone. In situations where raw emotion takes over and we are unable to express how we feel, all that can be done is to allow the person to calm in their own time and keep them safe. After such an event, a child may feel distressed or regretful about what has happened and perhaps seek comfort and reassurance. In such situations, it can be difficult for us to offer comfort, particularly if we have just been through the experience with them and have been injured or have pent-up feelings of our own. Nonetheless, do try to offer support and reassurance.

Try also to take a bit of time to deal with any residual feelings you have, and if possible talk to someone else and 'debrief'. This will help everyone involved to continue supporting your child in a consistent, constructive way. You may find that there are useful services, such as family support services, parent groups or counselling centres in your area.

Thinking about behaviour

Here are some questions that may help you to think about a particular behaviour:

- Is the child experiencing any pain, illness or physical discomfort (such as toothache, earache, digestion problems, allergies, seizures)?

- How does the child communicate their needs, wants and feelings? Could the behaviour be a way of compensating for communication difficulties?

- Have there been any recent changes in a child's life (e.g. a new teacher, moving house, disruption to routine)?

- Is the child experiencing any sensory differences which may be affecting them? This may be very subtle: a change in the washing powder you use, for example.

Remember, more overt behaviour can also be a coping strategy. For example, a repetitive movement such as rocking or hand-flapping could help your child to cope with a stressful situation, to relax, or to deal with sensory over- or under-stimulation. It should also be noted that responses to stress can be varied. At times, people may withdraw or lose communicative abilities that they would otherwise be able to draw upon.

Lets look at an example:

An autistic young man is taken to the supermarket but finds the environment very distressing because of the sensory stimuli present (harsh lighting, background music, the number of people) and his own worries about what is expected of him.

As a result, the young man becomes highly stressed and begins biting his hand and hitting himself. This behaviour could serve several purposes: a coping strategy, a way of blocking out other stimuli, or a way of avoiding or escaping from the situation altogether. The young man has learnt that this behaviour is likely to result in him being taken away from the supermarket to a quieter place to calm down.

It may be tempting to interpret this as manipulative or that he is trying to control the situation. However, if we again consider that this environment is threatening to him, we can consider his response within a coping framework. By doing this we can also re-consider what we are trying to achieve here.

What is the purpose of going to the supermarket? If it is to obtain shopping, then can this be done in an alternative shop where there are less sensory stimuli?

How have we prepared this young man? If it appears that he gets anxious and we feel it is due to anticipation, we should examine how we prepare him for the environment. We may wish to audit what we have done so far: do we offer pictures of what the shop will look like? Do we tell him what to expect? Do we provide him with enough information?

Monitoring behaviour

Autistic people can't always express their feelings through facial expressions, body language or speech. Instead, these feelings may be expressed through other means.

Your child might be trying to tell you that they are tired, stressed, annoyed by something that happened earlier, or in need of some time alone – but if this isn't always immediately obvious, how do you find out what they want?

It can be helpful to use a behaviour diary to try and determine the reason for a particular behaviour, however a word of caution here. Without being able to ask the person directly as to why they present the way they do, interpretation of the diary is always purely subjective and so you should rely more on your relationship with your child and being attuned to them. A behaviour diary allows you to monitor a child's behaviour over time, simply to notice patterns that you can then cross reference with your own feelings of a child's needs as you relate to them.

The author Philip Whitaker (2001) suggests thinking of behaviour as an iceberg: the behaviour you are actually seeing is the tip of the iceberg but there's a lot more going on under the surface. Here are some questions you can ask yourself to determine the underlying causes of behaviour:

- What behaviour is occurring?

- How often does it occur?

- What happens before and after?

- Are other environmental variables affecting behaviour?

Other things that you can consider include:

- The time of day.

- The temperature.

- The sound level.

- The people around you.

- Your location.

When you are completing a behaviour diary, or monitoring a child's behaviour in some other way, try to focus on *the actual behaviour that is occurring*. Therefore, rather than describing a child as 'getting angry while watching TV', think about:

- exactly which point did your child started to get angry?

- where you were?

- what you were doing immediately beforehand?

- how exactly your child behaved, i.e. did they hit out at a particular person? In what way?

At this point it is also useful to look at how factors in the environment may have affected a child's behaviour. Was the television on really loud when the behaviour occurred? Were other people in the room at the time? What were they doing? Does the child engage in other behaviour that perhaps serves a similar purpose, for example does a similar thing happen whenever they want to avoid a particular task or gain access to a desired item or activity?

However, all of this comes with a huge health warning for parents: don't over burden yourself! If you feel that you do not have the energy, time or are just too exhausted and this is another thing for you to do, then just being available to your child is enough. The reality is that we can place a lot of pressure on ourselves by feeling we need to do more. You may find that some of these suggestions are helpful, but you do not have the internal resources to create diaries. That is ok, just being available to interact with your child is enough. If you feel that you can adopt some monitoring strategies, then perhaps you can create some type of diary that gives some information but does not go into great detail. Remember, you are the expert when it comes to your child.

In this chapter we try to offer a balanced view, and look at the relative merits of different approaches. This is to enable you as a parent or practitioner to choose approaches that work for you in your situation. As such, an alternative to a diary that focuses on situations where a child was in distress, is a diary that records when they are engaged, happy, content and able to self soothe. This can often be more helpful as it can provide information that helps the child regulate their emotions.

Helpful strategies

Proactive strategies (that is, strategies that are planned and developed in advance) are a very important part of supporting your child to regulate their levels of arousal. They are more effective in the long-term than reactive strategies (reacting to a situation that is already happening), as they aim to prevent distress rather than responding once it arises. Proactive strategies can be time consuming to put in place and often require a lot of work.

If a particular behaviour represents a threat to safety, then sometimes a quick decision has to be made. However, if the behaviour is something that is undesired but not immediately threatening (e.g. spitting), then it may be better to gradually suggest alternatives. Remember, a behaviour that we find challenges us possibly helps your child to cope – so taking it away could make them more stressed and anxious. Also, a person will not replace one behaviour with another if it doesn't actually meet the same purpose for them.

With self-injurious behaviour it is important to intervene, but you may find that a child needs to finish the behaviour before being able to move on: it may serve a meaningful purpose for them. If there is a threat to your child's health or safety, or that of those around them, measures may need to be taken immediately to reduce risk. This responsibility should not fall solely on you. Emergency interventions can be planned for as well and so you should seek professional advice to help you draw up a plan to manage these situations. There should also be an onus here on social services providing families with adequate support.

Adapting the environment

We have already looked at how autistic people can experience sensory processing difficulties, and how stimuli in the environment (such as certain noises or colours) may cause stress and anxiety and result in distress. Often, fairly simple adaptations can help to make the environment much more manageable. For example, if the sound of a lawnmower makes your child distressed, could the lawn be mowed while they are out at school or college? Or could your child wear ear-defenders? Alternatively, you might also use music that is gradually increased in volume until it matches that of the lawn mower.

Where children are faddy eaters, new foods can be introduced through fun touch and taste sessions in the kitchen. Here children learn to explore food through texture and smell as well as taste, in a non-threatening manner where getting messy (if the child enjoys it) is a new way of relating to food. Some aversions to smell and taste once entrenched can become lifelong stressors, and so caution is also advised. Again, if a child's diet becomes unhealthily restricted, then you should seek professional advice.

Another way to help reduce stress and anxiety is by creating a low arousal environment. This might mean having clear, uncluttered rooms (not too many pictures or ornaments on display), low levels of light, calming music, or a quiet area or chillout room so that your child has a place to go to relax. The low arousal approach extends to thinking about our own behaviour, too, and the way we interact with children. We can promote a low arousal environment by being calm and consistent.

You may also be able to identify things in the environment that repeatedly trigger a particular behaviour. It may be best to remove the trigger if possible to prevent the behaviour, then to consider a planned, step-by-step process to reintroduce it if necessary.

For example, if a child pours pepper all over their dinner because the pepper pot is on the table throughout the meal, try offering pepper at the beginning of the meal then putting it away. This may mean that you don't have to remind the child not to use too much pepper, thereby saving them from becoming agitated or stressed.

Introducing structure

As we have already said, many autistic people become stressed or anxious if they cannot predict what will happen next, or if they are unsure how to behave in a particular situation. For this reason, your child may prefer a structured, predictable environment. It is possible to introduce structure at home using some simple strategies. It should also be remembered that structures need to be put in place that help understanding and reduce stress. Imposed structures and routines that do not make sense to an autistic person can increase stress and resultant anxiety.

Visual supports can help to address behavioural difficulties by reducing some of the anxiety that people on the autism spectrum experience when they are not sure what to expect.

Daily or weekly visual timetables can show clearly what a child will be doing in the day or week ahead. Timetables can be adapted to suit a child's level of understanding. You could use picture symbols or words, and different media – a diary, a wall planner or the calendar function on a smart phone may all be suitable. It depends what works for that particular child.

Other forms of visual supports include **now and next cards**. Again, these could contain words or pictures.

Here is an example of how Ali's parents used visual supports:

Ali loved his swimming lessons, which were held every Tuesday afternoon. However, his parents were finding it increasingly difficult to cope with the constant questioning by Ali about his next lesson. Each day, Ali would insist it was swimming day and get his swimming costume and towel ready. Sometimes Ali would get very distressed when told that he wasn't going swimming that day.

His parents decided to try a strategy that Ali's teacher was using successfully at school: a weekly timetable with picture symbols showing different activities that took place throughout the week. The swimming symbol was placed under Tuesday.

Ali's parents stuck the visual timetable on a wall in the kitchen and, each time Ali asked to go swimming, his parents would refer him to the timetable which reminded him of the day's activities and showed him how many days remained until his next swimming class.

After a week of redirecting Ali to the timetable, the constant questioning gradually reduced and Ali started referring to the timetable independently. The distress also decreased as Ali could clearly see when he would be able to go swimming again and what activities he would be doing on the days before that.

Comic strip conversations

Comic strip conversations are another way of visually representing the different levels of communication that occur during a conversation. They might include stick characters with thought bubbles and speech bubbles to show the different elements of a conversation, for example the difference between the words we say and our inner thoughts and feelings. Comic strip conversations can also be a useful way to explore differing perceptions of a situation (where possible), if they are mutually created. Such activities can therefore also help build understanding and rapport.

Intensive Interaction

Intensive Interaction is a technique that was originally developed for use for people with learning disabilities, but has been adapted by practitioners such as Phoebe Caldwell for those who are also autistic. These techniques involve building a dialogue with an autistic person in their own 'language' (or way of communicating and relating). Such methods can be useful in building rapport and relating better to how a child may be experiencing the world around them.

Technology

Technology has now quickly become part of our lives and there are a range of technologies, from apps to digital cameras, that can be helpful. You can take photos and videos to use as visual supports and colour-coded diaries can be helpful to many people, either on phones or tablets.

One particular approach, Video Interactive Guidance (VIG), helps parents examine interactions with their children. Parents benefit by receiving constructive feedback where opportunities for interaction may have been missed. By using this technology and approach, parents are able to adapt their behaviour to assist and support their child's development and engagement, as well as understand how their child communicates.

Visual supports

Visual supports may really help a child to communicate. A number of systems, such as Widgit, Boardmaker or the Picture Exchange Communication System (PECS), allow a child to communicate a short sentence, for example 'I want a drink'. They can gradually build up a library of symbols to communicate more and more complex sentences.

If a child is becoming stressed or anxious, they can use PECS or another form of visual communication to tell others that they are feeling and if they would like to go to a quiet area to calm. Some people may find electronic communication aids helpful and there are now a range of portable electronic devices that can produce either synthetic or digital speech for the user.

The incredible five-point scale is a simple idea that is popular with children and young autistic people, as many find it quite hard to talk about feelings, but easier to relate to a numerical scale. Making feelings and emotions – both rather abstract concepts – more 'concrete' can be helpful. For example, if your child is a 1 it means they are feeling relaxed and happy. If they are at a 5 it means they're extremely anxious. You can then link the numbers back to physiological changes in the body, for example 'When I'm at a 5 I'm clenching my teeth and my fist'.

Once your child recognises where they are on this numbered scale, you can develop strategies for them to use in each situation. Here is an example.

	What I do	How it feels	What I can do
5	■ Swearing ■ Breaking stuff ■ Clenched teeth	■ I have to break ■ something ■ I need to leave	■ Get someone to help me leave or take a walk ■ with me
4	■ Swearing	■ Cross	■ Leave the room, with permission, to go to a safe place
3	■ Not talking ■ Pacing ■ A little swearing	■ Upset	■ Go to bedroom
2	■ Keeping to myself ■ Still talking with others	■ Not happy	■ Talk to a safe person ■ Get a drink ■ Go for a walk
1	■ OK	■ OK	■ No action needed

You may also be able to use numbers to help manage a situation, even if you do not have the numbered chart to hand.

A young autistic girl was in a restaurant with her mother. She began to get anxious and her mother, noticing this, put three fingers on the table. This helped her daughter to understand that she was getting anxious and was 'at a 3', without the need for anybody to say anything. Their strategy, which they'd previously worked out, was to go back to the car for five minutes to calm down.

This kind of strategy can take time to put together and won't produce results overnight but, in time, the focus is on supporting your child to recognise when they are in a heightened emotional state and what they can do to manage it. How you use it will depend on the level of understanding a child has.

Some autistic people may prefer to use pictures rather than numbers. One child used a picture of a house to explain and communicate his feelings: the ground floor represented feeling uncomfortable, the first floor was 'warning time', and smoke coming out of the chimney meant he felt he had lost control and was very scared.

Relaxation techniques

Relaxation techniques may help your child to manage their anxiety levels and stress. Techniques include:

■ breathing exercises

■ progressive muscular relaxation

■ mindfulness

■ redirection to pleasant, calming activities such as taking a bath, listening to relaxing music, aromatherapy, rocking and twiddling with objects, swinging or jumping on a trampoline.

Jennifer always seemed to be extremely agitated when she got home from school in the afternoon. She would often shove furniture around, yell at family members and physically lash out if anyone got too close to her.

Jennifer's mother realised that this was her way of coping with high stress levels caused by a day of concentration and stimulation at school. She decided to structure a period of relaxation time into Jennifer's schedule when she arrived home. In Jennifer's case, this meant spending 45 minutes alone listening to how water from the tap dripped into an old tin cup that Jennifer had found one day on a walk.

Physical exercise

There is a wealth of evidence that shows the benefits of exercise in elevating mood and reducing stress and anxiety levels. Going out on strenuous walks, running, cycling or even spending time on a trampoline are not only good for general health but have been found helpful for many autistic people to regulate their arousal.

Responding to crises

Sometimes a child's behaviour may escalate to the point where their own safety or the safety of others is at risk. This is particularly the case with aggressive and self-injurious behaviour.

While the best strategy is prevention before the behaviour escalates, this is not always possible and at these times it is important to have a range of strategies that can be used to try to defuse the situation and help a child to calm down.

Being aware of potential factors that increase stress and avoiding these as much as possible, as well as recognising the 'indicators' that a child is becoming increasingly distressed, can help to avoid such situations.

The 'low arousal' response

All of the strategies we have mentioned can form part of a **low arousal** approach. Essentially, this means staying calm when faced with behaviour perceived as challenging – not always easy, but a calm and consistent approach can really help you to manage situations effectively.

The low arousal response is:

■ take a break

■ reduce verbal and non-verbal communication

■ give space

■ give a choice

■ give warnings.

An important part of the low arousal approach is recognising how our behaviour might increase the likelihood of distress developing and – on the other hand – how we might be able to reduce the chances of a meltdown happening.

For example, when a child is in a heightened state of arousal and feeling extremely anxious, they are likely to be less able than usual to process verbal or non-verbal information. We all know how our ability to process information is reduced when we are angry or stressed. Too much verbal engagement at this stage may only serve to raise anxiety levels further.

In contrast, if you can recognise the signs of increasing anxiety early, this could be a good time to redirect your child to a quiet area or an activity that they find calming. Think about your body language at this time, too. Direct eye contact can appear threatening or confrontational. If a child is already in a state of anxiety this may make them more anxious. Sometimes it can be a good idea to avoid directly confrontational words like 'no' or 'stop'. These words can trigger further arousal, especially if your child associates them with feeling anxious. Find other words to use or try visual symbols instead. You can also think about personal space: try to give a child a bit of space and be aware that they may try to avoid physical contact and interaction with others, possibly because they are very sensitive to touch.

If necessary, think about removing objects or other people so that everyone can remain safe. Removing people from the room also reduces the 'audience effect' which can make a child more anxious.

Remember, people's safety is of paramount importance. Sometimes there is nothing else that can be done except to make sure everyone is safe and okay. Once a child has begun to calm down they will enter a recovery period. During this time their arousal levels drop.

References and recommended further reading

Caldwell P (2014). *The Anger Box*. Hove: Pavilion Publishing and Media.

Dunn Buron K and Curtis M (2008). *The Incredible 5-point Scale*. London: The National Autistic Society.

Hirstein W, Iversen P and Ramachandran VS (2001). *Autonomic Responses of Autistic Children to People and Objects*. Royal Society, London.

Jones G and Hurley E (Eds) (2014). *Good Autism Practice: Autism, happiness and wellbeing*. BILD.

Lawson W (2010). *The Passionate Mind: How people with autism learn*. London: Jessica Kingsley.

Milton D (2012). *So What Exactly is Autism?* [resource linked to competency framework]. Autism Education Trust.

Milton D, Mills R and Jones S (2016). *Ten Rules for Ensuring People with Learning Disabilities and Those on the Autism Spectrum Develop 'Challenging Behaviour'... And maybe what to do about it*. Hove: Pavilion Publishing and Media.

Whitaker P (2001). *Challenging Behaviour and Autism: Making sense, making progress*. London: The National Autistic Society.

Woodcock L (2010). *Managing Family Meltdown: the low-arousal approach and autism*. London: Jessica Kingsley.

Chapter 18: Challenging Behaviour(ists) – Neurodiverse Culture and Applied Behaviour Analysis

By Owen McGill, MSc, BSc (Hons), School of Education, University of Strathclyde

'In the history of autism studies, expertise has been claimed by many differing academic schools of thought, practitioners, parents, quacks and so on. Yet, the one voice that has been traditionally silenced within the field is that of autistic people themselves.' (Milton, 2014)

Introduction

The Neurodiversity Movement has expanded knowledge, awareness and acceptance of identity through celebrating autism and positive portrayal of autistic lives. Vitally moving from the long-publicised idea of tragedy, Autistic-led organisations and charities continue to advocate for awareness and change while combating negative and stereotyped views of autistic people. Extensions of autistic and neurodiverse advocacy have begun to question the methods and perceived need for early and behavioural intervention. In particular, the debate around the use of approaches from Applied Behavioural Analysis (ABA) has been fought vigorously on both sides. Autistic experiences frame an eloquent movement against behavioural intervention from lived experiences, while an exuberant evidence-base from case studies, reports and group research argue the case for ABA's efficacy. From its broad evidence base, ABA has been continually seen as the 'gold-standard' for autism interventions. Such conclusions suggest ABA as having a positive impact on developing skills and improving quality of life. Despite the improvements seen in targeted behaviours through applying behavioural conditioning, the long-term impact of ABA remains unexplored from the perspective of the participants. Peer-reviewed literature draws on examples of high-quality methods and outcomes, particularly exampled in the *Journal of Applied Behaviour Analysis*. It could be argued, however, that the sources of these conclusions portray a practitioner's view of ABA as effective through limited reports rather than based on a collective conclusion drawn with the input of participants. In this chapter I aim to explore the debate between the autism community and ABA advocates. I will address the perspectives of apologists, parents and the vitally needed autistic expertise in understanding the unexplored long-term impact of Applied Behaviour Analysis. The chapter will also discuss the current debate on ABA outcomes within empirical literature and the need for autistic voices to form a vital part of future research outcomes.

Neurodiversity: a celebration

Since its inception, the neurodiversity movement has promoted the celebration of autism, and other developmental conditions, as a difference inseparable from the individual. First explored by Judy Singer (Ortega, 2009; Singer, 1999), the movement firmly challenges the idea of causality and cure, as promoted by the medical model (Kapp *et al*, 2013). For many, celebrating individuality and positivity in identity (Baker, 2011; Jaarsma & Welin, 2012) creates an understanding of neurodiversity as *human diversity* rather than tragedy in difference. Unfortunately, the continued focus on cause and cure from medical perspectives and the projection of autism as 'tragedy' have increased eugenics-focused research (Orsini & Smith, 2010) meaning the removal of funding for vital support networks for many autistic people (Pellicano & Stears, 2011).

There is a growing need for research to create a developed and critical understanding of autistic experiences and invest in research which impacts the daily lives of autistic people. Looking to recent research, the debate around terminology in addressing those who are diagnosed or identify as autistic represents the steps future research should endeavour to take – positioning identity-first language compared to 'person first' terminology used to address identity (Orsini & Smith, 2010; Kenny *et al*, 2016) as preferred by many, while acknowledging individuality in identity for those who prefer person-first. The use of identity-first language has been expressed by a large percentage of those in the autism community in the UK as favourable over the medically preferred person-first language. However, Kenny's (2016) research also reflects on the need to understand and respect individual preferences in identity language. A small step, such research moves forward, indicating a broader acceptance and awareness of the autistic voice through identity and the value that involving autistic individuals within autism research has in helping us understand issues which are meaningful to their lives. Bringing autistic voices and experiences into academia and political policies creates stronger rooted evidence, based on the expertise of autistic individuals (Milton, 2014).

Social media has a huge offering of autistic expertise on their daily lives and experiences. Social discussion pages such as 'Ask Me I'm Autistic' and 'Autistic Allies' allow autistic individuals to express their experiences while helping them to learn and gain knowledge through other people's lived experiences. From these and additional advocacy groups, opposition to techniques and philosophies that use behavioural modification can be expressed in a safe environment. ABA uses learning progression and stimulus fade in to adjust the sensory reactivity, communication and behavioural presentation of participants, approaching autism as a condition to be influenced or changed through the application of ABA. The aim to change or 'cure' autistic participants demonstrates a reductive understanding of autism in its attempts to reduce and remove anxiety reducing self-soothing techniques (e.g. stimming) (Lowery, 2017). Moving to negate the need for stimming and self-autonomy requires an engagement with those who are impacted by such reductive approaches to understanding. Viewing autism as removable (and, in some groups, requiring change) runs counter to the philosophy of acceptance and the celebration of the Neurodiversity Movement, bringing into focus the reason for challenging such ideologies.

Lived expertise

The societal barriers faced by many autistic individuals show the need for a deeper understanding and acceptance of autism. Autistic self-advocates, academics and other members of the autism community have highlighted the need for autistic voices to be heard, acknowledged and valued in matters which impact not only their lives, but the lives of all autistic individuals. In no way an easy challenge, autistic accounts have elucidated what had been coined as *impairments* or *deficits* as *difference* and part of the *autistic identity*. Autistic advocates and academics have built different inroads to understanding autistic lives. Comprehending the barriers in communication between autistic individuals and neurotypical individuals, Milton (2012) conceptualised these through the Double Empathy Theory, while Woods (2017) highlights shortcomings of the social model of disability in promoting autistic identity. From the side of autistic advocacy, promoting understanding and acceptance of autistic identity and promoting knowledge (Agony Autie/Sara Jane Harvey) and challenging 'autism cures' and pseudoscience (Autism Inclusive Meets/ Emma Dalmayne) are only a fraction of the knowledge to be drawn from autistic identity and the autism community.

Despite the positivity being represented by autistic viewpoints, there are still those who would challenge and oppose neurodiversity as an identity and as a movement. The medical model of disability continues to conceptualise autism in terms of deficit, impairments and inability (Jaarsma & Welin, 2012). Such a perspective creates environmental approaches where early intervention is not only palatable, it is seen as a vital necessity. The need for early and behavioural intervention stems from ABA literature which frames autistic children as only developing social skills, increasing quality of life and forming meaningful relationships (Dawson, 2008; Warren *et al*, 2011) through behavioural intervention. We remain societal and cultural level where autistic individuals face an increased vulnerability for autistic people in terms of professional/medical practice and intervention(s). Conclusions reached by the OHCHR ('Discrimination against autistic persons, the rule rather than the exception – UN rights experts', 2015) conceive that such intensive intervention could be classed as violating basic human rights, as many approaches aren't based on strong, robust science. For many who both practice and advocate for early intervention, the practice-based evidence and literature provide evidence that applying behavioural modification techniques are necessary to autistic children's development.

The techniques and approaches synonymous with ABA have been challenged as being abusive, torturous and as leaving many who have been through the intervention with post-traumatic stress symptoms (Kupferstein, 2018). Applied Behaviour Analysis aims to target, change and remove certain behaviours, while promoting the learning of new skills, social awareness and improving overall communication, knowledge and quality of life (Foxx & Meindl, 2007; Dillenburger & Keenan, 2009). For those who explore ABA's approaches in depth, perceptions of its effectiveness and the outcomes it achieves differ on either side of the ABA debate. From a behavioural perspective, intervention is needed to allow autistic children to progress socially, behaviourally and academically. Many autistic individuals have heavily disputed the need for such intervention, as the functions of some behaviours, such as stimming, aid in necessary anxiety reduction, self-regulation and expression (Nolan & McBride, 2015). The difficulty arises in ABA when such self-regulation may be seen by some behavioural therapists as unnecessary or distractive to learning (Dillenburger & Keenan, 2009) and are therefore targeted for change or removal. The semiotics and need for stimming have been consistently discussed by autistic individuals – particularly within Yergeau's (2012) video 'I Stim, Therefore I am', and Agony Autie's YouTube content. Both advocates define and show the power of stimming for an individual's expression and identity. What forms part of the perceived need for ABA intervention relates to such misinterpreted *challenging* or *complex behaviour*.

Who is challenged? Who is complex?

Looking at the longstanding evidence-base of ABA, the approach towards 'severe' and challenging behaviour is well documented (Newcomb & Hagopian, 2018). Through the many ways in which autistic individuals are 'characterised', categorised and labelled, the use of the terms such as 'challenging behaviour' and 'complex' is constant, confusing and aggravating for many. Challenging behaviour is summarised as *'culturally abnormal behaviour(s) of such intensity, frequency or duration that the physical safety of the person or others is likely to be placed in serious jeopardy, or behaviour which is likely to seriously limit the use of, or result in the person being denied access to, ordinary community facilities'* (Emmerson, 2001, p3). Further examples include aggression, self-injury and stigmatised behaviour (Nicholls *et al*, 2019). Factoring into the definition of challenging and complex, what is actually being expressed and communicated by the individual can be consistently misunderstood or ignored through the methods applied by ABA. Confusion, frustration, sensory or information overload, alongside a pressured environment where the participant has little to no control, may cause fight or flight reactions that are seen as non-compliance or as *challenging behaviour*.

In looking to my current writing, I feel it important to address two key elements which resonate with the problematic nature of the ABA debate; the 'Double Empathy Problem' and defining behaviour. Interactions and equal reciprocation are reliant on each individual comprehending the motions and interplay of the interaction. In the context of socialising, understanding meaning and cues from the other individual is vital for communication to be understood (Milton, 2012). In interactions between autistic individuals and the neurotypical (NT), there is a tendency to bypass the communication of the autistic individual in favour of the 'normal', and this creates problems in reciprocity as equality isn't met, being a 'double problem'. Understanding from both parties is critical to attaining understanding and social comfort for both individuals. Recent research has also highlighted the differences and difficulties between neurotypes as autistic individuals don't face issues of double empathy in neurodiverse circles, whereas such issues arise in neurodiverse circles. Despite this logical thought process, ABA takes a less inclusive stance. Behaviour is interpreted by the behaviour analyst who may hold preconceived notions as to which behaviours and communication methods are acceptable. Tying in with Double Empathy highlights the problematic outset of the therapy, as assuming one understands an individual without involving them begins with a sense of removing autistic self from the participants. Given that the majority of autistic individuals who participate in ABA are children who may not use verbal communication and don't get to make the choice of participation, the approach's intensity can have damaging and lasting implications for future mental health (see Kedar, 2011 & ABA Controversy Autism Discussion UK, 2017).

The second element of this section looks to behavioural interpretation and defining 'problem' or 'challenging' behaviour. Conclusions on what warrant this definition include 'physical aggression, self-injury... disruption' (Horner *et al*, 2002, p423). Given that behaviour can reflect emotion, communication or self-expression, judging 'autistic behaviours' relating to frustration or confusion as aggression reduces an individualised understanding on the part of the neurotypical therapist. The (mis)translation of behaviour through a neurotypical lens further stigmatises and labels the bahviour. Through the (mis)translation of behaviour in ABA, the shattering of equality in the communication between therapist and participant highlights the concept of Double Empathy within behavioural modification techniques. In a similar manner, the use of *complex* to describe autistic individuals can also serve to remove some of the difficulties professionals are facing in passing responsibility onto the person being supported. Emotion, reaction, expression and stimming can all be attributed to labelling an individual as *complex* or *challenging*, though *who* is challenged is rarely accounted for. The complexities of social language, cues and trends can be difficult for many to follow (Crompton, 2019 – *Neurodiverse Interaction*). Reflections from members of the autism community have stressed the differences in social language between neurodivergent and neurotypical communities. Catherine Crompton's recent research on social interactions highlighted that there is a *difference* in social cues and understanding between autistic people and autistic-to-neurotypical people. Though novel in terms of academic conclusions, the outcomes mirror what the autism community has been saying for some time. The *complex* and *challenging* labels placed on autistic individuals serve to bolster the perceived need for behavioural intervention, while advocacy from the Neurodiversity Movement suggests that more mentored and autistic-led approaches are a far more constructive.

ABA: a discourse in 'right'?

Following noted guidelines (e.g. NICE guidelines), many professionals call for early intervention for autistic children in order to create conditions for the best possible quality of life and well-being. Within the 'gold standard' of these approaches, ABA is supported by a significantly large quantity of research, much of which advocates and promotes the effectiveness and need for behavioural intervention. Some challenge the veracity of these claims, questioning the lack of engagement with and input from autistic participants, with autistic individuals who speak out against ABA labelled as a minority (Davison, 2018). Practices within ABA that are heavily criticised by anti-ABA groups are those which focus on removing soothing and self-managing (Gibson & Douglas, 2018) through the use of punishment (also seen as a reward system) (Cook, 2018; Leaf *et al*, 2019). Despite the growing number of voices speaking out against ABA, there remains a stable lobby from behavioural therapists, parents and professionals promoting the effectiveness of ABA.

Many behavioural therapists have reflected on the positive benefits they believe their work and intervention has brought the children they have supported (e.g. ABA4ALL). A growing number of behavioural therapists continue to promote the apparent positive impact of ABA on children's quality of life, social interactions and personal progression. An indicator of placing such value on ABA lies with the intensity and individualisation of the methods. Developing participants' skills while being adaptive, focuses on improving the participants' ability to learn new skills and replicate these in their daily lives. Empirical outcomes mirror such thought on adaptability and encompasses the well disseminated positive impacts on participants (Fein *et al*, 2013). For each individual partaking in ABA, the method is individualised by the Board-Certified Behavioural Analyst to ensure the child is achieving core learning developments that are central to their needs (Leach, 2010; Reichow & Volkmar, 2010). As neurodiverse individuals, we can look at the impact of high intensity intervention and see the continued reductivist misinterpretation of our personal processes. The veracity of ABA as being able to incorporate an understanding of the individual, while continuously forcing change, has galvanised the challenge to behavioural intervention.

Progressing culture: voice versus veracity

Cultural understandings of the application of ABA (and the need for intense interventions) are heavily influenced by the understanding society has of autism and how it perceives or imagines autistic lives. For many, the stereotyped and stigmatised image of 'Rain Man' or Dr Sean Murphy encapsulate the binary and closed perceptions that society at large has of autistic individuals. Many don't, or indeed can't, envision the autistic academic, the activist, the parent, the employee, the company owner, as stigma tells them that autistic individuals can't be things. Despite such reductive thought, the development and recognition of autistic culture has grown vastly in the last two decades, from the beginnings of cultural developments changing the public's recognition of autistic individuality (Dekker, 1999) to having a vital impact on research and outcomes (Kenny *et al*, 2016; Ellis, 2017; Spiel *et al*, 2017). Evaluating the efficacy of ABA within different cultures is impacted by a number of factors; the social perception of autism; the 'need' to change behaviour; and where the behavioural adjustments will target learning (Keenan *et al*, 2010).

Though cultural awareness of autism has continually grown, there is simply little to no record within empirical data on the personal effects and impacts felt by the autistic individuals who have participated in ABA. The short-term outcomes concluded through longitudinal research (Fenske *et al*, 2005) suggest a positive relationship between behaviourally applied skill learning and improved social awareness. These alone begin to form a strong enough argument to advocate for consistent ABA intervention for autistic children. There are those autistic individuals who have flourished following ABA, those who find it detrimental and those who oppose the changing of autistic children to 'fit in' and pass as neurotypical. Autistic people are diverse and individual. Why, then, is one intervention seen as the 'gold standard' for such a diverse group? In the perpetual debate on the need for ABA intervention, there are people whose experiences have driven them to either side. Rarely addressed are those whose attitudes towards early intervention have changed through their personal experiences and those of autistic adults and children.

Apologists and parental perspectives

'The underpinning of cultural discord in relation to ABA can be seen fundamentally within debate between the autistic community and academic outlooks, with some ABA practitioners reversing their views on the overall effectiveness and impacts of the intervention.' (Socially Anxious Advocate, 2015)

As cultural change has edged its way forward, the Neurodiversity Movement and autistic voices have drawn attention to factors not previously acknowledged or explored. As autistic reflections of ABA participation have become more involved in current thought and debate, some advocates or ABA practitioners have changed trajectories through aligning these with their own experiences in practicing behavioural intervention. Labelled as apologists, these individuals have reflected heavily on what they believe to be *malpractice*. One former-therapist (birdmadgrrl, 2017) spoke of her belief that her time practicing ABA supported the learning development of the autistic children she worked with. In time, her view of the positive impact of the approach changed, through being consistently forced to decide between the communication and needs of participants and applying the behavioural intervention. Hers is not the only such account. Others, such as *Why I Left ABA* (2015), have described feeling abusive for punishing behaviour that is a natural reaction to stress and fear, and forcing the continued participation of the child. Many children are typically exposed to the intervention through parental consent, not their own. Many children are therefore placed in a very intense environment from which they are (typically) unable to leave of their own accord and have their enjoyments taken away in order to be used as rewards, without being aware of the process or having a choice as to whether they take part. From these apologists, a certain backing and insight into the 'behind closed doors' approaches of some (not all!) behavioural therapists has progressed the argument put forward by many from the autism community.

Beyond apologists and reflections on the need for change, many parents have also become opposed to and advocate against ABA following their child's intervention.

Some have moved their advocacy online and promote the need for autistic-led methods (see ABA Controversy Autism UK on Facebook). Zurcher's (2012) account brings to light the misunderstanding that can be seen between the autistic child and the therapist. In their account, there were several discrepancies between their child's participation (or rather disengagement) with the intervention and how this was interpreted by the therapist. Such (mis)interpretation places many non-verbal individuals at a further disadvantage as communication is set by the therapist. Further, those who become selectively non-verbal during high stress environments can be viewed as *non-compliant*, placing the child at fault rather than the therapist's approach (Zurcher, 2012). For those parents who reflected on their reasons for removing their children from ABA intervention, there are similarities to Zurcher's (2012) issues. Parents may see their child's attempts at communication not being recognised or acknowledged, and being in a state of distress throughout the processes of ABA. In turn, they themselves are told to accept these stresses as part of the process, leading many parents to turn their backs on the intervention. As is argued, however, these techniques may be used only by the minority of therapists. Given the broad application of ABA, there will be those whose understanding of autism as inability may increase the risk of their participants' stress. Misinterpretation, or admonishing, of communication which lies outside the parameters of the therapist's learning makes participants vulnerable, stressed and potential voiceless. In turn, these individuals may be forced to comply to ensure they complete the sessions, learning to survive rather than thrive.

Opposingly, some parents remain focused on the need for ABA and its perceived benefits, leading some to suggest that ABA is of more benefit to parents than autistic children. Much of the debate from parental perspectives is founded on two factors. First, it has been suggested that those who speak out against ABA are either *not autistic enough* to have warranted an intervention, therefore having no real knowledge of its workings. Second, that those who advocate through their own experiences are only able to communicate their experiences because of ABA intervention. There are also some members of parental and professional groups who suggest that those who are in advocacy and academia should not be involved in these debates. Such ideology reflects the idea that the Neurodiversity Movement is not representative of non-verbal individuals (Clements, 2017). Such views do little to calm the ferocity of the debate. These instead fuel ableism and the repression of autistic voices, while failing to acknowledge that the advocacy and positivity of the Neurodiversity Movement community is made up of more than those who use verbal communication. Many have indeed failed to acknowledge the empowerment that online and social media forums offer non-verbal advocates. Additionally, many fail to understand the empowerment that can come from augmented and alternative communication technology, which allows non-verbal autistic voices to advocate and be heard. Significantly, those who have been through ABA have been able to express their expereinces on the elements they have found unfavourable (e.g. Kedar and Lowery).

ABA and autism: (un)acknowledged outcomes

Differences in attitudes towards the intensity of ABA reflect the substantial elements of the debate between the autistic community and empirical research. Depending on the beliefs about a participant's needs, the intervention can use a highly intense level of therapy of up to 40 hours a week. Despite the push from ABA literature and the Behaviour Analyst Certification Board that there is a need for this level of intensity, intervention-focused literature suggests that 25 hr/wk has as significant an impact as 40 hours (Warren *et al*, 2011). Despite the argument for lowering hours, much of the debate deriving from the experiences of the autistic community challenges the need for children to experience such intensity. Additionally, several social media sites aim to facilitate discourse between pro and anti-ABA voices, promoting autistic reflections and opinions in order to inform behavioural intervention practice (Autistics and BCBA's for a Reformed ABA), while autistic individuals have used blogs and other mediums to express their experiences.

Several self-authored experiences address many of the negative aspects of their ABA experiences. Much of the negativity focuses on the removal of autistic identity, self-preserving processes and the lack of connection to the individual as unique and having humanity beyond their diagnosis (Kedar, 2011; 2017). Such a disconnect forms part of the opposition to ABA (and behavioural therapies in general). Voicing personal experiences provides an evidence base for the challenges facing ABA. Together, these reflections build the foundations for opposing the treatment of autistic children in any context outside of physical illness. An argument could here be made, however, that the need to learn and remove dangerous behaviours, such as self-injurious behaviour or road safety, are effectively taught through ABA more quickly than other methods. The justification that children need to understand the concept of danger requires little argument, though the need for an intensive and potentially (mentally) damaging intervention is highly debatable. Regarding the required change within societal and professional attitudes towards autism, Lowery, in their reflection of undergoing ABA intervention states: 'We are different… it's who we are, and this should be respected' (2017). Their message portrays the need for an understanding of neurodiversity in order to move from a lack of respect or recognition of autistic participants agency and autonomy. Bringing such views into the processes of intervention would advance the well-being of autistic individuals considerably through self-acceptance of their strengths compared to negative societal perceptions of their weaknesses.

Looking to Kupferstein's (2018) seminal work on challenging the outcomes of ABA, her conclusions reflect the voices of autistic adults who have participated in early life ABA. The veracity of Kupferstein's work and findings has been criticised, and indeed will be for some time to come for those who advocate the efficacy of ABA. While critics look to the difficulty and effectiveness of diagnosing Post-Traumatic Stress Disorder and the possibility of bias within her work (Leaf, Ross, Cihon & Weiss, 2018), Kupferstein replicates the views and challenges put forward by autistic voices. On the other side of the argument, Kupferstein is simply looking to research that which the Autism Community has been suggesting for some time. Taking a stance on one side of such a long-standing debate would always impact the reception of her research, though it seems both sides wish to either completely exonerate or fully embrace her findings.

While many past participants have advocated against ABA, there are those who believe the intervention has advanced their development and lives and now promote and advocate in favour of ABA for autistic children. In comparison to Kupferstein's (2018) conclusions, these individuals feel that behavioural therapy has changed their lives in a positive manner. Some of these individuals would give credit to the intervention for their ability to now voice and express their experiences. Further, ABA has allowed them to be part of the broader autism community, being in education and allowing them to seek 'meaningful' employment. It is these individuals who many groups (such as ABA4ALL) seek out in order to combat the vilification of the therapy, instead drawing their narratives as a reason for all autistic children to participate in ABA. One example lies in Lerner's blog, *How ABA Saved My Life*, reflecting on the positivity and enjoyment they experienced through the continued learning, self-development and reinforcement of their progression and the positive impact ABA had on their life. In addition to this positive promotion, these reflections from autistic participants mirror the success found in empirical conclusions within research: improvements in behaviour, social awareness, intelligence and communication skills (Lerner, 2019). For those opposing ABA, these individuals may be viewed as internally ableised, while those in support would hold these reflections up as evidence of the efficacy of ABA. There is no doubt that the debate will continue to be fought on both sides for some time to come. While autistic individuals rightfully advocate for the safety of the wider community, parents will continue to seek what is best for their children. The key lies not in a middle ground or no-man's land, but the empowerment of autistic voices. Continuing the examples of current research, behavioural therapists should seek to develop an understanding of autistic lived expertise to ensure inclusion, communication and consent are maintained.

What next?

The question for many of those looking for better ways than ABA is how to enable their voices to be heard and acknowledged with empirical research. Such an accomplishment would allow for the autism and ABA debate to be evidenced empirically, enlightening both sides of the debate. It is therefore the suggestion of the author that research which engages with autistic voices on both sides of the debate be conducted to further our knowledge of the consequences and efficacy of ABA, and to continue to promote the autistic voice. While conclusive academic evidence would bolster the understanding of outcomes, the fact remains that those who stand on either side of the ABA and autism debate are unlikely to be moved. It is only the experiences of autistic people who have experienced ABA who can truly understand and explain the long-term outcomes of ABA intervention and verbalise what is unseen by professionals and parents.

References

ABA Controversy Autism Discussion UK. (2017). Retrieved from https://www.facebook.com/ABAUKAutismDiscussion/

Baker, D. L. (2011). *The politics of neurodiversity: Why public policy matters*. Boulder: Lynne Rienner Publishers.

birdmadgrrl. (2017). I Abused Children For A Living. Retrieved 27 August 2019, from https://madasbirdsblog.wordpress.com/2017/04/03/i-abused-children-for-a-living/

Clements, T. (2017). The Problem with the Neurodiversity Movement - Quillette. Retrieved from https://quillette.com/2017/10/15/problem-neurodiversity-movement/

Cook, K. B. (2018). Applied Behavior Analysis (ABA): Dispelling the Myths.

Crompton, C. (2019). Diversity in Social Intelligence. Retrieved 29 August 2019, from http://dart.ed.ac.uk/research/nd-iq/

Davison, S. (2018). Does ABA Harm Autistic People? | Autistic UK. Retrieved from https://autisticuk.org/does-aba-harm-autistic-people/

Dawson, G. (2008). Early behavioral intervention, brain plasticity, and the prevention of autism spectrum disorder. *Development and psychopathology*, 20(3), 775-803.

Dekker, M. (1999, November). On our own terms: Emerging autistic culture. In *Conferencia en línea*.

Dillenburger, K., & Keenan, M. (2009). None of the As in ABA stand for autism: Dispelling the myths. *Journal of Intellectual and Developmental Disability*, 34(2), 193-195.

Ellis, J. (2017). Researching the Social Worlds of Autistic Children: An Exploration of How an Understanding of Autistic Children's Social Worlds is Best Achieved. *Children & Society*, 31(1), 23-36.

Emerson, E. (2001). *Challenging behaviour: Analysis and intervention in people with severe intellectual disabilities*. Cambridge University Press.

Fein, D., Barton, M., Eigsti, I. M., Kelley, E., Naigles, L., Schultz, R. T., ... & Troyb, E. (2013). Optimal outcome in individuals with a history of autism. *Journal of child psychology and psychiatry*, 54(2), 195-205.

Fenske, E. C., Zalenski, S., Krantz, P. J., & McClannahan, L. E. (1985). Age at intervention and treatment outcome for autistic children in a comprehensive intervention program. *Analysis and Intervention in Developmental Disabilities*, 5(1-2), 49-58.

Foxx, R. M., & Meindl, J. (2007). The long term successful treatment of the aggressive/destructive behaviors of a preadolescent with autism. *Behavioral Interventions: Theory & Practice in Residential & Community-Based Clinical Programs*, 22(1), 83-97.

Gibson, M. F., & Douglas, P. (2018). Disturbing Behaviours: Ole Ivar Lovaas and the Queer History of Autism Science. *Catalyst: Feminism, Theory, Technoscience*, 4(2).

Horner, R. H., Carr, E. G., Strain, P. S., Todd, A. W., & Reed, H. K. (2002). Problem behavior interventions for young children with autism: A research synthesis. *Journal of autism and developmental disorders*, 32(5), 423-446.

Jaarsma, P., & Welin, S. (2012). Autism as a natural human variation: Reflections on the claims of the neurodiversity movement. *Health Care Analysis*, 20(1), 20-30.

Kapp, S. K., Gillespie-Lynch, K., Sherman, L. E., & Hutman, T. (2013). Deficit, difference, or both? Autism and neurodiversity. *Developmental psychology*, 49(1), 59.

Kedar, I. (2011). *Ido in Autismland. Climbing Out of Autism's Silent Prison*. Amazon.

Keenan, M., Dillenburger, K., Moderato, P., & Röttgers, H. R. (2010). Science for sale in a free market economy: but at what price? ABA and the treatment of autism in Europe. *Behavior and Social Issues*, 19(1), 126-143.

Kenny, L., Hattersley, C., Molins, B., Buckley, C., Povey, C., & Pellicano, E. (2016). Which terms should be used to describe autism? Perspectives from the UK autism community. *Autism*, 20(4), 442-462.

Kupferstein, H. (2018). Evidence of increased PTSD symptoms in autistics exposed to applied behavior analysis. *Advances in Autism*, 4(1), 19-29.

Leach, D. (2010). *Bringing ABA into Your Inclusive Classroom: A Guide to Improving Outcomes for Students with Autism Spectrum Disorders*. Brookes Publishing Company.

Leaf, J. B., Townley-Cochran, D., Cihon, J. H., Mitchell, E., Leaf, R., Taubman, M., & McEachin, J. (2019). Descriptive Analysis of the Use of Punishment-Based Techniques with Children Diagnosed with Autism Spectrum Disorder. *Education and Training in Autism and Developmental Disabilities*, 107.

Lerner, P. (2019). How ABA Saved My Life. Retrieved from https://medium.com/@pmlerner2000/how-aba-saved-my-life-b468bff23a7b

Lowery, A. (2017). What I Liked (and Didn't Like) About My ABA Experience. *The Mighty*. Retrieved from https://themighty.com/2017/02/aba-therapy-autistic-perspective/

Milton, D. E. (2012). On the ontological status of autism: the 'double empathy problem'. *Disability & Society*, 27(6), 883-887.

Milton, D. E. (2014). Autistic expertise: a critical reflection on the production of knowledge in autism studies. *Autism*, 18(7), 794-802.

Newcomb, E. T., & Hagopian, L. P. (2018). Treatment of severe problem behaviour in children with autism spectrum disorder and intellectual disabilities. *International Review of Psychiatry*, 30(1), 96-109.

Nicholls, G., Hastings, R. P., & Grindle, C. (2019). Prevalence and correlates of challenging behaviour in children and young people in a special school setting. *European Journal of Special Needs Education*, 1-15.

Nolan, J., & McBride, M. (2015). Embodied semiosis: Autistic 'stimming' as sensory praxis. In *International handbook of semiotics* (pp. 1069-1078). Springer, Dordrecht.

OHCHR | Discrimination against autistic persons, the rule rather than the exception – UN rights experts. (2015). Retrieved from https://www.ohchr.org/EN/NewsEvents/Pages/DisplayNews.aspx?NewsID=15787

Orsini, M., & Smith, M. (2010). Social movements, knowledge and public policy: the case of autism activism in Canada and the US. *Critical Policy Studies*, 4(1), 38-57.

Ortega, F. (2009). The cerebral subject and the challenge of neurodiversity. *BioSocieties*, 4(4), 425-445.

Reichow, B., & Volkmar, F. R. (2010). Social skills interventions for individuals with autism: Evaluation for evidence-based practices within a best evidence synthesis framework. *Journal of autism and developmental disorders*, 40(2), 149-166.

Sallows, G. O., & Graupner, T. D. (2005). Intensive behavioral treatment for children with autism: Four-year outcome and predictors. *American Journal on Mental Retardation*, 110(6), 417-438.

Singer, J (1999) 'Why can't you be normal for once in your life?' From a 'problem with no name' to the emergence of a new category of difference. In: Disability Discourse, Corker, M and French, S (eds), Buckingham/Philadelphia: Open University Press.

Spiel, K., Frauenberger, C., Hornecker, E., & Fitzpatrick, G. (2017). When Empathy Is Not Enough: Assessing the Experiences of Autistic Children with Technologies. In *Proceedings of the 2017 CHI Conference on Human Factors in Computing Systems* (pp. 2853-2864). ACM.

Socially Anxious Advocate. (2015). *Socially Anxious Advocate*. Retrieved from https://sociallyanxiousadvocate.wordpress.com/

Warren, Z., McPheeters, M. L., Sathe, N., Foss-Feig, J. H., Glasser, A., & Veenstra-VanderWeele, J. (2011). A systematic review of early intensive intervention for autism spectrum disorders. *Pediatrics*, 127(5), e1303-e1311.

Woods, R. (2017). Exploring how the social model of disability can be re-invigorated for autism: in response to Jonathan Levitt. *Disability & society*, 32(7), 1090-1095.

Why I Left ABA. (2015). Retrieved from https://sociallyanxiousadvocate.wordpress.com/2015/05/22/why-i-left-aba/

Zurcher, A (2012) *Tackling that troublesome issue of ABA and ethics*. Retrieved from http://emmashopebook. com/2012/10/10/tackling-that-troublesome-issue-of-abaand-ethics/

Chapter 19: 'Zero tolerance' of black autistic boys: are schools failing to recognise the needs of African Caribbean boys with a diagnosis of autism?

By Olatunde Spence

I am a Black[41] parent of two Black autistic children of African-Caribbean heritage (1999) attending mainstream schools. I am also an art psychotherapist working with autistic students in a mainstream inner-city school that serves a predominantly black and minority ethnic community.

Two years ago my son was permanently excluded from his secondary school because of his behaviour, behaviour I suspected arose from his undiagnosed autism. However, the school insisted that my son was defiant, disobedient and unwilling to follow school rules. Because the school believed his behaviour was chosen, they refused my requests for an educational psychology assessment. According to the Special Educational Needs and Disability Code of Practice (Dept of Education, 2014) this assessment should have been initiated because of his long record of disruptive behaviour.

---

41 British Sociological Association, Anti-Racist Language: Guidance for Good Practise (undated, unacknowledged authorship) Black- This term has taken on more political connotations with the rise of black activism in the USA since the 1960s and its usage now implies solidarity against racism. The idea of 'black' has thus been reclaimed as a source of pride and identity (Price, Shildrick, 1999, p61)

To justify the permanent exclusion, they carried out a risk assessment,
characterising my son in stereotypical ways e.g. potential risks of involvement in
gangs, substance misuse, carrying a weapon and violence to others. None of these
claims were substantiated. This was the first indication we had that my son was
being subjected to a form of racial profiling.

Ultimately though, we successfully challenged the school and the local authority,
the decision was overturned and my son returned to his school after 15 months,
with an autism diagnosis and with appropriate support. It is this experience that
led to my research into the experience of black boys with an autism spectrum
disorder diagnosis and how racism, micro-aggressions of racism, and ableism[42]
intersect and damage the life chances of black autistic boys in the UK.

In the report, ironically titled *They Never Give Up on You*, the Office of the
Children's Commissioner, School Exclusion Inquiry (2012), identified:

*'A black Caribbean boy eligible for free school meals who also has special
educational needs (SEN) is 168 times more likely to be permanently excluded
than a white British girl without SEN and not eligible for free school meals.'*

This claim recognises the compounding impact of discrimination known as
'intersectionality'. Crenshaw (1989) first coined the term when describing the
specific issues for black women facing racial and sex discrimination in employment.
She described the failure of the court to recognise how racial discrimination and sex
discrimination intersect and affect black women. She gives this example:

*'Consider an analogy to traffic in an intersection, coming and going in all four
directions. Discrimination, like traffic through an intersection, may flow in one direction,
and it may flow in another. If an accident happens in an intersection, it can be caused
by cars traveling from any number of directions and, sometimes, from all of them.
Similarly, if a Black woman is harmed because she is in the intersection, her injury
could result from sex discrimination or race discrimination.'* (Crenshaw, 1989, p149)

In a later article she concluded:

*'When it comes to thinking about how inequalities persist, categories like
gender, race and class are best understood as overlapping and mutually
constitutive rather than isolated and distinct.'* (Crenshaw, 2016)

---

42   For the purpose of this article, the term 'ableism' is: 'the discrimination or dehumanisation of a disabled
     person. The ableist societal world-view is that neurotypical or able-bodied people are the norm in society
     and therefore essential and fully human. In contrast, people who have diversities or disabilities are
     largely seen as invisible 'others', in a diminished state of being human…' (Identity-First Autistic, 2016)

In this article I intend to raise awareness about the complexities of racism and the
intersection with ableism and how this links to the high rates of school exclusions
for African-Caribbean boys.

Introduction

My dad arrived in England from Jamaica in 1955. At the time, because Jamaica
was a colony of the British Empire, he was a British citizen. He came because, after
World War Two, Britain was short of workers and needed to rebuild its economy
(McDowell, 2018). Men and women were invited to Britain from the Caribbean to
work in manufacturing, public transport and the NHS. However the welcome was
conditional, and it was commonplace to see racist notices in homes and businesses
saying 'No Blacks no Irish and no dogs' (Verma, 2018). The recent Windrush
scandal, reported by *The Guardian* newspaper in 2019, has demonstrated again
how racism and the hostile climate continues to affect African Caribbean people.
Black British citizens who are descendants of my dad's generation continue to face
disproportionate disadvantages in all aspects of their lives.

Before I had children, I was a community activist challenging racism and
institutional practices that undermined the rights of black people. I had long
experience of supporting black people who had faced racism in school, employment,
housing, the criminal justice and health care systems. As a black woman and
activist, 'institutional racism' as a concept was not new to me.

After the racist murder of Stephen Lawrence in 1993, Doreen Lawrence's tireless
campaign to bring his killer to justice led to the MacPherson Inquiry (1999). This
Inquiry exposed the racist attitudes and practices of the police when investigating a
racially motivated murder. The inquiry found that institutional racism was present
within institutions that govern all aspects of life in Britain:

*'For the purposes of our Inquiry the concept of institutional racism which we
apply consists of: The collective failure of an organisation to provide an
appropriate and professional service to people because of their colour, culture,
or ethnic origin. It can be seen or detected in processes, attitudes and behaviour
which amount to discrimination through unwitting prejudice, ignorance,
thoughtlessness and racist stereotyping which disadvantage minority ethnic people.*

*Racism, institutional or otherwise, is not the prerogative of the Police Service. It
is clear that other agencies including for example those dealing with housing and
education also suffer from the disease. If racism is to be eradicated there must be
specific and coordinated action both within the agencies themselves and by society*

*at large, particularly through the educational system, from pre-primary school
upwards and onwards.'* (McPherson, 1999, Para. 6.34 and 6.54)

It has now been 20 years since the MacPherson (1999) inquiry. Has anything changed?

Challenging institutional racism in the school and health systems

I now want to critically reflect on how racism impacts black autistic boys accessing
health and education services. I had long suspected that my son was autistic. From
a young age he found unfamiliar social situations stressful, he had difficulties with
changes in routine and struggled with eye contact. His behaviour in primary school
suggested that he wasn't coping with the school environment, especially adapting
to changes. In secondary school this became more apparent as he had to adapt to a
much bigger community with more rules, different subjects in different rooms and
new teachers. He was expected to concentrate for longer periods, it was noisier and
busier, and more attention was paid to following rules and instructions.

My son was the tallest student in his year and this made him more noticeable,
which meant that teachers had expectations about his emotional maturity. As a
consequence, by year nine he had a behavioural record that the school wanted to
act on. The disciplinary process of fixed term exclusions began. The school regarded
my son's behaviour as 'chosen' and that his 'defiance' and inability to follow rules
contravened the school behaviour policy and required disciplinary action.

Even though I raised concerns that my son may have undiagnosed special
educational needs (SEN), the school began the process of permanently excluding
him. Throughout this process I continued to assert that my child may have an
undiagnosed condition that was impacting on his behaviour, however this was
dismissed by the school governors and the local authority appeals panel.

I believe the procedures that led to his permanent exclusion were based on their
stereotypes of black boys. For example, the completed risk assessment form they
used in their submission characterised my son in the following ways: potential risks
of involvement in gangs, drugs, carrying a weapon and violence to others. None of
these risks were substantiated or evidenced and instead the risk assessment was
used as a tick list of risks to justify permanent exclusion. More importantly, his
vulnerabilities were not given equal weight.

I believe my son's sensory sensitivities lay at the root of some of his challenging
behaviour. However, some of the school staff interpreted his behaviour as 'chosen
bad behaviour'. This language and perspective was used repeatedly in descriptions
of incidents recorded in his behaviour log. In my experience, schools do not regard
disruptive behaviour as indicative of an expression of unmet needs. Our experience

of the school is supported by findings in the National Autism Society's (NAS) *Diverse Perspectives* report:

'Some parents felt that there was an assumption that black boys are badly behaved and more liable to social exclusion. Participants felt that further assumptions are made that families are to blame for bad parenting that causes behaviour.' (2014, p8)

As a result, he was denied access to an assessment for autism before this irrevocable action was taken. He did not get the support he needed to stay in his school, as he was entitled to under equalities legislation. These attitudes and practices, at all levels of the disciplinary and appeals processes, led to my son being placed in a Pupil Referral Unit (PRU).

Challenging the school's decision to permanently exclude my son has been devastating for my family. As a black family, in the face of a predominantly white, middle-class environment, we felt our views and evidence were disregarded and our voice unwelcome. I can certainly identify with the comments made by parents in the NAS' Diverse Perspectives report:

'White families meet white professionals and seem to be on personal terms. We are made to feel like outsiders. – Parent'

'Black parents are often branded as trouble makers. – Parent.' (2014, p18)

Their refusal to accept my concerns about unmet needs was reflected in the experiences of parents highlighted in the *Diverse Perspectives* report (2014):

'They said that it was hard to convince schools, even following a diagnosis, that autism was the cause of behaviour.' (2014, p18)

In discussion with my son following the permanent exclusion, he told me he wanted to go back to where he belonged: his own school with his friends and sister. We began a long struggle to support his expressed need to return to a familiar environment. This could only be accomplished by seeking acknowledgement that he had been unlawfully excluded due to unmet needs. We decided to bring a case of disability discrimination to the SEND First Tier Tribunal – HM Courts & Tribunals Service. My family, like most families finding themselves in this situation, did not have any experience of the complex tribunal process. However, when we sought legal advice and representation from the Equalities and Human Rights Commission (EHRC), we were advised that representation would not be available as it would be very difficult to prove disability discrimination as my son did not have a formal 'diagnosis'. In order to challenge the school's decision, I was told I had to prove at the time the decision

was made he was, in fact, disabled. In these circumstances I felt I had no option but to
seek a psychiatric diagnosis of Autism Spectrum Disorder (ASD)[43] to substantiate my
claim of disability discrimination (this proved not to be the case).

We persisted and, with some guidance from the EHRC and the National Autistic
Society, I submitted an appeal against the school and we were granted a hearing at
the Special Educational Needs and Disability First Tier Tribunal. At the hearing,
for the first time we felt we were listened to with respect and understanding. The
tribunal panel found that it was not necessary for there to be a formal diagnosis for
a person to be deemed disabled. For the school, the case hinged on the fact that my
son did not have a formal diagnosis and they were resistant to the determination
of the panel that they should have acted differently. However, at this stage we
had also received confirmation of the formal diagnosis, which we were able to
bring to the attention of the panel, despite the school's attempts through their
legal representatives to prevent the panel from seeing the letter. At the end of the
hearing, in their final submission, the school and their legal representative still
pleaded that, whatever the outcome of our claim for disability discrimination, they
opposed his reinstatement. In spite of this, the tribunal found the school to have
discriminated against my son on the grounds of disability, and the permanent
exclusion was overturned. The tribunal found that, because the school had not
triggered an assessment of needs based on my concerns, they had therefore failed in
their duty under the SEND Code of Practice (2014) and the Equalities Act (2010).

This vindication of our position resulted in my son returning to the school, where
he managed to complete his education and to get his GCSEs. Further, the school
was required to apologise for their actions and for staff to undertake training in
disability discrimination and autism awareness.

It is important to note that the lack of a formal diagnosis, the point the school saw
as most important to their case, proved not to be the reason the school was found
to be in breach of equalities legislation. It was enough that they did not appreciate
that his behaviours were in themselves indicative of unmet needs and should have
been recognised and responded to.

Because of this experience, I decided it wasn't enough to just fight back; this
difficult and challenging experience motivated me to complete a Post Graduate
Certificate in Education in Autism and Asperger's Syndrome at Sheffield Hallam
University. Here, I began to explore and investigate the intersectionality of racism
and ableism in relationship to autism (Annamma *et al*, 2018). I read the findings
of the *They Never Give Up on You* report (OCC, 2012) (see above). This report

---

43 For the purpose of this article I am using the diagnosis of ASD from the Diagnostic and Statistical
  Manual-5 (DSM-5, 2013), which includes the following criteria: social

highlights the disproportionate use of permanent exclusion of black boys, especially those receiving free school meals (FSM) with a SEN. They were describing my son's experience and I wanted to know why this had happened to him.

'Zero tolerance' and exclusion policies

Schools' behaviour policies set out what is expected of students and the sanctions they will face if they break the rules. Exclusions are applied where poor behaviour is persistently disruptive and does not improve. Schools are concerned about increasing levels of verbal and physical aggressive behaviour and the consequent disruption to learning. In response, zero tolerance policies to support schools to develop robust behaviour policies were implemented in 2010. This was reinforced in 2014 by Michael Gove's message to teachers to 'get tough' on bad behaviour in schools (reported by *The Guardian*, 2014).

This policy has direct consequences for students with a diagnosis of Autism Spectrum Disorder (ASD) and they are now disproportionately represented in school exclusions. This is despite schools being expected to '*consider whether continuing disruptive behaviour might be the result of unmet educational or other needs*' (Dept of Education, 2016, p7).

The impact of the 'get tough' message can be seen from these statistics. In 2011/12 the numbers of children with an ASD diagnosis excluded from school was 2,831; by 2015/16 this had risen to 4,485, up by 60% (Hazell, 2018; Lasota, 2018). It is not clear from these figures how many of these pupils are black. However, government statistics for 2018 do show that the rate for permanent exclusions of black Caribbean pupils was nearly three times the rate of white British pupils (Department for Education 2018). Black and mixed ethnicity pupils had the highest rates of both temporary and permanent exclusions (EHRC, 2018).

What is becoming clearer is that these policies have direct consequences for young people with an autism diagnosis, however we don't know the numbers of black boys with an autism diagnosis in the UK and how they may have been affected.

We do know the situation of African Americans. In 2007, a study by a team at the Center for Autism and Developmental Disabilities Research and Epidemiology, University of Pennsylvania, found that African-American children were 5.1 times more likely to be mis-diagnosed with conduct disorders before being diagnosed with ASD. This shows that black children in the UK, as in the US, may well be under-represented in autism diagnoses and we know they are over-represented in school exclusions.

I now want to consider the long-term consequences of the 'get tough' policy for
African Caribbean boys' mental health and to critique the ideology that underpins
the 'get tough' zero tolerance approach.

Evans and Lester (2012) describe zero tolerance as an approach taken from
criminal justice systems, and they argue that:

*'Zero tolerance policies often restrict this view of student behaviour and require
teachers to follow mandatory policies regarding punishment for certain behaviours.
How do teachers manage to honour the **unique needs** of their students while at the
same time adhering to uniform school discipline policies?'* (2012, p109)

Sullivan and Johnson (2016) challenge school responses to behaviour management
and state that:

*'…policy is informed by ideology not evidence. If zero tolerance approaches are
informed by criminal justice practices we know already that African Caribbean
communities are disproportionately represented in arrests, stop and search
and sentencing. If minsters are using this ideological approach to school
discipline the evidence shows that African Caribbean students will undoubtedly
be disproportionately affected. According to Eleanor Busby's article in The
Independent Education News 2018, reporting from the National Education Union
(NEU) conference, teachers believed that zero tolerance approach to bad behaviour
amount to child abuse. Teachers attending the conference spoke out saying these
polices **'punish Black children and working class children the most'**.*

The question then becomes, is this ideology racist? In Black Parents Speak Out: The
school environment and interplay with wellbeing, Ochieng's research identified that:

*'…a number of key factors were viewed as compromising the wellbeing of African
Caribbean adolescents in schools; these were identified as experiences of racism,
the delivery of a Euro-centric curriculum, and reliance on suspension and
exclusion as a form of discipline at school. Participants also believed that
because African Caribbean boys suffered worse educational achievements
and the consequences of racism, this led to a significantly poorer
wellbeing in comparison with the girls'* (Ochieng, 2010, p176)

Sensory differences and behaviour policies

I now want to consider the guidance from the Department for Education (2016) on
school behaviour policies. In my view, in applying their behaviour policies, schools
are failing to meet their requirements under the Equality Act (2010). This is because

they are not making reasonable adjustments to behaviour policies and the school environment in order to meet the needs of autistic students. I believe this leads to disproportionate rates of exclusion. The guidance stresses that the policy must be *applied consistently* (Department for Education, 2016). However, the needs of a student with a diagnosis of ASD are not recognised and therefore they are disadvantaged, and this causes harm. For instance, if a school has a uniform policy that requires that *all* children must wear a tie and blazer, stand in lines and be learning ready, these expectations can present challenges for children with ASD diagnoses whose experiences and reactions may be as a result of their sensory and perceptual differences (such as not being able to tolerate the texture of the fabrics, finding close contact with people in crowded situations and moving classrooms overwhelming). Sensory sensitivities can also cause anxiety, pain and discomfort, which can lead to behaviour that challenges. This is poorly understood by most teaching staff. Beardon argues:

'...if we apply a concept that works for people in general and then apply it to the autistic population then the risk of harm goes up.' (Beardon, 2018)

I understand sensory sensitivities and reactions to sensory environmental stimulus as being at the heart of the difficulties of social communication and cognitive differences experienced by autistic people (Beardon, 2016; Delacato, 1984; Bogdashina, 2016). An explanation of what is sensory and how it impacts on individuals is described by Dellapiazza *et al* (2018), who cite Dunn's (1997) model for understanding sensory processing, the sensory experience and the link to behavioural responses:

'...the process during which the central nervous system receives, interprets, and responds to sensory inputs. Sensory stimulation can arise from each modality: auditory, tactile, visual, olfactory, vestibular, gustatory, or proprioceptive. Dunn's model takes into account interactions between neurological sensory thresholds and behavioural responses.' (2018, p78)

In my work, I share this perspective with teaching staff through discussions, training and in staff meetings. I share this perspective to combat some of the myths about autism and to encourage staff to think about the environmental stimuli that might have led to behaviour that challenges.

I work with students with an ASD diagnosis, a majority of the students are from black and minority ethnic communities. Students are often referred to me for behaviours that are preventing them from getting the best out of the learning environment (e.g. conflicts with peers or staff, aggression, anxiety and withdrawal from lessons). Behaviour that challenges within school is often experienced as disruptive. However, I argue that behaviour is a form of communication and, in my experience, unmet needs are often being expressed. For instance aggressive behaviour can be understood as a reaction to unresolved past issues (Leiberman, 2008); an emotional reaction to conflict (Kaplan, 2006); and a symptom of underlying issues (frustration, fear, anxiety, unfair treatment, injustice, pain or discomfort) (Hobson 1985; McKenzie-Mavinga, 2009; Bogdashina, 2016).

Poor behaviour within schools is often framed as an individual transgression of school rules. Hodge (2015) argues against this concept and counters that behaviour that challenges can be understood in the same way that we think about a social model of disability. Hodge states:

'...many teachers are currently operating within an **Individual Model of Behaviour** that always positions the problem of the behaviour in the pupil... this model leads to the application of ineffective and oppressive behavioural strategies' (2015, p1)

I have found this approach helps students, teaching staff and parents to explore behaviour that challenges within the context of sensory sensitivity. This has helped to identify the stressors that led to anxiety much earlier, reducing the number of incidents. As a parent advocate, sharing my knowledge of my children's sensory sensitives, anxiety and their behaviour has raised the awareness of school staff and led to positive changes in their teaching practice (Beardon, 2016; Bogdashina, 2016).

Racism, racial micro-aggressions and anxiety

I want to consider how racism contributes to 'the frustration, fear, anxiety, unfair treatment, injustice, pain or discomfort' (described above) experienced by African Caribbean autistic boys. To begin with, Beardon (2017) suggests there is a higher prevalence of anxiety within the autistic adult population as a whole. He states that this could be due to environmental factors, sensory sensitivities, communication differences and masking. Studies have also linked racial discrimination to increased anxiety levels in black populations (Graham, West, Roemer, 2015 citing Breslau *et al.* (2006) found:

'...a 24.7% lifetime prevalence rate of anxiety disorders among Black individuals. In addition, a replication of the National Comorbidity Study found anxiety disorders to be more persistent in Black individuals when compared to White individuals' (2015, p553).

In *Three Golden Rules for Supporting Autistic Students*, Beardon describes:

'... practical processes that schools can abide by that ensure the autistic child's needs are met:

1.   *Autism plus the environment equals the outcome. That outcome might be positive or negative, but the person who is autistic remains the same, it is the environment that leads to the outcome. So if you want a successful outcome, and you recognise the person with autism cannot change their brain, then the only thing you can change is the environment. And that often, but not always, means the people within that environment.'*
(Beardon, 2018)

Applying this rule to black autistic boys is helpful. My children's experience of racism within the school environment has given me cause to consider how their levels of anxiety and responses to perceived racism compounds their stress and behavioural responses.

I now want to consider 'racial micro aggressions' as part of the anxiety creating environment for black autistic boys. In this context, the NAS (2014) report *Diverse Perspectives* identified teacher's attitudes and perceptions toward black boys' behaviour as a significant area of concern. Do these attitudes include 'racial micro-aggressions'?

Micro-aggressions are factors in the everyday lives of black people and are described as:

> *'...verbal, non-verbal, and environmental slights, snubs, or insults, whether intentional or unintentional, which communicate hostile, derogatory, or negative messages to target persons based solely upon their marginalized group membership. In many cases, these hidden messages may invalidate the group identity or experiential reality of target persons, demean them on a personal or group level, communicate they are lesser human beings, suggest they do not belong with the majority group, threaten and intimidate, or relegate them to inferior status and treatment.'* (Wing Sue, 2010, paragraph 2)

The research by Abdullah and Graham (2016) describe anxiety in relation to racism as follows:

'An individual's perception of control over life contexts, safety, and environment is directly linked to stress and anxiety. We are not responsible for our experiences of racism, and we have very little, if any, control over whether or not we experience racism. So in the context of racism, racist experiences, can elicit understandable perception of lack of control of one's environment, therefore contributing to the development and maintenance of stress and anxiety.'

Through my own lived experiences and that of my children, racial micro-aggression are experienced every day: tone of voice, facial expressions, use of language and

body language are absorbed through the senses. The daily micro-aggressions
described by Wing Sue (2010) lead me to conclude that racism for black boys is an
embodied sensory experience and that this is not generally recognised. As a result,
they are being disproportionally affected by the stress of the school environment
and the wider impact of multiple disadvantages and discrimination.

This is an example of how micro-aggressions in relation to race and disability
intersect and compound the impact on the black autistic student. A student uses their
timeout pass regularly, they are often challenged in the corridors by teachers who
say, 'What are *you* up to?' They are not doing anything wrong, however the child is
being treated with suspicion. The student 'feels' this and experiences it as a slight and
reacts to it by saying, 'I'm not *up* to *anything*'. In the following discussion with the
teacher the student does not maintain eye contact and replies abruptly, and this is
interpreted as defiant and suspicious behaviour. The anxiety and distress affects the
rest of the student's day as they feel it was unfair and bottle it up.

In the next section I will consider how can we reduce these negative experiences
and how can we increase black autistic students' resilience and positive self-regard
to prevent low self-esteem.

Exploring a positive black autistic identity

Developing a positive black autistic identity is integral to my role as a mother of
black autistic children, and in my role as a psychotherapist and activist.
A large part of my work and practice is to support young black people to develop
a positive identity that increases a sense of belonging, value and self-worth. As
a practitioner working within a black perspective[44], it is a very important to me
that I address this challenge in a holistic way (Best, 2005). This involves continual
learning to understand the theories and the systems in relation to autism. This
journey has helped me to develop a black and non-clinical perspective.

Too often, black students do not experience a positive sense of self in the school
environment and curriculum. This is especially true in addressing the damaging
effects of racism. I have explored and used the *Black Identity Development Model*
(Jackson, 1975; 2001) as a means to support the development of a positive black
identity. This model has been further adapted by Atkinson *et al* (1998) to include a
Minority Identity Development Model, which is useful for working with all autistic

---

44 Black perspective: 'A black perspective recognises the collective capacity of black people to define,
develop and advance their own political, economic, social, cultural and educational interests. 'Black'
provides an historical and cultural context, whilst 'perspective' supplies the unique analysis and
consciousness-raising tool for action. A black perspective equips black people to continue the fight
for self-emancipation and create a body of knowledge, develop strategies that contribute to their
intellectual freedom and political liberation (Best 2005)

young people. By adapting this model to work with black autistic students I have been able to support young people to explore a positive black autistic identity.

In the school where I work I prioritised influencing the staff to consider how they could be part of directly increasing the visibility of black and autistic people. In the school, while there are many posters that celebrate the achievements of black and minority ethnic people and other minority groups and yet the poster that celebrated the achievements of autistic people only represented successful white people, mainly scientists e.g. Marie Curie, Albert Einstein, Steve Jobs etc. I started a discussion about whether it reflected the lives of students in the school. As a result of this discussion, over a year, awareness was raised and a new poster was designed of notable people that all young people could relate to. The poster includes people that have described themselves as having an autism or ADHD diagnosis. For example:

- Simone Biles, Olympic athlete.

- Stephen Wiltshire, a black artist from the UK.

- Lionel Messi, a talented footballer.

- Talia Grant, playing an autistic character in Hollyoaks.

- Anne Hegarty of 'The Chase'.

Lionel Messi is included as it is rumored that he was diagnosed with Asperger's syndrome as a child. The new poster has become a valuable resource that generates discussion about the experience, challenges and successes of the people in the poster. It also encouraged students to find out more about black autistic people and to have different conversations about their own experience of autism. The display of contemporary media and sports personalities has also been an invaluable resource for working with students who can see positive black and autistic role models.

In developing knowledge and resources, I share articles, research and new findings that appeal to student's specific interests.

For example:

- Looking at the theory that autism can be traced back to the ice age[45].

- Viewing YouTube videos about autistic people's lives has opened up a new conversation with a positive slant on their own understanding and their feelings about themselves as autistic young people. For instance, Stephen Wiltshire's videos about the cities that he has visited and the kind of art he makes.

---

45 At this time of human evolution, it is argued that autistic people had important assets; their capacity for focus, heightened sensory awareness and attention to detail, and it is hypothesised that autistic people played an important role in cave painting, food gathering and arrow making (Keys, 2018).

■ For Black History Month[46], staff have specifically looked for black people in history who had extraordinary talents and lives like the blind pianist Tom Wiggins.

This proved invaluable when students expressed their feelings of isolation, of being called names and not receiving positive messages about their unique differences. Students were shocked when they discovered that there are notable and successful autistic people. I have found that providing students with a range of information opens up opportunities to talk about issues in their lives. The issues they bring may well be about stress, low self-esteem, isolation, invisibility and negative stereotypes.

My aim is to counter the widely held belief that challenges encountered by autistic people are the result of having a 'diagnosed disorder' rather than 'difference' (Beardon, 2018). I do this by facilitating a process of enabling the students to value and celebrate their 'difference'.

Reframing behaviour that challenges through art therapy

In my experience, the reason my son's school refers students for art therapy is related to behaviour that challenges. However, the issues that are brought by the students are often about family conflict, belonging and identity issues, self-hatred, low self-esteem, loss and grief, anger, fear and traumatic events. Art therapy can be a very useful way of supporting the students to communicate their distress about the challenges and difficulties they face in a safe, supportive, non-judgmental and confidential environment.

Art therapy is a described as a form:

'... of psychotherapy based on the belief that the creative process in artistic self-expression can help individuals resolve conflicts and problems, develop interpersonal skills, manage behaviour, reduce stress and increase self-esteem. It can be preferable to counselling for those who are unable to verbalise the emotional and mental effects of bereavement, domestic violence, a broken home or identity problems.' (Keating, 2007, paragraph 5)

In my practice, my aim is to work with students, staff and parents to understand behaviours within the context of high levels of anxiety. I use an assessment process to help identify the triggers for anxiety. I then explore with them any relationship

---

46 Black History Month is an established, nationally recognised observance that honours the lives, experiences and history of African-Caribbean people.

between the expression of the anxiety and behaviours that create challenges for
them and the school. This approach enables students, parents and teaching staff to
reframe behaviours within a context of appreciating the underlying issues facing
the student. The relevance of this work to my psychotherapeutic practice is that it
helps me to identify the range of factors that may be leading to their anxiety, which
can lead to behaviour that challenges.

My art therapy practice is responsive and tailored to the needs of autistic students.
I use the creative process as described above to explore issues. Where possible I
use art materials, however for a number of my students art materials may trigger
anxieties related to touch and tactile sensitivity (Alter-Muri, 2017). This is not
in itself a barrier because students have the opportunity to talk about what is
affecting them when using the materials during the sessions.

The art therapy room is therefore a quiet space where students can get support to
make sense of their experience through:

- aiming to provide a calm space where students can relax and explore

- providing a range of materials that may stimulate sensory pleasure and/or
  discomfort (Beardon, 2016)

- encouraging discussion about sensory sensitivities to support the student to
  better understand their own sensory experiences (Brown & Dunn, 2010)

- providing a range of multicultural art materials including a range of different skin
  tone paints, crayons, masks, pictorial representations of diverse communities.

The benefits of exploring high levels of anxiety and disruptive behaviour using a
creative process can be illustrated by work I did with an autistic Muslim student.
He was concerned about how I viewed Muslims, stereotypes of Islam, the rise of
Islamophobia and how he experienced this through the media. He brought these
issues to the therapeutic space and would challenge me. I considered the negative
impact this had for his sense of self and identity and engaged with him by sharing
my understanding of multiple disadvantages.

Initially his high levels of anxiety and low self-esteem prevented him from feeling
safe in the art therapy room. He often left the room for short periods during the
session and this behaviour led to teaching staff questioning if he was using art
therapy appropriately. However, I persisted and encouraged him to work with
materials that he liked. He chose masks that can be decorated and worn. Initially,
he didn't decorate the masks but used them to hide his face. 'Hiding' became an
important theme in our work together. He then began decorating the masks and to
explore feelings that he couldn't easily express, for instance the way he decorated a

mask led to a discussion about sadness and crying. This exploration eventually led to a trusting relationship between us.

This trusting relationship enabled him to share with me his underlying difficulties and links to behaviour that challenged. For example, he wanted to have a girlfriend and this was against his family's values. This made him angry, especially because of the restrictions placed on him as a result of his diagnosis and perceived vulnerability. This resulting inner conflict; his need to be seen to be as a good Muslim; his family values and his lack of opportunities for developing his independence led to high levels of anxiety and was connected to his disruptive behaviour in the school. It was important for me to recognise the importance of how intersectional issues of racism, Islamophobia and ableism impacted on this young man's life. The process supported him to explore his identity as a young Muslim, as an autistic man and to better understand the connection between his emotions and behaviour. By finding a way to explore these difficulties, he was better able to acknowledge his distress.

Conclusions

In this article I have examined whether schools are failing to recognise the needs of black autistic boys. In doing this, I have sought to explain how racism, micro-aggressions of racism, and ableism intersect and ultimately damage the life chances of black autistic boys in the UK and leads to high rates of schools exclusions.

The high rates of permanent exclusions of black boys from mainstream schools, coupled with the recent 60% rise in exclusions for autistic students, is alarming, but does not specifically reflect the experience of black autistic boys. This requires further exploration.

Further, the OCC's *They Never Give Up on You* report (2012) states that:

'A black Caribbean boy eligible for free school meals who also has special educational needs (SEN) is 168 times more likely to be permanently excluded than a white British girl without SEN and not eligible for free school meals.'

It is unlikely that this statistic takes into account the experience of black autistic boys, a particularly vulnerable group that we do not know much about.

The rise in youth offending and the possible links to school exclusions are raising concerns at a governmental level, as can be seen by a recent Home office report that has warned that school expulsions could be fueling a rise in youth crime (*The Telegraph*, 2018). This was certainly a concern I had: by permanently excluding my son from school and isolating him from his peers I felt they put him at greater risk of involvement in crime. My motivation for returning him to mainstream school was both to challenge the discrimination he faced as a black autistic student and to keep him out of the criminal justice system. I regard permanent exclusion from school for black autistic boys as a potential 'pipeline to prison'. Keeney Parks (2018), a black mother and researcher in the US, shares my concerns. She writes about the day-to-day lives and experiences of black parents who have a child diagnosed with autism. Her recent online blog identifies similar realties to those I have experienced:

'The disparities faced… by African-Americans receiving special education services, which is the case with the majority of autistic children, are especially disconcerting… but even more so for kids in special education, who are often segregated from typical peers into special classes, juvenile justice and criminal justice systems are deprived of an appropriate education that could have changed their School-to-Prison Pipeline trajectory.'

In the UK context, The Lammy Review (2017) found that:

'Despite making up just 14% of the population, BAME men and women make up 25% of prisoners, while over 40% of young people in custody are from BAME backgrounds. There is greater disproportionality in the number of Black people in prisons here than in the United States.'

I believe that this a sign that black autistic boys are in danger of being on the same trajectory as the African Americans that Parks describes.

A confidential government briefing paper was recently leaked (*The Guardian*, 2019) addressing the concerns arising from their determination to continue with a 'get tough' stance on poor behaviour. According to *The Guardian*, the Department for Education's paper:

'…includes a major focus on poor behaviour in schools, said to be driven by No 10's view that recent polling has shown strong public support for policies taking a tougher line. The announcements will include explicit support for head teachers who use 'reasonable force' in their efforts to improve discipline. '…While the DfE expects members of the public will welcome 'a harder narrative on discipline', the document warns key stakeholders will be worried the policy could result in increased rates of permanent exclusion, which have in any case been climbing since 2012.

'The document notes police and crime commissioners 'worry about rates of exclusion driving knife crime' and acknowledges concerns it will impact disproportionately on

*children from some ethnic minority backgrounds, in particular black
Caribbean boys, and those with special educational needs (SEN).'*

The prevailing culture of the government is creating a hostile climate for black
autistic boys that says 'we have given up on you', rather than the promise implied
in the OCC's claim in *They Never Give Up On You*, in which they state:

*'Permanent exclusion has a negative effect on an excludee's life for far longer
than the period immediately after exclusion. We knew a minority of schools
exclude informally and therefore illegally but for the first time in this
Inquiry have this on record. Whilst most schools work far beyond the call of
duty to hold on to troubled and vulnerable children, a minority exclude
on what seems to the observer to be a whim. And for whatever reasons, many
of them explored in this report, we have not sufficiently challenged the failures
and brought about the changes required. We must do so now.'* (OCC, 2012)

I challenged the school to get justice for my son by successfully overturning the
school's decision to permanently exclude him. This included making decisions I wasn't
always comfortable with such as imposing a psychiatric diagnosis of a disorder on
my son, and supporting him to appreciate why this was important. This journey
has been extremely difficult for me and my whole family, especially for my son. He
has missed out on important aspects of adolescence with regard to friendships and
relationships at school. The result of my son attending a PRU for 15 months meant
he was only able to access a limited curriculum, reducing his scope for GCSE subjects
and qualifications. This experience has impacted on his life chances.

To change this situation for my son and other black autistic boys, I have shared my
learning with you. What I hope will happen as a result of this article is that there
will be great efforts to:

■ address the gaps in the research into the experience of autistic African
  Caribbean boys and their families

■ reduce the rising rates of permanent exclusions that disproportionately affect
  black and autistic students

■ better understand how the intersection of ableism and racism impacts on African
  Caribbean boys' life-long well-being.

In these ways we can begin to better understand the challenges facing black
autistic boys and to give them the life chance they are entitled to.

References

Abdullah T & Graham J (2016) The Link Between Experiences of Racism and Stress and Anxiety for Black Americans: A Mindfulness and Acceptance-Based Coping Approach accessed online 23rd. January 2018 at https://adaa.org/learn-from-us/from-the-experts/blog-posts/consumer/link-between-experiences-racism-and-stress-and

Annamma SA, Ferri BA, Conner DJ (2018) Disability Critical Race Theory: Exploring the Intersectional Lineage, Emergence, and Potential Futures of DisCrit in Education. Sage 42 (1) 46–71.

Atkinson DR, Morten G & Sue DW (Editors) (1998) Counseling American Minorities: A cross cultural perspective (5th Edition) [online]. McGraw. Hill Company. Available at: www.covwarkpt.nhs.uk/download.cfm?doc=docm93jijm4n468.pdf&ver=580 (accessed July 2020).

Beardon L (2017) Autism and Aspergers Syndrome in Adults. Sheldon Press, London.

Beardon L (2018) Is Autism a Disorder? [online]. Available at: https://blogs.shu.ac.uk/autism/2018/07/17/is-autism-a-disorder/ (accessed July 2020).

Beardon L (2018) Three golden rules for supporting autistic pupils [online]. Accessed on 20th August 2019 at https://schoolsimprovement.net/three-golden-rules-for-supporting-autistic-pupils/

Bennett Brown N., Dunn W. (2010) Relationship Between Context and Sensory Processing in Children With Autism, Volume 64, Number 3 - American Journal of Occupational Therapy,

Best J. (2005) A Black Perspective in Community and Youth Work, Community Work Unit, School of Education, University of Manchester

Bogdashina O. (2016) Sensory Perceptual Issues in Autism and Asperger Syndrome Jessica Kingsley Publishers London and Philadelphia

Busby E. (2018) Zero tolerance approach to bad behaviour in schools amount to 'child abuse', teachers claim Education News. The Independent accessed online 3rd. January at https://www.independent.co.uk/news/education/education-news/strict-behaviour-school-punish-children-child-abuse-teachers-national-education-union-a8283276.html 17.01.2019

Crenshaw, K. (1989) Demarginalizing the Intersection of Race and Sex: A Black Feminist Critique of Antidiscrimination Doctrine, Feminist Theory and Antiracist Politics, University of Chicago Legal Forum: Vol. 1989: Iss. 1, Article 8.

Available at: http://chicagounbound.uchicago.edu/uclf/vol1989/iss1/8

Crenshaw K. (2016) TedWomen accessed 1st august 2018 https://www.ted.com/talks/kimberle_crenshaw_the_urgency_of_intersectionality

Delacato C. H. (1984) The Ultimate Stranger: The Autistic Child Ann Arbor Publishers

Dellapiazza F., Vernheta C., Blanc N., Miota S. Schmidtd R., Baghdadlia A. (2018) Links between sensory processing, adaptive behaviours and attention in children with autism spectrum disorder: A systematic review Psychiatry research, 2018 – Elsevier accessed online at https://scholar.google.co.uk/scholar?hl=en&as_sdt=0%2C5&as_vis=1&q=Links+between+sensory+processing%2C+adaptive+behaviours+and+attention+in+children+with+autism+spectrum+disorder%3A+A+systematic+review&btnG=

Department of Ed (2014) Statutory guidance SEND code of practice: 0 to 25 years -

Department for Education and Department of Health and Social Care

Department of Education (2016) Behaviour and discipline in schools - Guidance for Head teachers

Department for Education (2018) Pupil Exclusions Ethnicity Facts and Figures accessed on 11th August 2019 at https://www.ethnicity-facts-figures.service.gov.uk/education-skills-and-training/absence-and-exclusions/pupil-exclusions/latest#permanent-exclusions-by-ethnicity

Equalities and Human Rights Commission (2018),Race report- Statistics and analysis to accompany the race report: Healing a divided Britain accessed 17th August 2019 at https://www.equalityhumanrights.com/en/race-report-statistics

Equality Act 2010, Government Equalities Office

Graham, West, Roemer, 2015 A preliminary exploration of the moderating role of valued living in the relationships between racist experiences and anxious and depressive symptoms

Hobson R. F. (1985) Forms of Feeling – The Heart of Psychotherapy Tavistock Publications London and New York

Hodge N. (2015) Labels like autism and ADHD are nothing to shout about. Times Educational Supplement

Hazell W. 2018 Exclusions of autistic pupils up 60 per cent TES accessed July 2019 at https://www.tes.com/news/exclusions-autistic-pupils-60-cent

Identity - First Autistic (2016) Effecting Social Change through Language accessed 20th August 2019 at https://www.identityfirstautistic.org/about1-c1oqk

Kaplan F (2006) Art Therapy and Social Action- Jessica Kingsley Publishers

Keating M (2007) A place to hide and heal – The Guardian Education. Accessed Jan 2019 at https://www.theguardian.com/education/2007/nov/13/schools.uk3

Keeney Park S (2018) How Racism Impacts Black Kids with Autism: From the Clinic to the Classroom – Speak Up Blog accessed 20th January 2019 at http://speakupparents.org/blog/2018/8/2/how-racism-impacts-black-kids-with-autism-from-the-clinic-to-the-classroom

Keys D (2018) Prehistoric autism helped produce much of the world's earliest great art, study says, The Independent, accessed 15/02/2019 at https://www.independent.co.uk/news/science/archaeology/prehistoric-autism-cave-paintings-barry-wright-penny-spikins-university-of-york-a8351751.html

Lammy D. (2017) The Lammy Review: An independent review into the treatment of, and outcomes for, Black, Asian and Minority Ethnic individuals in the Criminal Justice System, HM Government, accessed 24th August 2019 at:

https://assets.publishing.service.gov.uk/government/uploads/system/uploads/attachment_data/file/643001/lammy-review-final-report.pdf

Lasota J. (2018) Ambitious about Autism responds to Government exclusions review https://www.ambitiousaboutautism.org.uk/understanding-autism/ambitious-about-autism-responds-to-government-exclusions-review

Leiberman (2008) Art Therapy and Anger – Jessica Kingsley Publications

McKenzie, Mavinga I (2009) Black Issues in The Therapeutic Process – Palgrave Macmillan

McDowell L. (2018) How Caribbean migrants helped to rebuild Britain accessed 29th July 2019 at https://www.bl.uk/windrush/articles/how-caribbean-migrants-rebuilt-britain

MacPherson, W. (1999). The Stephen Lawrence Inquiry, The Stationary Office UK. Available at: http://webarchive.nationalarchives.gov.uk/20130814142233/http://www.archive.official-documents.co.uk/document/cm42/4262/4262.htm [Accessed 4 Jan. 2016].

Ochieng B.M.N. (2010) Black parents speak out: The school environment and interplay with wellbeing- Health Education Journal 70(2) 176–183 School of Health studies, University of Bradford, UK sagepub.co.uk/journalsPermissions.nav DOI: 10.1177/0017896910373143 hej.sagepub.com

Office of the Children's Commissioner (2012) 'They never give up on you', School Exclusions Inquiry – response from the Department for Education

Price J and M Shildrick (1999) My body Myself How Does a Black Woman Do Sociology? Feminist Theory and the Body: A Reader Routledge

Sullivan A, Johnson B (2016) Challenging Dominant Views on Student behaviour at school...Answering back - Springer Science + Business Media Singapore

The Guardian 2019 'Windrush Scandal' accessed July 2019 at https://www.theguardian.com/uk-news/windrush-scandal

The Guardian (2019) 'Micheal Gove Urges 'traditional punishments for school mis-behaviour' accessed 21st January 2019 athttps://www.theguardian.com/education/2014/feb/02/michael-gove-traditional-punishments-school-misbehaviour

The Telegraph (2018) School expulsions fuel rise in youth crime, say experts accessed 24th August 2019 at: https://www.telegraph.co.uk/news/2018/04/10/school-expulsions-fuel-rise-youth-crime-say-experts/

Verma R. (2018) 'It Was Standard To See Signs Saying, 'No Blacks, No Dogs, No Irish' - Human Rights News, Views & Info accessed on 19th August 2019 at https://rightsinfo.org/racism-1960s-britain/

West J. R., Roemer L. M. (2013) The Experience of Racism and Anxiety Symptoms in an African-American Sample: Moderating Effects of Trait Mindfulness Graham Published online: 29 April 2015 Springer Science + Business Media New York

Wing Sue D. PhD (2010) Micro-aggressions: More than Just Race - Psychology Today accessed online 28th January 2019 at:

https://www.psychologytoday.com/gb/blog/microaggressions-in-everyday-life/201011/microaggressions-more-just-race

Chapter 20: Neuroqueering music therapy

Observations on the current state of neurodiversity in music therapy practice

By Jessica Leza, MA, MT-BC

Acknowledgements: The author would like to thank James Hays, CJ Shiloh, Rachel Reed, Sierra Norris, Anastasia Canfield, Kristin Abbott, Allison Burns and Roia Rafieyan for their support.

Author's note: This essay is intended as a collection of observations from one board-certified, neurodivergent music therapist who currently serves neurodivergent students in the public school system. As a clinician deeply embedded in the profession of music therapy (MT), and one who is as beholden to bias as any other human, this essay is not intended to be an objective or exhaustive assessment of current music therapy practice, history or theory, and is instead offered as an expedition in special interest hyperfocus – an 'autistext' in a scholarly dialect – inspired by the tradition of autie ethnography as described by Melanie Yergeau in Authoring Autism (p24).

What is music therapy?

Music therapy is the art and science of using music within a therapeutic relationship to assist a client in achieving specific and measurable goals and objectives. Music therapists are extensively trained musicians who play professional-quality instruments to create live music experiences. Music choices are always guided by the client's unique preferences and needs. Music therapists also use recorded music and other ways of engaging in the various cultural definitions of music. Clients typically participate in active music making while being guided and assisted by the therapist, who both uses music as an accommodation and creates accommodations to access music, according to the client's strengths, needs and cultural values. It is an allied health profession, similar to speech-language pathology (SLP), occupational therapy (OT), or physical therapy (PT), and in the US it requires a potential therapist to earn a bachelor's degree in music therapy, complete a 1,040 hour internship, and pass a written exam overseen by the

Certification Board for Music Therapists (CBMT). Once a music therapist achieves their MT-BC credential, they must prove they have participated in at least 100 hours of continuing education and professional development activities to maintain certification for another five years.

According to the CBMT's website, there are just under 8,400 music therapists in the US who are currently maintaining their certification. Music therapists serve clients of all ages, from birth to death, and clients do not need to have training or special musical abilities – just an interest in and enjoyment of music. Music therapists provide services in people's homes, schools, nursing homes, hospitals, private clinics, churches, day cares, shelters and other locations in the community.

Music therapy will always be forged out of the contexts and cultures in which it is located. As a result, even though most but not all music therapists have served neurodivergent clients at some point in their careers, most music therapists seem to struggle in identifying how neurodiversity impacts their clinical practice, and the field of music therapy has been criticized (Straus, 2014) for overall '[positioning] itself squarely within the medical model of disability, … and offering music as a source of normalization, remediation, and therapy toward a possible cure.'

A brief overview of the history of music therapy and neurodiversity

Throughout the nascent years of the neurodiversity movement, the field of music therapy plugged along, for the most part cultivating an idle unawareness of the cultural currents stirring in the autism, mental health and disability communities. Around five years ago, a steady trickle of information about neurodiversity began to percolate slowly throughout the global music therapy community. In 2012 and 2013, disability rights activist and music therapist CJ Shiloh gave a series of presentations at regional and then national conferences about Sensory Friendly Concerts, sometimes joined by Sunny Cefaratti, autistic advocate and co-founder of The Musical Autist (Shiloh, 2019).

In 2014, Michael Bakan's 'Ethnomusicological perspectives on autism, neurodiversity, and music therapy' was published in *Voices*, a world forum for music therapy. In it, Bakan proposes a 'paradigm shift from pathology to neurodiversity', from which 'therapy, in this manifestation, would be achieved not by targeting Autistic ways of being for change, but rather by targeting change through the embrace of Autistic ways of being'.

2014 also saw the publication of Shiloh and LaGasse's 'Sensory friendly concerts: A community music therapy initiative to promote Neurodiversity' in the *International Journal of Community Music*. In it, the authors describe 'Sensory Friendly Concerts®️ (SFCs), a music enjoyment and making venue that promotes the social acceptance of each individual, specifically of those who identify as 'autistic' and seek to develop an autistic culture and community' (p113). These events are based on a collaboration between music therapists and community musicians, as facilitated by The Musical Autist, a non-profit that strives for anti-oppressive practice in part 'by developing fine arts concert venues where naturally occurring autistic behaviours are readily accepted' and an autistic community can be built (Shiloh & LaGasse, 2014, p116). In the autumn of the same year, nonspeaking Autistic advocate Josh Berkau joined Shiloh, LaGasse and DePriest to give a well-received presentation to a crowded audience of music therapy professionals at the American Music Therapy Association's (AMTA) national conference, titled 'Presuming Competence in our Clients' (Shiloh, 2019).

In 2015, the AMTA held 'Improving Access and Quality: Music therapy research 2025', a research symposium that invited breakout groups to discuss considerations for future research in selected clinical topics, including autism spectrum 'disorder' (Bumanis, 2015). Sierra Norris and CJ Shiloh successfully 'rallied for neurodiversity to be acknowledged in the long-term strategic goals of music therapy research', with valuable encouragement from Annette Whitehead-Pleaux. The following year, the journal *Music Therapy Perspectives* would publish some of Shiloh's reflections on the experience in a piece called 'A Clinician's Response: Considering Our Clients' Voices'. Throughout 2015 and 2016, Shiloh continued to provoke consideration for the role of neurodiversity in music therapy through presentations given at the AMTA national conference and the Online Conference for Music Therapy, this time focusing on 'Ethically Navigating Hot Button Topics in the Autism Community' (Shiloh, 2019).

In 2016, autistic musician Henny Kupferstein and music therapist Susan Rancer published their book *Perfect Pitch in the Key of Autism: A guide for educators, parents, and the musically gifted*. Sierra Norris presented a paper to the International Society for Music Education (ISME) Commission on Special Music Education and Music Therapy titled 'Disability as identity and culture: Implications for music educators and researchers' (Norris, 2019). That summer, New York University's Nordoff Robbins Center for Music Therapy hosted a symposium titled 'Neurodiversity, Music Therapy, and the Autism Spectrum', in which therapists and autistic advocates argued for abandoning Nordoff and Robbin's concept of the 'music child' – a musical version of the outdated image of a non-autistic child trapped inside an autistic 'shell' – in favour of a concept of 'core musicality' (Reynolds, 2016).

In 2017, music therapist Ken Aigen gave several keynote speeches, including 'Music therapy and neurodiversity: A progressive platform for future practice' and 'Autism and the Neurodiversity Movement: Implications for music therapy research', the latter presented at the University of Bergen in Norway (Aigen, 2017). That same year he was awarded the Arthur Flagler Fultz Research Award from AMTA, allowing him to begin a research project called 'Music in Everyday Autistic Life: The Significance of Music for Autistic Adults' with Jon Fessenden, Rachel Reed, CJ Shiloh, Stephen Shore and Marla Hodermarska (Shiloh, 2019). Meanwhile, Sierra Norris brought 'Neurodiversity and positive niche construction in the music classroom' to the Arizona Music Educators Association (Norris, 2019).

In early 2018, Columbia University held a symposium titled 'New Frontiers in the Study of Music, Autism, and Neurodiversity', where Aigen spoke about moving beyond the medical model of disability. That April, CJ Shiloh, Sunny Cefaratti and Rachel Reed hosted a roundtable discussion for the Mid-Atlantic Region of AMTA where they '[shared their] experiences working together as an autistic advocate, neurotypical music therapist, and autistic music therapy intern in developing a community music therapy program' (Shiloh, 2019).

In the fall of 2018, AMTA announced the controversial hire of a new executive director. Lee Grossman came to AMTA after spending time at the head of several organisations, most notably the Autism Society of America (ASA). Grossman's public statements had historically placed him as a pathologising agent in autism advocacy, and his reputation as an anti-vaxxer preceded him. Music therapists across the country quickly began to raise a furore. Discussions on social media exploded, complaints were registered to the AMTA board, and some members chose to resign their membership.

In hindsight, Grossman's hire may have been just the needling the music therapy profession required in order to take the next steps in becoming true allies and advocates for the neurodivergent and autistic community. The heated discussions that took place over the months drew out a burgeoning awareness among professionals that, among other things, neurodivergent and specifically autistic music therapists exist; neurodivergent and autistic music therapy interns exist; neurodivergent and autistic music therapy students exist.

Then, as now, many music therapists seem to be unaware that a human being could have autistic neurology and *yet also* be a talented musician capable of earning college degrees and working in an allied health field. Once again, we see that the same issues of ableism that appear in the broader world also impact many therapists' understanding of neurodivergent lives and potentials.

The controversy over Grossman's hire did not burn out until his sudden and unexpected resignation in May 2019, when he left to take a position at another organisation. The growing community of neurodivergent and/or autistic music therapy students and professionals and dedicated allies did not retire alongside Grossman's involvement. Instead, efforts at activism and community building have only increased. Grossman's controversial anti-autistic views revealed for many the need to cultivate a deeper understanding of neurodiversity, and many in the field have risen to the challenge.

Training and education sessions on topics in neurodiversity are becoming standard fare on the conference docket in 2020. I spoke about 'Embracing Neurodiversity: Advocacy and Allyship' at the Southwestern American Music Therapy Association (SWAMTA) conference in March 2019 to a packed and responsive room, at much the same time that Alyssa Wilkins and Ava Marvin were leading a workshop about 'Finding the Beauty in Neurodiversity' at the Institute for Therapy through the Arts (ITA) Integrative Creative Arts Therapies Conference. The European Music Therapy Conference in June 2019 held a roundtable of five therapists who discussed 'What can the neurodiversity movement offer Music Therapy?' (Thompson *et al*, 2019). The Central Texas Music Therapy Association (CTMTA) held a mini-conference in September 2019 for which they specifically sought out a presenter who could speak on neurodiversity. Neurodiversity was the subject of a Continuing Music Therapy Education (CMTE) course at the national AMTA conference in November 2019, followed by an additional educational session on the topic during the Online Conference for Music Therapy (OCMT) in December 2019. The new text *A Spectrum of Approaches: Music therapy and autism across the lifespan* includes a chapter from Beth Pickard (2019) in which she explores the 'therapeutic aim of developing autonomy' as one way to 'value neurodiversity'. And in South Africa in 2020 the World Congress of Music Therapy will host a roundtable of six music therapists, again discussing 'What can the neurodiversity movement offer music therapy?' (Shiloh, 2019).

In addition to these professional trainings and publications, undergraduate and graduate music therapy students are focusing on topics that integrate the neurodiversity paradigm into music therapy through their graduate thesis, student research projects and student music therapy conferences. Amanda Scranton is currently analysing the data already collected for her graduate thesis regarding 'music therapists' perceptions and awareness of neurodiversity and their descriptions of practices and beliefs'. At the undergraduate level, neurodivergent music therapy students are completing research projects on topics that directly impact the lives of neurodivergent clients, such as alexithymia or the trauma potentials of Applied Behaviour Analysis (ABA).

Some music therapy students are even comfortably 'out' as autistic in their academic programmes, and have spoken about the positive experience of support and accommodations they have received through their university (although others find themselves in less tolerant and accommodating programmes). These anecdotes can be taken as indicators that the field is moving towards a more open acceptance of diverse neurologies and disability, but I would be remiss if I did not acknowledge that the vast majority of neurodivergent MTs and MT students seem to feel safer by engaging in forms of masking and privacy surrounding diagnosis, and instead engage in advocacy and education without personally disclosing to the field at large. There are certainly many ways in which the profession can feel hostile to neurodivergent music therapists, something that may reflect the cultural contexts that music therapy exists in, as much as anything else.

In spite of (or perhaps because of) this potential for hostility, a community of allies and advocates has nonetheless continued to grow rapidly. Several music therapists and music therapy students founded the 'Neurodiversity for Music Therapists' website and public Facebook page in early summer 2019, as well as a closed Facebook group for music therapy professionals and students to discuss professional issues and create learning modules that privilege the lived experience and expertise of neurodivergent and/or autistic people. This community has also begun the work of compiling resources and reading lists for colleagues who want to learn more through independent study; there are also plans for this community to create additional resources such as a toolkit for music therapy professionals in academia and supervision to help faculty successfully support neurodivergent and autistic music therapy students and interns. Many in the music therapy community have also discussed the need for an edited anthology that will introduce the concepts of neurodiversity to music therapy students and professionals.

Musicking neurodivergence and the neuroqueering of music therapy

Often when music therapists communicate about neurodiversity, the focus is on what music therapists can do for neurodivergent people in therapy, rather than what might be called the act of neuroqueering music therapy – or disrupting any stigmatising and oppressive 'standards of practice' by inviting the neurodiversity paradigm *in* and leaving the pathology paradigm *out*.

Nick Walker (2015) defines several ways that one can neuroqueer, for example by 'being neurodivergent and actively choosing to embody and express one's neurodivergence (or refusing to suppress one's embodiment and expression of neurodivergence) in ways that 'queer' one's performance of gender, sexuality, ethnicity, occupation, and/or other aspects of one's identity'. Most music therapists would probably state that they consider it a responsibility to create a therapeutic environment and relationship that allows their neurodivergent clients to freely express themselves, and may even consider this skill of embodying and expressing oneself as described by Walker to be a serious and legitimate goal for therapy. In many instances, a client's ability to neuroqueer in therapy might be seen as the foundation or pathway for mastering increasingly more complex and nuanced goals.

Another aspect of neuroqueering is defined as, 'working to transform social and cultural environments in order to create spaces and communities – and ultimately a society – in which engagement in [neuroqueering] is permitted, accepted, supported, and encouraged' (Walker, 2015). It is this explanation of neuroqueering as a verb, an act in search of a moving target, through which it might be easiest to see how we have already begun the radical act of neuroqueering music therapy.

At its core, neuroqueering requires that clinicians approach autistic and neurodivergent people with a sense of cultural humility, and honour disabled people as experts in their own needs and experiences. It also seems that this is a radical act that carries the potential to upend the inherent power imbalances that exist within therapy, and therapists who are heavily dependent on these traditional power structures to enact a 'successful therapy' may find the suggestion that we should actively neuroqueer our music therapy practices to be a radical one.

But music therapy is already radicalised.

We are already a profession that habitually abandons spoken, verbal communication in exchange for a radical rattling, a shaking, stuttering, victorious chant; a strumming, stimming, ticcing, thumping, stomping, clapping, wordlessly ringing and thunderous musicking.

We already radicalise echolalia out of its pathologised language of impairment and music it into a vibrant and multidimensional context that displays its natural expressive and aesthetic form, an artful repetition, a snap-crackle-pop call-and-answer that communicates and validates our shared human experiences together in song and recitation.

We already radicalise 'stereotypy' and 'self-stimulatory behaviours' into a spinning, jumping, drumming stimdance indigenous to the autistic spirit; a repetitive motion unleashed into a magnificent wave of choreography.

We are already radicalised, a profession that prides itself on knowing that communication doesn't only happen through words. We are already the therapy that 'doesn't seem like therapy', the one that 'looks like you're just playing around', the therapy that is itself often misunderstood and undervalued. We are already radicalised, and so many music therapists are already actively musicking neurodivergence in full concert with their clients, whether in a formalised fashion such as occurs in Nordoff Robbins' music therapy or in a community music programme such as those facilitated by The Musical Autist.

In 2014, Bakan described what might be considered a vision of what happens when music therapists move beyond musicking neurodivergence and begin to actively neuroqueer music therapy:

'If we were to privilege listening to what our Autistic interlocutors had to say about what they think they need and what matters to them over acting on the assumption that our main responsibility is to change them 'for the better' in accordance with the conventions of a pathology-based model of wellness and functionality, think how radically altered the landscape of therapeutic interventions might become.'

The music therapy field as a whole seems to be poised on the edge of this 'radically altered [landscape]', with many self-identifying as stranded by the gaps between theory and practice.

From where I stand, Bakan's 'radically altered landscape' looks like 'autistic space' by another name, and both resemble the 'public concerts and events that [promote] a safe and understanding environment where different responses to music are respected' described by Shiloh (2014, p118). In fact, the gaps between theory and practice may not be as daunting as some picture them, and by turning the full spotlight of neurodivergent hyperfocus on the subject, I have collected and sorted and lined up the following thoughts about translating the neurodiversity paradigm and its related concepts and values into clinical music therapy practice.

How to neuroqueer your music therapy[47]

Neuroqueering music therapy by putting 'nothing about us, without us' into practice doesn't only charge therapists with listening to neurodivergent voices when it comes to setting research priorities, designing a treatment plan, or choosing the language used in documentation. It first demands developing an understanding of who this 'us' is. Before a music therapist can neuroqueer their practice, they must familiarise themselves with the patterns and consequences of misdiagnosis, the atypical presentations of autism that often present in girls, women, and trans and

---

47 *The idea that I can tell you how to neuroqueer your music therapy is almost as absurd as claiming that I can teach you how to tomato your unicorn, but I have always found that absurdity has a comfortable home in music therapy, so why not proceed? These thoughts are meant to help clinicians and others conceptualise and describe current methods for integrating the neurodiversity paradigm into music therapy. Further research is required to clearly delineate what exactly might be meant by neuroqueering music therapy.*

nonbinary people, and explore the high incidence of overlap between autistic people and LBGT+ people. Staying up to date with best practices for serving the LGBT+ community is a minimum standard – there's no such thing as neuroqueering if you leave the queers behind. Therapists may need to engage in supervision or use other tools to examine their practice and ensure clients are not being assumed or pressured to be straight and cis-gendered merely because they are disabled, and that gender non-conforming behaviours are respected and celebrated, not pathologised or 'put under extinction'. Therapists may also need to put in the work of learning new terms (such as 'autigender' and 'gendervague') to help communicate in a fluent way regarding a client's gender or sexuality.

Getting to know the 'us' in 'nothing about us, without us' also mandates the acknowledgement that diagnostic descriptions and clinical case studies often focus on children, especially boys – and most especially white boys. Intentionally learning from autistic people of colour, especially autistic women and nonbinary people of colour, is an important way to pursue the neuroqueering of music therapy. Neurodivergent people of colour might face unique challenges that include difficulty accessing services, facing both racial and ableist discrimination, and/or experiencing the cumulative pressure to assimilate to both mainstream US culture and to neurotypical culture. An additional complicating factor arises when others attribute social and communication differences to a minority cultural status, and this leads to misdiagnosis. Finally, many ethnic and religious communities serve as a refuge where someone is free to be openly neurodivergent, while others may be a source of harsh backlash for violating confusing social rules (Ashkenazy, 2017, p xxxiv-xxxv).

Neuroqueering music therapy by celebrating the 'us' also mandates an acknowledgement of autistic and neurodivergent culture. Many music therapists already construct activities around holidays and special events, making it a natural fit to pay tribute to Autism Acceptance Day (April 2), Autism Acceptance Month (April), Autistic Pride Day (June 18), Autistic Dignity Day (August 8), Autistics Speaking Day (November 1), Autistic History Month (November), and the Disability Day of Mourning (March 1). Music therapists can also neuroqueer their therapy spaces by rejecting the omnipresent blue puzzle piece symbol in favour of the rainbow infinity symbol.

This idea of a neuroqueered space naturally leads to concrete modifications in the physical environment intended to accommodate diverse neurologies. Maybe this means getting rid of flickering fluorescent lights and opening the blinds to let in indirect natural light. Maybe it means keeping a baseball cap available for clients to borrow when you can't change the lighting. Maybe it means turning off and unplugging unnecessary electronics that make buzzing sounds, even if you don't notice the noises yourself. Maybe it means leaving your essential oils at home, no matter how pure they are.

It probably means making the therapy room a safe place for stimmy activities. It probably means creating a sensory kit of non-musical items that can help neurodivergent people 'actively [choose] to embody and express [their] neurodivergence' (Walker, 2015) and then exploring the ways that stimming can be integrated into musical play, performance, composition, conducting and other relevant tools of music therapy 'intervention'. It probably requires the therapist engage in actively cultivating empathy by reflecting on their own stims, how stimming makes them feel, and the role this stim plays in their life. The therapist probably needs to privately try out an unfamiliar stim and consider the aesthetic values of a stim; after all, the repetitive nature of stimmy movements makes them ideal for conceptualising in terms of their potential for music making.

'Maybes' and 'probablys' aside, there is no singular, correct way to design autistic, neuroqueered spaces; instead, the neuroqueering of therapeutic space requires the flexibility to make ongoing adjustments to meet the changing needs of an individual or groups of individuals.

There are so many ways in which the responsive nature of music therapy is already so closely aligned with the needs of neurodivergent clients. Performing live music means the tempo, articulation and other musical characteristics can be modified in response to a client's sensory needs from moment to moment. Music therapists are proficient at playing across a wide selection of genres and styles on multiple standard instruments such as guitar, piano, autoharp and percussion, as well as each therapist's specialisation, such as the oboe, tuba, or operatic singing. This allows therapists to bring in a client's preferred instrumental timbres.

Music therapists are also already on the front lines of respecting and enabling alternative and non-traditional forms of communication, as all music therapists come to the field first as musicians who are proficient in the non-verbal language of music. As musicians, we also have extensive practice with the sitting-in-silence that patience often demands, the series of whole rests that must be allowed between a question and an answer, and many music therapists are already enacting a radical patience in their therapeutic spaces.

Neuroqueering communication in music therapy might ask the music therapist to not only validate a client where their skills and strengths are at during the session, but to consciously and purposely neuroqueer outside of the therapy session by advocating for the creation of autistic communication space in sly ways. For one therapist, this slyness might present as using both spoken language and simultaneous sign when communicating about the schedule with the abled receptionist – acting to neuroqueer the school environment by subverting expectations about who uses sign, and when. For another therapist, this sly neuroqueering might look like an overt and firm advocacy in a team meeting that a client has access to an AAC device/VOD 24/7. For another therapist, sly neuroqueering might manifest through the spontaneous musicking of neurodivergence that occurs when singing a child's familiar verbal stim, turning it into a joyful song while walking across the playground.

Much of the sensitivity required in neuroqueering music therapy is in determining relevant and respectful goals and objectives. Instead of employing the medical model's standards for therapeutic objectives, one can radically abandon those 'skills' that autistic people have identified as being unhelpful or even painful – such as forcing eye contact – and instead focus on those areas that the individual autistic person experiences as disabling or distressing. Bakan (2015) says, 'It is about letting people be who they are, not trying to measure their aptitudes and change them in ways that will make them more 'normal' or 'acceptable' in the eyes of others' (p142). Straus (2014) elaborates on this concept, saying:

'Instead of seeking to normalize autistic people, music therapy might instead acknowledge their distinctive sorts of musical interests and attitudes and offer to enhance their indigenous culture in an atmosphere of mutual respect. Instead of normalization and cure, music therapists might seek enhanced self-expression, knowledge, and pleasure through mutual music-making.'

The repetitive movements called stimming may be the one of the expressions of autism that most often becomes a stomping ground for compliance therapies that insist a strict mask of 'normalcy' be plastered over autism's sensory depths. By neuroqueering music therapy, stimming and other neurodivergent responses to sensory needs, such as covering ears, lying on the floor, flapping hands, rocking or humming, can be respected as self-accommodation and self-advocacy (Merrero, 2012; Shiloh, 2014). Merrero (2012) describes the way an autistic musician named Lyra sometimes covers her ears during performances in this way: 'her autistic aesthetics are considered behaviours of her disability, but if one views these behaviours as aesthetic choices, then her accommodation becomes an art, specifically her style of art' (p46).

When Merrero speaks of Lyra covering her ears as a self-accommodation, or Shiloh writes of hand flapping as self-advocacy, the authors are neuroqueering by presuming competence, something that is: 'not a completed act. It is an exercise, a constant work in progress. In order to practice this principle, you need to keep your heart open to being wrong' (Allen, 2017, p32). But presuming competence 'doesn't mean to assume that a person faces no barriers, and it is never an excuse for withholding supports and accommodations' (Sparrow, 2016, p20).

Adjacent to the neuroqueering act of presuming competence is an active re-examining of the meaning of dependence and independence. Cal Montgomery (2012) explains, 'independent can mean self-governing. It can also mean self-reliant... Dependent can mean controlled by others. It can also mean requiring the support of others' (pp80–81). Therapists might neuroqueer their practice by abandoning the binary of dependence vs. independence, and instead seek 'independence [as] a moving target', the pursual of which naturally manifests in music therapy as an interdependent interplay, a mutually responsive duet of assisting and accepting assistance (Thomas, 2017, p183).

One of the most viscerally important aspects of neuroqueering therapy for neurodivergent people emerges as a confrontation with and fundamental rejection of behavioural-based compliance therapies that coerce a performance of neurotypicality out of young children through the use of repetitive, irrelevant tasks, aversive stimuli, dangerous restraints and punishments. In the essay 'Change the world, not your child' Lei Wiley-Mydske says, 'therapies that value compliance and normalcy or sameness amongst peers are not respectful of your [client's] dignity, individuality, and autonomy' (2017, p57). Self-advocacy becomes a more suitable target than compliance, and an honest acknowledgement of the high rate of abuse of neurodivergent people reveals the survival value of noncompliance. 'I need to have the power to say no', Bridget Allen (2017) explains, 'Autonomy is dignity... Make sure I know my rights' (pp31-32). Lei Wiley-Mydske (2017) elaborates, stating that:

'Teaching me to fight for my rights was more important than forcing me to fit in...
I spent a lot of time learning to deny my natural impulses and feelings in order
to conform to what was expected of a 'good girl'. In doing so, I opened myself up
to become a victim of both emotional and sexual abuse from adults and intense
bullying from my peers. The way I experienced the world around me was supposedly
wrong, and there was no argument. So I remained silent, always.' (p55)

Valuing a neurodivergent person's 'no' in therapy can bring an ironic type of joy to a music therapy session that could include a regular process of offering a child a non-preferred instrument, and providing them with the support they need to reject it, and then allowing them to return to their preferred instrument to improvise, practice and compose.

Neuroqueering music therapy can sound like a steady stream of rejection,
a litany of echoing:
a 'no,'
    'I don't like that,'
'no,'
    'not that one,'

'no,'
 'put it away,'
'no,'
 'stop it,'
'no,'
 'move,'
'no,'
 'go away,'
'no,'
 'don't touch me,'

… and finally …

'STOP!'

And then a crash of drums and laughter to tell you that this was an elaborate, abstracted song and dramatic play all along, or as Kassiane Sibley (2017) writes: 'every day of childhood is practice for adulthood. We're vulnerable. We need extra boundary-setting practice. We need to learn this skill with people who would never hurt us, so when we need to stand up to those who would, we know how. And we need to know that we deserve to be safe' (p45).

Active neuroqueering creates opportunities to practice a variety of safe and healthy ways to reject those things that do not express or embody their authentic selves. 'Thoreau taught it, Martin Luther King Jr. taught it, and you can teach it: when demands for compliance become unreasonable, it is a fundamental human right to say no' (Sparrow, 2016, p84).

There is much ado about the language used to describe neurodivergent, disabled, autistic people. While many autistics prefer identity-first language, some do not, and the fact remains that there is no list of 'correct words' that a music therapist can employ that allows them to check a box marked 'task completed' and move on. As Lydia XZ Brown (2017) says in the anthology *All the Weight of Our Dreams*, 'we must hold ourselves accountable for examining and deconstructing ableism in all its forms in our work, our communities, our personal lives, and our relationships with each other' (p144).

While we are neuroqueering music therapy by deconstructing the preconceived and colonialist notions of the language of diagnosis and disorder (Mills, 2013), we can also busy our deconstructing hands by challenging preconceived and colonialist notions of instrumentation, or what types of objects deserve the label 'musical instruments' and which of these objects are suitable materials for therapy. Merrero

(2012) gives special attention to the non-traditional instruments played by teen autist Lyra, describing her process of choosing pots, pans and jars, as well as her techniques for playing on kitchen cabinet doors and various chairs (p8). This openness to playing non-traditional instruments or playing traditional instruments in non-traditional ways is a common way of musicking neurodivergence and creating an environment where neuroqueered people are free to be themselves while also being in contact with supportive (and artistically relevant) community. In this case, neuroqueering music therapy can also mean letting go of the idea of playing a series of 'songs as therapy', instead using the concept of 'song' itself to validate and communicate with an autistic child who creates a subtle art.

A neuroqueered hit song, a Play-It-Again-Sam-Super-Number-One-Single, might sound like pouring dozens of egg shakers through the loop of a door handle into an upside-down drum waiting below, all the while whistling and vocally stimming with a vibrant sustained note. These neuroqueered compositions, like Egg-Pouring-Song, are my favourite kind of 'music therapy song'.

In Egg-Pouring-Song, a non-speaking autistic explores ways to use their voice in a safe environment, experimenting with the way that each small change in the position of their mouth or tongue causes barely perceptible changes in tone. Hold a posture just so, and you can sing 'bee, bee, bee' in a way that makes your entire face buzz like a hive of bees, bees, bees have taken over your skeleton, all while you watch the colourful shaker eggs pour, tumble and thud.

I have another favourite music therapy song, when a student lines up the instruments and sensory toys and household objects, and I join in, and we spend the time together lining up objects, making symmetrical, musical, ever changing art, admiring our work contentedly, then making furious, scrambling changes. I will admit to tearing up when a non-speaking student feels comfortable enough during our Lining-Up-Music-Art song to sing, and I hear their perfect, quiet hymn of neurodivergent communion. These are the types of poignantly, radically beautiful moments of music therapy that bring musicians into the fold of therapy to begin with.

In *Music therapy as psychospiritual process in palliative care*, D Salmon (2001) elaborates on some of these qualities and consequences of music that draw us to the profession, saying, 'music speaks ... the language of the deep, evoking imagery and memory, resonating with feeling, and transporting one beyond the bounds of ordinary awareness'. Here we find the poetics of neuroqueering music therapy, by diving wildly into music's 'language of the deep' only to find yourself immersed in the 'deep love' of autism, explained by Maxfield Sparrow in *The ABCs of Autism Acceptance:*

'The way I love? It is deep. Autism is deep love.
People write it off as special interest or obsession, but even if it's not
something I can excel at, I can excel at loving what I love, loving what I do,
loving who I love. Autism is being able to be consumed by love and interest,
it is giving 100% because it is an insult to the thing one loves to give
any less. Autism is going big or going home' (Sparrow, 2016, p72).

'Autism is deep love.'
    ('Music speaks the language of the deep.')
'Autism is deep love.'
    ('Music speaks the language of the deep.')
'Autism is deep love.'
    ('Music speaks the language of the deep.')
'Autism is deep love.'
    ('Music speaks the language of the deep.')

Autism is deep love and it's time to go big and go home:
tl;dr The truth is… I can't actually tell you how to neuroqueer your music therapy.

References

Aigen K (2017) *Autism and the Neurodiversity Movement: Implications for music therapy research.* Presented at Grieg Research School in Interdisciplinary Music Studies, University of Bergen, Norway.

Allen B (2017) Acknowledge vulnerability, presume competence. In: EB Ballou, K Thomas & S daVanport (Eds) *What Every Autistic Girl Wishes Her Parents Knew* (pp29–32). USA: DragonBee Press.

Ashkenazy E (2017) Foreword: On Autism and Race. In: LX Brown, E Ashkenazy & MG Onaiwu (Eds) All the Weight of Our Dreams: On living racialized autism (pp. xxiii-xxxix). Lincoln, NB: DragonBee Press.

Bakan MB (2014) Ethnomusicological perspectives on autism, neurodiversity, and music therapy [online]. *Voices* **14** (3). Available at: https://voices.no/index.php/voices/article/view/2220/1974 (accessed May 2020).

Bakan MB (2015) The musicality of stimming: Promoting neurodiversity in the ethnomusicology of autism [online]. *MUSICultures* **41** (2). Available at: https://journals.lib.unb.ca/index.php/MC/article/view/22914 (accessed May 2020).

Brown LX (2017) Why the term 'psychopath' is racist and ableist. In: LX Brown, E Ashkenazy & MG Onaiwu (Eds) *All the Weight of Our Dreams: On living racialized autism* (pp137–144). Lincoln, NB: DragonBee Press.

Bumanis A (2015). MTR 2025 Progress Report. American Music Therapy Association. Available at: https://www.musictherapy.org/mtr_2025_progress_report/ (accessed May 2020).

Kupferstein H & Rancer S (2016) *Perfect Pitch in the Key of Autism: A guide for educators, parents, and the musically gifted.* Bloomington, IN: iUniverse.

Marrero E (2012) Performing neurodiversity: Musical accommodation by and for an adolescent with autism (Master's thesis, Florida State University). Available at: https://diginole.lib.fsu.edu/islandora/object/fsu:182997/datastream/PDF/view (accessed May 2020).

Mills C (2013) *Decolonizing Global Mental Health.* New York, NY: Routlage.

Montgomery C (2012). Critic of the Dawn. In: J Bascom (Ed) *Loud Hands: Autistic people, speaking* (pp71–87) Washington DC: The Autistic Press.

Norris S (2019) Re: I have a published paper… [online forum comment]. Available at: https://www.facebook.com/groups/700110057079405/ (accessed May 2020).

Pickard B (2019) Valuing neurodiversity: A humanistic, non-normative model of music therapy exploring Roger's person-centered approach with young adults with autism spectrum conditions. In: E Coombes, H Dunn, E Maclean, H Mottram & J Nugent (Eds) *A Spectrum of Approaches: Music therapy and autism across the lifespan*. London: Jessica Kingsley Publishers.

Reynolds E (2016) 'What can music do?' Rethinking autism through music therapy. NYU News. Available at: https://www.nyu.edu/about/news-publications/news/2016/july/autism-and-neurodiversity-at-nordoff-robbins-center-for-music-th.html (accessed May 2020).

Salmon D (2001) Music therapy as psychospiritual process in palliative care. *Journal of Palliative Care* **17** (3) 142–146.

Sibley KA (2017) What your daughter deserves: Love, safety, and the truth. In: EB Ballou, K Thomas & S daVanport (Eds) *What Every Autistic Girl Wishes Her Parents Knew* (pp44–49). USA: DragonBee Press.

Scranton AR (2019) *Music therapy and neurodiversity* (Unpublished master's thesis). The State University of New York, Fredonia NY.

Shiloh CJ (2019) Re: Here is info … [Online forum comment]. Available at: https://www.facebook.com/groups/700110057079405/ (accessed May 2020).

Shiloh CJ & LaGasse AB (2014) Sensory friendly concerts: A community music therapy initiative to promote Neurodiversity. *International Journal of Community Music* **7** (1) 113–128. Available at: https://www.ingentaconnect.com/content/intellect/ijcm/2014/00000007/00000001/art00007 (accessed May 2020).

Sparrow M (2016) *The ABCs of autism acceptance*. Fort Worth: Autonomous Press.

Straus JN (2014) Music therapy and autism: A view from disability studies. *Voices* **14** (3) Available at: https://academicworks.cuny.edu/gc_pubs/415/ (accessed May 2020).

Thomas K (2017) A thank you letter to parents of autistic girls. In: EB Ballou, K Thomas & S daVanport (Eds) *What Every Autistic Girl Wishes Her Parents Knew* (pp183–185) USA: DragonBee Press.

Thompson GA & Elefant C (2019) 'But I want to talk to you!' Perspectives on music therapy practice with highly verbal children on the autism spectrum. *Nordic Journal of Music Therapy* **28** (4) 347–359.

Thompson G, Elefant C, Roginsky E, Metel M & Pickard B (2019) What Can the Neurodiversity Movement Offer Music Therapy? European Music Therapy Conference, Aalbog, Denmark.

Walker N (2015) Neuroqueer: An introduction. *Neurocosmopolitanism*. Available at: https://neurocosmopolitanism.com/neuroqueer-an-introduction/ (accessed May 2020).

Wiley-Mydske L (2017) Change the world, not your child. In: EB Ballou, K Thomas & S daVanport (Eds) *What Every Autistic Girl Wishes Her Parents Knew* (pp55–59). USA: DragonBee Press.

Yergeau M (2018) *Authoring Autism: On rhetoric and neurological queerness*. Durham, NC: Duke University Press.

Chapter 21: From difference to diversity in school

By Dr Rebecca Wood

Debates rage over terminology in relation to autism. Words such as 'disorder' (Kenny *et al*, 2016), 'condition' (Broderick & Ne'eman, 2008) and person-first language e.g. adult with autism (Gernsbacher, 2017) are considered stigmatising, although there is by no means a consensus on this. Meanwhile, rather quietly in the background, the word 'difference' has been carrying out some heavy lifting, thought to be a more constructive way of conceptualising autism than the term 'disorder'. For example, Lawson (2011, p41) posits that autism should be thought of 'as a cognitive difference or style' and Baron-Cohen (2002, p181) deliberates whether Asperger syndrome 'should necessarily be viewed as a disability or, from a difference perspective, as a difference'. This apparently more positive framing has been adopted within education practitioner training contexts: according to the Autism Education Trust (2019), autism consists of 'four areas of difference' which school staff need to understand in order to support autistic pupils.

Yet for such a commonplace and anodyne word, subject to multiple meanings and inferences, its polysemic nature is often underestimated. What you and I understand by 'different', when referring to certain individuals, groups of people, or even ourselves, will almost certainly not be the same, and naturally will depend on our own situations and dispositions. If you're a funky, alternative sort of person, perhaps it's a positive descriptor. But if you prefer to blend in with the crowd, then 'difference' might have unwelcome connotations of being 'weird', 'strange', 'not like us'. Indeed, the metaphors of difference abound in the autism context (Broderick & Ne'eman, 2008): *Does your child swim in the opposite direction of the shoal of fish?* I remember reading in a leaflet I was given, shortly after my son was diagnosed with autism, aged three.

So, it's worth thinking about how being 'different', as well as autistic, operates in our schools, where for most settings in the UK, uniformity is highly prized. After all, most pupils literally wear 'a uniform', and punishments can be meted out for the wrong kind of shoe or length of trouser. Children and young people are expected to line up, to sit down in rows, and chant in unison in the assembly hall. And so for anyone who won't, or can't conform to this requirement for sameness, their difference is viewed as problematic (Wood, 2018). After all, 'persistent disruptive behaviour' is one of the main reasons autistic pupils are excluded from schools in England (Department for Education, 2019).

When I asked the school staff (n = 36), parents of autistic children (n = 10) and autistic adults (n = 10) in my PhD study into the educational inclusion of autistic children to describe autism, their responses, positive, negative, or something in between, were often entangled with notions of difference. For example, some parents, who described their children as 'different', were concerned that others would find them 'odd' or 'weird', especially as they got older, citing hand-flapping, making noises and limited speech as being characteristics that might mark their children out as strange, leading them to be shunned socially by their peers. Moreover, the view that children become less tolerant the older they are was reflected by a number of the adults in my study. One autistic adult asserted that even between infants and junior school, children start to 'notice your difference' and so become 'meaner', a circumstance which gradually worsens in secondary school and beyond as 'people's tolerance of difference gets smaller'. As a result, she said, for most of her life she had been made to feel like she 'didn't fit'.

Meanwhile, another autistic adult said that at primary school, she was made to feel 'like an alien' to such an extent that she was almost convinced that she was 'not human'. This sense of alienation and estrangement also applied to some parents, as one complained that she was stared at as if she was 'an alien or something, like weird' for helping her daughter, who had motor planning difficulties, down some steps at the local cinema. Moreover, having read books about autism in a drive to understand their children better, some parents found little help in these sources of information, as the descriptions of autism, especially when framed negatively, did not match their own offspring. This led one parent to conclude that not only was her child 'different' by dint of being autistic, but that he was 'different to every other child'.

For some school staff, autistic children, by their very nature, are somehow psychologically elsewhere. According to a SENCo (Special Educational Needs Co-ordinator), autistic children 'are prone to drift off', and a teaching assistant commented that they 'live within their own world far more than they do in the world that we do'. Moreover, this apparent disconnectedness was associated with 'severity' of autism, whether a child was 'high' or 'low functioning' on the 'spectrum', terms I did not initiate in interviews. A SENCo said that autism 'sits on a spectrum', and 'at the top end there is Asperger's' while 'at the extreme end, they're in a complete bubble'. One teacher said that she could not understand how a highly able autistic boy in her class who 'functions perfectly well without support' even received a diagnosis of autism, while by contrast, according to one parent, 'a low functioning child' would 'really freak, like, roll around the floor and scream'. In other words, unless autism manifests itself as a highly problematic form of difference, it doesn't really exist. Nevertheless, according to one teaching assistant, all autistic children have difficulties, regardless of where they sit on the 'scale':

'There are so many different types. You have the ones at the lower end of the scale, they've got no life skills, no retention. You've got the ones at the higher end of the scale, they are very bright, but not able to get on with their peers. They all don't get on with their peers, they have trouble with that.'

Therefore, in these accounts, ideas about difference are enmeshed with negative conceptualisations of autism and the sense that autistic children are somehow 'other'. However, none of the autistic adults in my study used the term 'spectrum', only one employed functioning labels and none of the parents who used the descriptor 'low functioning' felt their own children fell into this category.

Furthermore, not all participants problematised the apparent disconnectedness and 'otherness' of autistic people and indeed associated difference with positive attributes. One parent, who thought that her son was in 'a little world of his own', rather admired this about him, and wished she could 'get into his head for an hour or so, or even a day', because in her view, he was 'completely awesome'. Another parent felt that her autistic son had taught her to 'look at the world differently' and that this was 'very positive'. Moreover, half of the autistic adults considered autistic people have specific abilities deriving directly from being autistic, particularly in relation to attention to detail. Indeed, two of the autistic adults thought that autistic traits, such as not wasting time on small talk, have contributed to the evolution of the human race. One autistic adult said that autism enables her 'to see the world differently' in a revelatory, enlightening way, 'rather like a pair of glasses which give someone the ability to see', and a SENCo asserted that some autistic people have 'amazing skills' which can be associated with genius. Therefore, in these instances, difference was very much seen as a quality.

In addition, some school staff asserted that the presence of autistic children in class provides an important, instructional benefit for the rest of the pupils. One teacher stated that autistic pupils enable classmates to 'not be afraid of children with differences', while another teacher asserted that their presence helps pupils to 'understand everybody is different … understand different behaviour' and therefore 'respect it'. Even so, one teacher was of the view that autistic children don't especially benefit from this scenario:

'You know this whole idea about it helps the other children be more understanding and maybe that works, but I don't know if the autistic child always gets a lot out of it.'

The problem, according to one parent, was that schools simply aren't doing enough to teach pupils about differences and present them with disabled role models:

'There's no heroes as in a disabled person. You know, you've got your Winston Churchills, but … it's always about typical people… Like about the Paralympics and things like that, the Paralympics was on BBC 2 and the Olympics was on [BBC 1]… do you know what I mean? You just think to yourself well hold on a minute… this is society.'

These comments suggest that, while autistic children might aid the understanding and empathetic development of other pupils, there is little reciprocal benefit to them from being positioned as 'different'. Within this dynamic, they are still perceived as somehow being of second order.

According to three of the autistic adults, meanwhile, autism is a 'neurological difference' which impacts on how people think, process information and respond to the environment, a view which was shared by some school staff and parents. One autistic adult stated that even though autistic people are different from each other, she felt 'connected' to all autistic people nonetheless, as it is non-autistic people who are 'odd' in certain respects. Indeed, for another autistic adult, the problematisation of autism results from the fact that autistic people are a minority, different from the norm, and so subject to prejudice and exclusion. And perhaps surprisingly, given that this interview took place relatively recently at the end of 2015, only one participant – an autistic adult – used the term 'neurodiversity', which was introduced rather hesitantly: 'I was wondering if I should mention neurodiversity'.

So where does all of this leave us? It would seem, in the context of autism and education at least, that notions of difference become inevitably enmeshed with ideas about ability – or the lack of it – the problems that autistic children seemingly create and their apparent failure to engage with the real world, which is assumed to be distinct and knowable. Even when autistic traits are admired, attitudes stray uneasily close to notions of othering (Devlin & Pothier, 2006; Hughes, 2009) exoticism (Arnold, 2013) and 'fishbowling' (Moon, 2014). Indeed, too often the notion of 'difference' as manifested in schools equates to individual deficit models (Liasidou, 2012), creating 'a problem and a spectacle of difference, to be managed and tolerated' (Allan, 2008, p21) by teachers. As a result, the presence of children positioned as 'different' is potentially contingent on their ability to provide an instructional service for their classmates.

Describing certain individuals or groups as 'different' also creates the problem of norm referencing, raising the question of 'different to what?' (Allan, 2008; Ravet, 2011). Such representations can be 'constructed through binaries, with one being the norm, and also superior' (Williams & Mavin, 2012, p161), meaning that in schools, some children will unavoidably be perceived as deficient. These attitudes in turn have been associated not only with negative conceptualisations of autism, but with repressive and damaging interventions designed to somehow normalise autistic people (Milton, 2017; Wood, 2018; 2019). Moreover, contradictory attitudes towards difference can cause pupils to 'mask' in school in order to try to 'fit in', causing them to supress their true nature, a process which can be at a significant emotional cost (Cook *et al*, 2017).

And so, in education and no doubt other contexts, the word 'different' appears to be crumbling under the sheer weight of the contradictions and complexities it is expected to carry. Perhaps, therefore, we need a better, more fluid terminology. The autistic adults in my study provided insights into the value of intra-autistic communication, of challenging our conception of normality and understanding 'diversity and difference as part of everyday normal' (Lawson, 2011, p26), rather than as somehow separate to it. Here, the diversity of the autistic population is something to be celebrated and embraced, so that we can be alive to 'the positive characteristics of autism that contribute to human diversity and creativity' and so understand how autism can facilitate the development of 'new social identities' (Grinker, 2015, p345).

Taking this a step further, the concept of neurodiversity, even while its meaning is still contested, could help us to understand that autism is a manifestation of human diversity, regardless of any associated impairments (Kapp *et al*, 2013), a view echoed by some of the autistic adults in my study. Within education contexts, such a conceptualisation drives a shift of focus onto the multiplicity of learner needs (Liasidou, 2012) and the right to varied representation. Moreover, understanding that 'difference' is no longer fit for purpose also suggests caution in the use of the term 'neurotypical', a concept not yet clearly defined sociologically or neurologically. Therefore, instead of marking some children out as 'different', 'special', or even 'typical', we must consider how best to support all learners and their diverse dispositions in school, whether or not they follow the crowd. After all, if the shoal of fish was swimming into the mouth of a shark, you wouldn't want to just tag along, would you?

References

Allan J (2008) *Rethinking Inclusive Education: The philosophers of difference in practice*. Dordrecht: Springer.

Arnold L (2013) The social construction of the savant. *Autonomy, the Critical Journal of Interdisciplinary Autism Studies* **1** (2) 1–8.

Autism Education Trust (2019) *What is Autism?* [online]. Available at: www.autismeducationtrust.org.uk/what-is-autism/ (accessed May 2020).

Baron-Cohen S (2002) Is Asperger syndrome necessarily viewed as a disability? *Focus on Autism and Developmental Disabilities* **17** (3) 186–191.

Broderick AA and Ne'eman A (2008) Autism as metaphor: narrative and counter-narrative. *International Journal of Inclusive Education* **12** (5-6) 459–476.

Cook A, Ogden J and Winstone N (2017) Friendship motivations, challenges and the role of masking for girls with autism in contrasting school settings. *European Journal of Special Needs Education* **33** (3) 302–315.

Department for Education (2019) *Permanent and fixed period exclusions in England 2017 to 2018* [online]. Available at: www.gov.uk/government/statistics/permanent-and-fixed-period-exclusions-in-england-2017-to-2018 (accessed May 2020).

Devlin R and Pothier D (2006) Introduction: Toward a critical theory of dis-citizenship. In: Pothier D and Devlin R (eds) *Critical Disability Theory: Essays in philosophy, politics, policy, and law*. Vancouver: UBC Press, pp1–22.

Gernsbacher MA (2017) Editorial Perspective: The use of person-first language in scholarly writing may accentuate stigma. *The Journal of Child Psychology and Psychiatry* **58** (7) 859–861.

Grinker R (2015) Reframing the Science and Anthropology of Autism. *Culture, Medicine and Psychiatry* **39** (2) 345–350.

Hughes B (2009) Disability activisms: social model stalwarts and biological citizens. *Disability & Society* **24** (6) 677–688.

Kapp S, Gillespie-Lynch K, Sherman L and Hutman T (2013) Deficit, difference, or both? Autism and neurodiversity. *Developmental Psychology* **49** (1) 59–71.

Kenny L, Hattersley C, Molins B, Buckley C, Povey C and Pellicano E (2016) Which terms should be used to describe autism? Perspectives from the UK autism community. *Autism* **20** (4) 442–462.

Lawson W (2011) *The Passionate Mind: How people with autism learn*. London: Jessica Kingsley Publishers.

Liasidou A (2012) *Inclusive Education, Politics and Policymaking*. London: Continuum International Publishing Group.

Milton D (2017) Challenging the ideology of idealised normalcy. In: Milton D and Nicola M (Eds) *Autism and Intellectual Disabilities in Adults, Volume 2*. Hove: Pavilion Publishing and Media, pp7–10.

Moon L (2014) Fishbowling, Commodification and Lenses. Theorising Autism. Centre for Research in Autism and Education.

Ravet J (2011) Inclusive/exclusive? Contradictory perspectives on autism and inclusion: the case for an integrative position. *International Journal of Inclusive Education* **15** (6) 667–682.

Williams J and Mavin S (2012) Disability as constructed difference: A literature review and research agenda for management and organization studies. *International Journal of Management Reviews* **14** (2) 159–179.

Wood R (2020) The wrong kind of noise: understanding and valuing the communication of autistic children in schools. *Educational Review* **72** (1) 111–130.

Wood R (2019) Autism, intense interests and support in school: From wasted efforts to shared understandings. *Educational Review* doi: 10.1080/00131911.2019.1566213

Chapter 22: 'I'd like to tell them what gets left-out or 'unsaid': Autism, neurodiversity and employment experiences in neoliberal times

By Sharon Elley, Angie Balmer, John Wilson and Akiva Secret

Introduction: walls are there because someone forgot to consider us

This chapter provides ethnographical accounts of our personal and anecdotal experiences of being autistic in workplace settings and organisations. It connects our autobiographical stories to research about the wider political, cultural and social meanings and understandings associated with employment relations and autism. Autoethnography offers ways to reflect and write about relations and contexts, or as Stuart Hall (1996, pp107–8) suggests, our 'local hopes and local aspirations, local tragedies, and local scenarios that are the everyday practices and the everyday experiences of ordinary folks'. The chapter is formatted as a collective letter which draws on new and emerging research about autism and our lived experiences with respect to neurodiversity as a biological fact and paradigm within the context of neoliberalism. In modern times, letter writing has been exceeded by email, which demands instance responses, and formal or informal published works usually subscribe to strict or loose conventions to express or share ideas, research and messages. Regardless of contexts, letter writing is undervalued as a method to make data creatively accessible to audiences. This is despite how letter writing as a means of communication has historically played a role in the reproduction of ideas and writing as an art since the times of Ancient Greece (Blake & Bly, 1993).

The following letter is a collective and considered deliberation from the authors which offers a critical dialogue about the systematic shortcomings of organisational structures, processes and relations. This chapter is not about any one organisation or workplace setting, and it is not applicable to all contributors' experiences, but provides a means to share politically and collectively what it means to be autistic, neurodivergent and employed in neoliberal society. Its contents are also more broadly applicable to other disability groups. The chapter aims to highlight the complex strengths and challenges of autism, including ableism in the workplace, and the so-called social 'compensatory' (Livingston *et al*, 2019) strategies exercised in being and staying employed. It critically engages with 'reasonable adjustments'. The strengths of autism are less well understood in research or how they connect to employment patterns, relations and identities, with even less known about autistic strategies. The neurodiversity movement offers new ways to rethink ourselves and our experiences, and how we relate to employment practices, service-provision and broader society. The chapter concludes by raising some new questions and avenues of inquiry; perhaps some of which would be unnecessary if we all lived in a world that accepted the 'terms and conditions' of each person according to their identity, each person according to their ability, and each person according to their need.

Letter: sent without prejudice

Dear Directors, Supervisors, Managers, Human Resource Personnel and Policymakers (or to whom it may concern),

We would like to thank you for our meetings over the years to discuss reasonable adjustments, our role(s) in our workplace settings and any personal or performance-related issues we may be experiencing. Some of the issues raised we felt unable to immediately answer given that we are autistic and benefit from reflective time and space to process the information and discussion. We would like to take this opportunity to now respond in the hope that we can convey the strengths and challenges of being neurodivergent autistic employees in educational, governmental, media and legal contexts. We are committed to finding ways for neurotypical managers to understand our lived autistic experiences in ways that are mutually informative, supportive and beneficial. The following provides the different key points that have been typically raised during our various meetings, offers an informed and measured response, and makes suggestions for moving forward on an individual, collective and structural level.

We would like to introduce you to our autism in the workplace

This is because our meetings have left the impression that you may know very little about autism, disability or neurodiversity. Autism is extraordinarily complex and notoriously heterogenous. The medical model of disability problematically defines autism spectrum 'disorders' (ASD) as a set of complex neurological developmental conditions (DSM-5), leading to intellectual and behavioural challenges throughout the lifespan. This is prolifically challenged by the social model of disability (Barnes, 1994) and compatible neurodiversity model (Davidson & Orsini, 2013; Walker 2013) which instead suggests that autistic people experience social, attitudinal and infrastructural barriers and frequent discrimination, disadvantage and social exclusion in employment and broader society. This is often due to the difficulties regularly experienced by neurotypical people in understanding and accepting 'autistic' differences in thinking, moving and interacting, and in sensory and cognitive processing as exemplified in ableist structures, policies and practices (Hersh & Elley, 2019). Despite our respective organisations' public pledge of signing-up to the 'social model' of disability, we often find this may not translate so well into actual practice and the move to recognise neurodiversity in the workplace is slow.

We suspect that you may know little about neurodiversity and we offer an explanation. The neurodiversity movement challenges medical and deficit positions of cure and causation, instead celebrating autism as inseparable from identity. Neurodiversity regards atypical neurological development as a 'normal' and natural human difference (Singer, 1989). This means granting rights and value to being autistic alongside recognition and acceptance. Affirming and recognising our 'natural' neurological and/or behavioural differences means, as Graby (2015) suggests, accepting all types of human diversity and challenging supposedly 'universal' assumptions about 'human nature' that privilege majority and historically dominant groups (also see McWade et al, 2015). We claim a positive identity by virtue of being autistic, but we find that we are routinely disabled by the societal barriers, attitudes and structures which serve the majority population.

You may be unaware that we are a neurominority group with only 1% of the population worldwide diagnosed as autistic. Correspondingly, the National Autistic Society, UK, report that only 16% of work-aged autistic adults are employed full-time in Britain and this is the lowest disability figure when compared to other disability groups. However, we suspect that autistic employment figures are much higher given the reluctance to disclose to employers or under-diagnosis, particularly among women and ethnic minority groups. The authors have worked in various low and high-status positions, mostly full-time, throughout our lives from as young as 13 years old in settings ranging from chip shops and factories to the legal and educational professions. We all received a late diagnosis of autism in our 30s-50s, which may partly explain how some of us left school with few to no qualifications due to family disruption or poverty or did not complete degrees due to educational systems letting us down. Others of us successfully completed typical educational trajectories and progressed directly into professional employment, while others returned to education as mature learners. Collectively, we have been diagnosed autistic from three to seven years ago and inadvertently fall into the so-called 'abled-disabled' category (Titchkosky, 2003). While we have been successful, thrived or survived, most of the time, our success can be fragile, unstable and contingent on social and institutional relations, practices and organisational structures as well as our own individual characteristics and biographies.

You may not be aware that the neurodiversity movement positions acceptance and legal protection for neurological differences alongside differences associated with race, sexuality and gender. Equally, Walker (2014) points to the social dynamics of neurodiversity which should be understood comparably to ethnicity and class. We draw your attention to the idea of intersectionality (Crenshaw,1991) to elucidate our sentiments. Intersectionality enables an understanding of how multiple categories of difference and identity depend on one another and are mutually associated with outcomes. We are white, working-class women and men who are diverse and differently abled. We are directors, lawyers and educationalists; however, we work in professional organisations that are still not always welcoming or designed for the 'likes of us' (see for example, Reay *et al*, 2005) in terms of our classed identities or autistic (dis)abilities. We may accrue material resources and still lack access to the social, cultural and emotional capitals legitimately recognised and afforded other (privileged/advantaged) professionals. This offers a partial explanation as to why our autistic strengths and challenges may play-out in relation to different autism traits, individual characteristics and identities. It also partly explains how we can ambiguously seem to slip from one socially stigmatised identity to another or attempt to perform non-pathologised forms of identity in context-specific situations. These aspects are enmeshed and moderated by power relations, structures and contexts which legitimate and value majority ways of being while ascribing others as inferior or less worthy.

With this in mind, we would like to mention an academic idea which is increasingly gaining popularity. Ableism is an elastic term used variously in different contexts usually to denote discrimination against disabled people. Academically speaking, it is described as a set of beliefs, practices and processes that produce, based on perceptions of a person's abilities, a particular understanding of self, relations with others and the environment, and includes being judged by others (see Wolbring, 2008). We often encounter the assumed stability of disability as something we are or are not or how we are an 'exclude-able type' (Titchkosky, 2003). We can find that, while ableism works to exclude and marginalise us by rendering us 'abnormal', the neoliberal organisations in which we work attempt to 'normalise' us. While neoliberalism remains a contested term, it goes beyond economic values and involves a 'governing rationality that disseminates market values and metrics to every sphere of life' (Brown, 2015, p176). As such, neoliberal rationality necessitates that individualism and competition become the defining features of social relations (Coco, 2013, p602). Within the neoliberalisation of disability relations, bodies and subjects, we become valued as 'the abled-disabled' (Titchkosky, 2003): that is, as productive individualised subjects, resources and consumers. Rather than falling into clear-cut lines by which our (dis)ability is demarcated, we are both abled and disabled, valued and devalued, fortified and debilitated.

We understand that you value our workplace contributions and strengths

We thank you for mentioning during our various meetings that we are incredibly committed, diligent, honest and reliable. For us, work is about our status, our place in the world, our sense of meaning, identity, belonging and well-being as useful members of society. We often use our atypical processing, perception and cognitive abilities to distinguish patterns and details that others may overlook, and retain facts and figures (Grandin, 2012; Cannon, 2018). We are usually creative, compassionate and empathic towards colleagues and customers. We may dislike chaos and bring order to systems; we often prefer to not work in practices and processes that are irrational, and use logic and reasoning to develop them to efficiency and capacity. We also bring ideas from 'the edges' because we are autistic, and not despite being autistic. However, as you are probably aware, we can encounter challenges.

For instance, an over-load of information can be overwhelming. Our perfectionist tendencies may make it difficult for us to judge which autistic traits we can attempt to manage, or when to reduce our hyper-focus to give less time to, for example, a task or if to seek direction or support. High levels of anxiety and stress or uncontrollable or unexpected events effect everyone, but we likely feel the effects magnified. Conversely, recent research shows that autistic strengths and challenges that have traditionally been conceptualised as dichotomous and either 'good' or 'bad' cannot necessarily be isolated as solely strengths or challenges.

We would like to draw your attention to the work of Russell *et al* (2019), which highlights how the same autistic tendencies may be beneficial in some circumstances and unhelpful in other situations. For example, hyper-focusing on tasks or duties with tenacity and perseverance to the exclusion of others advantageously produces high standards and completed work. However, this may mean excluding other people's interests and priorities or being unable to distinguish between priorities. Equally, attention to detail enables task completion to excellent standards, but our perfectionism can become problematic within time constraints (Russell *et al*, 2019).

Moderating influential factors that mitigate against strengths being an advantage
or disadvantage are also dependent on our contexts, based on (individual) extent
and controllability of circumstances, alongside our personal/professional and your
perspectives (ibid). Equally, you may also not be aware of recent research that points
to the so-called 'compensatory' strategies we choose or forcibly use.

While we are not in complete agreement with this research, because it sits within
a deficit position, it does usefully capture some of the specific strategies we may
use to disguise autism at the surface level (see Livingston *et al*, 2019). It also
goes someway to answering your questions about how we can 'appear normal',
'not autistic' or how we have 'managed to do this before'. Compensatory strategies
involve using intellectual and executive thinking to regulate social behaviour
such as social norms and switching between social rules. These are difficult to
sustain, become more difficult when anxious, distressed or stressed, and only
function in some situations or can be slow and inflexible in fast-paced interaction
(ibid). Compensatory strategies are akin to a rubber band that binds our attempts
to push our boundaries based on how far the band will stretch before it snaps us
back into our reality.

We would also like to highlight the association between compensation, anxiety
and depression (see Dean *et al*, 2017; Cage & Troxell-Whitman, 2018). We are not
detached and unemotional, but very socially motivated and use compensatory
strategies which, if unsuccessful, reduce our self-esteem, self-confidence and
well-being. Compensations beneficially enable us to successfully interact, socially
communicate and fulfil face-to-face roles (see also Livingston *et al*, 2019). They
can be rewarding and worthwhile, but can also come at a personal cost such as
tiredness or exhaustion, and depleted energy levels or even (mini) burn-out. These
are necessary strategies for us to avoid rejection and feelings of shame or reduce
pressures to conform or bullying. Compensatory strategies can result in our social
cognitive differences going unnoticed, our intellectual abilities fatigued, and
support needs being overlooked or underestimated in organisational structures and
workplace settings (ibid).

We are sure that you will understand that this produces contradictory messages
about our disability, ability and feelings of ambivalence towards the types of
inclusion, support and accommodations we are entitled to receive or expect. While
we may feel valued as colleagues, particularly when over-performing in workplace conditions which play to our strengths, we are perhaps less so if questions
are raised about our ability in relation to the challenges we may be experiencing
in other work-related duties. Nonetheless, we thank you for recognising the
advantages we do bring to the workplace and organisation. As McGuire (2013)
suggests, though, the idea of advantageous or disadvantageous exists only in

relation to the values of neoliberal society. For us, the question, then, is how are
management structures going to distinguish between our abilities, talents and
what is a strength or challenge or (un)acceptable compensation so as to inform
reasonable accommodations?

We would like to raise the question of reasonable adjustments or accommodations

In neoliberal times, we agree and thank you for emphasising that reasonable
accommodations may not be straightforwardly understandable for the 'abled-
disabled'. We also recognise the difficulties organisations are currently facing in
terms of time and resource shortages. We understand that employment practices
have changed over recent decades, particularly since the economic recession of
2008 onwards resulting in intensified competition and increased expectation
to 'do more with less', and subsequently 'everyone is struggling'. However, we
are not sure that this equates to our everyday struggles and feel that it may
relativise and diminish our disability or provide further challenges. Being
neurodivergent within neuronormative organisations can be a daily battle. We
are expected to 'fit in' and 'stand out' in our respective roles. Neoliberalism
demands excellence to succeed and we must go beyond what is required in
order to be outstanding (Davies, 2014; 2015). Many of us are already pushing
our personal boundaries and comfort zones because of workplace normative
expectations. While it may not appear so, we are like swans gliding on the pond
but fervidly paddling underneath to stay afloat.

We are very glad to hear that some organisations celebrate diversity and
difference, and that this is clearly laid out in workplace diversity and inclusion
policies. For some of us, though, presenting as (non)conforming in our roles has
potentially led to miscommunications, misunderstandings, perceived bullying
and stigma. For example, our perfectionist tendencies and bluntness have led
to accusations of 'purposely undermining colleagues' and 'people not wanting to
work with' us. In some organisations, which arguably are increasingly becoming
more managerialist, bureaucratic, constraining and less autotomised, we fear
that not all of us will fair equally. While we may outwardly discredit myths about
autistic deficit and inability, we continue to be measured against performance
and promotion criteria very likely created by, and for, neurotypical people. Our
own experiences of fitting into boxes that, let's face it, people who are not autistic
often struggle to fit in, alongside decreasing flexibility in a preference for ever-
more bureaucratic 'rules' is worrying. Most of us like rules; we are then clear
about boundaries, expectations and roles. However, we find **clear** rules which
work helpful rather than simply *more* rules, which can make us frustrated and
anxious. Some of us also prefer to operate in the blurred boundaries and spaces

afforded professional autonomy which are, however, increasingly being eroded by standardisation. Many autistic people are sceptical of how they will 'measure-up' in neoliberal times and there seems to be little account in our discussions or assessments of the multiple complicating factors which impact our experiences or potentially our performance.

We are sure you will find that settings in organisations are controlled by rigid expectations, mass communications and the production of standardised knowledge. There are virtues placed on being present, the ability to participate, and to engage in collegiality (Nishida, 2016). This can exclude those who encounter challenges figuring out and adapting to unspoken social norms, face-to-face interaction and expressing appropriate emotions at appropriate times (Price, 2011). Reasonable adjustments that sanction non-attendance or participation at, say, meetings, or printing off a large volume of emails (time-consuming), or reduced contracts are, therefore, not necessarily inclusive or helpful. This intersects with 'compensating' for our different accents, our different values and our different backgrounds which can drive attempts to avoid further stigmatisation. Coupled with being neurodivergent and not necessarily fitting into processual or organisational cultures can lead to doubly (i.e. disability and class) or triply (i.e. with gender) experiencing challenges or disadvantage. These issues interact with one another to create distinct consequences. This means not only acknowledging a layering of different conditions or identities but how they interrelate, and thinking about (bio)social categories in institutional contexts and cultures alongside individual characteristics.

We believe you will agree it is evident that the exchange between employer and employee compromises a structure of 'rights, obligations, formal and informal social relationships' which impact daily experiences (see McGovern *et al*, 2007, p12). Most workplace interactions are based on a host of unwritten rules, assumptions and expectations on both sides (Blyton *et al*, 2004). Violation of these unwritten social rules are seldom tolerated (Nishida, 2016). This is less about our own individual failings, challenges or deficits, but how we arrived in our professional positions already 'fish out of water' (Bourdieu, 1984; 1986) and sometimes intellectually 'dancing to our own tune'. Intersecting identities and social injustice make even sharper distinctions of how privilege, recognition and power are distributed across organisations and experienced differently (Nishida, 2016). Despite reasonable adjustments, worker productivity is understood within a framework of normative and individual capability, ability and competency. Failure to keep up with such demands can become an individual's responsibility to fix or compensate.

You will have observed that our minds and bodies are sometimes exhausted, injured, and they retain our trauma as well as stress (also see Van der Kolk, 2014; Nishida, 2016). We are brave (rather than confident) most days, but we are also frightened and anxious to get 'it' right. We may try to not stand out but blend into the corridors knowing we somehow got 'it' or said 'it' or did 'it' wrong (Hendrickx, 2015). It is frightening being in organisations that may not understand autism or neurodiversity but which make 'informed' decisions about what we can and cannot do, what is 'suitable' for us or where 'we do or don't fit'. We may well have lost our confidence and esteem by virtue of trying to 'boundary cross' into pre-existing normative patterns of behaviour and thinking, or constantly looking to others for social cues and reassurance we have behaved, responded or acted according to 'conventions'.

We feel hurt and we feel unsafe when our autism is inadvertently written off or we encounter suggestions to 'try harder'. This is despite how we regularly try to avoid becoming troublesome or complaining for fear of being identified as 'the problem' (Ahmed, 2019), but remain troubled or vulnerable. This can accumulate in anxiety and trepidation about potentially losing our jobs, being performance-managed-out or isolated. Reasonable adjustments are not a 'wicked problem' – a complex problem that evades easy solutions – nor a magical wand to organisational, cultural and attitudinal barriers. They can be valuable, nonetheless, if not conceived as a solution to broader organisational or societal ills or be *practically* effective for some people, in some circumstances, in some contexts, some of the time. We understand that it might be difficult to 'trust' our assessments of our needs, which can sometimes seem ambiguous, that is, autism is not visible like a broken arm that mends but a hidden disability which affects us in different contexts or circumstances. Equally, it is assumed we should trust your judgments unequivocally about what you think we need or can and cannot do. We appreciate that it may be confusing because we cannot be defined by a specifically exact 'limitation' or strength or challenge, and these can be mutable and interchangeable.

We would like to offer ways that organisations can think about reasonable adjustments and embracing neurodiversity

Loomes (2019), in consultation with the autism community, offers a useful list of 25 reasonable adjustments or accommodations. These range from straightforward suggestions of providing us with clear expectations or detail and context if asked questions, to more complex matters of 'optionally' working part-time or working from home. However, these are currently divorced from context, and what can seem as uncomplicated accommodations are often less so in practice. Negotiating adjustments can feel scary, and can be risky and incredibly difficult given our late diagnoses and relative successes. This includes how identity factors (i.e. resourcefulness) are integral to us dealing with social, emotional and structural obstacles or inequalities since birth. Some of us would not be contributing to this letter today if we had 'given-up' or relied on systematic support or legal entitlements. We are sure you can understand that securing reasonable adjustments is very dependent on organisational knowledge of autism, individual willingness to see beneath the surface or 'performances' that are embedded in our psyche, and understanding that we may experience accommodations as a threat or loss of identity. It is also difficult to predict when adjustments need to be in place or which would be helpful at what times (Kerschbaum *et al*, 2017). Regardless, we may make requests, and we additionally suggest the following:

- Embedding neurodiversity into the fabric of our working practices, which means beginning from a place that recognises we are all diverse and all different instead of this being treated as an 'additional' or an 'afterthought'. This can include support or rights.

- Workplace training for everyone, delivered by autistic people as 'experts' or those who have personal experience of autism.

- Recognition that we may lack energy and the personal resources to perform on a certain day. We are reliable, but unfortunately our autism can be unpredictable. We also become deflated if we need to ensure the same reasonable accommodation is honoured and see this more as a shared responsibility. So, collectively agreeing to work-speed and the general impact on energy and work levels.

Recognition of our strengths and adapting performance or promotion criteria which is rigid and exclusionary to reflect a broader definition of intellectual and social ability, and make resources available.

- We wonder if you could think of how these issues map onto our work-life balance and policies? Given we regularly go home and sleep for anywhere from one to two hours, and spend weekends working to 'catch-up', or sleeping to recuperate, or sacrifice our personal and family relationships.

- We also hope that you may have some space for thinking about and questioning when a compensatory strategy becomes an entitlement for a reasonable accommodation?

We like or love our jobs (most of the time). And we trust this letter will be met with the same professional courtesy, kindness, compassion and generosity that we extend. We hope that given the power, status and prestige afforded by your positions and organisations, you will collectively encourage individuals, collectives and institutions to rethink the complex strengths and challenges of autism, how you can adapt or adopt compensatory strategies and recognise neurodiversity as a legitimate claim.

We sincerely look forward to hearing from you and working together to continue the conversation and resolve any issues for both ourselves and proponents of neurodiversity.

Kindest regards,
All.

Concluding comments: doors are there to be opened, shut or left ajar

Often, we are silent or silenced, sometimes through fear or perceived threat, but as Aude Lorde's (2017) book says: 'Your silence will not protect you'. This chapter has endeavoured to provide personal ethnographical accounts that highlight the systematic failings of organisational structures, processes and relations, and how power operates with regards to autistic experiences. Ideas about neurodiversity offer new ways to reconsider ourselves and our experiences, and question how we relate to employment practices, service-provision and broader society. Letter writing as a method alongside autoethnography has given us relative freedom to creatively express our thoughts, experiences and feelings, and comfortably fits within a neurodiversity paradigm that recognises unique difference and diverse abilities.

Collaborative discussion and letter writing enable solidarity and reflective space to heal our shared wounds and vulnerabilities, as our minds rally against the hidden injuries of social, attitudinal and infrastructural barriers, dis/advantage and inequalities. Our minds, bodies and identities are always both 'inside and outside the margins', always speaking multiple languages of existence, and always occupying different spaces (see Alshammari, 2016, p36). This means recognising how the neurodivergent mind-body-spirit are dependent on environments through which they materialise as fitting or 'misfitting' (Garland-Thomson, 2011, p598). This includes how stigmatised or unpredictable (dis)abilities are problematic because their 'appearance exposes the incongruent relationship between the two things…[and] the awkward attempt to fit them together'. Professional work requires minds that fulfil the 'essential functions' of a role and it is unclear whether autistic attributes, such as changes in cognitive processing speed or extensions of time, are an individual or reasonable organisational accommodation (Kerschbaum *et al*, 2017), or when strengths are recognised and valued. Reasonable adjustments can struggle with an ambiguous state of being such as the so-called 'successful' professional autistic, and we often sit between the disjuncture of the 'abled-disabled'.

Our autistic strengths intertwine with our (dis)ability, and the boundaries between our strengths and our challenges are unclear and interchangeable. This includes how our personhood intersects with other valued or devalued categories of identity such as class and gender. As Russell *et al* (2019) equally suggest, it is difficult to separate out cognition, behaviours and attributes as 'autistic' from those behaviours that are attributable to self/identity. This leads to the problematic self/autism divide and includes strengths and challenges as a false dichotomy. The potential utility of ableism is its explanatory power, which allows an exploration of how some abilities are conceptualised as flawed or inferior in comparison to the majority, and how this can translate into structures, practices and processes of disablement. In neoliberal times, organisations that want to 'innovate' may be either resource-short or resource-rich environments which want to harness autistic abilities and strengths but can fail to support any challenges. There are also injustices at work in 'business as usual' models, and a 'minimum standards' or 'compliance model' (Kerschbaum *et al*, 2017, p322). In such contexts, we find the focus is often exclusively on outcomes and products rather than organisational, structural and individual processes, equity and power dynamics. This can result in a negative impact on our well-being as we are driven by neurotypical society's expectations of what marks out intelligence, behaviour and value. Basic straightforward reasonable adjustments are rational, but can also be complex and appear irrational, both practically and in terms of consequences, particularly in neoliberal, austere times of competition, individualism and metrics. Yet, as Foucault (1991, p343) aptly reminds us:

'Our point is not that everything is bad, but that everything is dangerous, which is not exactly the same as bad. If everything is dangerous, then we have something to do. So my position leads not to apathy but to hyper- and pessimistic activism.'

Autistic strengths and challenges are 'in the eyes of the beholder'. Under neoliberal 'terms and conditions', advantageous or disadvantageous can, for some, only exist in relation to the values of neoliberal society. Ideas of reasonable adjustments may well provide a veneer of support, and autistic strengths or challenges shore up power and privilege in subtle ways. That is, superficially provided without fully making a difference, and sometimes used in ways to rework and reframe power, privilege and ableism. Using power and status to embrace neurodiversity, bestow recognition and rights, and reach acceptance will also mean being open to challenge and critique, and thinking differently about individuals, power structures and relations. With this in mind, we leave with some inspirational thoughts about never giving-up in the face of adversity and the drive for change:

'And when they seek to oppress you. And when they try to destroy you.
Rise and rise again and again. Like the Phoenix from the ashes.
Until the lambs have become lions and the rule of [neoliberal]
Darkness is no more.' (Maitreya, *The Friend, The Holy Book of Destiny*).

We will leave the light on.

Acknowledgements
We thank the editors of this collection for their patience and for enabling us to express ourselves in creative and non-conforming ways which we and audiences can find more accessible. We would equally like to encourage other publishers to

loosen conventions. We finally thank our employers and good colleagues over the years who have encouraged us to simply be ourselves, recognised our strengths and embraced their and our challenges in a two-way equal process.

References

Ahmed S (2019) *Living a Feminist Life*, Durham: Duke University Press.

Alshammari S (2016) A hybridized academic identity: negotiating a disability within academia's discourse of ableism. In: SL Kerchbaum, LT Eisenman and JM Jones (Eds) *Negotiating Disability: Disclosure and higher education*. University of Michigan Press.

Barnes C (1994) *Disabled People in Britain and Discrimination: a case for anti-discrimination legislation*, London: Hurst and Company.

Brown W (2015) *Undoing the Demos: Neoliberalism's stealth revolution*, New York: Zone Books.

Bourdieu P (1984). *Distinction: A social critique of the judgement of taste*. Harvard: Routledge and Kagan Paul Ltd.

Bourdieu P (1986) The forms of capital. In: JG Richardson (Ed) *Handbook of Theory and Research for the Sociology of Education*. New York: Greenwood Press.

Cage E and Troxell-Whitman Z (2018) Understanding the reasons, contexts and costs of camouflaging for autistic adults. *Autism and Developmental Disorders* **14** (5) pp1899–1911.

Cannon H (2018) *Autism: The positives*, University of Leeds, February, 2018.

Crenshaw K (1991) Mapping the margins: Intersectionality, identity politics and violence against women of colour. *Stanford Law Review* **43** pp1241–1299.

Davidson J and Orsini M (2013). *Worlds of Autism: Across the spectrum of neurological difference*. University of Minnesota Press: Minneapolis.

Davies W (2014) *The Limits of Neoliberalism: Authority, sovereignty and the logic of competition*. London: Sage.

Davies W (2015) *The Happiness Industry: How the government and big business sold us wellbeing*. London: Verso.

Dean M, Harwood R and Kasari C (2017) The art of camouflage: gender differences in the social behaviours of girls and boys with autism spectrum disorder. *Autism* **21** (6) pp678–89.

Foucault M (1991) On the genealogy of ethics: an overview of work in progress. In: P Rabinow (ed.) *The Foucault Reader: An introduction to Foucault's thought*, pp. 340–72. Harmondsworth: Penguin.

Garland-Thomson R (2011) Misfits: a feminist materialist disability concept. *Hypatia* **26** (3) pp591–609.

Graby S (2015) Neurodiversity: Bridging the Gap between the Disabled People's Movement and the Mental Health System Survivors' Movement? In: H Spandler, J Anderson and B Sapey (eds) *Madness, Distress and the Politics of Disablement*. Bristol: Policy Press.

Grandin T (2012) *Different…Not Less: Inspiring Stories of Achievement and Successful Employment from Adults with Autism, Asperger's and ADHD*. Arlington: Future Horizons.

Hall S (1996) *Critical Dialogues in Cultural Studies*, New York: Routledge.

Henrickx S (2015) *Women and Girls with Autism Spectrum Disorder: Understanding life experiences from early childhood to old age*. London: Jessica Kingsley Publishers.

Hersh M and Elley S (2019) Barriers and enablers of inclusion for young autistic learners: lessons from the polish experiences of teachers and related professionals. *Advances in Autism* **5** (2) pp117–130.

Kerschbaum SL, O'Shea AM, Price M and Salzer MS (2017) Accusations and disclosures for faculty members with a mental disability. In: SL Kerchbaum, LT Eisenman and JM Jones (eds) *Negotiating Disability: Disclosure and higher education*. University of Michigan Press.

Lawson W (2009) *Single Attention and Associated Cognition in Autism*, PhD thesis Deakin University.

Livingston LA, Shah P and Happe F (2019) Compensatory strategies below the behavioural surface in autism: a qualitative study. *Lancet Psychiatry*.

Loomes (2019) 'Reasonable Adjustments' for #AutisticsInAcademia: The Community Speaks… [online]. Available at: https://voicespaces.co.uk/2019/07/18/reasonable-adjustments-for-autisticsinacademia-the-community-speaks/ (accessed May 2020).

Lorde A (2017) *Your Silence Will Not Protect You*, London: Silver Press.

Maitreya, The Friend (2011) *The Holy Book of Destiny*, USA: Kaivalya International Sanctuary.

McGovern R, Hill P, Mills C and White M (2007) *Market, Class and Employment*. Oxford: Oxford University Press.

McGuire AE (2013) Buying time: the s/pace of advocacy and the cultural production of autism. *Canadian Journal of Disability Studies* **2** (3) pp98.

McWade B, Milton D and Beresford P (2015) Mad studies and neurodiversity: a dialogue, *Disability and Society* **30** (2).

Nishiada A (2016) Neoliberal academia and a critique from disability studies. In: P Block, D Kasnitz, A Nishida and N Pollard. *Occupying Disability: Critical approaches to community, justice and decolonizing disability*. New York: Springer.

Price M (2011). *Mad at School: The rhetoric of mental disability and academic life*. University of Michigan Press: Ann Arbor.

Reay D, David ME and Ball S (2005) *Degree of Choice: Social class, race and gender in higher education*. Stoke on Trent: Trentham Books.

Russell G, Kapp SK, Elliot D, Elphick C, Gwernan-Jones R and Owens C (2019) Mapping the autistic advantage from the accounts of adults diagnosed with autism: a qualitative study. *Autism in Adulthood* **1** (2) 124–133.

Singer J (1999) Why can't you be normal for once in your life?: From a 'Problem with No Name' to the emergence of a new category of difference. In: M Corker and S French. *Disability and Discourse*. Buckingham: Open University Press.

Titchkosky T (2003) Governing embodiment: technologies of constituting citizens with disabilities. *Canadian Journal of Sociology* **28** (4) 517–542.

Van der Kolk B (2014) *The Body Keeps the Score*, UK: Penguin Random House.

Walker (2014) Neurodiversity: Some Basic Terms & Definitions [Online]. Available at: https://neurocosmopolitanism.com/neurodiversity-some-basic-terms-definitions/ (accessed May 2020).

Chapter 23: A literature review exploring the efficacy of person-centred counselling for autistic people

By Lisa Cromar

With thanks to The Person-Centred Association's Person-Centred Quarterly who originally published this article.

Introduction

This literature review investigates the suitability of Person-Centred Counselling (PCC) for autistic clients, a subject of particular importance to the author as an autistic person currently training to become a PC counsellor and having experience of this approach as both client and practitioner on placement with an autism charity. The PC Approach (PCA) and autism have been well documented, however literature exploring the efficacy of PCC for autistic people is minimal; Buck and Buck (2006) and Rutten (2014) give a useful description of the PC intervention and the autistic condition.

This review is important due to the known higher prevalence of poor mental health in the autistic population than in the neurotypical population, as can be seen in Figure 23.1, below. Understanding how effective PCC is in supporting this vulnerable client group is vital, and to explore whether adaptations to the approach would be beneficial.

For comparison, this review will begin by exploring the efficacy of Cognitive Behavioural Therapy (CBT) with adaptations on offer for autistic clients,

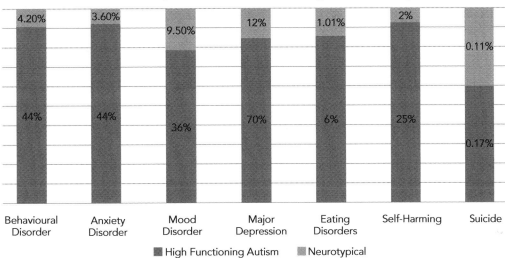

Figure 23.1. A comparison chart of co-morbid psychiatric disorders commonly found in people with high functioning autism/Asperger's syndrome, alongside the same disorders found in the neurotypical population. Data for high functioning autism; for behavioural disorder, anxiety disorder, mood disorder, and major depression, from Lake et al, (2014), for eating disorders (minimum of) from Howlin and Magiati (2017) and for self-harming, from XI Autism-Europe Conference (2016). Data for Neurotypical; for behavioural disorder and anxiety disorder, from Emerson (2003), for mood disorder, from Insel & Fenton, (2005), for major depression, from Andrade et al., (2003), for eating disorder, from Qian et al (2013), and for self-harming, from XI Autism-Europe Conference, (2016). Data for suicide for neurotypical and high functioning autism, from Kirby et al., (2019).

including any barriers, and commenting on the research available. It will then explore whether PCC is *enough* for autistic people, focusing on Rogers' (1967) core-conditions of the relationship, empathy, unconditional positive regard (UPR) and congruence, and how these fit with this client group, including any barriers, progressing to examine what adaptations might be required to make the PCA more accessible to autistic clients. Finally, the quality of the research will be examined, with recommendations for improvements suggested by Vossler and Moller (2015) and Booth *et al* (2016).[48]

Methodology

For this review, a full systematic search was carried out, predominantly using ebsco-host. A reference list check was then completed, then the authors, including Mick Cooper and Chris Abildgaard, were contacted to establish if other research was available.

---

48 This review reflects on autism research dating back ten years when functioning terms were more commonly used, so to ensure accuracy they were included. However, the author would like to acknowledge that functioning labels can be hurtful and unhelpful to the autism community and future research should avoid this type of terminology.

What is included is believed to be a complete list of all available literature relating to PCC and autism. However, in summary, 55 pieces of literature were saved for further scrutiny, with a total of 39 being included in the final review. However, there are areas, including gender differences and autism with intellectual disability (ID), which were excluded but particularly merit further research in relation to autistic people; these will be further addressed in the Further Research section of this review.

How does PCC compare in effectiveness to CBT? Is CBT a panacea for the autistic client group?

CBT Advantages

Most of the literature available concerning counselling and psychotherapy for autistic people relates to CBT. Prominent authors in this field being Attwood (2015), a staunch CBT advocate, Paxton and Estay (2007) and Purkis *et al* (2016). To highlight the disparity of literature on therapy for autistic people, a search on the ebsco-host database brought up 4,013 results with the search parameters 'CBT OR Cognitive Behavioural Therapy AND autism OR Autism Spectrum Disorder OR ASD', compared with four results with the search parameters 'Person Centred Counselling AND autism OR Autism Spectrum Disorder OR ASD'. It seems to make sense that the popularity of CBT as the primary therapy offering could be driven by this disproportionate weight of empirical evidence.

This was supported by Koenig and Levine (2011) who contend in their case study that 'behavioural approaches have solid empirical support with respect to helping individuals with ASDs modify behaviour and improve functioning' helping with 'addressing anger management/obsessive thinking' (p33). This argument is further supported by Lake *et al* (2014), stating 'the effectiveness of CBT in addressing anxiety, anger and social deficits... is well documented in the literature... and case studies... suggest CBT is a promising treatment for depression and anxiety in this population' (p4). Furthermore, Rogers (2016) maintains that 'the unique skills of this client group', including 'strengths related to the need for structure, and a scientific way of thinking, lend themselves to learning opportunities in behavioural experiments' (para 5-6). The empirical evidence appears positive for CBT being effective for the autistic client group.

Adaptations

This evidence comes with a caveat. Similarly to findings by Cooper *et al* (2018), Blainey *et al* (2017) found in their study of 81(N) autistic adults with no ID, that results indicated 'preliminary evidence' showing 'CBT-based psychological therapy provided *within a specialist service* may be effective at reducing general psychological distress in adults with Autism Spectrum Disorder (ASD) and co-morbid mental health difficulties' (p01479). These results support the National Institute for Health and Care Excellence (NICE, 2012) recommendations, which advise: adaptations to the delivery method of CBT will need to be met for the autistic client's cognitive and social communication needs when treating mental health conditions. What seems clear from the literature, is that standard CBT training is not suitable for autistic people; indeed, adaptations to meet the needs of this group are recommended.

A study by Cooper *et al* (2018) of 54(N) psychological therapists aimed to ascertain 'their current knowledge and past experience of working within a cognitive behavioural framework with autistic people' (p44). Results demonstrate the need, as posited by other authors, such as Rosslyn (2018), Murphy *et al* (2017) and Attwood (2015) for adaptations to CBT. All 54(N) participants reported making some adaptations, including 'an increased use of written and visual information' (p43). In line with NICE (*2012*) guidelines, the participants 'emphasised behavioural change over cognitive approaches, having well explained guidance and rules of therapy' (p43). They recommend 'involving a friend, family member or carer, having breaks, incorporating special interests and avoiding ambiguous use of language' (p44). Cooper *et al* (*2018*) acknowledge that a weakness of this report is that it is not representative of all CBT therapists working with autistic clients. The participants were surveyed while attending a training event to learn how to adapt CBT for autistic clients. Therefore, they are likely to already have a specialist interest and knowledge in this group. This has caused result bias, which Booth *et al* (2016) would posit has 'erroneously influenced the conclusions' (p153) of this group. This has potentially given an inaccurately high view of the level of therapist confidence in working in this group; Cooper *et al* (2018) recommend 'future studies should recruit a wider range of therapists' (p49). Regrettably, many autistic people will not be fortunate enough to find themselves placed with a therapist with autism specialism, especially as Hearst (2014) explains, 'most adult autism is undiagnosed' (p26). The report also highlights many other barriers of CBT for autistic clients.

Barriers

Cooper *et al* (2018) found many 'barriers' to the effectiveness of CBT for autistic clients, largely around the 'cognitive' element. The CBT practitioner participants reported 'the most frequently reported barrier… was rigidity of thinking or Black and White thinking'… and 'found that the cognitive style of autistic people was not always amenable to this approach' (p48).

The American Psychiatric Association (APA) (2013) details rigid thinking patterns in autism in the Diagnostic and Statistical Manual of Mental Disorders (DSM-

5). In a report by Rogers (2016) that investigated how to adapt CBT for children with autism, it was disclosed that Rogers will not offer CBT 'if the child … has an extremely rigid thinking style' (para 10). Cooper *et al* (2018) insist that if a therapist were to pursue the cognitive element of CBT with an autistic client, the therapist and the client could become quite frustrated and contribute to, as Eaton (2018) further argues, the client's experiences of 'a high level of social rejection… this would to some extent, serve to reinforce their negative beliefs' (p116-p117) which they hold about themselves.

Negative beliefs can be further adversely affected by poor executive functioning commonly experienced by autistic people. Ross (2018) explains that, 'executive-functioning deficits affect planning, time management, organisation, prioritisation, inhibition, focus, task initiation (and persistence), transitions, working memory and attention to detail' (p7). This explains why the CBT practitioner participants in Cooper *et al*'s (2018) study reported challenges with the 'pacing of therapy and completing of homework' (p48).

The literature suggests that, unless allowances and adaptations are made to CBT to make it accessible to autistic people, the results could be detrimental and lead to, as Cooper *et al* propose, 'a less favourable therapeutic outcome' (2018, p48).

Research

Most of the research seems to be based on adapted versions of CBT. Attwood (2015) agrees with Paxton and Estay (2007), arguing, 'there has been evidence that this is an effective approach with persons on the autism spectrum' (p12). However, there appears to be some weakness in this evidence. Weston *et al* (2016) agree with Murphy *et al*'s (2017) counter-argument, stating that the available studies are 'problematic, as there are no large-scale definitive trials in this area making use of robust methodologies. As such, the conclusions reached within this meta-analysis and previous meta-analyses are potentially limited' (p51).

Furthermore, it is a limitation that most of the trials of CBT detailed in the literature, as Murphy *et al* (2017) explain, saw CBT tested most commonly against 'active' or 'passive' controls (usually defined as 'waitlists'). This argument is supported by Weston et al (2016), whose meta-analysis of 48(N) studies 'investigating the effectiveness of CBT when used with individuals who have ASD' (p41) had no comparisons to other therapy modalities.

This review found only one study comparing CBT to PCC, namely a study by Murphy *et al* (2017), which was a very small-scale randomised control trial (RCT) with 47(N) participants. This produced interesting results; despite the acknowledged benefit of adaptations being applied to CBT (in this case the adapted version of CBT was Multimodel Anxiety and Social Skill Intervention (MASSI)), unadapted PCC fared equally well, demonstrating similar efficacy. This begs the question, if adaptations had been made to PCC, would it have been shown to be more effective than CBT?

Summary

Murphy *et al* (2017) and Lake *et al* (2014) agree with Blainey *et al* (2017), arguing that, 'although CBT is the intervention with the greatest evidence-base, alternative forms of psychotherapy could be explored for people with autism spectrum condition (ASC), enabling parity of choice' (p01483). It seems unjust and discriminatory that, despite the British Association of Counsellors and Psychotherapists (BACP) (2019) detailing 30 different therapy modalities, only one type, CBT, is targeted towards autistic people.

There are useful adaptations being made by CBT practitioners to make it more accessible to autistic people. However,7 it is possibly not a panacea for all autistic people and has its limitations. The evidence-base is weak, with larger-scale reviews required, including more comparisons to other therapies, including PCC.

Is person-centred counselling enough for autistic people? What are the barriers?

The data available to judge whether PCC is 'enough' for autistic people is minimal and qualitative in nature, and could be viewed as falling significantly short, compared to the more predominantly empirically based quantitative data available for CBT.

For this review, due to the piecemeal nature of the evidence which is available, research cannot be disseminated in an objective way; therefore inferences will need to be made in the collation of this limited data. Despite uneven data, the qualitative data which is available is promising, particularly around the benefits of Rogers' (1967) core conditions, the first of which is the relationship between the counsellor and client.

Relationship

The significance of the relationship is proposed by Purkis *et al* (2016) who state, 'the therapeutic alliance is particularly important for people with autism. They may have issues trusting others and have more difficulty than neurotypical people in knowing who is and isn't trustworthy' (p188). Hodge and Rutten (2017) further purport that autistic people 'experience a very limited number of positive relationships; the act of regular and predictable engagement with another person that enables being heard and feeling understood... might go a long way to raising self-esteem and improving quality of life' (p514).

The therapeutic alliance may take more time and work to form, as Keonig and Levine (2011) argue 'a lack of, or much under-developed, "sense of the other"… for those with ASD' means 'establishing and maintaining relationships is an effortful process that requires understanding and patience on the part of all participants' (p29). Accepting and prizing the client for who they are phenomenologically, with Rogers' (1967) unconditional positive regard (UPR), may provide a strong base in forming this therapeutic alliance.

The PC core conditions

Autistic people may have experienced very little prizing in their previous relationships. Knibbs and Rutten (2017) claim that autistic people 'are subject to heightened conditions of worth' (p2). Research suggests that being different from peers and society as a whole can have a negative impact on mental health, as demonstrated by Lester (2014), who found that, for autistic people, 'there is a lot of negative stigma generated by society at large. Stigma has been associated with normal/abnormal dichotomy, with those oriented to as 'abnormal' often being stigmatised' (p187). Furthermore, a study by Cooper *et al* (2017) of 272(N) explores factors that could interfere with the development of positive social identity' (p844), which would lower personal self-esteem and increase depression and anxiety. This study posits that having a negative social identity directly and negatively affects self-esteem.

Rutten (2014) further explains that for autistic people 'whose difficulties are largely in the social domain, life is likely to start off with disadvantages… it is probable that social interactions with significant others in early life present people with autism with very high levels of conditionality. Whilst conditions of worth and incongruence develop' (p81). It seems autistic people are often subjected to largely unachievable externally imposed conditions of worth. The ensuing struggle to try to 'fit-in' to societal expectations results in them living incongruently and increasing the likelihood of experiencing a high degree of failure in this respect.

The PCA, offering Rogers' core conditions of a counsellor giving UPR, empathy and congruence, could help a client to experience a relationship which gives them what Cooper *et al* (2017) describe as 'a positive social identity', which has the potential to increase their 'personal self-esteem, and in turn, would reduce depression and anxiety' (p846). In the mini society which exists in the counselling room, the autistic client would hopefully experience a positive identity within the therapeutic alliance. In finding more acceptance of themselves and, as Cooper *et al* (*2017*) term their 'autism identity', the hope would be that with the support of a congruent and non-judgmental counsellor, they could become free to be happier in their identity, and therefore more congruent in their own way of being.

Buck and Buck (2006) carried out a case-study reflecting on an autistic client's experience of PCC, when the sessions came to an end, they report that the client 'discovered that the therapist was really interested in him and for the first time in his life nobody judged' (p71). Buck and Buck believe the therapy was useful to this client, reporting that 'the potential for a more fulfilling life is more likely now' (p71). The PC counsellor gave him the trust to discover 'the most suitable way forward for himself' with his own 'unique way of seeing the world' (p71). The client was able to move to a place of congruence.

Rogers (1951) believed that seeing the world through the client's eyes empathically is fundamental to the PCA. Hodge (2012) further argues that it is important to 'appreciate what being in the world might mean to a client who is on the autism spectrum', warning counsellors to be aware that often the 'problem' is not within the 'individual, rather in the environments that clients inhabit…'. Failing to appreciate this might cause counsellors to 'try to restore a "normal self" within a client who is not necessarily biologically configured in ways that will allow him/her to ever meet the requirements of being "normal"' (p106). Perhaps it is enough to reflect that a client can struggle, sometimes, in what can be a confusing society to an autistic person, and so it is beneficial to avoid directing them in ways in which they can become more 'normal' to enable them to 'fit-in'.

Purkis *et al* (2016) add that it is important that autistic clients have access to a counsellor who can 'understand the particular needs not only of autistic people generally, but also the autistic individual they are working with, [which] can be seen as essential to a good therapeutic alliance for autistic people' (p188). Each autistic person needs to be treated as a unique individual who is the expert and driver of their own life.

Knibbs and Rutten (2017) reiterate, 'as described in detail elsewhere, person-centred theory presents core beliefs that the client is expert; this maps neatly on what people on the autism spectrum say they need from practitioners' (p5). Buck and Buck (2006) agree with Knibbs and Rutten (2017), arguing that 'the person-centred perspective is central in recognising each individual's uniqueness, and in achieving true empathic understanding.' It 'also provides a model for considering the complex conditions of worth and accompanying challenges for individuals with social learning difficulties' (p1). In their work with autistic clients, they aim to 'achieve conditions where clients feel accepted and valued, listened to and understood, not judged or required to conform to inappropriate expectations' (ibid). PCC offers conditions which have the potential to be an effective therapeutic approach that is 'enough' for helping autistic people, but it is not without some possible barriers.

Barriers

The autistic client

There appear to be significant barriers to autistic people benefitting from counselling. Vogan *et al*'s (2017) study assessing the experiences of 40(N) autistic people, highlights difficulties accessing health services. They found counselling to be the most 'commonly accessed health service beyond a family doctor' (p267). Despite this, participants reported there were 'overwhelming steps to finding and obtaining services' (p268). Hodge (2012) agrees: '…there are barriers for disabled people to even get as far as the counselling room in the first place. The cost can be prohibitive… for disabled people who often have fewer financial resources' (p106–107). Arriving at counselling can be challenging for the autistic client group.

Once an autistic client has managed to navigate these obstacles and arrived at counselling, there can be further barriers, including, as Hodge (2012) and Cooper *et al* (2017) argue: '…some autistic individuals see the condition negatively and attempt to distance themselves from the autism label' (p844), possibly leading to masking and ultimately incongruence. Autistic clients may struggle to find words for feelings, a condition known as alexithymia. Blainey *et al* (2017) explain that 'alexithymia, or difficulty understanding internal states such as thoughts or feelings, is well documented amongst people with ASC' (p01481).

Alongside the difficulty in accessing and describing thoughts and feelings, they may also have a tendency to blame others and not take accountability for their own actions. Hodge (2012) explains that 'some people with autism may focus on the need for the world to change' (p106–107).

The autistic person presenting to the counsellor could be quite confusing to the counsellor as a result of these complications, particularly around the struggles with feelings, accountability and possibly the negativity and defensiveness towards their own autism, possibly causing masking behaviour and incongruence.

The counsellor

The sometimes unfamiliar dichotomy of the experiences and worldview of an autistic person, compared to those of a neurotypical counsellor, can present further barriers. There was an overwhelmingly common finding in the research that autism knowledge, training and the confidence of counsellors who found themselves working with autistic clients was lacking.

Cooper *et al* (2018), Hodge and Rutten (2017) and Purkis *et al* (2016) agreed with Brookman-Freeze *et al* (2012), who conducted a survey that assessed 13(N) therapists' 'perceptions of their knowledge and confidence serving children with

ASD' (p1656). They found that 'therapists have limited training in ASD and are highly frustrated serving this population' (p1652).

The danger is that this frustration and lack of confidence may show itself in the counselling room. Unsurprising, then, that many autistic people, as Vogan *et al* (2017) report, have 'negative experience of professionals' (p268). Purkis *et al* (2016) further claim that 'lack of knowledge in itself is not a barrier to being a good therapist, a lack of acceptance and understanding the experiences of an individual with autism... should be an indicator that the therapist may not be the right person to help' (p186).

Unfortunately, due to a chronic lack of counsellors trained in autism, this makes accessing appropriate therapists very difficult for the autistic population. Not only does awareness and training need to develop in the counselling profession, including in PCC, to make it 'enough' for people with autism, but counsellors also need to gain approval and confidence in adapting their approach, where necessary, to make counselling accessible to autistic people.

Summary

Although empirical research is lacking in the area of efficacy of PCC for autistic people, the available literature supports the benefits of the counsellor offering of Rogers' core conditions: relationship, UPR, empathy and congruence. This may be the first time an autistic person has experienced a relationship of this type.

There are, however, some barriers to overcome for an autistic client entering into counselling, such as the difficulties a client may have initially reaching the counselling room, and their struggles describing thoughts and feelings (alexithymia), for example. Additionally, there is a general lack of confidence and training in autism among counsellors.

Nevertheless, with the right training and knowledge, it looks promising from the literature that PCC is 'enough' for autistic clients, with the caveat that adaptations may need to be made.

What adaptations can/need to be made to PCC to make it 'enough' for autistic clients?

The UK government have recognised that health and care services need to be adapted to make them more suitable and accessible to autistic people. They have launched a consultation with a proposal for 'learning disability and autism training for health and care staff' (2019). The proposal states that all health and care staff working in the NHS will have 'mandatory learning disability and autism training' (para. 1). This will bring counsellors who work in the NHS up-to-date with the Autism Act (2009) and the Equality Act (2010), which states that, as Rowe (2017) also advises, 'anyone working with a person who has ASD ought to make reasonable adjustments to the way they work' (p79). The hope is that this will contribute to improving counsellor confidence when working with autistic clients and give them the ability and skills to adapt appropriately to meet the needs of these clients.

Personal and body language

It is hoped that any autism training packages would include recognising and responding appropriately to different body language and personal language of autistic individuals. Mearns and Thorne (2007) comment: '...as the counsellor learns the personal language of her client his behaviour becomes progressively easier to see and to accept' (p102). Rosslyn (2018) purports that, for the neurotypical counsellor, it can be 'bewildering ... to find a client on the spectrum carefully avoiding eye-contact ... giving ... one-word replies ... bundled up in their outdoor coat ... and on the edge of their chair ... playing with a shoelace... they may seem reluctant to engage' (p29). Rosslyn explains that an experienced counsellor would know this autistic client 'is in a state of high anxiety and sensory alert...' Such a client knows 'they will be alone with a stranger for an hour, having to simulate eye contact and follow another person's expectations' (p290). Aston (2011) agrees that autistic clients 'are working hard just to keep up to speed with interactive communications' (para. 11). Rosslyn (2018) explains that this more unusual body and personal language could lead a counsellor to make assumptions based on more neurotypical behaviour, leading them to think their client could be 'depressed, traumatised' or 'hostile' (p29). Lester (2014) asks 'who and what positions behaviour as "normal" and "abnormal"?' and calls for 'careful attention to the consequences for how, when and where notions of "normalness" are made "real"' (p190). Counsellors and researchers need to show caution in relation to the assumptions that they make, not least around eye-contact in autistic people.

Guest and Ohrt's (2018) study into the effectiveness of client-centred play therapy (CCPT) for autistic children took eye-contact as a positive outcome, commenting that an autistic participant's 'eye contact improved' (p162). This outcome is alarming, as a study by Hadjikhani *et al* (2017) found that 'constraining individuals with ASD to look into the eyes ... results in activation of the subcortical pathway', meaning 'direct eye-contact may be experienced as stressful in autism' (p3–4). Aston (2011) concludes that, for autistic people, 'making or maintaining eye-contact can be very difficult' (para. 13). A strategy for a counsellor to help their client feel more relaxed in therapy would be to give them permission not to have to maintain eye contact.

Communication

The 'learning disability and autism training for health and care staff' (2019) highlights the need to 'use appropriate communication skills when supporting a person with autism' (p10). Woods *et al* (2013) carried out a review of which adaptations counsellors were currently making for autistic clients. They propose that these clients, 'typically have problems with social communication, particularly conversation, non-verbal cues and reciprocal interaction… [and] have difficulties in empathy and theory-of-mind' (p34). Rogers (2016) adds that autistic people can 'interpret language in a literal manner' (para 13). Aston (2011) additionally comments that 85% of autistic people suffer from 'alexithymia … which simply means no words for feelings' (para 15). Autistic people can therefore struggle to describe their feelings. Woods *et al* (2013) and Rogers would agree with Aston's (2011) recommendations that autistic clients are given 'clear instructions and logical options to consider' (para. 16). Additionally, Abildgaard (2013) highlights it can be useful to introduce 'the concept of 'maybe' … for our more rigid thinkers…. The use of the word 'maybe' aims to create flexibility and is more proactive because it does not allow these clients to create just one picture in their heads related to how things are "supposed to go"' (para. 15).

Training above and beyond standard counsellor training is important for counsellors to understand the communication differences of the autistic client group. As Hearst (2014) argues: 'we can … see that a condition that affects social relationships would affect therapy … if this condition were not well understood, it would be difficult to conduct therapy effectively' (p28).

Environment/sensory input

Rosslyn (2018) explains that the autistic client may not have come to therapy for the purposes of forming 'a relationship, but for help – and until they receive some, they will not relax… they may be finding the environment stressful; overhead lights, coloured cushions, diffusers and small noises are all potential sensory problems' (p26-p27). Hearst (2016) adds that it is important to be 'aware of the sensory environment recommending not having clutter and providing "stim toys" (things to fiddle with)' (para. 4). Nicholson (2017) clarifies that 'autistic individuals lack the ability to adjust to sensory experiences that other people accept as normal' (para 9). Aston (2011) comments that if the client 'is comfortable and relaxed within the environment', this gives them 'the best possible chance of having a stress-free and beneficial therapeutic alliance' (*para.* 23).

Boundaries

As well as tending to the environment, boundaries may also need to be modified. Hodge and Rutten (*2017*) highlight that autistic clients might need 'a high level of consistency around room layout, dates and times … being more flexible about where sessions might take place and in what form ... some clients need more frequent, shorter sessions' (pp513-514). Nicholson (2017) suggests, however, that they might need longer sessions as 'this extended time period allows for cognitive flexibility and for theory-of-mind deficits' (para. 5).

Furthermore, it appears to be unhelpful for autistic clients to be restricted to the usual offering of six sessions. Research by Blainey *et al* (2017) found that an average of 20 sessions would be most beneficial. Further research by Jones (2013) recommends more relaxed boundaries, including 'the use of refreshments, humour and self-disclosure to facilitate the therapeutic relationship' (p197).

The aim in creating these 'friendlier relationships', Jones (*2013*) clarifies, is that autistic clients can then 'engage in the therapeutic relationship' (p197). Engagement in the therapeutic relationship can still be a challenge when working with an autistic client due to poor communication skills hampering the development of psychological contact, deemed necessary to form Rogers' first condition of the relationship.

Creative counselling

Stepankova's (2015) study of 6(N) autistic individuals investigates the use of Prouty *et al*'s (2002) pre-therapy contact reflections. For example, giving a bodily reflection verbally can be useful for autistic clients who are lower functioning and perhaps non-verbal, although this was out of the scope of this review, which focuses more on higher functioning autistic clients. The principles of pre-therapy to help aid psychological contact can be expanded upon, with creative counselling.

Ross (2018) argues that 'a creative, person-centred, and sensory sensitive approach to working with ASD students is essential... tactile and visual therapies such as drawing, sand-tray, and small figure work may be useful methods to explore' (p14).

Ross (ibid.) agrees with Nicholson (2017), commenting that it is common for autistic people to 'have a special interest' and it can be 'important to weave it into counselling communications, in order to encourage client engagement' (para 12). Aston (2011) recommends finding out 'from the client how they best prefer to communicate; they may prefer to write things down... to express feelings' (para 12). Abilgaard (2013) further explains that many autistic people 'are visual learners, using visuals is key to helping these clients' (para 5). Additionally, Jones (2013) recommends working in a 'creative and flexible way ... to benefit in developing the therapeutic relationship' (p198).

It is hoped that these creative tools will enable the autistic client to enter into a therapeutic relationship with his counsellor where psychological holding is possible, and therapy can take place.

Summary

The qualitative, case study and anecdotal research for this review has highlighted that many adaptations are already being made by PC counsellors. They may include being more aware of differing communication styles, personal language and body language, providing support in the counselling room, for example, being more aware of sensory issues, flexibility around boundaries and providing creative tools to aid in communication to ultimately help in building a therapeutic relationship with adequate psychological holding.

This review has provided evidence that adaptations *can* and *need* to be made to PCC to make it 'enough' for autistic clients. However, to make it available to greater numbers of autistic people, it is promising that the UK government propose making autism training mandatory. This will hopefully give a greater number of PC counsellors the training to make them more confident in making the necessary adaptations.

Conclusion

Summary of main results

The literature gathered for this review demonstrates that CBT, with adaptations, can be an effective therapy of choice for autistic clients, however it is not without barriers and is not a panacea for all. This review agrees with Blainey *et al* (2017) who recommend 'a parity of choice' (p01483) is given to the autistic client group. Furthermore, there is a need for greater comparisons with other therapies in future CBT research, and for larger-scale studies.

There was minimal empirical research exploring the efficacy of PCC for autistic people. This review agrees with Harris *et al* (2010), who argues that autism research is still in its 'infancy'. However, promising evidence was available to demonstrate Rogers' core-conditions of PCC: empathy, UPR and congruence as being of therapeutic value to this group. The review also agrees with Knibbs and Rutten (2017), that PCC is an ideal platform for helping autistic people who can be subject to 'heightened conditions of worth' (p2).

Although this review could not say that PCC is *enough* for autistic clients in its classical form, it has provided evidence that it could be enough with adaptations, such as using creative counselling to aid in forming the psychological contact necessary for the vital relationship between counsellor and client, and for the counsellor to be sensitive to sensory sensitivities in the client and differing communication styles. Most importantly, counsellors need to receive adequate training in autism. This review supports the government plans to provide mandatory training on learning disability and autism training for health and care staff (2019).

It is important that all therapy approaches, including PCC, are adapted and made available to the autistic client group, and to not discriminate by excluding any therapy choices from them for reasons of inaccessibility, not least due to poor mental health being more prevalent in the autistic client group. It is unjust that only CBT is currently being adequately adapted to meet the needs of this group. We can, however, learn lessons from CBT practitioners as to how to standardise research to make the evidence-base stronger in the promotion of PCC and how to more adequately adapt the approach.

Future research

Although excluded from this review due to being beyond its scope, gender differences appear to warrant further research. A recent report by Kirby *et al* (2019) highlights that autistic females are three times more likely to commit suicide than neurotypical females. It is important that further research is carried out to understand both the causes of this increased risk, and the mental health issues leading to this tragic outcome. Although the gender split for this review is overall well-balanced, at 60% male and 40% female, where gender was disclosed, autism research tends to be heavily male orientated. For example, studies by Blainey *et al* (2017) had 60 males and 21 females, and Lester (2014) had 11 males and one female. We need to ensure that future research represents females fairly if we are to understand how they can be better supported and to decrease the risk of suicide in this group.

Another area excluded from this review, but which requires greater research, is autism with ID; most research focused on high-functioning autism with no ID, despite findings by Russell *et al* (2019) that 50% of autistic people have ID. Indeed, 'Eight out of ten studies demonstrated selection bias against participants with ID' (p1). Further research is required to examine the efficacy of mental health support currently on offer for this group.

This review agrees with research by Buck and Buck (2006), who argue that further research is needed in 'practical therapeutic process to understand how the basic concepts of client-centred theory can be used to describe and understand the experiential world of clients with ASD better, and thus help them to optimise their lives' (p72). This review has highlighted how Rogers' core conditions could be beneficial to autistic clients and there is scope for this to be researched further, particularly if adaptations can be agreed.

Potential bias

The author of this review is training in PCC. Therefore, there was a risk of what Vossler and Moller (*2015*) term 'the allegiance effect' (p37) giving a bias towards favouring PCC. This effect was mitigated against by adding a comparison with CBT, which is better researched. Both approaches were carefully addressed, scrutinising both the benefits and barriers of each.

References

Abildgaard C (2013) Processing the 'whole' with clients on the autism spectrum [online]. *Counseling Today*. Available at: https://ct.counseling.org/2013/12/processing-the-whole-with-clients-on-the-autism-spectrum/ (accessed May 2020).

American Psychiatric Association (2013) *Diagnostic and Statistical Manual of Mental Disorders* (5th Ed). American Psychiatric Publishing.

Andrade L, Caraveo-anduaga J, Berglund P, Bijl R, Graaf R & Vollebergh W, Dragomirecka E, Kohn R, Keller M, Kessler RC, Kawakami N, Kiliç C, Offord D, Ustun TB and Wittchen HU (2003) The epidemiology of major depressive episodes: results from the International Consortium of Psychiatric Epidemiology (ICPE) surveys. *International Journal of Methods In Psychiatric Research* **12** (1) 3–21. doi: 10.1002/mpr.138

Aston M (2011) Understanding Asperger syndrome. *Therapy Today* **22** (7).

Attwood T (2015) *The Complete Guide to Asperger's Syndrome*. London: Jessica Kingsley Publishers.

Blainey S, Rumball F, Mercer L, Evans L & Beck A (2017) An evaluation of the effectiveness of psychological therapy in reducing general psychological distress for adults with autism spectrum conditions and comorbid mental health problems. *Clinical Psychology & Psychotherapy* **24** (6) O1474–O1484. doi: 10.1002/cpp.2108

Booth A, Sutton A & Papaioannou D (2016) *Systematic Approaches to a Successful Literature Review*. London: Sage.

British Association of Counsellors and Psychotherapists (2020) Types of counselling and psychotherapy [online]. Available at: www.bacp.co.uk/about-therapy/types-of-therapy/ (accessed May 2020).

Brookman-Frazee L, Drahota A & Stadnick N (2012) Training community mental health therapists to deliver a package of evidence-based practice strategies for school-age children with autism spectrum disorders: a pilot study. *Journal of Autism & Developmental Disorders* **42** 1651–1661.

Buchan L (2015) Axia-ASD Conference: The 1st of Dr. Buchan's Presentations [online]. Available at: http://axia-asd.co.uk/axia-asd-conference-the-1st-of-dr-buchans-presentations/ (accessed May 2020).

Buck D & Buck M (2006) Asperger's syndrome: a client-centered approach. *The Person-Centered Journal* **13** (1–2) 63–74.

Cooper K, Loades M & Russell A (2018) Adapting psychological therapies for autism. *Research in Autism Spectrum Disorders* **45** 43–50 doi: 10.1016/j.rasd.2017.11.002

Cooper K, Smith L & Russell A (2017) Social identity, self-esteem, and mental health in autism. *European Journal of Social Psychology* **47** (7) 844–854. doi: 10.1002/ejsp.2297

Eaton J (2018) *A guide to mental health issues in girls and young women on the autism spectrum* (1st ed). London, UK, and Philadelphia, USA: Jessica Kingsley Publishers.

Emerson E (2003) Prevalence of psychiatric disorders in children and adolescents with and without intellectual disability. *Journal of Intellectual Disability Research* **47** (1) 51–58. doi: 10.1046/j.1365-2788.2003.00464.x

Guest J & Ohrt J (2018) Utilizing child-centered play therapy with children diagnosed with autism spectrum disorder and endured trauma: a case example. *International Journal of Play Therapy* **27** (3) 157–165. doi: 10.1037/pla0000074

Hadjikhani N, Åsberg Johnels J, Zürcher N, Lassalle A, Guillon Q, Hippolyte L, Billstedt E, Ward N, Lemonnier E & Gillberg C (2017) Look me in the eyes: constraining gaze in the eye-region provokes abnormally high subcortical activation in autism. *Scientific Reports* **7** (1) 1–7. doi: 10.1038/s41598-017-03378-5

Harris H, Durodoye B & Ceballos P (2010) Providing counseling services to clients with autism. *Counseling & Human Development* **43** (2) 1–15.

Hearst C (2014) Autism in the therapy room. *Therapy Today* **25** (1) 26–30.

Hearst C (2016) Identifying autism [online]. Available at: www.bacp.co.uk/bacp-journals/private-practice/autumn-2016/identifying-autism/ (accessed May 2020).

Hodge N (2012) Counselling, autism and the problem of empathy. *British Journal of Guidance & Counselling* **41** (2) 105–116. doi: 10.1080/03069885.2012.705817

Hodge N & Rutten A (2017) *The SAGE Handbook of Counselling and Psychotherapy* (Chapter VII_ Therapeutic Specialisms) (4th ed.). London, UK: SAGE Publications Ltd.

Howlin P & Magiati I (2017) Autism spectrum disorder: outcomes in adulthood. *Current Opinion in Psychiatry* **30** (2) 69–76. doi: 10.1097/yco.0000000000000308

Insel T & Fenton W (2005) Psychiatric epidemiology. *Archives of General Psychiatry* **62** (6) 590. doi: 10.1001/archpsyc.62.6.590

Jones R (2013) Therapeutic relationships with individuals with learning disabilities: a qualitative study of the counselling psychologists' experience. *British Journal of Learning Disabilities* **42** (3) 193–203. doi: 10.1111/bld.12028

Kirby A, Bakian A, Zhang Y, Bilder D, Keeshin B & Coon H (2019) A 20-year study of suicide death in a statewide autism population. *Autism Research* 1-9. doi: 10.1002/aur.2076

Knibbs J & Rutten A (2017) *The Handbook of Person-Centred Therapy and Mental Health: Theory, research and practice* (2nd ed.). Monmouth, UK: PCCS Books.

Koenig K & Levine M (2010) Psychotherapy for Individuals with Autism Spectrum Disorders. *Journal of Contemporary Psychotherapy* **41** (1) 29–36. doi: 10.1007/s10879-010-9158-9

Lake J, Perry A & Lunsky Y (2014) Mental Health Services for Individuals with High Functioning Autism Spectrum Disorder. *Autism Research and Treatment*. 1-9. doi: 10.1155/2014/502420

HM Government (2019) Learning disability and autism training for health and care staff [online]. Available at: www.gov.uk/government/consultations/learning-disability-and-autism-training-for-health-and-care-staff (accessed May 2020).

Lester J (2014) Negotiating abnormality/normality in therapy talk: a discursive psychology approach to the study of therapeutic interactions and children with autism. *Qualitative Psychology* **1** (2) 178–193. doi: 10.1037/qup0000013

Mearns D & Thorne B (2007) *Person-centred Counselling in Action*. Los Angeles: Sage.

Murphy S, Chowdhury U, White S, Reynolds L, Donald L, Gahan H, Gahan H, Iqbal Z, Kulkarni M, Scrivener L, Shaker-Naeeni H & Press DA (2017) Cognitive behaviour therapy versus a counselling intervention for anxiety in young people with high-functioning autism spectrum disorders: a pilot randomised controlled trial. *Journal of Autism And Developmental Disorders* **47** (11) 3446–3457. doi: 10.1007/s10803-017-3252-8

NICE (2020) CG142: Autism spectrum disorder in adults: diagnosis and management [online]. Available at: www.nice.org.uk/guidance/CG142/chapter/1-Guidance#interventions-for-autism (accessed May).

Nicholson E (2016) What works when counselling autistic clients. *Healthcare Counselling and Psychology Journal* **16** (4).

Paxton K & Estay I (2007) Counselling People on the Autism Spectrum. London: Jessica Kingsley Publishers.

Prouty G, Werde D & Pörtner M (2002) *Pre-therapy*. Ross-on-Wye [UK]: PCCS Books.

Purkis J, Goodall E & Nugent J (2016) *The Guide to Good Mental Health on the Autism Spectrum* (1st ed.). London UK and Philadelphia, USA: Jessica Kingsley Publishers.

Qian J, Hu Q, Wan Y, Li T, Wu M, Ren Z & Yu D (2013) Prevalence of eating disorders in the general population: a systematic review. *Shanghai Archives of Psychiatry* 25 (4) 212–223. doi: 10.3969/j.issn.1002-0829.2013.04.003

Rogers C (1951) *Client-centered Therapy*. London: Constable.

Rogers C (1967) *On Becoming a Person*. London: Constable.

Rogers S (2016) Creative CBT with autism spectrum disorder [online]. BACP. Available at: www.bacp.co.uk/bacp-journals/bacp-children-young-people-and-families-journal/september-2016/creative-cbt-with-autism-spectrum-disorder/ (accessed May 2020).

Ross H (2018) The pastoral care of high-functioning ASD students. *New Zealand Journal of Counselling* **38** (1) 1–21.

Rosslyn F (2018) On the spectrum and in the room. *Therapy Today* **29** (5)

Rowe A (2017) *Adapting Health Therapies for People on the Autism Spectrum*. London, UK: Lonely Minds Books.

Russell G, Mandy W, Elliott D, White R, Pittwood T & Ford T (2019) Selection bias on intellectual ability in autism research: a cross-sectional review and meta-analysis. *Molecular Autism* **10** (1) 1–10. doi: 10.1186/s13229-019-0260-x

Rutten A (2014) *Person-centred Work at the Difficult Edge: A person-centred approach to counselling clients with autistic process*) (1st ed., pp74-87). Monmouth, UK: PCCS Books Ltd.

Štěpánková R (2015) The experience with a person with autism: phenomenological study of the experience with contact and contact reflections. *Person-Centered & Experiential Psychotherapies* **14** (4) 310–327. doi: 10.1080/14779757.2015.1038396

Vogan V, Lake J, Tint A, Weiss J & Lunsky Y (2017) Tracking health care service use and the experiences of adults with autism spectrum disorder without intellectual disability: a longitudinal study of service rates, barriers and satisfaction. *Disability and Health Journal* **10** (2) 264–270. doi: 10.1016/j.dhjo.2016.11.002

Vossler A & Moller N (2015) *The Counselling and Psychotherapy Research Handbook* (1st ed.). London, UK: Sage Publications Ltd.

Weston L, Hodgekins J & Langdon P (2016) Effectiveness of cognitive behavioural therapy with people who have autistic spectrum disorders: a systematic review and meta-analysis. *Clinical Psychology Review* **49** 41–54. doi: 10.1016/j.cpr.2016.08.001

Woods A, Mahdavi E & Ryan J (2013) Treating clients with asperger's syndrome and autism. *Child and Adolescent Psychiatry And Mental Health* **7** (1) 32. doi: 10.1186/1753-2000-7-32

Chapter 24: Autism and addiction

By Tania Browne

Let me introduce myself. My name is Tania Browne; I'm an alcohol and addiction researcher at the University of Stirling, and at the sprightly age of 46 I found out I was autistic.

Now, this is hardly a dramatic revelation. In fact, it's increasingly common here in the UK. Many people from past generations, like me, have slipped through the diagnostic net. In recent years there has been an increasing demand for diagnosis of people with suspected autism spectrum condition (ASC) in adult mental health services (Crowley *et al*, 2018).

There are several reasons why we adults with ASC may not have been diagnosed in childhood. Firstly, until recently there was quite simply a lack of awareness in the educational and health care communities. Autism wasn't recognised in the DSM until 1980, and Asperger syndrome in 1994 (though it's worth noting that in the latest edition of DSM, Asperger syndrome has been removed as we realise the broad variety of autistic adults and their 'spiky' profiles).

Some of us are misdiagnosed with other conditions for long periods of time, until one day the penny drops; obsessive-compulsive disorder, ADHD, and (in my own case) bipolar disorder are all common, and women especially are often misdiagnosed with borderline personality disorder. Our parents may have thought there was something 'a bit odd' about us, but they may have been unwilling to pursue a diagnosis due to the stigma and discrimination that autistic people still face. There is also a racial bias in diagnosis. A study in the USA in 2007 found that white children were over twice as likely to be diagnosed with an ASC than their African American peers. These children had very similar symptoms, but were more likely to be diagnosed with ADHD (Mandell *et al*, 2007).

Many of us will have been considered a little 'shy' or 'introverted' as children, but without what many people think of as the 'classic' symptoms of autism. Our problems dealing with the world might only have become apparent as we grew into adulthood and faced social demands in the world of work, and the need for executive functioning skills (skills such as timekeeping and the ability to organise yourself). It's now thought that women in particular learn 'masking' skills to conceal their autism, especially mimicking small-talk, rehearsing expected conversations, and having more 'feminine' special interests (Cage & Troxall-Whitman, 2018).

There has been a lot of talk in the media about how diagnosis of ASC is increasing, and from this some people deduce that the condition itself is on the rise. However, there is no evidence to support this – the illusion is created by changing rates of diagnosis, rather than an increase in autistic people. There has only been one large-scale study in the world measuring prevalence of autism in adults. In 2011, Terry Brugha and colleagues at the University of Leicester found that while the prevalence of autism in the population was not age dependant, the rate of existing diagnosis did correlate with the age of participants. In other words, autism rates are pretty constant over time, it's just that we're better at spotting it than we used to be. Brugha's best estimate was that around 1 in 75 people of all ages are on the autism spectrum. In their conclusion, he and his colleagues write that:

'In our clinical experience, providing ... social care to adults with a diagnosis of ASD leads to improvements in quality of life and reductions in the inappropriate use of high-cost hospital services... A great deal more research should be directed at the epidemiology and care of adults with this condition.' (Brugha et al, 2011)

This last quote is important, because the general health of autistic adults has rarely been studied and, as I've discovered during my own research, there's barely any published evidence at all about autistic adults and addiction to alcohol and drugs. The assumption that an autistic person would rather read a nerdy website all night in their room than party hard might prevent people, including medical staff, from suspecting substance use in autistic teens and adults. In my case they'd be absolutely right, but everyone is different. As the saying goes, 'If you've met one autistic person... you've met one autistic person'. The fact is that autistic people can and do use alcohol and drugs. Even the briefest scan of Reddit autism forums will show many discussions among those who self-experiment with cannabis, cocaine and MDMA to see if it alters their personal 'symptoms', as well as those who are seeking advice as they drink to combat their loneliness. Of course, this doesn't necessarily lead to addiction, but if combined with other conditions such as depression and anxiety, it can be a slippery slope.

Though screening for a substance use disorders is common for many mental health conditions, it is not routine for those with ASC. Arnevik and Helverschou (2016) surveyed previously published scientific studies and identified only 18 examining the association between ASC and substance use disorders. The results of these showed rates of adults diagnosed with ASC with substance use problems varied widely between 0.7% and 36%. However, all of the identified studies were on small, specialised populations, such as offenders and patients in mental hospitals. The samples were also predominantly male, which makes drawing comparisons and establishing a good estimated rate difficult.

A population-based study trying to establish the rate of substance use disorders in a general population of autistic adults was not published until 2017. In a Danish study of almost 27,000 individuals, Butwicka and colleagues documented a doubled risk of alcohol and substance use-related problems among autistic adults when compared to the general population. A population study such as this had never been done previously, and it provides stark contrast with the studies of niche samples gathered by Arnevik and Helverschou. It suggests that prevalence of substance use disorders in autistic people may be much higher than previously estimated – something that I myself am keen to study further.

There are several good reasons why we should make the effort to establish the rates of autistic people having problems with alcohol and drugs, and to further study the links between autism and addiction:

■ The perceived 'protective factors' of autism are overstated.

■ Depression is strongly linked to substance use, and a higher proportion of autistic people experience depression and anxiety than in the general population.

■ Social isolation and anxiety are shared common factors in both ASC and substance use disorders.

■ There is a significant discrepancy between need and support for autistic adults.

■ Let's go through these points in turn.

Perceived 'protective factors' of autism are overstated

The protective factors of an autism diagnosis may appear to outweigh the risk of alcohol and substance use. For example, many might assume that autistic people tend to be strict rule-followers, and the idea of social boundaries or breaking the law would be unthinkable. Sensory processing sensitivities could make the taste of alcohol unpleasant and the concept of snorting, smoking or injecting drugs abhorrent (Kunreuther & Palmer, 2017). The assumption that an adult with ASC doesn't want to socialise or feel accepted may prevent primary care staff from suspecting substance use in autistic adults.

It has sometimes been argued that there is no link between autism and substance use disorders, and some studies identify autism as a protective factor for alcohol or drug addiction (eg. Ramos *et al*, 2013). However, such studies often use young people in specialist care settings, and not those in general education. Kunreuther and Palmer (2017) point out that if an autistic adolescent is in a mainstream school, then the desire to 'fit in' may still lead to experimentation with alcohol and substance use. More and more children diagnosed with ASC are being 'mainstreamed', so are more readily vulnerable to social situations, peer pressures, relationship issues and school (and employment) successes and failures. This is important, as alcohol and substance use disorders in adulthood frequently begin in adolescence (Levy & Sundaram, 2018).

Clarke *et al* (2016) also note that there is a significant discrepancy in past studies regarding substance use in autistic adults. Most studies didn't factor in any kind of desire for social interaction, but in their own thematic analysis of eight interviews they found that the theme of social difficulties dominated their overview. The desire to 'fit in' with their peers appeared to be an important motivator in the participant's use of substances, including alcohol, cannabis, codeine, cocaine and MDMA.

Depression is strongly linked to substance use and a higher proportion of people with ASC experience depression and anxiety than in the general population

A systematic review reported by Rydzewska et al suggest that depression, bipolar disorder, schizophrenia, suicidal thoughts and behaviour, and non-affective psychosis are more common in autistic adults than other people (Rydzewska *et al*, 2019).

In their 2018 study, Wang et al note that there is a well-established connection between depression and substance use in neurotypical people. They suggest a mechanism through which the stress of stigma relating to mental illness may lead to 'emotional dysregulation', and maladaptive coping strategies such as alcohol and drugs. Wang *et al* suggest that this stigma undermines self-esteem, increases isolation and deters people from seeking help – this may equally be a factor when considering the stigma of autism, especially when seeking diagnosis as an adult (Kunreuther & Palmer, 2017). However, it's important to note that Wang and colleagues also acknowledge that the line of causation may be the other way around – substance use might lead to emotional dysregulation and maladaptive coping.

Symptoms of anxiety and depression are commonly reported by adults diagnosed with ASC, and this can make core autism symptoms worse and lower a person's quality of life. Hollocks *et al* (2019) reviewed a total of 35 studies of anxiety and depression in autistic adults published between 2000 and 2017, and found a pooled estimate of current anxiety and depression of 27% and 23% respectively in clinical studies. This was considerably higher than would be expected, based on estimates of 1–12% in the general population. The finding was similar for pooled *lifetime* estimates of anxiety (42%) and depression (37%). Hollocks *et al* also found that specific anxiety disorders, particularly social phobia and obsessive compulsive disorder (OCD), were more common in autistic adults.

Murray *et al* (2019) found that 46% of 205 British adults who received a diagnosis of ASC in adulthood reported symptoms that reflected moderate or severe anxiety and/or depression. Cassidy *et al* found that in a large sample (n=374) of newly diagnosed British adults, 66% had contemplated suicide, significantly higher than both the general population (17%), and patients with psychosis (59%). Further, 35% had attempted suicide, higher than previous estimates of attempted suicide in general (2.5%) and university (10%) populations (Cassidy *et al*, 2014). A later research paper from Cassidy suggests unique contributors to suicide in autism when compared to the general population, which need to be addressed in addition to important well-known factors such as mental health, employment and living arrangements (Cassidy *et al*, 2018).

In Sweden, Bejerot *et al* (2014) discovered a higher rate of self-reported social anxiety in 50 autistic adults when compared to the general population. A systematic review of 25 papers also found strong links between autism and social anxiety (Spain *et al*, 2018).

Social anxiety can produce a higher risk of problem drinking and drug use, particularly when autistic adults are accustomed to using masking behaviours. Masking is defined as camouflaging particular aspects of one's behaviour from others to 'pass' in social situations, and is common in autistic people navigating the non-autistic world (Bargiela *et al* 2016; Cage & Troxell-Whitman 2019). Peer influence has been shown to be a predictor of alcohol use among college students and young adults. Perceived norms are considered a strong predictor of alcohol use and alcohol related negative consequences among young adults (Villarosa *et al*, 2016).

While the studies above can be seen as a first step in furthering our understanding, the sampling and methods chosen are extremely homogenous. None of the studies included adults with ASC tendencies but without diagnosis, or adults who had not been in contact with clinical services. This means that they may not fully represent adults with ASC in the whole population. They might possibly be of value in clinical practice settings, but they have limited value to an understanding of the relationship of autism to anxiety and depression in the wider community.

Social isolation and anxiety are shared common factors in both ASC and substance use disorders

Many adults with ASC and related mental health issues report a sense of loneliness and social isolation. Todd *et al* (2004) defined 'social exclusion' as having housing problems, being unemployed, having a lower education level and being isolated (i.e. living alone). All of these factors regularly occur as a result of the executive functioning problems frequently reported by autistic adults, leading to a more chaotic lifestyle than the general population (Hollocks *et al*, 2014).

Drake *et al* (2002) noted that the biological emphasis formerly placed on investigating people dually diagnosed with substance use disorders and mental health disorders meant that vital issues such as social networks, boredom, poverty, dysphoria and expectations of drug effects were neglected. The reasons may be complex, but the desire to fit in with peers plays a key role in substance use among those with psychiatric disorders. Boredom, loneliness and stress have been cited as key reasons why people with mental disorders may use (and relapse into using) substances (Laudet *et al*, 2004). Participants in Laudet's study also mentioned other reasons why they used substances – to increase happiness, energy and emotions, and to reduce feelings of anxiety and depression.

Agwu *et al* (2016) note the role of social capital in substance use disorders, defining social capital as a multidimensional concept 'operationalised as economic, cultural, and social assets, civic engagement, solidarity, trust and reciprocity'. Importantly, Kunreuther and Palmer (2018) suggest that becoming involved in drinking and drug subcultures may be a way for autistic people to gain social capital among other marginalised groups when they feel rejected by mainstream culture.

Clarke *et al* (2016), in their interviews with eight adults with ASC, come to the conclusion that some socially oriented adults with ASC feel isolation and a lack of connectedness, and will use substances to aid communication with others, and to gain a sense of social inclusion. They conclude that, '...*contrary to the protective factors of autism contained within earlier literature, the presence of... [ASC]... leaves an individual as vulnerable to the development of SUD as the wider population, and perhaps arguably more so*'.

There is a significant discrepancy between need and support for autistic adults

It's now widely recognised that ASC is severely underdiagnosed in the adult population, and that as a direct result of this there is very limited support available for newly diagnosed adults. Similarly, adults diagnosed with ASC during childhood, *'find themselves "falling off a cliff" into unstructured and overwhelming adult environments for which they lack the tools for successful integration'* (Wallace *et al*, 2016). All physical and mental health outcomes for autistic adults are poor, which puts them at risk for alcohol and other substance use.

The autistic advocate John Elder Robison writes that outcomes for autistic adults range from institutionalisation to seamlessly 'blending' into the community. This means that there's a wide range of implications for support and services (Robison, 2019). There's still a great deal of stigma attached to an autism diagnosis which, combined with a distinct lack of post-diagnostic support and services, may discourage people who suspect that they're autistic from seeking psychiatric confirmation. Robison further points out that if the currently undiagnosed community have similar outcomes to those with a diagnosis, the implications for future health outcomes and the need for tailored treatments are sizeable if we consider Terry Brugha's prevalence estimate of 1 in 75 people in the UK.

The lack of monitoring and social support networks for autistic adults may ultimately be a major factor in drinking and other substance misuse, and it's an issue that needs to be addressed. But how?

Adults with ASC may be under-served in mainstream addiction services [A-head] Arnevik and Helverschou (2016) point out that little is known about successful interventions for autism and substance use disorders. They postulate, in fact, that typical interventions may do more harm than good. Forced involvement in group sessions or community-based programmes could make autistic people anxious and cause them to drop out. This could lead to further feelings of failure and alienation in autistic adults, leading to more substance misuse; a self-perpetuating cycle that would be very hard to break.

Attwood (2018) agrees with this general view, stating that rehabilitation services often rely on social living and group therapy and activities, and provide limited opportunities for personal space and solitude. Autistic people might need solitude, guidance and support in the social and disclosure requirements of group therapy. They may have difficulties recognising social and personal boundaries, converting their thoughts and feelings into speech, knowing when to talk in a group, and understanding how to show that they acknowledge the experiences and emotions of other group members with substance use issues who may not be autistic.

Much investigation still needs to be done to establish the scale of the problem of autistic people with alcohol and substance use problems. What studies have been done are on small, niche populations, which are too varied to provide a comparison even between themselves, and certainly not representative of the adult autistic population in general. What's more, the only existing population study focuses on adults who have received a diagnosis, when it is known from Brugha that a large proportion of autistic adults don't have an official diagnosis.

The next steps are therefore to establish:

- a clearer picture of a general community prevalence of substance use disorders among autistic adults

- an initial scoping picture of the rate of alcohol and substance use among people who are not officially diagnosed, but who suspect they have ASC

- the experiences of treatment so far; or if treatment has not been sought, the perceived barriers to seeking help

- how clinicians may be able to tease apart the often mixed presentations of ASC and substance use disorders in order to provide more tailored effective treatments.

Research already shows that autistic adults are more likely than the general population to report unmet medical needs and dissatisfaction with their care (Nicolaidis *et al*, 2012) as well as barriers in accessing medical care (Raymaker *et al*, 2017). Additionally, only 38% of GPs report having had any training in ASC, and even those who have report a lack of confidence in caring for their adult patients with ASC (Unigwe *et al*, 2016). However, little has been published on how to improve healthcare access and delivery for autistic adults. As the adolescent and adult populations with autism spectrum conditions continue to grow, it becomes increasingly important that we seek a better understanding of their health care needs (Rydzewska *et al*, 2019; Robison, 2019).

In a series of focus groups and an online survey of almost 2,000 stakeholders, Pelicano *et al* found almost unanimous disappointment that autism research is still primarily limited to the basic science – neural and cognitive systems, genetics and other potential risk factors. As one autistic adult said, '…it represents the priorities of neurotypical people, not autistic people' (Pelicano *et al*, 2014). All stakeholder groups agreed that much more research is needed in in services and support, and they unanimously called for evidence-based services and interventions.

Any research on alcohol and substance use disorders would contribute to such an evidence base, for both the development of brief interventions directed at autistic adults, and for more effective and 'user-friendly' recovery services. There is clearly a need for specialist staff within community mental health and addiction services who have received training in the core issues surrounding autistic adults, and it has even been suggested that a model of 'ASC hub' workers be adopted. This would co-ordinate autistic people's mental health and recovery with psychosocial supports such as future life/career planning, further education and independent living skills (Crowley *et al*, 2018).

In a 2018 paper about the co-production of research, Sue Fletcher Watson *et al* describe activities necessary to build a culture where autistic people and their allies can have meaningful roles in research. These included changing the language describing autism, modifying or identifying physical spaces to enable autistic participation, and adapting the structures and bureaucracy of academia to facilitate autistic involvement and leadership in research. A similar approach needs to be taken by the medical profession and addiction services, to provide a more autism-friendly space for those seeking help with problem alcohol and drug use. The health of autistic people, and in some cases even their lives, may depend on it.

References

Agwu, E., Magura, S., and Coryn, C. (2016) Social Capital, Substance Use Disorder and Depression Among Youths. *American Journal of Drug and Alcohol Abuse*, **42** (2) pp. 213-221.

Arnevik, E.A. and Helverschou, S.B. (2016) Autism spectrum condition and co-occurring substance use condition - A systematic review. *Substance Abuse: Research and Treatment*, 10, pp. 69-75.

Attwood, T. (2018) 'Introduction'. In: Kunreuther, E. and Palmer, A. eds. *Drinking, drug use, and addiction in the autism community*, London, Jessica Kingsley Publishers pp 7-11.

Bargiela, S., Steward, R. and Mandy, W. (2016) The Experiences of Late-diagnosed Women with Autism Spectrum Conditions: An Investigation of the Female Autism Phenotype. *Journal of Autism and Developmental Conditions*, **46** (10), pp. 3281-3294.

Bejerot, S., Eriksson, J.M. and Martberg, E. (2014) Social anxiety in adult autism spectrum condition. *Psychiatry Research*, **220** (1), pp. 705-707

Brugha, T.S., McManus, S., Bankart, J., Scott, F., Purdon, S., Smith, J., Bebbington, P., Jenkins, R. and Meltzer, H. Epidemiology of autism spectrum disorders in adults in the community in England. *Archives of General Psychiatry*, **68** (5), pp. 459-466.

Butwicka, A., Laangstrom, N., Larsson, H., Lundstrom, S., Serlachius, E., Almqvist, C., Frisen, L. and Lichtenstein, P. (2017) Increased Risk for Substance Use-Related Problems in Autism Spectrum Conditions: A Population-Based Cohort Study. *Journal of Autism and Developmental Conditions*, **47** (1), pp. 80-89.

Cage, E. and Troxell-Whitman, Z. (2019) Understanding the Reasons, Contexts and Costs of Camouflaging for Autistic Adults. *Journal of Autism and Developmental Conditions*. Available: https://link.springer.com/article/10.1007%2Fs10803-018-03878-x [Accessed January 25th 2019]

Cassidy, S., Bradley, P., Robinson, J., Allison, C., McHugh, M. and Baron-Cohen, S. (2014) Suicidal ideation and suicide plans or attempts in adults with Asperger's syndrome attending a specialist diagnostic clinic: a clinical cohort study. *The Lancet Psychiatry*, **1** (2), pp. 142-147.

Cassidy, S., Bradley, L., Shaw, R. and Baron-Cohen, S. (2018) Risk markers for suicidality in autistic adults. *Molecular Autism*, 9 (1), pp. 42.

Clarke, T., Tickle, A. and Gillott, A.(2016) Substance use condition in Asperger syndrome: An investigation into the development and maintenance of substance use condition by individuals with a diagnosis of Asperger syndrome. *International Journal of Drug Policy*, **27**, pp. 154-163.

Crowley, N., O'Connell, H. and Gervin, M. (2018) Autistic spectrum condition without intellectual impairment in adult mental health services - Fostering new perspectives and enhancing existing services. *Irish Journal of Psychological Medicine*. Available: https://www.cambridge.org/core/journals/irish-journal-of-psychological-medicine/article/autistic-spectrum-disorder-without-intellectual-impairment-in-adult-mental-health-services-fostering-new-perspectives-and-enhancing-existing-services/6BFC6D0812842A924695AC41899F1A84 [Accessed: February 18th 2019]

Drake, R.E., Wallach, M.A., Alverston, H.S., and Mueser, K.T. (2002) Psychosocial Aspects of Substance Abuse by Clients With Severe Mental Illness. *The Journal of Nervous and Mental Disease*, **190** (2) pp. 100-106.

Fletcher-Watson, S., Adams, J., Brook, K., Charman, T., Crane, L., Cusack, J., Leekam, S., Milton, D., Parr, J.R., and Pellicano, E. (2018) Making the future together: Shaping autism research through meaningful participation. *Autism*. Available: https://journals.sagepub.com/doi/10.1177/1362361318786721 [Accessed November 12th 2018]

Hollocks, M.J., Jones, C.R.G., Pickles, A., Baird, G., Happe, F., Charman, T. and Simonoff, E. (2014) The Association Between Social Cognition and Executive Functioning and Symptoms of Anxiety and Depression in Adolescents With Autism Spectrum Conditions. *Autism Research*, **7** (2), pp. 216-228.

Hollocks, M.J., Lerth, M.W., Majiati, I., Meiser-Stedman, R., and Brugha, T.S. (2019) Anxiety and Depression in Adults with Autism Spectrum Disorder: A Systematic Review and Meta-Analysis. Psychology of Medicine, 49 (4) pp. 559-572.

Kunreuther, E. and Palmer, A. (2018) eds. *Drinking, drug use, and addiction in the autism community*, London, Jessica Kingsley Publishers.

Laudet, A.B., Magura, S., Vogel, H.S. and Knight, E.L. (2004) Perceived Reasons for Substance Misuse Among Persons With a Psychiatric Disorder. *American Journal of Orthopsychiatry*, **74** (3), pp. 365-375.

Levy, S., Sundaram, S. (2018) Adolescence: A High Risk Time for Substance Use Disorders. *Harvard Health Blog* 7th August. Available: https://www.health.harvard.edu/blog/adolescence-a-high-risk-time-for-substance-use-disorders-2018080714402 [Accessed March 25th 2019]

Mandell D.S., Ittenbach R.F., Levy S.E. and Pinto-Martin J.A. (2007) Disparities in diagnoses received prior to a diagnosis of autism spectrum disorder. *Journal of Autism & Developmental Disorders*, **37** (9), pp. 1795-1802.

Murray, C., Kovshoff, H., Brown, A., Abbott, P. and Hadwin, J.A. (2019) Exploring the Anxiety and Depression Profile in Individuals Diagnosed With an Autism Spectrum Disorder in Adulthood. *Research in Autism Spectrum Conditions*, **58**, pp. 1-8.

Nicolaidis, C., Raymaker, D., McDonald, K., Dern, S., Boisclair, W.C., Ashkenazy, E. and Baggs, A. (2012) Comparison of Healthcare Experiences in Autistic and Non-Autistic Adults: A Cross-Sectional Online Survey Facilitated by an Academic-Community Partnership. *Journal of General Internal Medicine*, **28** (6) pp. 761-769.

Pellicano, E., Dinsmore, A., and Charman, T. (2014) What should autism research focus upon? Community views and priorities from the United Kingdom. *Autism*, **18** (7) pp. 756-770.

Ramos, M., Boada, L., Moreno, C., Llorente, C., Romo, J. and Parellada, M. (2013) Attitude and Risk of Substance Use in Adolescents Diagnosed with Asperger Syndrome. *Drug and Alcohol Dependence,* **133** (2), pp. 535-540.

Raymaker, D., McDonald, K., Ashkenazy, E., Gerrity, M., Baggs, A., Kripke, C., Hourston, S., and Nicolaidis, C. (2017) Barriers to healthcare: Instrument development and comparison between autistic adults and adults with and without other disabilities

Robison, J.E.(2019) Autism prevalence and outcomes in older adults. *Autism Research*, **12** (3) pp. 370-374

Rydzewska, E., Hughes-McCormack, L.A., Gillberg, C., Henderson, A., MacIntyre, C., Rintoul, J. and Cooper, S. (2019) General health of adults with autism spectrum conditions A whole country population cross-sectional study. *Research in Autism Spectrum Conditions*, **60**, pp. 59-66.

Spain, D., Sin, J., Linder, K.B., McMahon, J. and Happe, F. (2018) Social anxiety in autism spectrum condition: A systematic review. *Research in Autism Spectrum Conditions*, **52**, pp. 51-68

Todd, J., Green, G., Harrison, M., Ikuesan, B., Self, C., Pevalin, D. and Baldacchino, A. Social exclusion in clients with comorbid mental health and substance misuse problems. *Social Psychiatry and Psychiatric Epidemiology*, **39** (7), pp. 581-587.

Unigwe, S., Buckley, C., Crane. L., Kenny, L., Remington, A., and Pelicano, E. (2017) GPs' confidence in caring for their patients on the autism spectrum: an online self-report study. *British Journal of General Practice*, **67** (659) pp.445 - 452

Villarosa, M., Kison, S., Madson, M., and Zeigler-Hill, J. (2016) Everyone Else is Doing it: Examining the Role of Peer Influence on The Relationship Between Social Anxiety and Alcohol Use Behaviours. *Addiction Research & Theory*, **24** (2) pp. 124-134.

Wallace, G., Kenworthy, L., Pugliese, C., Popal, H., White, E., Brodsky, E. and Martin, A. (2016) Real-World Executive Functions in Adults with Autism Spectrum Disorder: Profiles of Impairment and Associations with Adaptive Functioning and Co-morbid Anxiety and Depression. *Journal of Autism & Developmental Disorders*, **46** (3), pp. 1071-1083.

Wang, K., Burton, C.L., and Pachankis, J.E. (2018) Depression and Substance Use: Towards the Development of an Emotion Regulation Model of Stigma Coping. *Substance Use and Misuse*, **53** (5) pp. 859-866.

Chapter 25: Establishing neurodivergent authorship in the sexual violence debate

Dr Susy Ridout (Associate Lecturer (Neurodiversity and Inclusion), Oxford Brookes University)

Aside from being a sector of society who has a right to a voice, the presence of neurodivergent voices in the sexual violence debate is imperative on many levels. These concern establishing:

■ agendas which acknowledge the experiences of all individuals who have been sexually violated

■ inclusive practice and the development of appropriate and relevant services and research

■ systems that acknowledge the different ways in which our diverse neurologies respond generally, as well as to trauma.

This chapter takes the position that all brains are different and therefore 'neurodiverse', and that an understanding of social dynamics, in particular context and the location of power, sets 'the neurodiversity paradigm' within social models of disability.

One approach to ensuring space for neurodivergent voices in the sexual violence debate might be to explore three distinct strands. The first strand concerns taking a sociological view on the provision of services to all victim-survivors of sexual violence, and one which embraces humanity as being neurodiverse (having different brain neurologies). The second strand then enquires into the provision of services to neurodivergent individuals as a subset of this, and looks into the arguments informing this. The third strand would investigate how strands one and two interrelate in order to facilitate neurodivergent authorship in the debate on sexual violence. It can be argued that this would assist the establishment of a much-needed space for neurodivergent voices.

Background

Inclusive services are imperative in responding to and tackling sexual violence, and the location of intersectional and neurodivergent voices is integral to addressing diversity. This location of identity includes the voices of autistic individuals and explores the location of power and context within our narratives of sexual violence.

Within specialist services, there is already a clear presence from sectors of the community, such as LGBTQ+ and BAME individuals and those from different age and faith backgrounds, for example the Rape and Sexual Violence Project (RSVP), Women's Aid, the Survivor's Trust and Mermaids. However, representation from disabled individuals and individuals who are neurodivergent is still not apparent at any level including the establishing, management and delivery of these support services.

This may or may not have a direct relationship to the fact that neurodivergent individuals do not disclose this identity when they disclose sexual violence or if they do, this is ignored. As such, only 29% of those accessing specialist services are recorded as being disabled, but data regarding those that are neurodivergent is not transparent (Social Care, Local Government and Care Partnerships, Mental Health and Disability Division, 2014). Nevertheless, statistics will never truly reflect the quantity of incidents as disclosure rates are extremely low (BBC News, 2019; Rape Crisis, 2018), and since 2013-2014, fewer cases are being referred by the police to the CPS for prosecution (Barr, 2019). A worrying feature is a lack of clarity as to whether these statistics include neurodivergent voices, whether they incorporate our voices under the umbrella identity of 'disabled', or whether our individual voices are omitted altogether.

This provides an opportunity for non-autistic voices to argue that it is unnecessary to include neurodivergent perspectives within specialist service provision as it already exists, albeit as a hidden factor. A further worrying aspect feeding into the current debate on sexual violence is that research to date, while recognising autistic individuals within conversations around risk and sexual violence, has had a tendency to focus on autistic individuals as dangerous and challenging (Beardon, 2008), with no further exploration around this data. The resultant imbalance results in the exclusion of the real life experiences of neurodivergent victims of sexual violence from crime statistics.

The 'nothing about us without us' campaigning slogan should herald the way to informing and shaping services with the inclusion of neurodivergent voices at its heart. This is also true in the provision of services for neurodivergent victim-survivors of sexual violence, yet in the UK this is currently not the case. This is problematic on many levels, but particularly in the establishment of inclusive services (Ridout, 2018). Lack of transparency permits the gaslighting of experiences of neurodivergent narratives of sexual violence and our intersectional identities. Furthermore, this style implements a practice whereby, with support requirements unaddressed, neurodivergent victim-survivors are less likely to disclose incidents or receive support that addresses the agenda of the individual or that is appropriate or effective.

As a society, it could be argued that with the initiation and momentum of the #me too movement, we are moving forwards in the sexual violence campaign and debate. Yet this campaign, initiated by a woman from the BAME community (Burke, 2017) has been hijacked by celebrity voices and an agenda that serves to offer a broad lens and lack of detail as to the diverse intersectional identities of victim-survivors. This too leaves us guessing as to the position or existence of neurodivergent voices in the debate. Biased representation of victims can be witnessed in the portrayal of the numerous victim-survivors at the hands of celebrities over decades, as they are only afforded the identity that the media wishes to impose, primarily that of victim status (Jacob, 2018). The discrepancy between identities means that neurodivergent victim-survivors of sexual violence are fighting numerous imposed outsider power narratives, namely those around neurodiversity and neurodivergence and those around trauma (Ridout, Serious Media and RSVP, 2019). These fail to acknowledge our individually expressed intersectional identities and do not enable us to make sense of our experiences at any one moment or at our own pace.

The neurodiversity paradigm, social dynamics and neurodivergence

Neurodivergent individuals are often perceived within a medical model framework (Milton & Moon, 2012; Reeve, 2004), so from the outset, outsiders impose an agenda of dysfunction. This is frequently without there being any additional accompanying narrative aside from neurodivergent, so perhaps it is unsurprising when a traumatised neurodivergent victim-survivor of sexual violence is disbelieved or signposted to the wrong services, namely mental health services.

It has long been argued by non-autistic people and practitioners who adopt a medical model approach, that neurodivergence falls outside an accepted 'norm'. So neurodivergent victim-survivors are arguing against a concept of blame on two fronts: first because of our neurdivergence; and second due to being victim-survivors of sexual violence. Nonetheless, the concept of 'individuals' is one that embraces unique identities and intersectionalities, each requiring an understanding of its nature, characteristics and preferred types of approach required in support and service provision.

Since the emergence of the debate on neurodiversity in the late 1990s (Singer, 2017), the conversation around neurodivergence has continued to have a leaning towards autism as a singular and separate neurological difference in relation to social dynamics such as context and power. However, since the advent of the international neurodiversity movement, a broader agenda of neurological differences has been established. This provokes enquiry into social factors impacting on the naturally occurring and diverse brains of individuals (including ADHD, ADD, epilepsy, dyslexia, dyspraxia, Irlen syndrome and dyscalculia). In addition, it switches attention from victim-blaming to one of surrounding and differential contexts, location of power and grassroots activism. A more flexible approach to addressing perceptions of trauma, responses to trauma, processing trauma, and moving forwards allowing insider experiences to lead the way, might be plausible with the introduction of this agenda based on the real life experiences of neurodivergent victim survivors as set within this framework. Success in this venture means that, as a society and as individuals, we must acknowledge and accept the right of neurodivergent individuals to have a voice. If not, then the individual and collective narrative trauma agendas of vulnerable people are automatically excluded.

Social diversity requires numerous responses to trauma and distress, which in turn requires recognising and understanding support required in terms of social context, location of power and identity/identities, so there can never be one single approach to addressing these. In my experience, most services offer counselling and support without informing individuals of the approach taken, and this can impose a wholly inappropriate framework (Ridout, 2018). There are several examples of this which I will draw on from a range of experiences. First, the range of mental health services that victim-survivors can be whisked through, barely given time to process what is happening or the appropriateness of it anyway, can provide a layer(s) of additional trauma to that already experienced due to the sexual violence. Within these services, the location of power is often clearly in the hands of the individual therapist or counsellor, such was my experience, and the outcome of each was predictably an individual (me) who did not conform with the system and allocated identity which gaslit my narrative of sexual violence. Another example can be seen with the recent advent of the Power, Threat, Meaning Framework (2018), which has had minimal involvement from autistic victim-survivors, and which is now incorporated by some specialist services. While it is reasonable to argue that some victim-survivors would not wish to explore types of counselling and support available, their vulnerable position at this point whereby any support is better than no support should not be exploited. A system should be in place whereby all victim-survivors can inform themselves at a glance of the nature and content of support on offer, should they wish to. This would also facilitate a more inclusive approach whereby neurodivergent individuals, and others, who needed additional time to process information could have it. It is therefore essential that we reflect on the nature of this type of system in terms of its characteristics and delivery and the whole conversation around sexual violence.

Provision of services to victim-survivors of sexual violence

Vital to establishing any service is evidence (formal or informal) to support its requirement. In the case of neurodivergent victim-survivors, this absence of data is evident (RCEW, 2018). However, sexual violence has no boundaries and it can therefore be argued that statistics will inevitably include neurodivergent individuals on some level, whether or not they are accurately or overtly recorded in the breakdown of figures.

An understanding of the numbers of people likely to access a service (or who already are) is also of paramount importance, and for the service to be successful, appropriate and effective, it needs to embed the individuals on whom it impacts at every level. This does not solely mean in terms of gender, sexual orientation, race, heritage, age, faith or disability, but should also include those who identify as neurodivergent and who bring these intersectional identities to the fore (SCLGCP, 2014; NICE, 2010).

Current and long-standing issues concern a lack of reporting, cases not being handled seriously or accurately (Barr, 2019), a failure to identify statistics relating to neurodivergence/autism within this, and the challenges faced by specialist services to obtain funding or address training issues and to be fully inclusive. Therefore, it is very much a matter of chance as to whether any support a victim-survivor receives is relevant to their unique collection of support needs.

It is a fact that, due to a lack of essential funding, many sectors of the community are unable to access support from specialist services (RCEW, 2015), even with a boost from the government purse this year (2019). Furthermore, it can be argued that, aside from a lack of recording, other influencing factors range from:

- a failure to include service users in the informing, shaping and delivery of support services
- a lack of attention to detail in the establishment of an enabling and neurodivergent-friendly environment in which to report and also to receive support
- failure to address the location of power within a service hierarchy
- failure to acknowledge and tackle institutional discrimination
- the adoption of a tokenistic approach
- a requirement to switch from the provision of an overarching service to one which focuses on the individual

- a lack of attention to the real lived experiences and agendas of the service users themselves.

Consequently, services, from reporting to supporting following disclosure, and to follow-up support, frequently fail to address their target audience.

Worryingly, the cases most likely to be ignored are those where the victim is experiencing mental health problems, and this has raised concerns around consent and police engagement with victims (Barr, 2019). The experience of many victim-survivors is that their insider experience of sexual violence is afforded a mental health label by outsiders concerned only with addressing their own professional working agenda (Ridout, 2018). This results in a situation whereby the natural trauma response of a victim-survivor to an unacceptable invasion of their body and privacy is gaslit, and this is carried out by many in society, be they family, friends or service providers (Ridout *et al*, 2019). Since autistic/neurodivergent individuals often experience high levels of anxiety, they are frequently already labelled as having mental health problems. Research also shows that incidents of mental health problems and suicidality are high among autistic individuals (Cassidy, 2015), although the origins of these experiences have yet to be explored and merit urgent attention. If a typical practice trend is to see autistic/neurodivergent individuals as different and having mental health problems, rather than exploring other influencing factors, there may be an ensuing gaslighting of other identities such that access to relevant support services becomes restricted. This is highly questionable practice.

Provision of services to neurodivergent victim-survivors of sexual violence

Within specialist services, there is already an acknowledgement of the distinct social dynamics, power dynamics and contextual dynamics that impact on some communities, and this arises in the highlighting of provision of specialist support workers from the BAME or LGBTQ+ communities in particular. However, in my experience as a victim-survivor, there also needs to be an emphasis on promoting neurodivergent specialists, too, and I would argue this on a number of levels.

Disclosure

Following disclosure, the amount of information that one is required to process is immense. First, the victim-survivor has to deal with the instance of disclosure itself and whether or not to report the incident(s) formally. Second, the counselling on offer, the style of counselling, its purpose and what it can offer, is a fairly nebulous process which, although it might be explained verbally, must take account of our communication preferences and needs to reflect before we can make an informed choice. Third, the decision to follow the report to court process can be overwhelming, and while it can be really useful if someone such as an ISVA (Independent Sexual Violence Advocate) steps in and manages the information flow, understanding the entire process and having ongoing options to manage things for oneself or alongside an ISVA is critical. This is easier if they understand neurodiversity and diverse ways of processing of information, and the need for time to engage with and reflect on this process. The report to court booklet is also overwhelming, and in order to understand the process, it is essential for victim-survivors to have some understanding of this in order to instil some measure of control over any anxiety and their ability to engage with others involved throughout (police, witness care, barristers, for example) at any one time. The simplification of this book, informed/led by neurodivergent individuals, would acknowledge and encompass communication preferences. Fourth, a familiarity with the role of an ISVA assists with accessing the available support most relevant or desired within the specialist service, and their liaison between the victim and all aspects of the CJS can be an integral part of bringing a perpetrator to justice. All of these elements are greatly enhanced by having neurodivergent individuals embedded within specialist services. This empathetic approach in terms of both neurodivergence and trauma should at least be available as it is arguably more appropriate.

Neurodivergent staff

To have experienced being let down by practitioners is not an uncommon occurrence for those who identify as neurodivergent, and this includes in a variety of contexts and by an array of individuals, and this can be due to a number of factors including the double empathy problem (Milton, 2012). Therefore, having the option to establish trust with a neurodivergent practitioner within a support service would greatly facilitate the building of a meaningful working relationship. Under the Equality Act (2010) (HMSO, 2010), the Autism Act (2009) (HMSO, 2009) and the National Strategy for Autistic Adults in England (2010) and the Updated Statutory Guidance (2015), neurodivergent/autistic people have a right to be included in services that impact on them. My experience of this is that lip service does not work. While many outsiders might be good practitioners, eventually this position, coupled with a lack of training, will result in ineffective support for a neurodivergent victim-survivor.

The alternative to this is working with someone who understands the need to establish a sense of control in one's life and the considerable anxiety caused should this not be the case. This may originate from an agenda of difference where the individual had all control taken away by practitioners, educationalists and even, at times, (well-meaning yet ill-informed) parents. A neurodivergent support worker will more likely comprehend this perspective either through lived experience or through networks and friendship groups. Issues such as setting your own agenda in relation to neurodivergence, trauma and the wider theme of identity is therefore often better understood by neurodivergent practitioners themselves as they may well have lived experience of discrimination or barriers to inclusion. This is why neurodivergent/

autistic people argue that training on autism and issues impacting on us should be delivered by autistic people themselves (Ridout, 2018; 2016). This needs to be extended to provide increased opportunities for neurodivergent practitioners.

The need to provide information in visual, written and spoken formats which can be accessed iteratively, as and when required, is key to providing an inclusive support service and would address the range of resources available. This process encourages debate around additional facilities and resources that could be added to accommodate new and additional support requirements and establish a flexible system of engagement.

Monotropism

As neurodivergent individuals may tap into a monotropic means of accessing and processing information, as described by the monotropism theory (Murray *et al*, 2005), all staff working with neurodivergent victim-survivors of sexual violence would benefit from an understanding of this concept, which requires an ability to shift the object of attention to a broader focus (Murray, 2019; Chown, 2017, p219). While research is yet to be done regarding this theory, it resonates with me in terms of my experiences as a survivor with attention to detail as opposed to a preference for looking at the bigger picture. This might also explain the experience of hyperawareness. Such attention would give credence to challenges experienced due to a difficulty shifting from a single internal focus of interests (in this case the experience and impact of trauma) due to being neurodivergent. Consequently, the experiences of neurodivergent victim-survivors would be afforded a wider acceptance than the current approaches, which are victim-blaming (Eaton, 2019), gaslighting (Ridout, 2018) or which employ a medical model perspective (Ridout, 2018).

Double empathy problem

Central to the provision of services to neurodivergent individuals is the ability to have empathy. A lack of this is seen in a situation characterised by the double empathy problem (Milton, 2012), and in the context of sexual violence, might arise at a number of points: trying to describe your experience; understanding and processing the report to court process; and understanding the court experience itself. However, the aftermath is a little-mentioned space where feelings and emotions may require additional and specific support.

At whatever point in the process after disclosure, and whatever choices individuals make, having an empathetic listener is essential. Preferences will vary between individuals, but it is essential that neurodivergent specialists are included within the range of support workers to validate our voice.

Language is my language

Inclusion within authorship would recognise the language and terminology used by any individuals, and within this those that identify as neurodivergent. This is integral to people being able to voice their experiences in the way that they wish. Essential tools to working with victim-survivors concern recognition of choice of language to describe their experience as a neurodivergent individual and that of their experience. This facilitates meaningful engagement by challenging any imposed power dynamics, while at the same time recognising the double-empathy problem. This latter stresses the need for an empathetic standpoint from service providers and one which enables contextualisation of points made.

At a time in a victim-survivor's life when they have had control taken away, lost self-esteem and confidence and been devalued, recognition of their language and terminology is key to their validation. Care needs to be taken not to impose power in a manner which, although well-meaning, is also disempowering. For example, having someone refer to you as a 'victim-survivor', when there are many days where you feel more like a victim and need to manage accompanying feelings. We need to be able to choose our language to reflect our contextualised feelings at any one moment, and that is something that can be challenging. It is inappropriate for well-meaning people to state that we have survived and are thriving simply because that is the corporate tagline, when inside we may be experiencing huge struggles. And many of us may be unable to voice this. It is essential, therefore, that we can choose the applicable language to reflect any one moment in our pathways to recovery, and this accepts, that for some, any incident may be one from which they do not recover.

As a society we have a responsibility to hear these uncomfortable narratives, without putting a positive spin on them, for they are so often redolent of the experience of individuals in disenfranchised, marginalised communities. These narratives reflect the implicit, dirty side of sexual violence that society does not wish to see.

Communication preferences

It is particularly true that neurodivergent individuals show more marked and diverse communication preferences (Ridout, 2016), and my experience as a survivor was that being able to use a diversity of ways of voicing my experiences was useful. This is something from which all survivors may benefit, but as it is frequently a prerequisite to our successful communication and voicing of experiences, the inclusion of neurodivergent individuals among support services at every level would address this point more immediately. Use of mixed expressive media, sensory mapping (before and after the event as a point of comparison) and narrative diaries could assist and enhance the expression of our experiences and provide a means to a process whereby we can reflect on what we are saying more effectively (Ridout, 2016; 2018).

Morphing recovery and survival

Recovery and survival morph continually as we encounter new circumstances and engage with these. Previous triggers may always be there, or we may have dealt with them successfully. Context and environment greatly impact on these and neurodivergent individuals may be masking struggles on a daily basis. For this reason, the additional stress of masking trauma can only be imagined by those outside our experiences. Within the neurodiversity framework, the debate on sexual violence would benefit from neurodivergent authorship as it would encompass the numerous challenges and barriers faced by a more diverse population. These challenges would acknowledge the breadth and depth of experiences, which in turn would better inform service provision.

The coping and masking veneer frequently employed by neurodivergent individuals to navigate social settings often goes unrecognised by outsiders. Gradually, it succumbs to overwhelming pressures which we then feel obliged to explain in the context of our different identities as well as our experiences of trauma. Yet incorporating neurodivergent authorship in the sexual violence debate would allow society to include individual narratives regarding strategies employed to cope with and manage unacceptable behaviour imposed on our bodies. This authorship would give everyone a voice and offer informed support to a wider sector of society than is currently the case.

Anxiety and support cut-off points

With anxiety running high, and increased due to the whole court experience, victims do not need additional fears that their support will be cut once sessions are completed. One way round this is to have a re-entry system that acknowledges that individuals will often wish to access additional support due to issues such as a changes in circumstances or feelings of being overwhelmed. This plays to the support preferences voiced by many in the Cygnet Mentoring Project (2016), and gives neurodivergent individuals room to negotiate the length of sessions and their spacing. While this related to a mentoring system, there is an argument that the style could also be transferred to specialist support systems as it provides a means for individuals to process and reflect on their thoughts, feelings and experiences.

Networks

It is necessary that individuals who work in a support setting are open to the fact that neurodivergent individuals may not have any support networks, either due to their neurodivergence or their experience of sexual violence. If a support network is assumed, this can be extremely isolating as many neurodivergent people struggle to socialise anyway, and families and friends often turn their backs. This situation can leave individuals feeling embarrassed and awkward as they find difficulty expressing this mix of feelings, and it is a situation that, despite having many friends and lovely children, I found difficult to voice.

Struggling with being overwhelmed

Neurodivergent people involved in establishing and delivering specialist services would be able to liaise with others in the Criminal Justice System (CJS) with and for the individual. This is critical in terms of describing their feelings of being overwhelmed. Hyper- and hypo-sensitivity might leave us in states of extreme sensory arousal or having no reaction at all. Rather than simply linking this to trauma, it may be a natural response due to being neurodivergent and one which falls into our general realm of daily responses to stressful situations. Being able to voice this to someone who is empathetic is critical and removes pressure arising due to the need for unnecessary repeated explanations.

Establishing neurodivergent authorship in the sexual violence debate

In pulling the above sections together, I have only touched on a few areas related to my experience and those of others. Nevertheless, I think it clarifies that there are many areas where a neurodivergent victim of sexual violence would struggle to navigate a system if they chose to report an incident should local services fail to understand their support requirements.

My personal experience is that the specialist service which supported me, and others in the CJS went out of their way to understand me, give me time and allow me plenty of opportunity to return and ask further questions using my ISVA. Others are not always so lucky, but it is our right and one for which we should fight collectively, as our voices need to be loud in this debate as it impacts on us too. Ultimately, there should be 'Nothing about us without us'.

References

BBC News (2019) https://www.bbc.co.uk/news/uk-49669760

Barr C (2019) Thousands of Rape Reports Inaccurately Recorded by Police. *The Guardian*, 19.9.2019

Burke T (2017) The 'Me Too' Campaign Was Created By A Black Woman 10 Years Ago. *Huffpost* 17.10.2017.

Cassidy S (2015) *Suicidality in Autism: Risk and Prevention*. University of Coventry: Centre for Research in Psychology Behaviour and Achievement.

Chown N (2017) Understanding and Evaluating Autism Theory, p219. London: Jessica Kingsley Publishers.

Eaton J (2019) 'Logically, I know I am not to lame, but I still feel I am to blame': Exploring and measuring victim blaming and self-blame of women subjected to sexual violence and abuse. University of Birmingham.

Gov.co.uk (2019) https://www.gov.uk/government/news/funding-boost-for-victims-of-rape-and-sexual-abuse

Jacob E (2018) *To Report or Not to Report: Survivor Testimony of the (In)Justice System*. Resonance Press.

Johnston L (2018) *Power, Threat, Meaning Framework: Science, Psychiatry and Social Justice* [online] Mad in America. Available at: https://www.madinamerica.com/2019/04/power-threat-meaning-framework-one-year/ (accessed June 2020).

Milton D (2012) On the ontological status of autism: the 'double empathy problem'. *Disability and Society* **27** (6) pp883–887.

Milton D & Moon L (2012) The Normalisation Agenda and the Psycho-emotional Disablement of Autistic People. *Autonomy, the Critical Journal of Interdisciplinary Autism Studies* **1** (1).

Murray D, Lesser M & Lawson W (2005) Attention, monotropism and the diagnostic criteria for autism. *Autism* **9** (2) pp139–156.

NICE (2010) Implementing 'Fulfilling and rewarding lives'. Statutory guidance for local authorities and NHS organisations to support implementation of the autism strategy. London: The Stationary Office.

Rape Crisis England and Wales (2018) *About Sexual Violence* [online]. Available at: https://rapecrisis.org.uk/statistics.php (accessed June 2020).

Rape Crisis England and Wales (2015) (RCEW) RCEW responds to news of lack of funding for specialist sexual violence services. Available at: https://rapecrisis.org.uk/news/latest-news/rape-crisis-responds-to-news-of-lack-of-funding-for-specialist-sexual-violence-services/

Reeve D (2004) 'Psycho-emotional dimensions of disability and the social model'. In: Barnes C and Mercer G *Implementing the Social Model of Disability: Theory and Research*. Leeds: The Disability Press.

Ridout S, Serious Media & RSVP (the Rape and Sexual Violence Project) (2019) *Empowering and Inclusive Support from a Specialist Support Service*.

Ridout S (2018) 'Involve neurodivergent survivors in shaping responses'. In: Mental Health Today. Hove: Pavilion Publishing and Media Ltd.

Ridout S (2018) 'Neurodivergence and the Gaslighting of Rape.' Conference paper at the Intimate Lives: Autism, Gender and Sex/uality. University of Birmingham.

Ridout S (2016) *Narrating experience: the advantage of using mixed expressive media to bring autistic voices to the fore in discourse around their support requirements* [onlne]. Available at: https://etheses.bham.ac.uk/id/eprint/6928/1/Ridout16PhD_Redacted.pdf (accessed June 2020).

Singer J (2017) *Neurodiversity: The Birth of an Idea*. Judy Singer

Social Care, Local Government and Care Partnership Directorate, Department of Health (2014).

Chapter 26: University through the eyes of autistic students and staff

Professor Nicola Martin. PhD London South Bank University (LSBU) Critical Autism and Disability Studies Research Group.

Dedication

This chapter is dedicated to Jo Krupa for her amazing proofreading talents and reference checking. As a neurodiverse academic, I rely on Jo's support with this aspect of my writing as well as lots of other things. Thank you, Jo.

Introduction

Work-related experiences of autistic university employees and freelance researchers receive scant research attention. This chapter seeks to slightly reduce the size of a very large hole into which this area of enquiry seems to have fallen by including information from a small scale survey of autistic lecturers and researchers involved with The Participatory Autism Research Collective (PARC). Research which aims to identify barriers to higher education participation identified by autistic students is a little more prolific and examples are discussed here. Striking overlaps between the narratives of autistic people working and studying at university emerge and conclusions are drawn from the available evidence about common approaches which could benefit autistic employees and learners alike. These shelter largely under the universal design (UD) umbrella and are generally obvious and uncomplicated. UD can potentially benefit everyone because the approach involves planning for diversity rather than being surprised that the mythical norm is imaginary. The ethos of UD is congruent with the anticipatory anti-discriminatory duty of The Equality Act (2010). A model that has acquired the acronym REAL is discussed as a way to conceptualize good autism practice within a UD paradigm with the potential to benefit everyone. The approach is informed by a commitment to equality as a social justice concern. REAL stands for: reliable, empathic, anticipatory and logical.

The emergence and purpose of PARC as a vehicle for autistic scholars to collaborate is discussed. Although the collective's reach is far greater now, PARC originated from The Critical Autism and Disability Research Group (CADS) at London South Bank University (LSBU). Participants regularly echo the contentions of autistic contributors to this paper that that they are seldom remunerated justly for their contribution to autism research. CADS operates within the Centre for Social Justice and Global Responsibility at LSBU and paid autistic co-researchers are always central to our autism research. This policy decision is a point of principle informed by a social justice ethos, the principle being 'nothing about us without us' (Charlton, 1998, p1). Further pertinent detail about PARC follows in the next section.

PARC background

PARC[49] originated (unfunded) in 2015 when Dr Damian Milton and I were working together at London South Bank University (LSBU) on the two-year Cygnet Mentoring Project, funded by Research Autism, which looked closely at effective mentoring and mentor training aimed at autistic adults (Milton *et al*, 2017; Sims *et al*, 2016). Our aim with PARC was to create a structure that would provide opportunities for autistic researchers to work together and influence autism research. PARC participants write together, apply for research funding together and conduct seminars and conferences which showcase autistic expertise. In addition to the prolific contribution of Dr Damian Milton[50], further examples of publications by PARC members include: Arnold *et al*, 2018; Chown *et al*, 2015; 2017; 2018; Loomes, 2017; 2018; Ridout, 2017; Ridout & Edmondson, 2017; Woods, 2017; Woods *et al*, 2018; Woods & Waltz, 2019. Common to each is insider perspective and a strengths-based approach which problematises deficit model thinking about autism in particular and neurodiversity more generally.

PARC meetings now take place across the UK and international collaborations are forming in Europe, America and Australia. Many PARC members do not have secure paid employment commensurate with their academic qualifications. Often, they work to further the collective in their own time, unremunerated. This is not a comfortable situation. Although PARC has highlighted the concern, nobody has yet systematically gathered evidence about how many autistic scholars are actually being paid properly for their contribution to research. Autistic university employees and researchers face myriad barriers to full participation (Chown *et al*, 2015; Martin, 2017), so it is little wonder that autistic voices are either almost silenced within the research arena or effectively giving their expertise for free.

---

49 https://participatoryautismresearch.wordpress.com/

50 https://damianmiltonsociol.wixsite.com/dmilton-autism/publications

PARC participants are generally extremely positive about the opportunities the collective provides. The following comments from PARC participants are typical:

'It gives me life. I feel incredibly isolated and disconnected from the university which has system that I find inaccessible in many ways. PARC events and the networks of autistic researchers and allies that maintain communication across Twitter give me a (albeit distant) sense of camaraderie and belonging, as well as provide a great source of inspiration and knowledge.'

'PARC. events are accessible (financially and expectation wise) and a great way to share differing viewpoints. The only thing is getting the confidence to go and finding such networks exist in the first place.'

The danger of over-promising and under-delivering was illustrated by an autistic academic who felt disappointed that PARC was not resourced to provide more practical assistance. Given the complete reliance on volunteers and lack of infrastructure or funding, PARC cannot provide any sort of bespoke service as it operates solely on good will and peer support. With funding and administrative backup, PARC could do so much more.

Since its inception at LSBU, as a result of the energy and commitment of autistic academics, PARC has gained traction in other universities in and beyond the UK (Milton *et al*, 2019). Seminars, researcher development events and conferences were increasing in frequency pre Covid, and plans are afoot to pick up once the pandemic crisis has eased. As most autistic people are not in lucrative employment (Barnham & Martin, 2017), events are always free, and this is made possible by the support of the universities hosting them. Many autistic scholars involved with PARC are self-funding doctoral candidates who cannot afford huge conference fees.

Further development of PARC is planned, particularly around influencing autism researchers about the apparently thorny issue of paying properly for autistic expertise. So far, no magic money tree has appeared to assist in this endeavor. In an ideal world, articulating the principle of fair pay when bidding for research funding would impress the funders, and even one day become the norm.

Universal design

Jorgenson *et al* (2013), Milton *et al* (2016) and others reflect on the origins and practices of UD and Universal Design for Learning (UDL). Milton *et al*'s paper focused specifically on the requirements of autistic people but reinforces the point that good autism practice is good practice for all. Put simply, UD and UDL involve planning based on the assumption that people are not identical and therefore will have a range of access requirements relating to environments, systems, interactions and everything else. Not making assumptions that everyone thinks, feels, learns and moves in the same way is a good starting point which is broader than a disability equity concern. Ramps and automatic doors for example, help anyone moving anything on wheels. Heteronormativity and gender normativity are not the default positions in UD, so gender neutral toilets reinforce belonging and 'they' is a helpful default pronoun. Intersectionality is understood as ordinary, so plans with a specific autism badge on them are less useful than those more sensitive to individuality. One PARC contributor who also has a physical impairment discussed either experiencing multiple oppression or acceptance of their embodiment as just ordinary. Understanding and appreciating the value to society of diversity, and utilizing UD to enable full participation of everyone, is the gold standard. Disability is, however, frequently problematized when other diversity strands under the Equality Act (2010) are celebrated (Martin & Fraser, 2012). UD de-problematizes difference by proactively planning for inclusion and is congruent with the anticipatory duty articulated in the Equality Act (2010). The following comment shared by the line manager of a PARC member is indicative of an unhelpful lack of understanding of UD and equality principles: 'He is an academic, he has to learn how to navigate the admin systems.' Later in this chapter the REAL model is proposed as a way of conceptualizing good autism practice underscored by UD thinking, with benefits beyond creating conditions for the effective and equitable participation of autistic people.

Emancipatory research principles and ethical concerns

In this section I reflect specifically on ethical considerations arising from a body of work that I authored or co-authored. I am not the only researcher in this arena by any means, but I am not well placed to critique in detail the ethical foundations of other studies because information provided about the ethical dimensions of the work is usually brief and somewhat anodyne. It is certainly very rare to see any sort of statement about paying autistic researchers.

Mindful of trying not to fall into the 'researcher as parasite' (Stone & Priestley, 1996, p699), I acknowledge that although I am disabled, I am not autistic and cannot therefore claim direct insider perspective. Emancipatory researchers emphasise the importance of insider perspectives, but there are arguments that the idea of insider is not necessarily impairment-specific (Barnes, 2014). Impairment-specific research runs the ethical risk of identifying labelled individuals as other, by reflecting the salient features of the othered identity while de-emphasising individuality (Madriaga *et al*, 2008). Interactions between systems and procedures which have not been equality impact-assessed under the Equality Act (2010), and my own neurodiverse cognitive style have certainly created problems for me in the workplace. My experience may well equip me with some degree of empathy with others who do not conform to the erroneously assumed neurotypical stereotype.

Emancipatory research is characterised by involvement of, control by and usefulness to disabled people (Barnes & Sheldon, 2007; Barnes, 2014; Barton, 2005; Oliver, 1997). While CADS aspires to emancipatory methodology, currently work emanating from the research group is at best participatory because of the level of control of the process by autistic people. Autistic participants in many of the studies with which I have been involved have provided their insights without any sort of incentive beyond selflessly making things better for others. (Examples include: Atkinson *et al*, 2011; Hastwell *et al*, 2012; 2013; 2017; Beardon *et al*, 2009; Madriaga *et al*, 2008; Martin, 2000; 2005; 2006a; 2006b; 2007; 2008a; 2008b; 2008c; 2011b; 2012; Martin *et al*, 2008; Milton *et al*, 2017; Sturgess, 2018). In keeping with the emancipatory principle of usefulness, findings have been reported jargon-free, mainly in practitioner journals, in order to reach people who are able to enact useful research-informed practice improvements. While steering groups of autistic people steer the ship, and paid autistic researchers are part of the team, CADS has yet to undertake a project led by an autistic principal investigator, so falls short of the emancipatory ideal in this respect, too.

Studies cited here with which I have been involved had ethical clearance of course, but these research outputs are not without ethical dilemmas. Alongside others I have gathered vast amounts of data over the years, some of which I feel we have not scrutinised as fully as we could have. Beardon *et al* (2009), for example, have only thematically analysed in depth one theme of the vast ASPECT report (Beardon & Edmonds, 2007). The moral responsibility to ensure that data analysis is detailed and informed by disabled people requires enough time to deeply and repeatedly engage with the process. Conducting unfunded research while navigating other time pressures does not negate the moral responsibility to do justice to the very personal information provided by participants.

Limitations around questionnaires are considered in Martin (2008a). Comparison between student interview data from Hastwell *et al* (2013) and Madriaga *et al* (2008), and questionnaire responses from Martin (2008a), evidence the relative richness of working with transcripts of interviews. I have tried not to fall into the ethical trap of over-generalising from questionnaires and interpreting responses of some people with a particular label as if they relate to a larger population. PARC participants are keenly aware of the danger of assuming homogeneity by impairment label. The interpretivist paradigm (Willis *et al*, 2007) which characterises my body of work signals a move from 'this is what I know' to problematising the notion of knowing, influenced by the contention that there is no such thing as shared objective truth, as 'knowing' (Cooper, 1981; Foucault, 1982; Peters, 2003).

A continuing ethical responsibility is incumbent upon researchers because once something is published it is 'out there'. Ethically, researchers need to be mindful of the potential on-going impact of work which is in the public domain (ideally being contactable to answer questions and address misconceptions and generalisations). Participant anonymity is particularly pertinent as people can change their minds over time about what they want to say. I always take great care to ensure that no research participant could be identified. I also harbour a concern that I might unknowingly cause anxiety on occasion because participants did not feel confident to let me know.

Foucault's work around power relationships is relevant to research in which the researcher, directly or indirectly, has power over the researched (Foucault, 1982; Goodley, 2010; McIntosh, 2002). Undertaking research with autistic students while being in a position to impact directly on their university experience has an ethical dimension. Research ethics is about more than filling in a form and seeking approval, and the concerns I have already raised about the exploitation of autistic researchers who are giving their expertise for free come under my personal research ethics umbrella.

Alongside Barnes and Sheldon (2007), Barnes (2014), Barton (2005), Milton *et al* (2019), Oliver (1997) and others, 'nothing about us without us' is an ethical principle in my book. The operation of respectful non-exploitative working practice is part of the equation within CADS research.

Many PARC participants are involved in HE as either doctoral students, researchers and/or lecturers. Contributors insights into a small-scale survey about their perceptions of barriers and enablers around university work in these roles inform the next section.

Insights about employment from autistic scholars

Contributors to this section completed a short questionnaire or wrote their ideas on Post-it notes at a PARC meeting The questionnaire was emailed by an autistic academic and asked open-ended questions around a loose set of themes designed to elicit comments about barriers and enablers in higher education employment. The following observations are only based on a small snapshot of 12 individuals of all genders between their mid-30s to mid-50s, and do not claim to be representative of anyone else. Unfortunately, there is no solid evidence base on which to build firmer conclusions. Nobody who replied had a full-time, permanent academic contract. Tangible parallels between staff and student experiences were immediately apparent from the small number of responses and the tiny amount of research focusing on staff experiences. Points from research gleaned using search terms such as autism, employment, university and autistic academics are included alongside direct quotes from questionnaire responses.

The employment of PARC participants is almost always fractional or hourly paid. Doctoral candidates often occupy a liminal space between university researcher, part-time lecturer and student. Their contribution is included here under the loose category of staff, but straddles rather uncomfortably the staff-student divide. More uncomfortable is the fact that some participants identified here as researchers are not really university staff in the traditional remunerated sense, as the university is not paying them, and neither is anyone else. Disappointingly, it is not uncommon for PARC members to leave university with a doctorate only to find themselves without a job related to their area of expertise. The following is not indicative of unbounded optimism in this regard:

'*IF* I make it through my PhD (which in itself will feel like an overly tremendous achievement) I do not know how I will find a place for myself in academia.'

Common characteristics of scholars associated with PARC are a genuine in-depth interest in their area of academic expertise, an immense capacity for hard work and a desire for their employment to make use of their talents. The follow comment illustrates a typically positive but cautious attitude:

'I hope I will be able to find a department where my needs will be taken into account and I will be supported to thrive and undertake work that, in turn, will hopefully benefit more autistic people both in its manner of engagement and co-production, and in terms of applications of findings.'

The advantages of having someone on the team who possesses these qualities hardly need to be spelled out. Despite evidence of academic excellence including peer-reviewed papers, typically, as revealed by the following comment, contributors did not assume that they would have a smooth trajectory into work commensurate with their talents and achievements:

'While universities might "traditionally" have been institutions that could have suited autistic academic employees very well, these days are long gone. Nowadays, the ever-changing face of Higher Education means that demands are myriad and varied, lack tangibility and could pose frustrating challenges to an otherwise exceptionally competent autistic academic.'

Pre-entry considerations focused on criticism of recruitment practices. Promotees found themselves disadvantaged again either by the difficulty of negotiating processes, which lacked transparency, or the feeling that procedures around progression were too daunting to even contemplate. Some talked with sadness about feeling that they might need to attempt to hide their autism in order to secure employment and then continue to do so in the workplace, at great personal cost. Their rationale was that this was a necessary evil in order to be able to fit in and avoid stereotyping and discrimination.

While most disabled students can access technological and other forms of assistance from the Disabled Student Allowance (DSA), and a range of in-house services, the lack of equivalent systems for employees was identified as a barrier by contributors. This concern is echoed in research which suggests that processes for assisting the transition to work of disabled students are inadequate (Barnham & Martin, 2017; Wilson & Martin, 2017).

Access to Work (AtW) (Sayce, 2015) is an imperfect employee-facing initiative which nevertheless has potential. Processes around AtW and similar initiatives were variously described as chaotic and not joined effectively with university systems. One participant suggested that they could hardly face trying to make AtW work for them because the interface between the scheme and the institution felt impenetrable, medicalised and othering, and confidentiality could not be guaranteed. This is unfortunate because AtW is designed specifically to assist disabled employees already in the workplace, as well as job seekers. The scheme offers a range of valuable resources including personal assistant-type support and training in assistive technology. Alarmingly, autistic scholars involved with PARC and trying to move into academic employment post doctorate have very little knowledge of AtW which suggests that nobody is telling them about it. The Equality Act (2010) applies to careers and alumni services and disabled students should have equal access to their resources post-graduation.

Autistic applicants particularly commented on the interview process, which did not routinely play to their strengths because of unspoken expectations around neurotypical approaches to communication. These included engaging in irrelevant chat, making sustained eye contact without staring, and deciphering convoluted and improbable lines of questioning. Feedback on the recruitment process for one research project commended the practice of providing straightforward written questions for the candidates, all of whom were autistic, half an hour before the interview. Doing so required minimum effort and could easily become routine, alongside things like thinking about the sensory environment and the clarity of information provided. Autistic people are best placed to advise on exactly what is required.
Promotees described similar issues around processes associated with promotion. Research evidence suggests that disabled people working in supportive teams certainly think twice about going for promotion, for fear of being unable to replicate hard-won supportive working conditions in another context (Roulstone & Williams, 2014).

Administrative procedures were found to be particularly challenging by autistic academics, many of whom felt that their induction had been inadequate, lacking in practical detail or even non-existent. A PhD scholar made the following comment, which is also relevant to staff:

'Administrative barriers are the most immediately stressful. Complex and convoluted online systems and programmes, and labyrinthine networks of people that you need to call or email to get things done or fixed… struggling and failing … through an impossibly challenging online system that was both visually impossible to navigate and not designed in a way that would be accessible to anyone…. It left me very much with the sense that – this system is not for "people like me". Either the university did not expect "people like me" to progress this far into education, or they simply don't want me here.'

Another respondent expressed exasperation about, *'a reluctance to provide explicit instructions, with the suggestion that it is up to the individual to make up their own way of doing things, which generally results in a later situation in which it is revealed that the only way to do things was their way (which they did not communicate).'*

Bureaucratic requirements were not experienced as value-free by the following contributor, who felt that the institution was not geared up to embrace difference practically and positively. Some might call this '(institutional) ableism', which is exemplified by a culture in which a 'mythical norm' dictates the way things are done and variance is not tolerated, let alone celebrated (Campbell, 2009; Jammaers *et al*, 2013; Kattari *et al*, 2018).

'Misunderstanding of my needs, negotiating bureaucracy and unwritten cultural expectations, jumping through hoops… there are many barriers to working in this sector.'

Assuming the ability to navigate impenetrable complexities about getting paid without road-testing the processes with people who might face disadvantage, as in the next example, suggests that systems may not have been equality impact assessed as required by The Equality Act (2010):

'Getting actually paid for work I had done was almost impossible. I had more than one contract because I had more than one role. I never saw these contracts so could not really work out what I was being paid for and whether I was paid at all for some of the work.'

The following description is of a situation that has gone horribly wrong:

'I've had a lengthy career outside academia… However, my one month in an academic post came to a grinding halt when I was found wandering in a daze outside the office…

I stopped … for the sake of my mental health. Although it hasn't always been the easiest, this is the one and only time I have been unable to cope with employment.'

Research with disabled staff in higher education indicates that administrative systems that are difficult to understand and technological requirements that are hard to pick up often create extreme stress. This is particularly so if accompanied by an inadequate induction underpinned by the expectation that the new person will just work it all out for themselves (Martin, 2017). Autistic scholars trying to negotiate inadequately explained work practices described being overwhelmed and completely stressed out by tasks which were apparently supposed to be simple. Being the one who is just not grasping the plot by mysterious, magical osmosis is an othering experience with which I am also quite familiar as a neurodiverse academic. I share the view of autistic colleagues that advice which includes the expression, 'It's easy, you will just pick it up as you go along,' is both annoying and alienating. Angell-Wells (2019) suggests that anxiety around getting to grips with workplace technology is by no means limited to disabled employees. Her research identifies an achingly wide gap in enquiry concerned with the affective dimensions of learning to handle intimidating and unfamiliar ICT systems.

Conferences are not routinely autism friendly. Networking demands social competences and motivations not necessarily traditionally associated with autistic dispositions. Small talk unrelated to the conference theme, for example, is often an unspoken expectation which not all autistic scholars enjoy. The following contribution illustrates that, before even getting there, paperwork and travel can pile on the stress:

'I spoke at three international conferences, all of which were incredibly terrifying and none of which were paid… I don't feel I can do that again without some practical support if the journey is to another part of the UK or abroad. I'm not sure how I will be able to get those kinds of accommodations, so I've put the ideas of conferences off for now.'

Although under-resourced and by no means perfect, PARC conferences on the other hand are led by autistic academics and organised with some understanding of the requirement for clarity and sensory sensitivity.

Environmental and sensory issues are revealed in the preceding and following quotations and exacerbated by open-plan offices, hot desking and similar practices. Equality impact assessment is relevant to environmental conditions as well as systems and all other aspects of university life.

'Physical barriers include the sensory environments being like hell… Strip lighting that makes a hideous whirring sound, supervisions in crowded areas or a broom cupboard…'

Clear communication is something contributors identified as essential. Ambiguity, miscommunication and unclear expectations in interactions with others caused obvious distress, such as in the examples provided below:

'The most prohibitive barriers related to communication… political games play out and some information is given to one, but conflicting information given to others… I find it all exhausting and confusing and has made me feel like quitting many times, even though I love my research and find the academic work itself not at all challenging.'

'Communication between colleagues is very rushed and focused on informal 'chats' between lectures rather than clear conversations with a possibility for clarification. The inability to switch between tasks to participate in these conversations is tricky.'

One contributor expressed frustration about having to tell colleagues again and again about the relatively straightforward reasonable adjustments they required in order to be effective:

'There is only so many times that I can clearly, kindly, explicitly explain my needs in relation to being autistic (sensory environment, a need for clear instructions and timeframes, etc…) and they are ignored. I am assuming that my difficulties are overlooked because I appear competent in other areas, I've explained in plain terms that I am a 'vulnerable person' to be told that my supervisor also thinks of himself as vulnerable (he has no disability).'

Woolly, ambiguous boundaries have created problems for the contributor who provided the following comment:

'Students expect an increasing amount of 'interaction' with lecturers, but often fail to grasp (or be consistently given) basic ground rules for such interaction. They do not always turn up for meetings or read feedback on their essays, and often see the 'seminars' as a chance for one-to-one conversations that could easily be conducted elsewhere. I find this clash between students' expectations (of having someone available as a 'buddy' rather than a teacher) and the realities of teaching (when they will be one of many students that the lecturer is responsible for), very distressing.'

Supportive colleagues were identified frequently by participants as a force for good. Relying on the better nature and helpfulness of co-workers was not seen as enough in itself. Addressing institutional obstacles arising from a culture of ableism was proposed as a sustainable approach.

'I have found some people to be very understanding, whereas others were not. I love learning, thinking, writing and playing with ideas and theories. I find it depends on the people and the team – in terms of vibe but also accessibility too.'

'A thing I have learned about oppression is that even when people or organisations are nice, you can't assume that it will continue. The rug can be pulled out at any time and this makes it hard to feel safe.'

Frustratingly, the reasonable adjustments autistic colleagues need in order to thrive are usually potentially very simple, but somehow get over complicated along the way. One contributor, for example, spoke of their delight at being enabled to just get on with their job without having to travel a long distance to the campus and join in with meetings that were only tangentially relevant to their role. This adjustment cost nothing.

While the work of CADS prioritises autism research, and autistic researchers are therefore usually recruited to CADS to research autism, PARC participants clarified that they often have expertise in unrelated fields. Just as Professor Stephen Hawking did not identify his discipline as Critical Disability Studies, contributors described getting a bit tired of being expected to take an interest in disability research when their academic interests lay elsewhere. The danger of being pigeonholed as an autism researcher with only insider perspectives to contribute is reflected in the following statement:

'We can address this barrier by making space for autistic researchers to do all kinds of autism-relevant research, informed by our perspectives as autistic people but not limited to sharing personal perspectives as autistic people.'

The expectation of flag-waving irritated disabled academics in Martin's (2017) study of the experiences of disabled leaders in higher education. Although this was problematised more by those with visible impairments, the following quote illustrates that autistic people are not immune to the expectation that they will fly the flag or pave the way for others:

'It has been absolutely gruelling. I feel, at every turn, particularly as an autistic PhD candidate in a small department, that I am carving the way for people like me and it is taking a significant effort.'

Although gathered from a small number of contributors, all these comments graphically illustrate the amount of effort required to navigate academic life as an autistic researcher or lecturer. Equality impact assessment undertaken by (paid) autistic researchers could identify potential obstacles and manifestations of ableism and pose solutions which could eradicate or at least diminish them and, in doing so, create a more conducive and less chaotic environment. To this end, some helpful ideas are presented in the next section in the form of questions an autistic person might ask. Representatives from academic institutions with the power to address some of the concerns illuminated by these questions, might wish to flex their empathy muscles and attempt to answer them from an institutional perspective.

Questions arising from staff facing research

Recruitment:

■ Am I sufficiently convinced that recruitment processes are non-discriminatory so referring to my impairment in advance will not disadvantage me?

■ Will the interview play to my strengths or will people make negative judgements about me based on social conventions around communication style?

Induction:

■ Is this induction going to be useful to me in that it will cover information I need, clearly, consistently and without contradictions?

■ Will I be able to explain what sort of support I need during the induction process and will this be acted upon effectively?

■ Does the organisation understand how to make processes such as accessing Access to Work support happen with minimum fuss?

■ Will my contract be clear and specific?

■ Will there be a named person who can help me if there is anything I do not understand?

Administrative systems:

■ Will the administrative systems I am expected to use be explained clearly and will they work effectively?

■ What sort of administrative support will I receive?

■ Will processes around getting paid work effectively?

Communication:

■ Will communications with colleagues be clear and logical?

■ Will communication systems be clear and logical?

Sensory environment:

- Will I have an appropriate space to work in that does not cause too much sensory overload?
- Will I be able to avoid hot desking?

Changing jobs/promotion:
- Will the fact that I am autistic mean that I am pigeonholed by the university as 'an autism researcher'?
- Will I be supported to progress in the organisation?

Insights from autistic students

Studies focusing on the university experience of autistic students include work by Cain *et al* (2016); Gellbar *et al* (2014); Lucas and James (2018); Madriaga and Goodley (2010); Newbutt *et al* (2016); Siew *et al* (2017); Taylor (2005); Taylor *et al* (2010); Van Hees *et al* (2015) and others. I have been directly involved in several projects over almost 20 years. Examples include: Atkinson *et al* (2011); Beardon *et al* (2009); Chown *et al* (2018); Hastwell *et al* (2012, 2013 and 2017); Madriaga *et al* (2008); Martin (2000, 2005, 2006a, 2006b, 2007, 2008a, 2008b, 2008c, 2011b); Martin *et al* (2008); Milton *et al* (2016, 2017, 2018); Sturgess (2018).

Despite differences of emphasis arising from the phenomenology of the researchers concerned, there is a striking degree of congruence between the findings of various studies in this field. Agreement that autistic people struggle with ambiguity and lack of predictability, for example, is widespread. While I prefer to lay problem causality at the feet of the unpredictable ambiguous institution, occasionally the tone of research is somewhat deficit model and locates 'the problem' firmly with the autistic person. Studies sometimes problematise the way autistic students present themselves and this does not sit particularly comfortably with me. I am not a fan of the term 'challenging behaviour' for example, as, in keeping with many autistic researchers, I prefer to look at communicative intent and factors within the environment which elicit distress responses. My ontological perspective leads me to see the world through an overtly social model lens (Oliver, 2013). I am clearly of the view that environmental factors which disadvantage autistic people need to be identified and addressed as a matter of social justice.

In my writing, I problematise the notion of pragmatic acceptance of labelling (as a gateway to services) while flying the flag for UD and UDL and inclusive practice which benefits everyone (Milton *et al*, 2016). Inclusive practice is based on the idea that the learning environment is conducive to all learners and that diversity is a beautiful thing to be celebrated (Martin, 2011a; 2011b). Inclusion is not about bashing square pegs into round holes, it is about having a wide variety of different-shaped holes and niches into which a wide variety of differently shaped people can snuggle down and feel comfortable and motivated. Maslow *et al* (1987) identified conditions for progress to self-actualisation a long time ago and students are not likely to be productive and reach their potential if they feel as if they do not belong. Here, 'belonging' is posed as a reductivist definition of inclusion, which embraces disability as a valuable diversity strand. Belonging implies community (Martin, 2017; Milton, 2017a).

Evidence of adverse impacts on self-esteem through social exclusion at university reminds us that what goes on in the classroom is only a small part of university life (Chown & Beavan, 2011; Chown *et al*, 2018; Hastwell *et al*, 2012; 2017). Autistic participants emphasised the need for a comfortable social environment and highlighted the difficulty around finding such a thing. Freshers' Week got several mentions because of the sensory overload of Freshers' Fair, leading to lack of access to the clubs and societies that have the potential to form the basis of a social life with like-minded people (Madriaga *et al*, 2008; Martin, 2008a; 2008b). 'Othering' (Cliff, 1983; Foucault, 1982; Richards, 2008) is an important concept when thinking about working effectively with students in a way that does not make them feel alienated and 'othered'.

Findings from the wide range of studies cited here coalesce around a series of common threads, which are most tangibly summarised into a list of questions for HE staff focusing on the student journey from pre-entry to post-exit. These questions reflect the concerns of autistic students and ideas that arose from the insider perspectives of research participants.

Pre-entry:
- How do I get clear information about courses?
- Can I come and visit and meet people who will be working with me?
- Can I visit the campus a few times to see how it feels?
- Who can help me decide?
- How do I apply for Disabled Student Allowance (DSA)?
- Who can help me apply for DSA?
- How does all the paperwork around enrolment work and who can help me with it?
- What's it like in halls of residence and can I visit before I move in and maybe stay the night?
- How do I sort out my student loan?

First few weeks:
- Can somebody meet me and show me where to go?
- How do I choose from different modules and options?

- Will it be possible to join clubs and societies?
- How do I find out about clubs and societies?
- How can I make friends?
- Where can I eat my sandwiches?
- What if the halls of residence are too noisy?
- How do I organise my time?

Assignments:

- What if I get a rubbish mark?
- How will I know if I'm doing ok?
- How can I ask my lecturer questions?
- How do I hand my work in?
- What if I'm working in a group and other people don't take it seriously?

Exams:

- What if I don't understand the question or instructions?
- What if I fail?
- What if it's noisy in the exam hall?

Placement:

- How do I find a placement?
- How do I get to my placement?
- What if it does not work out?
- How do I talk to people on placement?
- Who can help me if I get stuck?

Dissertation:

- How do I decide what to do?
- How do I plan my time?
- How do I organise all this information?

Finding a job:

- How do I know what sort of job I want?
- Who can help me decide?
- How will I manage the interview?
- What if I hate my job?
- Is there any sort of support at work?

Sources of help:

- How am I supposed to understand who can help me with what?
- How do I contact different services for different sources of help?
- What do I do if I need help that is not to do with my course?
- Who can I talk to if I feel worried?
- Will confidential information about me be shared?

This list of questions illustrates the sort of concerns research participants have raised but fails to reflect the fact that autistic students have a bucketful of strengths to bring to the academic party. These include application and a high level of motivation and interest (Hastwell et al, 2013). The flipside of seriousness and dedication is that autistic students often experience anxiety born out of perfectionism. On many occasions, I have found myself trying hard to persuade an autistic student that 75% is a very good mark. Group work anxieties often arise from the worry that other people are not pulling their weight and will bring down everyone's grade (Martin, 2008a; 2008b; Sturgess 2018). This can be easily rectified by assigning individual marks as well as credit for ensuring that every group member is included and has a clear role to play.

The need for clarity is a recurrent theme. Ambiguous information and impenetrable administration systems can cause high levels of anxiety. Instructions that are not clear can make it difficult for a student to focus on an assignment because they are worried that they might be getting it wrong. Badly written exam questions and instructions cause a great deal of stress. Reliability is something that autistic students' value. Over-promising and under-delivering create confusion, so it really helps if people just do what they say they are going to do. At a systemic level, a culture of reliability is helpful. If, for example, a class must be moved to a different room, notifying all students in advance routinely via an agreed system helps everyone, not just autistic students. Having named reliable people is valued, particularly when the roles of individuals are unambiguous. Having a mentor to help with navigation between people, roles and systems is something many students found helpful.

A focus on social aspects of university life such as living in halls and making friends illustrates a common preoccupation of autistic students. Some were keen on social groups with other autistic students, but others would run a mile and would much rather just join in with people who have similar interests. As mentioned, Freshers' Week was problematic for many because of the huge sensory overload of activities like Freshers' Fair. Joining clubs and societies online was helpful. Sensory overload concerns were frequently reported by participants, so a guided tour of the campus was recommended to help students find quiet comfortable spaces.

By paying attention to student's concerns it is possible to anticipate the sort of arrangements which are likely to reduce potential difficulties. Anticipating that applying to university is a big step, and potential students and their parents will have lots of questions, has prompted some universities to arrange pre-entry events that provide clear unambiguous information and opportunities such as pre-entry summer school. Knowing that job interviews can be a barrier, the employability team could work to make alternative arrangements with potential employers, such as work trials. Every step in between could also be equality impact assessed with input from autistic people.

Commonality between autistic students and staff

Research, and common sense, tell us that the whole student journey is important from pre-entry to post-exit. Equally, disabled staff face barriers at various points in their employment, including the stage prior to securing a job in the first place (Martin, 2017). The acronym REAL encapsulates the essence of studies discussed here. REAL stands for: reliable, empathic, anticipatory and logical (Martin 2008a). Enacting the REAL principle amounts to doing what you say you are going to do **reliably**, **empathising** with the world view of the individual, **anticipating** potential difficulties and addressing them before they arise, and communicating clearly and **logically** to avoid ambiguity. REAL encompasses many features of UDL /UD so is potentially useful beyond the original aim of trying to improve the university experience of autistic people.

Limitations

All the research discussed here has limitations of course. Much of it was unfunded and therefore poorly resourced. Gender was not isolated as a consideration and many other variables and intersectionality could have been considered more fully. Factors such as Social Capital (Bourdieu, 1986) were largely ignored or not named as such. Chown *et al* (2015), for example, considered the intersection between being autistic and the first in the family to embark on higher education in relation to the doctoral journey, but this exploration did not specifically draw upon Bourdieu's work on Social Capital. Differences between studying from home and while living away, the implications of being the first in the family to go to university, campus versus city locations, gender, poverty and so on and so on, are things that could have been considered and may be the focus of future research. Poverty is not a protected characteristic under the Equality Act (2010) but the idea of being autistic and managing either to study while not having two pennies to rub together or to budget on extremely low pay deserves consideration.

Lest we forget, much of the contributing autistic expertise within the research discussed here was unpaid, which is perhaps the biggest limitation of all. I am in the privileged position of being able to make proclamations such as 'the CADS research group will not undertake autism research without paid autistic researchers. As an ally, I feel that it is incumbent upon me to do so, but I also acknowledge that it is not too difficult from the relative safety of my salaried leadership position. Ethical statements within autism research papers are not required to provide information about whether the team included paid autistic researchers. Perhaps this systematic limitation could usefully be rectified. CADS will certainly not be party to such an omission.

References

Angell-Wells (2019): A hermeneutic phenomenological study of lecturers' lived experience of ipad adoption. Unpublished EdD thesis, London South Bank University.

Arnold, L., Milton, D., Beardon, L., and Chown, N. (2018) England and Autism. In: Volkmar, F. (Ed) *Encyclopaedia of Autism Spectrum Disorders*. New York, NY: Springer.

Atkinson, R., Evans, S., Gandy, C., Graham, C., Hendrickx, S., Jackson, V., Martin, N. (2011) A Buddy Scheme - Supporting transition and progression for students identified with Asperger Syndrome (AS). *Journal of Inclusive Practice in Further and Higher Education* 3(2), 109-126.

Barnes, C. (2014) What a difference a decade makes: reflections on doing 'emancipatory' disability research. In: Nind, M. and Rix, J. (eds.) *Ethics and Research in Inclusive Education*, pp. 55-70. London: Routledge.

Barnes, C. and Sheldon, A. (2007) Emancipatory disability research and special educational needs. In: Florian, L (ed) *The Sage handbook of special education*, pp.233-246, London: Sage.

Barnham, C. and Martin, N. (2017) Considering employment of young people with intellectual impairments and autism leaving school and college. In: Milton, D. and Martin., N. (eds.) *Autism and Intellectual Disability Volume 2*, pp. 51-53. Hove: Pavilion.

Barton, L. (2005) Emancipatory research and disabled people: Some observations and questions. *Educational review*, **57**(3), pp.317-327.

Beardon, L. and Edmonds, G. (2007) ASPECT consultancy report. A national report on the needs of adults with Asperger syndrome. www.shu.ac.uk/theautismcentre [accessed 01 July 2018]

Beardon, L., Martin, N. and Woolsey, I. (2009) What do students with Asperger syndrome and high functioning autism want from college and university – in their own words. *Good Autism Practice*. **10**(2), 35-44.

Bourdieu, P. (1986) The forms of capital. In: J. Richardson (ed.) *Handbook of Theory and Research for the Sociology of Education*, pp 241-258. New York, NY: Greenwood.

Cain, R.Y. and Richdale, A.L. (2016) Educational experiences and needs of higher education students with autism spectrum disorder. *Journal of Autism and Developmental Disorders*, **46**(1), 31-41.

Campbell, F.K. (2009) *Contours of ableism: The production of disability and abledness*. Basingstoke: Palgrave Macmillan.

Charlton, J. I. (1998) *Nothing about us without us: Disability oppression and empowerment*. Berkeley, CA: University of California Press.

Chown, N. and Beavan, N. (2012) Intellectually capable but socially excluded? A review of the literature and research on students with autism in further education. *Journal of Further and Higher Education*, **36**(4), 477-493.

Chown, N., Beardon, L., Martin, N. and Ellis, S. (2015) Examining intellectual prowess, not social difference: removing barriers from the doctoral viva for autistic candidates. *Journal of Inclusive Practice in Further and Higher Education*, **6**(1), 22-38.

Chown, N., Robinson, J., Beardon, L., Downing, J., Hughes, L., Leatherland, J. and MacGregor, D. (2017) Improving research about us, with us: a draft framework for inclusive autism research. *Disability & Society*, **32**(5), 720-734.

Chown, N., Baker-Rogers, J., Hughes, L., Cossburn, K. N. and Byrne, P. (2018) The 'High Achievers' project: an assessment of the support for students with autism attending UK universities. *Journal of Further and Higher Education*, **42**(6), 837-854.

Cliff, M. (1983). *Claiming an Identity, They Taught Us to Despise*. Watertown, MA: Persephone Press.

Cooper, B. (1981). *Michel Foucault. An Introduction to the Study of his Thought. Studies in Religion and Society*. Volume 2. New York, NY: Edwin Mellen.

The Equality Act (2010) https://www.disabilityrightsuk.org/understanding-equality-act-information-disabled-students [accessed 23 August 19].

Foucault, M. (1982) The subject and power. *Critical Enquiry*. **8** (94), 777-795.

Gelbar, N.W., Smith, I. and Reichow, B. (2014). Systematic review of articles describing experience and supports of individuals with autism enrolled in college and university programs. *Journal of autism and developmental disorders*, **44**(10), 2593-2601.

Goodley, D. (2010). *Disability Studies. An interdisciplinary introduction*. London: Sage.

Hastwell, J., Martin, N., Baron-Cohen, S. and Harding, J. (2012) Giving Cambridge University students with Asperger syndrome a voice: a qualitative, interview- based study towards developing a model of best practice. *Good Autism Practice* **13**(2), 56-64.

Hastwell, J., Harding, J., Martin, N. and Baron-Cohen, S. (2013) *Asperger Syndrome Student Project*, 2009-12: Final Project Report, June 2013. University of Cambridge. https://www.disability.admin.cam.ac.uk/files/asprojectreport2013.pdf [Accessed 28 Jun 2018].

Hastwell, J., Martin, N., Baron-Cohen, S. and Harding, J. (2017) Reflections on a university based social group for students with Asperger syndrome. *Good Autism Practice*, **18**(1) 97-105.

Jammaers, E., Zanoni, P. and Hardonk, S. (2016). Constructing positive identities in ableist workplaces: Disabled employees' discursive practices engaging with the discourse of lower productivity. *Human relations*, **69**(6), 1365-1386.

Jorgenson, L., Singleton, K. and Bennett, J., (2013), September. Universal Design for Learning in Higher Education. In: *Innovations in Teaching & Learning Conference Proceedings* (Vol. 5). [add online source? Available from: https://journals.gmu.edu/index.php/ITLCP/issue/view/189 [accessed 17 Aug 2019].

Kattari, S.K., Olzman, M. and Hanna, M.D., 2018. 'You Look Fine!' Ableist Experiences by People with Invisible Disabilities. *Affilia*, **33**(4), 477-492.

Loomes, G. (2017). The politics of autism: navigating the contested spectrum. *Disability and Society*, **32**(5), 761-762.

Loomes, G. (2018). Researching about us without us: exploring research participation and the politics of disability rights in the context of the Mental Capacity Act 2005. *Journal of medical ethics*, **44**(6), 424-427.

Lucas, R. and James, A.I. (2018). An evaluation of specialist mentoring for university students with autism spectrum disorders and mental health conditions. *Journal of autism and developmental disorders*, **48**(3), 694-707.

Madriaga, M., Goodley, D., Hodge, N. and Martin, N. (2008). Enabling transitions into higher education for students with Asperger syndrome. *York. Higher Education Academy*.

Madriaga, M. and Goodley, D. (2010). Moving beyond the minimum: Socially just pedagogies and Asperger's syndrome in UK higher education. *International Journal of Inclusive Education*, **14**(2), 115-131.

Martin, N. (2000) Widening opportunities for students with Asperger's syndrome. *Widening Participation and Lifelong Learning. The Journal of the Institute for Access Studies and the European Access Network. Open University* (2) August 2000:42-48.

Martin, N. (2005) Asperger's syndrome in the workplace. Potential difficulties and straight forward solutions. *The SKILL Journal*. 81: 30-34

Martin, N. (2006a) Strategies which increase the likelihood of success at university of students with Asperger's syndrome. *Good Autism Practice*, **7**(2), 51-60.

Martin, N. (2006b) At ruste studerende med Asperger's syndrome til at klare en universitetsuddannelse - god praksis for de ansatte. *Autismebladet* **2**,14-18.

Martin, N. (2007) Personal statements. Helping transition to further education and employment. *Good Autism Practice*, **8**(2), 17-21.

Martin, N, (2008a) REAL services to assist university students who have Asperger syndrome. *NADP Technical Briefing 10/08*

Martin, N. (2008b) A template for improving provision for students with Asperger syndrome in further and higher education. *NADP Technical Briefing 11/ 08*

Martin, N. (2008c) Empathy is a two-way street. In: Pollak, D. (Ed.) Neurodiversity in Higher Education: Positive responses to specific learning differences, pp.149-168. Oxford: John Wiley.

Martin, N. (2011a) Disability Identity. Disability Pride. *Perspectives: Policy and practice in higher education*, 16, 14-19.

Martin, N. (2011b) Promoting inclusive practice for PhD students near completion. *Journal of Inclusive Practice in Further and Higher Education*, **3**(2), 37-52.

Martin, N. (2012). Giving Cambridge University students with Asperger syndrome a voice: a qualitative, interview-based study towards developing a model of best practice. *Good Autism Practice*, **13**(1), 56-63.

Martin, N. (2017). Encouraging disabled leaders in higher education: recognising hidden talents. *Leadership Foundation for Higher Education.*

Martin, N., Beardon, L., Hodge, N., Goodley, D. and Madriaga, M. (2008) Towards an inclusive environment for university students who have Asperger syndrome (AS) *Journal of Inclusive Practice in Further and Higher Education*, **1**(1), 3-14.

Martin, N. and Fraser (2012) The First LSE Disability Identity Conference. Sample Abstracts and Evaluation Mat Fraser and Nicola Martin. *Journal of Inclusive Practice in Further and Higher Education*, **3**(1),5-10.

Maslow, A. and Lewis, K.J., 1987. Maslow's hierarchy of needs. *Salenger Incorporated*, **14**, p.987.

McIntosh D (2002). An archi-texture of learning disability services: the use of Michel Foucault. *Disability and Society*. **17**(1) 65-79.

Milton, D. (2017a) *A Mismatch of Salience: Explorations of the Nature of Autism from Theory to Practice.* Hove: Pavilion.

Milton, D. (2017b) Employment: a reflective review. In: Milton, D. and Martin, N. (eds.) *Autism and Intellectual Disabilities in Adults,* Vol. 2. Hove: Pavilion.

Milton, D., Martin, M. and Melham, P. (2016) Beyond reasonable adjustment: autistic-friendly spaces and Universal Design. In Milton, D. and Martin, N. (Eds), *Autism and Intellectual Disabilities in Adults,* Vol. 1, pp.81-86. Hove: Pavilion.

Milton, D., Sims, T., Dawkins, G., Martin, N. and Mills, R. (2017). The development and evaluation of a mentor training programme for those working with autistic adults. *Good Autism Practice*, **18**(1), 25-33.

Milton, D., Ridout, S., Kourti, M., Loomes, G. and Martin, N. (2019). A critical reflection on the development of the Participatory Autism Research Collective (PARC). *Tizard Learning Disability Review* [Online] 24:82-89. Available at: http://dx.doi.org/10.1108/TLDR-09-2018-0029.

Newbutt, N., Fabri, M., Andrews, P.C. and Pukki, H.K. (2016). Using design thinking to engage autistic students in participatory design of an online toolkit to help with transition into higher education. *Journal of Assistive Technologies*, **10**(2), 102-114.

Oliver, M., 1997. Emancipatory research: Realistic goal or impossible dream. In: Barnes, C. and Mercer, G. (eds) *Doing disability research*, pp.15-31. Leeds: The Disability Press.

Oliver, M., 2013. The social model of disability: Thirty years on. *Disability & society*, **28**(7), pp.1024-1026.

Peters, M. (2003). Truth-telling as an educational practice of the self: Foucault, Parrhesia and the ethics of subjectivity. *Oxford Review of Education*. **29**(2), 207-224.

Ridout, S. (2017). The autistic voice and creative methodologies. *Qualitative Research Journal*, **17**(1), 52-64.

Ridout, S. and Edmondson, M. (2017). 'Cygnet Mentoring Project: combined experiences from a mentor and a mentee.' *Autonomy, the Critical Journal of Interdisciplinary Autism Studies*, **1**(5). Available at: http://www.larry-arnold.net/Autonomy/index.php/autonomy/article/view/AR20 [accessed 23 Aug 2019].

Richards, R. (2008). Writing the Othered Self. Auto ethnography and the problem of objectification in writing about disability and illness. *The journal of qualitative health research*. **18**(12), 1717-1728.

Roulstone, A. and Williams, J. (2014). Being disabled, being a manager: 'glass partitions' and conditional identities in the contemporary workplace. *Disability and Society*, **29**(1), 16-29.

Sayce, E. (2015). *Access to Work review*. https://www.parliament.uk/accesstowork [accessed 13 Dec 2018].

Siew, C.T., Mazzucchelli, T.G., Rooney, R. and Girdler, S. (2017). A specialist peer mentoring program for university students on the autism spectrum: A pilot study. *PLoS ONE*, **12**(7), https://doi.org/10.1371/journal.pone.0180854 [accessed 23 Aug 2019]

Sims, T., Milton, D., Martin, N. and Dawkins, G. (2016) Developing a user-informed training package for a mentoring programme for people on the autism spectrum. *The Journal of Inclusive Practice in Further and Higher Education*, **7**, 49-52.

Stone, E. and Priestley, M. (1996). Parasites, pawns and partners; disability research and the role of non-disabled researchers. *British Journal of Sociology* **47**(4), 699-716.

Sturgess, S. (2018) *How do autistic physics undergraduate students experience working with others?* Unpublished MA dissertation, London South Bank University.

Taylor, M.J. (2005). Teaching students with autistic spectrum disorders in HE. *Education + Training*, **47**(7), 484-495.

Taylor, M., Baskett, M. and Wren, C. (2010). Managing the transition to university for disabled students. *Education + Training*, **52**(2), 165-175.

Van Hees, V., Moyson, T. and Roeyers, H. (2015). Higher education experiences of students with autism spectrum disorder: Challenges, benefits and support needs. *Journal of autism and developmental disorders*, **45**(6), 1673-1688.

Willis, J.W., Jost, M. and Nilakanta, R., 2007. *Foundations of qualitative research: Interpretive and critical approaches*. London: Sage.

Wilson, L. and Martin, N. (2017). Disabled Student Support for England in 2017. How did we get here and where are we going? A brief history, commentary on current context and reflection on possible future directions. *Journal of Inclusive Practice in Further and Higher Education* **9**(1), 6-22.

Woods, R. (2017). Pathological demand avoidance: my thoughts on looping effects and commodification of autism. *Disability & society*, **32**(5), 753-758.

Woods, R., Milton, D., Arnold, L. and Graby, S. (2018). Redefining Critical Autism Studies: a more inclusive interpretation. *Disability & society*, **33**(6), 974-979.

Woods, R. and Waltz, M. (2019). The strength of autistic expertise and its implications for autism knowledge production: A response to Damian Milton. *Autonomy, the Critical Journal of Interdisciplinary Autism Studies*, **1**(6). http://www.larry-arnold.net/Autonomy/index.php/autonomy/article/view/CO2 [accessed 23 Aug 2019]

Chapter 27: Accessing services and social interaction: strategies used by autistic people

By Marion Hersh, Sharon Elley, Zyggy Banks, Panda Mery, David Cowan & Cal Watson

Introduction

There are two main and very different approaches to the understanding of autism and autistic people: the medical model, based on deficits, and the social model of disability and compatible neurodiversity model. A deficit-based approach related to the medical model is still the most common. This focus on deficits affects the attitude towards research and the overall perception of autism and autistics by society as a negative phenomenon. The social model of disability and the compatible neurodiversity model both focus on autistic people rather than 'autism'.

Neurodiversity considers the diversity of human neurology (nerves and connections between them). This leads to the investigation of differences in thinking patterns, moving, interacting, and sensory and cognitive processing between autistics and the majority 'neurotypical' population, rather than one being better or worse than the other. Also, according to the social model of disability (e.g. Johnstone, 2001; Swain *et al*, 2003) autistic people experience social, attitudinal and infrastructural barriers and frequent social exclusion.

The idea for An Auternative Research Project (https://anauternative.uk/) originated in a Scottish Autism Research Group seminar in 2017. Several autistic participants felt that the over-focus on 'interventions' and the nature of these interventions showed a lack of understanding of real autistic lived experiences. The project was funded by Disability Research for Independent Living and Learning (DRILL).

It was autistic-led and the majority of the project team are autistic. Marion Hersh and Sharon Elley are a senior lecturer and lecturer at the Universities of Glasgow and Leeds. David Cowan is involved in projects for autistic people in Glasgow, and Panda Mery in London. Zyggy Banks supports autistic students at the University of Leicester. Callum Watson is an assistant psychologist who has formerly supported autistic students at the University of Leicester. David, Panda, Callum and Zyggy were all employed as research assistants by the University of Glasgow.

The project team was supported by an Advisory Board of autistic people who provided us with advice on all aspects of the project and also piloted the questionnaire. We have also now finished the follow-up research involving interviews and a diary exercise. The research project was based on the following two research questions:

1. How do autistic people use strategies, including logic, reasoning and rules, to understand social situations and other people's reactions, and to empower themselves?

2. What are the barriers, including stereotypes, misconceptions and systemic issues, to autistic people using their strengths and appropriate strategies to participate in decision making, the economy and the community?

These questions recognise that many and possibly most of the problems experienced by autistic people are due to the barriers they experience and that various measures will be required to remove or at least reduce them. We have produced a series of recommendations for decision makers, service providers and others. These recommendations can be found in the project reports at https://anauternative.uk/publications/.

However, this chapter will discuss some of the strategies autistic people themselves use to overcome barriers and facilitate social interaction and accessing and obtaining better outcomes from service providers. In line with the discussion in the next section, this recognises that autistic people are able to show agency and act with autonomy and self-determination, though they may require varying degrees of support to do this. We hope that other autistic people will find these strategies useful and that the chapter will encourage autistics to develop and share their own strategies, as well as using and modifying these strategies.

The next section will introduce the questionnaire and present a brief participant overview. The strategies used by participants are presented in section 3, which is divided into a number of subsections, and the conclusions follow in section 4.

Overview of relevant theoretical literature

The discussion in this chapter fits within the disability literature on self-determination, autonomy, independence and interdependence. Independence has generally been considered as the ability to carry out daily living activities without support (Hersh, 2013) or be 'financially self-sufficient' (Sprague & Hayes, 2000 p671). However, this is unhelpful to the many autistic and other disabled people who require support at least sometimes for daily living, choose to use support for daily living to free energy for other things, or who are not able to engage in paid employment. Thus, definitions of this type privilege activities many autistic and other disabled people require support for and may ignore their strengths. This can lead to them being treated as less than full adults or citizens and being disempowered.

In addition, we are all mutually dependent or interdependent (Reindal, 1999). Examples include an exchange of services. For instance, a doctor who treats the refuse collector who collects their waste or a teacher teaching the children of their dentist and the person who repaired their washing machine.

The disability literature has therefore investigated alternative approaches to independence, particularly autonomy and self-determination. Autonomy is the ability to 'make meaningful decisions about [one's] life and have also them happen' (Knight, 2007). Self-determination is about having agency and being able to make decisions and take action to maintain or improve quality of life (Wehmeyer, 2005). Autistic (and other disabled) students have been found to be less self-determined than non-disabled peers (Wehmeyer *et al*, 2010). Beliefs about their ability to be successful at school and a sense of personal autonomy and not being controlled by others have been shown to be important for developing self-regulation and motivation for both non-disabled and some groups of disabled schoolchildren (Deci *et al*, 1992). This probably also holds for adults and indicates the importance of measures to increase autistic people's sense of autonomy and awareness that they can succeed.

Self-determination has been linked to empowerment. It has been suggested that autistic and other people with developmental disabilities are disempowered by being made into 'objects without "selves", outside the context of interpersonal and social structural relationships'. They are then empowered by social relationships that facilitate self-development (Sprague & Hayes, 2000, p671). The project questions specifically consider the use of strategies by autistics as a means of empowerment. This links to the idea that disabled people can become 'vital contributors to their communities' (White *et al*, 2010). There has been some, sometimes slightly stereotypical, recognition that some autistic people have characteristics that could make them excellent employees (e.g. Hagner & Cooney,

2005). However, there has been relatively little discussion of the ways in which 'autistic' differences could enable autistic people to make creative and unusual contributions, and the loss to society as a result of the barriers which prevent this.

Unfortunately, space considerations do not permit a lengthy discussion of this literature or the differences between autonomy and self-determination. An interesting illustration is given by the life of Jamie & Lion (Knight, 2007), an autistic person who works for the BBC. He uses a variety of strategies, including the use of technology and support from carers, to enable him to work, contribute to the community and maintain his autonomy.

The Questionnaire

The questionnaire was drawn up by the whole project team. It was intended to be answered by autistic people, whether formally or self-diagnosed, or seeking a diagnosis. The final version consisted of seven sections with a mixture of open free choice answers and closed (choose answers from a list) questions. Five sections investigated participants' good and bad experiences, strategies and suggestions for improvements in the areas of: 1) diagnosis; 2) health service; 3) job search and employment; 4) benefits and 5) social interaction.

A further section covered participants' use of technology, including in interaction with service providers and in social and other situations. It also asked for suggestions for new technologies and modifications to, or better uses of, existing technologies. The final section collected personal data so we could determine the extent to which we had covered the whole autistic community and investigate the effects of factors such as gender or age on autistic experiences. All the questions were optional, other than the initial consent question which included a statement that the participant was autistic, whether formally or self-diagnosed or seeking a diagnosis.

Responses: participant overview

We obtained 223 responses, including eight from the initial piloting stage. Over half the participants (58%) were female, nearly a third (33%) male, 6% non-binary and 4% other. Ten percent had changed their gender from that assigned at birth. The relatively high percentage of both non-binary participants and trans participants is in line with the literature on the high percentage of autistic people who are trans and/or reject binary approaches to gender (Walsh *et al*, 2018). Another recent study had an even high percentage of female participants (Livingston *et al*, 2019), so it is possible that certain types of study may be attractive to autistic women. The previous low representation of autistic women in research makes this very welcome.

Participants had a good age distribution, though there were only a few participants aged 65 and older and none above 74. Nearly two fifths (37%) were in the 25-40 year age range and about a fifth in each of the 16-24 (19%), 41-50 (23%) and 51-64 (18%) age ranges. The lack of representation of older people was probably due to a combination of factors, including the lower diagnosis rates among this group compared to the rest of the population and the fact that they may be more difficult to contact, particularly by electronic means. The overwhelming majority (89%) were white, and this figure is very similar to that for the UK population (87.1%). Eight percent were black or mixed race, and 3% other.

There were considerably more middle class people (47%) than working class (37%), with a few considering themselves upper class and 14% other, generally because they were unsure where the fitted on the class spectrum or rejected the concept of class. The overwhelming majority (97%) of participants used spoken language most of the time. Nearly a fifth (19%) used another type of communication, either together with speech or on its own, with the most popular a communication system on a mobile device or PC and used by 12%.

Strategies used by autistic people

Participants used a variety of strategies in both social interactions and to support accessing and obtaining services. Several strategies were used in a number of different contexts. A number of these strategies are discussed in the following sections. They include a trusted/support person, hiding autistic traits and imitation, research and preparation, technology, logic and reasoning, stimming and relaxation, humour, interests and personality.

Presence of a trusted or support person

Support from another ('trusted') person was the second most commonly used strategy in social interaction, used by just over four fifths (82%) (with hiding autistic traits the most common). It was also used as a means of obtaining access to services and using them effectively. The comments about its effective use in social interaction were all very positive. The main problem, as several participants indicated indirectly, is that it that it cannot be implemented by the autistic person on their own, but depends on having access to a trusted person who is available to accompany them at particular times.

Therefore, participation in social activities could be affected by changes in another person's circumstances, such as moving house. At social events, participants preferred to interact with people they knew and keep out of the way otherwise. Typical quotes from participants included, 'I went out a lot more while my best friend still lived nearby... In family situations I won't go if my partner is not there' and, 'If I have to go to a social event, I stay out the way until I find someone I know then I stick with them'. As these examples illustrate, participants are showing agency and self-determination when using the 'trusted' person approach. In particular, using this strategy has enabled them to engage in more social activities. However, the comments do not indicate the impact, if any, of the presence of a trusted person on their enjoyment.

The indications from participants' comments are that they find this strategy empowering rather than that it makes them feel dependent. However, they could experience practical problems in finding another person. We would therefore suggest that, regardless of how independence is defined, the issue with carrying out activities with the assistance of a 'trusted' person is a practical one of having access to a suitable person rather than dependence.

The presence of a 'trusted person' was also considered a 'good idea' due to its effect on other people. 'Having a trusted person along is a good idea not because it makes me feel better, but because non-autistics might think you are more socially "acceptable" if another person is interacting with you'. This indicates the impact of stereotypes about autistic people and that some participants may have internalised them. The idea of lack of 'social acceptability' is very much counter to the premises of both the social model of disability and neurodiversity. Rather than human diversity being seen as a treasure and potential font of creative solutions to the world's problems, autistic differences become not socially 'acceptable'. This then diverts autistic energy from useful contributions to society to trying to appear more 'acceptable'. This is one of the areas where barrier removal in terms of changes in attitudes is required. It also raises the issue of the prevalence of feeling 'socially unacceptable' among autistic people and any impacts on self-confidence and self-esteem. It would seem more likely that this reduces rather than increases them.

A number of participants used a phone version of the 'trusted person' strategy. Where services could only be accessed by phone, some participants were prevented from using them if no-one was available to make phone calls for them. Another option was providing phone security information and then passing the phone on. However, participants did not indicate how they managed the phone security information. The comments indicate that some participants may have experienced objections to another person phoning on their behalf. Typical quotes included, 'Do not usually phone for myself' and 'I can't have spontaneous real-time conversations on the phone, so if that is the only option then I have to ask someone else to call for me or else give up on the service'. Another interesting issue, which participants did not discuss and therefore requires further investigation, is how they briefed the trusted person and ensured that misunderstandings did not occur.

Many participants experienced difficulties in accessing health services, with only 12.7% able to access the advice and treatment they needed for both mental and physical health, and just under half (47%) able to do this sometimes. Taking another person with them was the second most popular strategy for accessing health care, used by just over half of the participants (51%). A phone version of this strategy was used to obtain appointments, with 38% of participants asking someone else to phone for appointments on their behalf. The strategy of being accompanied to the appointment was also used by participants when going for autism diagnoses. The need of some autistic people for an accompanying person when accessing health services has been indicated in the literature (Nicolaidis *et al*, 2015), but not presented as a strategy.

Although it may initially seem a not very significant distinction, whether or not this is presented as a strategy does make a difference. Using strategies shows agency and self-determination. This is indicative of an autistic person taking an active role, investigating and identifying barriers and identifying and implementing solutions. On the other hand, being accompanied or using support could be seen as a passive approach, with the autistic person being dependent on someone else.

The 'trusted' person approach was also used in job searches and in the workplace. In particular, friends and relatives were used as support people in job applications, including to provide help with deciphering vague application forms and understanding hidden implicit meanings. Probably not unsurprisingly, participants do not mention the presence of a 'trusted person' at interviews and may have been concerned that this could be misinterpreted. However, the need for sign language interpreters for deaf people has been recognised. In the same way, recognition that some autistic people need communication interpreters could be helpful in overcoming interview barriers. Presenting the requirement in terms of a communication interpreter could be a way of overcoming the misunderstanding that needing assistance automatically implies that the autistic applicant is unsuitable for the job.

Strategies used in the workplace included using a 'front person' during interactions with colleagues and bosses and being accompanied everywhere. The strategy of using a 'front person' is similar to a strategy used by one of the project team, in which an intermediary is used to communicate with people they did not know about administrative and organisational issues when participating in high level meetings. It would be useful to investigate how a 'front person' is used and the benefits to the autistic person, as well as the role of the accompanying person. Another interesting question is whether, at some point, technology could take over, or the presence of another person is essential.

Among the strategies used for obtaining benefits, participants showed a preference for assistance from individuals, whether friends or professionals, and organisations. This typically involved someone making calls for the individual or explaining forms and acting as a 'translator'. This 'translator' role is probably similar to the front person role.

Individuals who provided help included support workers, disability employment advisors, family, friends and consultants. Organisations included trade unions and the Citizens' Advice Bureau. The ways support and assistance were provided included 'looking over forms and explaining things to me', and being accompanied, for instance, 'every time I went to the Benefits Office', and 'accompanied … when I had my PIP assessment'. Support was also important in getting benefits reinstated: 'help[ing] get them reinstated' when benefits were stopped 'for non-reasons'.

The situation was similar in benefits appeals. Here, obtaining advice from an organisation (64%) and help in completing the forms (61%) were the most commonly used strategies, followed by advice from an individual (57%) and being accompanied to the interview (57%).

Further research would be valuable on briefing 'strategies' to ensure the 'trusted person' has the correct information when, for example, organising appointments or providing evidence for benefits appeals. It would also be useful to investigate the characteristics required by a 'trusted person' and how this varies with the situation and autistic person being supported.

Hiding autistic traits (masking or camouflaging) and imitation

Hiding autistic traits was the most common strategy used in social interactions, used by over four fifths of participants (85%). It is probably linked to imitating other people, which was used by two thirds of participants (67%). Masking and imitation are among the more controversial strategies used by autistic people, both within the project group and in the literature.

Participants' comments about masking in social interaction were varied. However, overall, the considerable majority of the participants who commented found masking, sometimes expressed as 'fitting in', effective. On the negative side, and in line with the literature (e.g. studies reported in Hull *et al*, 2017), masking was frequently exhausting and/or damaging to mental health. Only a few participants commented on the effectiveness of masking without mentioning any costs. Several participants considered masking and imitation more successful in the short than the long term, due to their negative consequences over a longer period.

Typical participant comments included: 'Pretending to fit in works for a limited time. If I do it in a full time job it results in mental ill health'; 'I can mask very well but there is a terrible price to pay in the week following the event' and 'Masking and imitating I use on a day-to-day basis, but they are extremely draining.'

One participant expressed concerns about the pretence involved: 'it's... unpleasant to be liked for a false version of myself'. However, it is not clear what percentage of participants shared this perspective. It is probably not surprising that people prefer to be liked for themselves and find presenting a 'false version' distressing. However, this distress may be greater for autistic people due to particular concerns about honesty. There are indications of this in the literature (Hull *et al*, 2017), though further investigation is required. There are also suggestions in the literature that the element of 'deception' frequently involved in camouflaging could make relationships unsatisfying or unsustainable (Livingston *et al*, 2019).

Masking, hiding social differences and making eye contact were used by many participants as workplace strategies. They were often described to manage and maintain employment relations but at the cost of exhaustion and sometimes burnout. The use of 'appropriate' eye contact has been mentioned as a 'compensatory' strategy in the literature (Livingston *et al*, 2019).

The view that masking and imitation strategies can be effective but often come with a heavy price on mental health and exhaustion, but which can sometimes be successful without negative consequences, is borne out in the literature (e.g. studies reported in Hull *et al*, 2017).

Finally, a strategy of hiding autistic characteristics is likely to be a disadvantage when trying to obtain a diagnosis and necessary support, as it makes it less apparent the person is autistic. For instance, 'I think because I wasn't brought up being considered autistic, I had to conform more and learned to assimilate better. However, this was detrimental in other ways as my need for help, my struggles were hidden to an even greater extent.' Camouflaging has been suggested as a contributory factor in the late and missed diagnoses of women (e.g. Lai *et al*, 2015).

The mental health diagnostic manual DSM-5 has recognised that 'learned strategies' can mask 'autistic symptoms', but there are no guidelines for dealing with this (Livingston *et al*, 2019). There is thus a need for training for diagnosis professionals in seeing through masking. However, concerns have been expressed in the literature that publicising information about how to see through camouflaging might make autistics vulnerable to 'unfair' treatment, particularly in the workplace, as some autistic people use camouflaging as a protection against discrimination (Hull *et al*, 2017).

This raises the issues of the role of discrimination in camouflaging and whether the perceived need for it would be reduced or even disappear if attitudes to autistic people became more positive. A small number of participants seemed to be able to mask without costs and it would be interesting to know whether these participants and those found in other surveys share particular characteristics, use masking in a particular way or have just been 'lucky'. It would be valuable to investigate in more detail for a diverse sample of autistic people the balance between benefits and costs and the factors that affect this, as well the relationship between different types of autistic identity and the use of masking and, when used, its success and costs.

Research and preparation

Researching situations and preparation were used by participants to increase their chances of obtaining services, as well as in many other situations. Preparation in the form of social scripts and learnt small talk was used in social interactions. The use of notes and lists, as well as information from the internet had an important role in this strategy.

Many participants obtained evidence and prepared the case to support obtaining a referral or a diagnosis in advance. They used various sources of information to ensure they did not forget anything. Typical comments included, 'I would continue keeping notes and lists. I may consider using one of the online guides by autism support networks to make sure I think of every aspect that I may need to prepare for', and 'I made a list of reasons why I thought I was autistic, based on book about Asperger's syndrome'. Participants also used preparation to try and avoid communication problems in the stressful situation of diagnosis. Their comments included, 'writing notes – put on the spot, face-to-face, my brain goes blank and I stumble over any words that do remain. Being able to provide my feelings in writing makes it easier for both sides.'

Participants generally found this intense preparation useful. However, this raises the issue, which will need further research, of why participants considered such intense preparation to be necessary. A particular issue is whether autistics find it more difficult than it should be to obtain a diagnosis. Other issues relate to whether they have concerns about not being taken seriously, not being believed or having to justify trying to obtain an autism diagnosis. As the following comment indicates, people who think they may be autistic should be taken seriously and given appropriate support: '*Make the focus be more on helping the person than to just find if they're autistic or not and to never doubt that people have to say about themselves*'. We would suggest this should include much easier access to referrals and better training in communicating with autistic people for diagnosis practitioners.

The most popular strategy for accessing health care was having a prepared list of questions, which was used by nearly two thirds (66%) of participants. A related strategy, which was unfortunately not always possible in practice, was communicating with medical professionals before any appointments. Participants used this to provide information about their condition and a list of symptoms to avoid communication problems during the appointment. Email was the suggested way of providing this information. Typical participant comments were, 'Being able to email the GP before an appointment with the reasons for me going as I struggle to verbalise my issues when I'm stressed', and being able to email a list of issues and/or symptoms to medical practitioners in advance 'to make the appointment worthwhile if communication fails', and 'so less talking is required'. The use of notes to communicate with healthcare providers has been noted in the literature (Nicolaidis *et al*, 2015), but not identified as a strategy. While it may superficially not seem important, it does make a big difference whether or not something is considered a strategy used by autistic people. Developing and using strategies is a way of showing agency and developing self-determination and can therefore be important for increasing self-esteem and self-confidence.

Participants used research and preparation in job searches to improve applications and interview performance. They used strategies likely to be used by all job seekers and those more specific to autistic people. Strategies likely to be used by all job seekers included researching a prospective employer in advance (45.6%) and practising interview techniques (44%). A strategy more likely to be specific to autistics and some other groups of disabled people was asking for information and interview questions to be sent in advance to help them prepare (38%). Some participants also asked for photos. Another preparation strategy used by a minority of participants was training on managing in a work environment (14%). Participants' comments also mentioned other strategies. They included assertiveness training, 'looking at others' applications' and taking notes to interviews. It would be interesting to know how participants managed to get hold of other people's applications, whether they used the notes during the actual interview and the reaction to this.

Participants also used a wide range of techniques to increase their employability skills and chances of successful employment. These included reading body language books, asking for structured meetings and preparing lists. Other useful techniques included asking for feedback and keeping notes of examples of competence and scripts of how to respond in different workplace situations. However, these strategies sometimes had a personal cost, with some participants 'push[ing] self even if detrimental to health'. This raises issues of the time and effort participants are putting into research and preparation and the effect this is having on them.

The research and preparation approach used to support obtaining benefits and benefits appeals was similar to that used for job applications. It involved participants finding out what they were entitled to, learning the law regarding their entitlements and the systems and processes used by the benefits agency. The aims were maximising their chances of success and achieving a smooth transit through the system. While these strategies could also be used by non-autistic people, participants' approaches were probably considerably more thorough and in depth, including 'get[ting] to know the rules perfectly', but further research would be required to confirm this.

Another participant described their research in more detail: 'I have been proactive in researching my entitlements and legal background to obtaining benefits. I spend a lot of time reading forums online about benefits advice, and official guidance and publications on DWP/HMRC policies, so that I am clear about what I need to do in order to maximise my benefit entitlement.'

Research and preparation strategies used in social interaction included learnt small talk (72%) and prepared social scripts (57%). Although the applications are different, there is a relationship between using scripts in social interaction and the workplace. Although learnt small talk was used more frequently there were some indications that prepared social scripts may be more useful. More participants commented about social scripts than learnt small talk.

Scripts probably worked best for initiating conversations and rehearsing short interactions. They could reduce anxiety and uncertainty and make participants more secure in the direction of the conversation. Typical comments included 'Using scripts almost always gives assurance of how conversations will go and creates expected responses', and 'Using a pre-prepared script can give me a sense of security going into an interaction'.

Several participants found prepared social scripts useful to rehearse short interactions which they might otherwise find difficult. The following two extracts illustrate this, in interaction with a bus driver and a cashier: 'I also use scripts a lot, I have to rehearse what I need to say a little before I say it, for example saying thank you to the bus driver as I leave the bus, before I get up I will say it in my head', and, 'I rehearse scripts for situations that aren't normal socialisation but things like having to speak to a cashier when I buy something'.

Prepared scripts could reduce anxiety, but only so long as the other person followed them, which was unfortunately, but not surprisingly, not always the case: 'Pre-prepared social scripts lessen anxiety, but I panic when the other person deviates'. Difficulties in predicting the other person's reaction over longer conversations and the likelihood they would deviate from the script were the main disadvantages of this approach. This then led to problems with some participants finding it difficult to adapt to the new direction of the conversation. For instance, 'I panic when the other person deviates from what I expected them to say, and often I respond the way I had planned anyway, leading to confusion and embarrassment.'

A further problem of social scripts was making participants appear 'robotic'. This is possibly because they were not using natural dialogue. The approach could also create dependence on remembering or having access to the script: 'I am more likely to come across as robotic and it's more risky if I forget or lose or can't look at the paper I've written'.

In the case of small talk, one of the main limitations was the difficulties in preparing more than a limited amount of small talk. For instance, 'The prepared small talk works for a while but I often run out of conversation and it becomes difficult'. However, prepared small talk was not an option for all participants. Some people 'just can't do the small talk'.

Prepared social scripts and small talk are also mentioned in the literature, but as examples of 'compensation' rather than strategies in their own right. This included preparing questions about the other person to 'deflect' attention, and 'spending time' to prepare 'structured scripts' (Livingston *et al*, 2019).

One participant used a 'prepared script' type strategy initially in phone calls. However, unlike some of the participants who used social scripts in social interactions, they had worked out several follow-up strategies: 'I write out my first couple of sentences using the exact words and just read them off. Then I write down everything they say to read it through and check later. If it all gets too complicated and overwhelming I say I'll have to phone back another time, or I ask them to put it all in writing for me.' Writing things down is probably easier in phone conversations, as it's less obvious to the other person. However, this shows that at least some autistic people were able to combine strategies and prepare for their initial strategy becoming useable.

Both practical and psychological preparation could make it easier for some participants to make phone calls. Comments included, 'I like to use the telephone too but only once written details are available/confirmed' and 'will phone if required to (I need an hour to work up to it and to be in a private space)', and 'I have to psych myself up to call'.

Google was a popular source of information and used (excessively!) to search for resources and support across the internet 'whenever I have a question or a need' and 'to find resources in my area and to look up the locations of providers and which insurances they take'. The internet has the advantage of allowing participants to look up information 'without needing to speak'. Google Street View was used in travel planning to see what junctions look like. Participants also obtained information from autism groups on Facebook and an autism subreddit on Reddit. There are probably both similarities and differences in the way participants and the general population use Google for information. Participants were probably more thorough and detailed ('excessive') in their searches and found it necessary to search for information when other people would not have. Although this is not said explicitly, there is the possibility that participants' concerns about thorough preparation are drawing upon energy reserves that they need to participate in the activities they are preparing for.

Using technology

Email was particularly useful to a majority of participants, though it may be a preference rather than a 'strategy'. For instance, 'I prefer email, telephone if no other alternative'. Email (and messaging) could give participants greater control over the communication and avoid the immediacy and unpredictability of a phone call: 'I prefer email as it is a good way to take time to compose your needs'. Email's 'written record of evidence for both parties' was also valued. Participants generally preferred email to text, as it's 'quicker and easier to type', though they considered text 'more convenient sometimes'. However, emails also had problems, including for some participants taking 'a long time to write (up to eight hours) and when recipient misunderstands my query, will involve to & fro over days or weeks'. Several participants used online games as an alternative or more satisfying option than face-to-face socialising. Online games such as Second Life had the advantage of allowing mostly typed communication. Several participants commented positively on the ways in which online games allowed them to socialise. This included using Second Life, 'to socialise on a level impossible in person', getting their 'socializing in' by 'playing computer games with a group of online friends', using the voice chat platform Discord, and nightly online Skype games with friends. One participant said these are 'the only way I can socialise without it becoming very stressful. If I didn't do that I would go days at a time without socialising.' Several participants used social media to help counter isolation. Typical comments included, 'I socialize a lot in Facebook groups and Discord channels. I live in an isolated rural area, so they make me feel less lonely. I don't really have any friends here', and 'I am quite isolated socially so [social media] is a perfect way for me to keep in touch with family and a few friends'.

Some participants mentioned explicitly the importance of technology for socialising or networking with other autistic people. Examples included the #ActuallyAutistic community on Twitter where the participant had 'learnt a lot' and an online forum for autistic people 'as my main form of socialising'. Twitter was also used to 'follow autistic people & autism researchers'. Another participant used Google chat text to chat to two autistic friends: 'we support each other'. Facebook groups could be used to obtain 'support from other autistic people, especially women and other gender minorities' and were considered 'amazing'.

Some participants liked including visual media in their communications, for instance pictures 'as they're more expressive'. This included using WhatsApp to send a photo and emoji of what they were doing and using Facetime to talk to their parents, 'so I can see their faces and calm myself down'. Text, email and instant messaging were used to organise social events. Being on a WhatsApp group with their family made one participant feel 'more connected with them' and 'staying up to date with friends without having to contribute much myself. I can just sit quietly in the group, as I would in person'. Dating was rarely mentioned, but one participant used WhatsApp and Tinder for 'romance'.

These examples show participants being self-determined and using agency to find a type of social interaction that works for them. It also illustrates their familiarity and comfort with technology, though this should not be overestimated to imply that all autistic people are technology experts. The right of autistic (and other) people to choose how they prefer to socialise should also be recognised. For instance, it should not be implied that their online socialising is any less valid or satisfying than face-to-face socialising. Indeed many participants indicated that this would not be possible for them.

A small number of participants used technology to support face-to-face communication, including using AAC (Augmentative and Alternative Communication) devices and apps. This included both participants who used AACs as their main communication and those who used them occasionally. One application was communication with carers: 'I mostly communicate with my carers using AAC / SMS etc' or 'sometimes use a text-to-speech program on my phone'. AACs were also used on a part-time basis at work, socially and when 'shutdown'. 'I use AAC part time, including as a teacher and for social purposes' and 'AAC when shutdown (can be for weeks or even months)'. Another participant used their phone notes to support communication: 'When I cannot speak (and my communication cards do not apply to the situation), I often type into the notes in my phone'. This type of AAC use is also noted in the literature in a health service context, in this case depending on how clear their speech is at a particular point (Nicolaidis *et al*, 2015) rather than whether they feel able to use speech. Problems with doctors' reactions to AAC use have been noted in the literature (Nicolaidis *et al*, 2015), whereas our participants do not mention negative reactions to AAC use.

The use of AACs again shows agency and self-determination. Although participants do not mention this, as indicated in the literature e.g. (Zisk & Dalton, 2019) they may have had to overcome lack of acceptance of their use of AACs or negative assumptions about their intelligence and abilities. The use of an AAC by a teacher could have contributed to overcoming some of the negative attitudes to AAC use and stereotypes about AAC users among their students.

Technology was also used to communicate electronically in writing with service providers, but space constraints do not permit us to discuss this here.

Other strategies

A number of other strategies will be discussed very briefly here. Logic and reasoning were among the strategies we set out to investigate in the project. Analysing and reasoning was used both to try and understand situations and what was happening (80%) and understand emotions (66%). This was used more frequently than learnt strategies (42%) to understand emotions. Participants' comments indicated that analysing situations could be very useful for helping them understand what they should and should not do. This included observing the start of conversations before joining in. Participants could also over-analyse situations and this approach could be 'exhausting'. One participant commented very vehemently that the approach did *not* work.

Despite the large number of participants who indicated that they used this strategy, only a small number provided examples and indicated how successful it was. Of the comments provided, the balance seemed to be towards usefulness, if over-analysis was avoided, but further research would be required to confirm this.

To cope with stress in social situations, 60% used stimming and 31% relaxation techniques, including meditation. A high proportion of participants both tried to hide their autistic traits and used stimming (85%). The comments indicate that many participants carried out stimming unobtrusively, generally using objects such as hidden soft toys, fabric or nearby objects. This is in line with comments in the literature on masking including hiding stimming (Kapp *et al*, 2019; Wiskerke *et al*, 2018). However, participants did not comment on stimming (unobtrusive or otherwise) using body movements. Disadvantages included the possibilities of attracting unwanted attention and the focus on stimming itself sometimes leading to panic.

Humour (73%) and talking about (favourite) interests (64%) were popular strategies. Significant, but smaller, numbers used their personalities (47%) and identified and used their strengths (40%). Not unsurprisingly, using interests worked best with other people who shared a similar interest. Otherwise, problems could occur. However, participants did not mention looking for groups with common interests e.g. on the internet, possibly due to the way the questions were formulated.

Participants generally found humour and their personalities effective strategies. However, some of the comments indicated that they may work best for participants who are reasonably confident and/or who feel good about themselves. This could be problematical for autistic people, who are not necessarily confident. Humour did not always work, for instance for participants whose sense of humour was 'too subtle'. There is some anecdotal evidence, which requires further investigation, that 'autistic' humour may differ from neurotypical humour and unintentionally humorous comments could be the most successful.

Conclusion

There has been considerable discussion in the literature of the problems and challenges of autistic people. There has also been discussion of strategies for parents, teachers and other professionals, but minimal discussion of the strategies used by autistic people themselves. The limited previous research in this area has largely focused on hiding autistic traits and imitation e.g. (Livingston *et al*, 2019) and used a medical model perspective. Our research is wide ranging and from a social model neurodiversity perspective, informed by autistic people. A focus on autistic people's strategies is important, as it recognises that autistics can be autonomous and self-determined.

Much of the literature has presented autistic people as requiring action by others. Our research has shown that autistics can take action themselves and use strategies to improve their chances of obtaining and retaining employment, being able to access and successfully use services and having better social interactions. However, in line with the social model of disability we also recognise that autistic people face many barriers to full participation. Removing these barriers should be considered a human rights issue. We have developed recommendations aimed at service providers and decision makers for barrier removal or reduction. The recommendations can be found in the project reports at https://anauternative. uk/publications/. However, it will take time for our recommendations (or other approaches to barrier removal) to be accepted and implemented. There is still a lack of recognition that autistic people experience barriers rather than being the cause of problems and challenges and that action is possible at the collective rather than just the individual level.

Having strategies makes autistic people more autonomous and enables them to take action in the short term. While the removal of barriers will make life better for autistic people, they may always require strategies of some sort to maximise participation and increase quality of life.

The approach based on the recognition that autistic people develop and use strategies is in line with both the neurodiversity and social models and the disability literature on autonomy and self-determination. The social model focuses on barriers and the need for societal and collective action to remove them. However, this does not exclude action by autistic people in terms of the development of strategies. Neurodiversity recognises that autistic people's different ways of thinking and behaving can both lead to barriers, due to the problems experienced by the rest of society in adapting to them, and provide potential solutions. Developing and using strategies makes autistic people more autonomous and self-determined. The use of these strategies can maintain or improve quality of life by facilitating access to services and participation in social activities.

They include the use of a trusted person or technology to enable participants to carry out activities that otherwise would not be possible or that would be less satisfying. For instance, the trusted person strategy has enabled participants to participate in social activities, helped them understand and complete otherwise not easily comprehensible job application forms, and supported them in employment. The use of online and mobile games has enabled participants who might otherwise not have the means to socialise to do so, and helped them to find this socialising satisfying. The use of AACs (Augmentative and Alternative Communication devices) has enabled participants to communicate with others, either in general or occasionally, for instance when 'shutdown' occurs. It should be noted that support from a 'trusted' person should be considered an enabler which increases their autonomy rather than a sign of dependency.

Due to space constraints, we have only been able to present a selection of the strategies we obtained. However, we hope that the strategies we have presented will be useful to autistic people, help them to avoid the associated costs and encourage autistics to develop and share their own strategies. We also have a number of questions about the ways in which these strategies were used, the factors that influenced their effectiveness and any costs and ways to minimise these costs. We have investigated these issues in follow-up work involving interviews and a diary exercise. We also tried to use this further research to cover groups of autistic people under-represented in this stage, including older people and people with general learning difficulties. We discuss these and other issues in the project reports (https://anauternative.uk/publications/) and we hope to produce a number of papers where we discuss specific issues in more detail.

Acknowledgements

We would like to thank DRILL for funding us and their support throughout project, our Advisory Board, all the autistics who answered questionnaires, and everyone who helped circulate information about the questionnaire.

References

Deci EL, Hodges R, Pierson L & Tomassone J (1992) Autonomy andcompetence as motivational factors in students with learning disabilities and emotional handicaps. *Journal of learning disabilities* **25** (7) 457–471.

Hagner D & Cooney BF (2005) 'I do that for everybody': Supervising employees with autism. *Focus on Autism and Other Developmental Disabilities* **20** (2) 91–97.

Hersh M (2013) Deafblind people, communication, independence, and isolation. *Journal of deaf studies and deaf education* **18** (4) 446–463.

Hull L, Petrides KV, Allison C, Smith P, Baron-Cohen S, Lai MC & Mandy W (2017) 'Putting on my best normal': social camouflaging in adults with autism spectrum conditions. *Journal of Autism and Developmental Disorders* **47** (8) 2519–2534.

Johnstone D (2012) *An introduction to disability studies*. Routledge.

Kapp SK, Steward R, Crane L, Elliott D, Elphick C, Pellicano E & Russell G (2019) 'People should be allowed to do what they like': Autistic adults' views and experiences of stimming. *Autism* **23** (7) 1782–1792.

Knight J (2007) Spaced out and smiling, CSUN [online]. Available at: https://spacedoutandsmiling.com/presentations/autism-technology-csun-2017 (accessed July 2020).

Lai MC & Baron-Cohen S (2015) Identifying the lost generation of adults with autism spectrum conditions. *The Lancet Psychiatry* **2** (11) 1013–1027.

Livingston LA, Shah P & Happé F (2019) Compensatory strategies below the behavioural surface in autism: a qualitative study. *The Lancet Psychiatry* **6** (9) 766–777.

Nicolaidis C, Raymaker DM, Ashkenazy E, McDonald KE, Dern S, Baggs AE & Boisclair WC (2015) 'Respect the way I need to communicate with you': Healthcare experiences of adults on the autism spectrum. *Autism* **19** (7) 824–831.

Reindal SM (1999) Independence, dependence, interdependence: some reflections on the subject and personal autonomy. *Disability and Society* **14** (3) 353–357. doi: 0.1080/09687599926190.

Sprague J & Hayes J (2000) Self-determination and empowerment: A feminist standpoint analysis of talk about disability. *American journal of community psychology* **28** (5) 671–695.

Swain J, French S & Cameron C (2003) *Controversial issues in a disabling society*. McGraw-Hill Education (UK).

Walsh RJ, Krabbendam L, Dewinter J & Begeer S (2018) Brief report: Gender identity differences in autistic adults: Associations with perceptual and socio-cognitive profiles. *Journal of Autism and Developmental Disorders* **48** (12) 4070–4078.

Wehmeyer ML (2005) Self-determination and individuals with severe disabilities: re-examining meanings and misinterpretations. *Research and Practice for Persons with Severe Disabilities* **30** (3) 113-120.

Wehmeyer ML, Shogren KA, Zager D, Smith TE & Simpson R (2010) Research-based principles and practices for educating students with autism: self-determination and social interactions. *Education and Training in Autism and Developmental Disabilities* **45** (4) 475–486.

White GW, Simpson JL, Gonda C, Ravensloot C & Coble Z (2010) Moving from independence to interdependence: a conceptual model for better understanding community participation of centers for independent living consumers. *Journal of Disability Policy Studies* **20** (4) 233–240.

Wiskerke J, Stern H & Igelström K (2018) Camouflaging of repetitive movements in autistic female and transgender adults. *BioRxiv* 412619.

Zisk AH & Dalton E (2019) Augmentative and Alternative Communication for Speaking Autistic Adults: Overview and Recommendations. *Autism in Adulthood* **1** (2) 93–100.

Other titles from Pavilion Publishing

Mismatch of Salience: Explorations of the Nature of Autism from Theory to Practice
Dr Damian Milton

A Mismatch of Salience explores the communication challenges between people on the autism spectrum and neurotypical people and seeks to re-balance and celebrate this diversity.

For more information, visit: https://www.pavpub.com/learning-disability/autism/a-mismatch-of-salience

---

The Ten Rules Series: Challenging thinking and practice in autism and intellectual disability
Dr Damian Milton and Richard Mills

This unique range of powerful booklets aims to challenge thinking about the way we support and interact with autistic people and those with learning (intellectual) disabilities. The 'Ten Rules' concept sets out to be deliberately provocative by suggesting ways in which people, services and environments can unconsciously create problems and obstacles for those they seek to support.

Neurodiversity, Autism and Recovery from Sexual Violence: A practical resource for all those working to support victim-survivors
Dr Susy Ridout

An accessible, in-depth guide for those supporting autistic and neurodivergent women in their unique journeys towards recovery from sexual violence. The book provides a wealth of guidance and practical activities to assist in the exploration of issues to do with identity, safety, well-being, and the many effects of sexual violence.

Hall of Mirrors – Shards of Clarity: Autism, neuroscience and finding a sense of self
Dr Phoebe Caldwell

Drawing on Phoebe Caldwell's 40 years of experience and expert knowledge of autism and Intensive Interaction, Hall of Mirrors – Shards of Clarity marries recent neuroscience research evidence and practical approaches used in care to cover a wide range of vital subjects. Sense of self, confirmation, sensory issues, case studies and neuroscience findings are explored and weaved together in an inspired way which brings aims to bring theory into practice and vice versa, while at the same time listening to the voices of people with autism. The result is to allow everyone in the autism field to take a few steps forward with how they interact and support autistic people.

For more information, visit https://www.pavpub.com/health-and-social-care/health-learning-disability/hall-of-mirrors-shards-of-clarity

---

Autism and Mental Well-being in Higher Education: A practical resource for students, mentors and study skills support workers, 2nd Edition
Dr Susy Ridout

This book looks into the fact that, too often, autistic students and those with mental health needs struggle with higher education, often dropping out of courses because they do not receive the informed support that would help them to succeed. This much-needed manual addresses the provision of effective support via mentoring in order to build students' confidence and enable them to take control of their lives.

For more information, visit https://www.pavpub.com/health-and-social-care/health-autism/autism-and-mental-well-being-in-higher-education

---

Understanding and Resonding to Autism: The SPELL framework
Julie Beadle-Brown and Richard Mills

A fully revised, new edition of *Understanding and Responding to Autism: The SPELL Framework (2nd edition)* including new video, self-study guide and learner workbook. These new training and self-study resources reflect the changes in the autism context in the UK as well as in many other countries, and the valuable experience the authors have gained from many years of using the original resources for training in many different settings.

For more information, visit: https://www.pavpub.com/learning-disability/autism/understanding-and-responding-autism-spell-framework-2nd-edition